Outward Signs

Outward Signs

*The Powerlessness of External Things
in Augustine's Thought*

PHILLIP CARY

UNIVERSITY PRESS

2008

OXFORD
UNIVERSITY PRESS

Oxford University Press, Inc., publishes works that further
Oxford University's objective of excellence
in research, scholarship, and education.

Oxford   New York
Auckland   Cape Town   Dar es Salaam   Hong Kong   Karachi
Kuala Lumpur   Madrid   Melbourne   Mexico City   Nairobi
New Delhi   Shanghai   Taipei   Toronto

With offices in
Argentina   Austria   Brazil   Chile   Czech Republic   France   Greece
Guatemala   Hungary   Italy   Japan   Poland   Portugal   Singapore
South Korea   Switzerland   Thailand   Turkey   Ukraine   Vietnam

Copyright © 2008 by Oxford University Press, Inc.

Published by Oxford University Press, Inc.
198 Madison Avenue, New York, New York 10016

www.oup.com

Oxford is a registered trademark of Oxford University Press

Library of Congress Cataloging-in-Publication Data
Cary, Phillip, 1958–
Outward signs : the powerlessness of external things in Augustine's thought / Phillip Cary.
    p. cm.
ISBN 978-0-19-533649-8
1. Augustine, Saint, Bishop of Hippo. 2. Semiotics. 3. Signs and symbols. I. Title.
BR65.A9C285 2008
230'.14092—dc22   2007028376

9 8 7 6 5 4 3 2 1

Printed in the United States of America
on acid-free paper

In grateful memory of
Robert J. O'Connell, S.J.,
courageous and patient scholar

Preface

The concept of sacrament is not simply a kind of religious sensibility, what we might call a sacramental attitude toward the world. It belongs to a doctrine that is concerned not with the world in general but with particular places to find the grace of a particular God, which is Christ in the flesh. The formulation of the doctrine of the sacraments in the Middle Ages was a great achievement, I think, because in the Augustinian tradition within which it arose what matters most is inward and universal, whereas sacramental doctrine taught people to cling to things that are external and particular: not eternal realities or inner experience but flesh and blood, water and word. Precisely in its externality, sacramental doctrine is a great triumph of Christ over the philosophy of soul, inner presence, and spiritual experience, as well as other generalities such as "sacramental thinking," which tend to tyrannize over religious thought even in Christianity. (Most misleading of all is what has recently been called "incarnational thinking," another generalized attitude that contrasts sharply with the Christian doctrine of Incarnation, according to which the flesh of God is nothing but one particular Jew.) My ultimate interest here is to understand this triumph of the piety of the external and particular over the spirituality of the inward and universal, but this requires careful investigation of the unlikely conceptual context in which it occurred.

Powerless Externals

I was led into this investigation by Luther, that great enemy of the religion of inner spiritual experience. According to Luther, God gives himself to us through his external word, but not according to Augustine. My surprise at this contrast led me to write this book. For in this regard Luther is more Catholic than Augustine—certainly more of a medieval Catholic—while Augustine, if not exactly more Protestant than Luther, is closer to Calvin than Luther is on the issue of sacraments. At stake is nothing less than the nature of the Gospel, which for Luther has a sacramental kind of efficacy. "The words of Christ are sacraments by which he works our salvation," says Luther, because "the Gospel words and stories are a kind of sacrament, that is, *a sacred sign, by which God effects what they signify* in those who believe."[1] Luther's theology of the saving Word of God originates within the framework of medieval theology of sacramental efficacy.[2] His teaching that the Gospel of Christ is a divine promise effectually giving the salvation it promises grows out of the medieval conception of sacramental signs effectually conferring the inward grace they signify.

What initially surprised me was that Augustine had no such conception, even though he formulated the theory of signs within which Luther and the medieval theologians developed their theologies of word and sacrament. But perhaps I should not have been so surprised. When Calvin in his sacramental theology argued against Luther that external signs can have no intrinsic spiritual power, he insisted Augustine was on his side—and I now think Calvin was right about this. Yet the resulting fault line in Western Christianity is still unexpected and takes some getting used to: Calvin and Augustine on one side, Luther and Aquinas and medieval Catholicism on the other. In one sense, of course, all of Western theology is Augustinian, including in the matter of word and sacrament, both of which are conceived as outward signs of inner things. But the Augustinian framework assumes the superiority of the inner as well as the superficiality of the external, so it is striking when medieval theologians defend a piety that clings to external things and Luther follows them, while Calvin and the subsequent tradition of Protestant inwardness spurn this kind of externalism. The fault line opens up in the twelfth century when medieval theologians first define sacraments as external signs that not only signify an inner grace but confer it. Calvin, unlike Luther, rejects this confidence in the efficacy of external things and looks back past medieval sacramental theology to its deeper roots in Augustine.

Not that Augustine thinks exactly like Calvin. Of course how Augustine does think, exactly, is the topic of this book. While Calvin is concerned to "place no power in creatures,"[3] Augustine is convinced that bodily things have no power over souls. In other words, Calvin's denial of external sacramental efficacy stems from a distinctive view of creature and Creator (as if assigning spiritual power to creatures robbed God of his honor) while Augustine's stems from a Platonist view of body and soul, emphasizing the causal superiority of the latter. In Platonism, the soul gives form and life to the body, not the other way round. The inferiority of the body is tantamount to the powerlessness of external things over the inner self—so long as the inner self is morally pure, not defiled by carnal attachments and driven by earthly desires. Consequently external signs may have an appropriate spiritual use for those who are not yet pure, but clinging to them as if they had the power to save us merely reinforces our sinful tendency to love bodily rather than spiritual things.

Thesis and Argumentation

My contention is that Augustine the Christian Platonist invented the way we now think about outer and inner—not only the concept of a private inner world of the self, which was the topic of my first book, *Augustine's Invention of the Inner Self,* but also the concept of external signs expressing what lies hidden within the inner self, which is the topic of the present book. I call this new Augustinian conception of signs "expressionist semiotics," thinking of it as the distant origin of what George Lindbeck labels the "experiential-expressivist" model of Christian doctrine. The novelty of expressionist semiotics lies in the way it takes up the ancient philosophical theory of signs, which was originally a theory of scientific inference developed by empirically minded philosophers quite opposed to Platonism, and incorporates it into a Platonist metaphysics of body and soul, thereby inventing the new category of bodily signs that are communicative expressions of the soul. What I aim to understand is how concepts like inner self and outward expression first arose in Western thought, as well as why they did not originally allow for the sacramental notion of outward signs conferring inner gifts.

The overall thesis I argue for in this book is that Augustine's Christian Platonism has no room for such a notion, which I shall label "efficacious external means of grace." To arrive at this thesis, part I begins by examining Augustine's invention of expressionist semiotics, its philosophical roots (chapters 1 and 2) and epistemological consequences. The most important consequences are that words become a species of sign (chapter 3) and that signs cannot give us knowledge of what they signify (chapter 4). From this follows the theological implication that the Scriptures do not reveal God but consist of signs pointing out the way our souls must take to see God for themselves (chapter 5). This implication for the theology of the word is parallel to the implication for the theology of the sacrament: neither word nor sacrament can function as efficacious means of grace, because no sign can effectually give what it signifies.

Part II examines how this conception of the powerlessness of external signs applies specifically to Augustine's theology of the sacraments, and in particular how Augustine's concept of sacrament compares with that of his medieval successors (chapter 6), how his concept of baptism affirms traditional commitments to baptismal regeneration without assigning power to the outward ceremony of baptism (chapter 7), and how all the Christian sacraments are founded on Christ's coming in the flesh without assigning life-giving power to the sacraments or to Christ's flesh itself, which after all is an external thing (chapter 8).

Some Advice for Readers

The overall concern of this book is theological but its procedure often involves philosophical as well as theological exegesis. Readers interested primarily in theology, I would warn, might best begin reading later than chapter 1. I have dismaying visions of multitudes of readers getting bogged down in Hellenistic theories about the nature of signs and giving up somewhere in the middle of chapter 2, where the arcana of ancient philosophical semiotics meets the arcana of the early Augustine. Anyone who is as fascinated by this arcana as I am should dive in—I have done my best to make it accessible to the nonspecialist—but if your interest is strictly in Augustine the theologian, it would be better to begin with chapter 4, which contains quite enough semiotics for theological purposes. (If you also have an interest in Augustine's philosophy of language, you could begin with chapter 3). Or you could begin with the last chapter, indeed the very last section, entitled "Spiritual Eating," which will give you a good overview of the theological import of this book and its bearing on the fundamental issue of Christ in the flesh. From there, or indeed anywhere else in the book, it should be possible to follow whichever thread you like through the dense forest of this book's argumentation by using the many cross-references I have included in the footnotes, together with the summaries at the head of each chapter, which should help you locate the patches of this forest that most interest or provoke you.

The summaries summarize each chapter in order, section by section. You will find that most sections (marked by subtitles, to which the cross-references refer) are nearly self-contained, allowing you to read one at a gulp and then use a cross-reference to jump to another in a different chapter. I suppose many of us find it natural, as well as pleasant and instructive, to read scholarly works in this jumpy and nonlinear fashion instead of resigning ourselves to being taken on a forced march in a single direction by the author. I have simply done more than most authors to facilitate that kind of reading, in the hope that the book will lure more readers and gain more understanding that way. This is particularly necessary in that this book is not a series of reports on research but a single sustained exegetical argument woven of a great many threads, which have a way of disappearing for a while like strands in a braid and then coming back into view many pages later.

A few clarifications about terminology will perhaps be helpful even at this early point. I make no distinction between the terms "inner," "inward," "internal" and "interior," nor between "outer," "outward," "external," and "exterior," using them interchangeably as my sense of euphony suggests. Also, I do not usually make any distinction between "bodily" and "corporeal." Although the former often refers specifically to the human body, in a Platonist context it always does so by placing it at the same ontological level as other corporeal things, which for Augustine means it is a different kind of being from the soul. "Psychology," when used of Augustine's (or Plato's or Plotinus's) thought, means a philosophical account of the soul's kind of being, which is hardly what we now mean by the discipline of psychology. It is useful to start thinking about kinds of being as early as possible in reading this book, because the contrast between inner and outer, which defines expressionist semiotics, is an ontological contrast between levels of being. The level of being called "outward" can also be called "bodily" and "sensible," which is to say, every outward thing is corporeal and sensible, every sensible thing is corporeal and outward, and every bodily thing is external and sensible. This is not merely an equivalence of terms but a substantive ontological thesis characteristic of Platonism, which results in the three terms being, in modern logical parlance, co-extensive: they "cover" exactly the same things, even though they call attention to three different features of them.

What no clarification can accomplish, I have discovered, is to eliminate the possibility of provocation. Judging by my previous efforts, this book is apt to provoke those who like the inward turn in religion, as well as those who dislike it and would rather not think of Augustine as a hero of inwardness. I am in the latter camp myself, but cannot shake the conviction that the real Augustine is not quite what any of us want him to be. It is a dismaying conviction, very much like discovering your father is not all you hoped he was, and in that sense this is a book for grown-ups. It is probably not—what I wish it could be—edifying reading for those just learning theology. This is not to say any of us are in a position to stop learning from this father in the faith or even to stop admiring him—the man's mind and heart are deeper than mine, and I am a better Christian for having spent so much time with him—but our learning must often be by way of critical thinking. Augustine himself expected no less, bless his heart.[4]

Against Inwardness

But perhaps it will help if I explain what's not to like. Although I do not actually believe in the distinction between inner and outer (for I do not think we have a private inner world within us but rather live within the one world God has created) nonetheless if forced to accept such a distinction I am all for a piety that could fairly be called "externalistic," in which we cling to the external word, sacraments, and the flesh of Christ as the source of salvation, grace, and truth. If you like an inward spirituality or want to find God within, I hope I can make you think twice. This means I must ask you to question some fundamental intuitions you may have—intuitions that I contend did not exist before Augustine. I must ask you to consider that words may not so much express our experience as shape it and give it being, making it a distinctively articulate and human rather than animal experience. Although we often have intuitions prior to words (like mathematicians who first get an insight and later figure out how to explain it in words) we are the intuitive creatures we are because our minds are shaped by words (all the mathematicians on earth are speakers of some human language, their mathematical thinking formed by the habit of speech, without which they could never have learned mathematics at all). I would ask you to consider the possibility that our deepest intuitions could not have gotten into our hearts unless human words were there first. External things, I think, do exercise a wholesome power over our souls, not to control and coerce but to form and to teach, to bring our lives to the point where we may speak the truth and thereby engage in the work of thought. And if our souls are shaped by words, then words can give adequate expression to what is in them. Indeed, words are just the thing we need to be human, creatures made in the image of a God who speaks the truth.

Likewise, I agree with Luther in thinking there can be no Christ in our hearts unless he first gives himself to us in the external word of the Gospel. Christ is in us only to the extent that we cling to this word outside us. That, I think, is how it always is with persons. We get to know the people we love and bear them in our hearts not by looking within but by turning our attention outward and away from ourselves, hearing the word of these others, listening to what they have to say for themselves, and considering that it may be the truth. To know other persons *as* persons is impossible without honoring their authority to speak for themselves.[5]

Thus I add a belief in authority to my belief in externals. My inquiries into Augustine's thought will, I can only expect, seem rather scandalous at first to readers who think of belief in external authority as something we need to outgrow. I do not think this way, because the authority I am concerned with is the authority of other persons to speak for themselves, just as the exteriority of the word I am concerned with is ultimately the exteriority of other persons, those outside ourselves who can surprise and bless us with a truth that is not our own, a truth to which we have no access apart from their authority. Therefore to honor others as other, in their difference from ourselves, is precisely to embrace external authority. For this reason also faith, as Augustine rightly teaches, is a matter of authority rather than reason. But in contrast to Augustine, I don't believe we should aspire to a beatitude where faith in authority gives way to intellectual vision or (to make the usual translation into modern, Romantic terms) to direct inward experience. Persons are present for us not in our experience but in their flesh, and therefore knowing other persons, including God, is always dependent on external authority. The fact that this makes us dependent on what is outside us—a truth that comes to us only as a gift of the other—is the very goodness of it.

Inner Grace and Particular Election

Augustine can think differently, because his concept of inwardness allows for the possibility of finding the other within the self—looking inward and then upward, as I put it in my first book, *Augustine's Invention of the Inner Self*. This Platonist structure of Augustinian inwardness is particularly important for Augustine's doctrine of grace, which relies on a concept of divine help bestowed inwardly on the soul. Thus one of the most important ways in which this book swims against the usual current of Augustine scholarship is its assumption that Augustine's doctrine of grace is an outgrowth rather than a break from his Platonism. It is from the beginning and throughout his career a Christian Platonist doctrine of grace. This is an assumption I argue for at length in my second book, *Inner Grace: Augustine in the Traditions of Plato and Paul*, to which many of the cross-references in this book refer. There I show how key developments in Augustine's psychology of grace rely on his Platonist epistemology of inner teaching, and I argue that it was never the case at any point in his career as a Christian writer that Augustine thought he could arrive at wisdom and happiness without divine help bestowed inwardly upon his soul. That is just not how Platonists think.

The development of Augustine's doctrine of grace is thus not a story about how he becomes less Platonist and more Christian. For one thing, it is a story that has little to do with Christ incarnate, whom we must encounter in the flesh, not as an inner presence. To see where Christ in the flesh fits in, we must look at the authority of external things like words and sacraments, things that have the same kind of presence as flesh. At stake, ultimately, is our apprehension of a particular human being, Jesus Christ. This takes us in the opposite direction from Augustinian inwardness, which is not about embracing particulars. Hence a deepening appreciation of the authority of Christ as external teacher is an interruption in the trajectory of Augustine's early intellectual project, the source of what I regard as the most important change of direction in Augustine's thought, "the great shift in Augustine's teaching" as I call it here at the end of chapter 4.

The particularity of external things, especially those of the biblical story, give rise to the most fruitful challenges and the greatest difficulties in Augustine's thought. On the one hand, for example, his figural reading of Old Testament narratives is one of the most resourceful and astute to be found in any of the church fathers. But on the other hand, he cannot ultimately make sense of the particularity of divine election, the choices that God makes in history to call one person rather than another, one nation rather than another, as his favorite and beloved. In the Bible this is good news, because Israel is chosen for the blessing of all nations, and Christ is chosen for the salvation of the world. But when combined with Augustine's doctrine of the inner gift of grace, divine election becomes something to shudder at, an inscrutable depth in which some are predestined for salvation and others not.

In *Inner Grace,* I venture to argue that this is the fault not of Augustine but of the church, which had already aimed long before to replace or supersede Israel, constituting itself as the new Jacob, as it were, by stealing its brother's birthright as the chosen people so that Christians might be comforted and Israel excluded by the words of divine election, "Jacob have I loved but Esau have I hated." Ever since, the Jews have represented for Christian thought the kind of opaque particulars that must be seen through, transcended, and left behind—with only partial success, of course, leaving a residue of inscrutable depths in dark places such as Augustine's doctrine of election and predestination. This Christian effort to overcome Jewish particularity is a conceptual cousin of the attempt found so frequently in modern thought to overcome historical particularities and external authorities, including the authority of the divine other in holy Scripture. It is a terrible mistake.

Presence in the Flesh

From a modern perspective, what is strange about the biblical doctrine of election is its focus on particular flesh—Jewish flesh—a mere external thing, if you want to put it that way. There is something similarly strange about someone as Augustinian as Luther, at the beginning of modernity, clinging so tightly to external things like word and sacrament—very particular external words like the Gospel, and very particular sacraments like the bread of the Eucharist. Luther's theology is often treated as paradoxical, I think, because he uses expressionist semiotics to articulate this kind of outward turn, this clinging to external things, which goes very much against the grain of Augustine's motives for inventing expressionist semiotics in the first place. Most strikingly, Luther's emphasis on faith alone requires us to *believe* in the inner presence of Christ rather than *experience* it, which defeats the very purpose of Augustinian inwardness.

To agree with Luther about this is to be armed against the turn to experience in modern liberal Protestantism (as Karl Barth gratefully recognized)[6] and perhaps also against the kind of "metaphysics of presence" that is the target of many postmodern critics. For those interested in the latter, I should say that I do not believe in inner, intuitive, or phenomenal presence, just as I do not believe in Platonist souls or Augustinian inner selves. Except when I suspend disbelief and enter imaginatively into what seems to me the hallucinatory world of modern thinkers such as Schleiermacher or Husserl, I just cannot see why anyone would be very interested in what is present in our conscious experience. Consciousness itself, if there is such a thing, is of interest only insofar as it is directed to what is outside itself. That is to say, if words like "consciousness" and "experience" are any use at all, then their primary value lies in describing how we regularly go beyond the bounds of our previous experience or consciousness and come to be aware of new things. What's interesting is how we learn what is not yet present in our conscious experience. Thus any consciousness worth our trouble is oriented to what is not present to consciousness, and has no real interest in what some phenomenologists call "fullness of presence." To talk as if what "presence" really means is presence to, for, or within our conscious experience is therefore to jettison the only useful meaning of words like "presence," "consciousness," and "experience." Such talk in fact tends to turn our consciousness into a kind of prison, an inner world from which we can never really escape.

One of the advantages of not believing in the inner self is that one is free to regard such prisons as hallucinations, misguided philosophical inventions that never managed to achieve coherence, much less truth. One is free to believe that we do not live in an inner world of conscious experience but in the world God created—and that we should desire to learn what is really present in the flesh, not what is "fully present" to consciousness. The loveliest things in the world exist outside our conscious experience, and that is where any sane consciousness seeks them. If there are epistemological puzzles about how this works, part of the problem is surely our fondness for incoherent concepts of inner presence and conscious experience, which we would probably do better without. It has always seemed to me that there must be something wrong with our thinking if we find concepts like the inner world of consciousness easier to believe in than words and flesh, kingdoms and music, stars and trees and the like.

Sheer lack of interest in topics like "consciousness" and "experience" means also that I have never concerned myself with efforts to deconstruct something called "the metaphysics of presence." Still, it will be useful for those interested in these things to know that I think Derrida in particular gets the history of the metaphysics of presence wrong by focusing on speech as the purported locus of presence.[7] Here Augustine affords us much superior instruction in the meaning of metaphysics. It is true that his semiotics treats speech rather than writing as the primary form of the human word, but much more importantly it classifies both spoken and written words as merely external signs of a more fundamental inner presence. What is present to the mind, for Augustine as for Platonism in general and for all of expressionist semiotics, is metaphysically prior to the spoken word and everything corporeal, because it is a function of inner vision not outward speech. Seeing, not hearing, is the primary metaphor for presence in Platonism because the aim is to "see for ourselves" what is present to the mind rather than simply to believe what we hear about it secondhand.[8]

Hence also Luther's notion of an inner presence of Christ that is ours by the hearing of faith alone can only appear, in an Augustinian framework, as radical paradox. A Luther who was more biblical and less Augustinian would not look so paradoxical. Real presence is presence in the flesh, which most of the time is something we believe rather than see. Only in Platonism and its modern or postmodern descendants does this dependence on mere belief look like scepticism or paradox rather than ordinary human knowledge. For the fact is that we don't usually see or experience things for ourselves, but believe what we hear—where "hearing" is a synecdoche for all secondhand knowledge, reading as well as listening, which is dependent on what other people have to tell us. For the point is that our knowledge is normally not a matter of seeing for ourselves but rather one of the many kinds of debts we owe to persons outside us, stemming from an epistemic dependence on the testimony of others that befits creatures such as ourselves, whose lives are both fleshly and social.

Thanks to Others

Of course we do often see things for ourselves, but that too is something we could never have done without the external teaching of others. This is as true in Augustine scholarship as in mathematics: all of us who read and converse about Augustine or anything else are indebted to others for thoughts that are our very own. It is a debt therefore that frees us to be ourselves, and thus is a fit image of our owing our whole being to a gracious Creator. We thereby contract that most beautiful debt of thanksgiving, "still paying, still to owe," spoken of in Milton.[9]

Here I can only begin to tell what I owe to teachers and colleagues and other scholars. In the prefaces of earlier books I have thanked the people in whose company my thoughts were formed at Yale and Villanova, and here I would bring things up to date by mentioning with gratitude my colleagues at Eastern University, particularly Ray Van Leeuwen, Randy Colton, Steve Boyer, Dwight Peterson, Margaret Kim Peterson, Kent Sparks, Eric Flett, Carl Mosser, Jonathan Yonan, Chris Hall, and other members of the Christian Studies department, along with the many students who have had the hardihood to think carefully with me about Augustine—they too are scholars, even if only beginners, and because they are beginners they are learning more than the rest of us, which is something from which the rest of us have much to learn.

In my reading on the theme of Augustine's semiotics and its Platonist roots I owe most to the scholarship of Cornelius Mayer, whose great work on the concept of signs in Augustine's early writings also showed me the connection between semiotics and Christology, a point reinforced in a brief but profound article by Gérard Philips. After my own thinking had crystallized on these issues, I found support in the book of Ulrich Duchrow, who goes so far as to argue that, compared to a piety of "Biblical hearing," Augustine's semiotics displays *Sprachfeindschaft*, a critique of language that amounts to a kind of hostility.[10] It remains true, however, that my greatest scholarly debt in the realm of Augustine studies is to the work of Robert O'Connell, still the one whose writing did the most to free me to see with my own eyes.

A Note on Quotations and Citations

Unless otherwise indicated, all translations from primary texts are my own, as are all translations from secondary literature unless an English language edition is given in the bibliography. Italics in quotations are mine, introduced not for the sake of emphasis but simply to highlight the part of the quotation that is most important in my exegesis. Citations from ancient texts omit the chapter number where redundant: for example, *Confessions,* book 7, chapter 10, paragraph number 16 is cited "*Conf.* 7:16," not "*Conf.* 7:10.16."

Contents

Outward Signs

Introduction

Expressionist Semiotics and the
Powerlessness of the External

The inspiration for Augustine's theory of signs is Platonist. Augustine invents expressionist semiotics because his Platonist inward turn needs to give an explanation of the usefulness of external things like words. So he relates the outward to the inward by way of the concept of sign, which means he brings the theory of signs into the framework of a Platonist ontology of body and soul. He teaches the West to think of both word and sacrament as outward signs that give indispensable but inadequate expression to something higher and more inward. For words, being external, are bodily things existing at a lower ontological level than the inward things they express, which exist at the level of soul. This inner-outer contrast has an enormous impact on Western thought about bodies and souls, words and sacraments, meaning and grace, making many questionable connections seem obvious, such as the superficiality of the external, the depth of meaning, the hiddenness of divine grace, and the inwardness of experience. If we want to question these connections, we need to go back to the thinker who had the unrivaled ability to make such connections seem obvious.

Inadequate Platonist Signs

The key claims of this book, presented in the Preface, can also be formulated as theses about Augustine's Platonism. The thesis of part

I is twofold. First of all, Augustine invented expressionist semiotics because he was the first Platonist to have a semiotics. Secondly, he retains the Platonist insistence on the priority of the intelligible to the sensible even in the order of knowing, which means that sensible things such as signs cannot make intelligible things intelligible to us. This explains how he can be serious and consistent in upholding his own startling thesis in the treatise *On the Teacher*, which is that we do not learn things from signs. The thesis of part II is that the later medieval doctrine of the sacraments as efficacious external means of grace, signs that can confer the grace they signify, requires a departure from Augustine and his Platonist underpinnings.

In Augustine's Platonism words and sacraments have their significance and their use, but they cannot give us the inner good they signify. So it is not by turning to them that we find the knowledge of God but by turning inward, looking in a different dimension from all bodily things. The signs that belong to Christian faith have a way of negating themselves, as if they were saying "Not me!"—just like the whole of creation, whose message to those who seek God is "It's not me [*non ego sum*]—but He made me!" admonishing all who look to them that "we are not your God; seek above us!"[1] To this Augustine responds with the resolution, "through the soul itself I will ascend to him,"[2] undertaking an exploration of the inner space of the self. With this piety of the inward turn, I have argued, Augustine offers the West an alternative to finding the grace of God in external things such as the word of the Gospel and the sacraments of the church, not to mention the flesh of Christ.[3] In the latter Augustine sees an example of humility to follow as well as a kind of sacrament signifying the inward renewal of our souls,[4] but not the inner power of grace which alone makes that renewal and following possible. Such power is something Augustine does not find in outward things but in Christ's work as inner teacher and in the invisible community of souls called the church, which is Christ's spiritual Body. Being united with this community puts us in contact with the true inward channel through which grace comes to the soul, a channel of which the visible sacraments are merely outward markers.

Expressionist semiotics with its self-negating signs is of importance beyond theology, as it came to be taken for granted by philosophers of language in the Middle Ages and long afterward. It provides the framework for many modern theories of meaning and self, together with their postmodern deconstructions. Indeed, I do not think it too much to say that what "poststructuralist" postmodernists attempt to deconstruct is essentially Augustinian semiotics as represented by two of Augustine's modern philosophical heirs, Ferdinand de Saussure and Edmund Husserl. But as we shall see by the end of chapter 1, Augustine arrived at a version of this deconstruction long before any postmodernist. This I take it confirms the deconstructors' point. It has even been welcomed by theologians of a deconstructive bent.[5] Augustine himself is no deconstructor, yet he is not troubled by the deconstruction implicit in his semiotics because this is only a passing sceptical moment in a larger Platonist project of arriving at the presence of intellectual vision. A deconstructor is like a Platonist who thinks that such vision is endlessly deferred, who hints that such deferral is an inevitable feature of human language and may even be a good thing. Those who are neither deconstructors nor Platonists, on the other hand, are free simply to reject expressionist semiotics as an implausible account of how words get their meaning.[6]

Why the robust ontology of Platonism has superficially sceptical consequences is an important matter to consider, for it lets us see the origin of the pervasive sense in expressionist semiotics (both long after Augustine and long before deconstructionism) that the external signs whose very significance depends on expressing what lies within the inner self can never do an adequate job of it. Unlike many later versions of expressionist semiotics, in ancient Platonism the best part of the soul is not an unfathomable depth of feeling but a clear space of intellectual light shining from above. If our feelings are turbid and dark, Augustine believes, that is not because of the nature of the soul itself but because of its misguided attachment to external things, which compare to the inner world of the soul as shadows to light: opaque and insubstantial, hard to understand but only in the sense that they are not real enough to be objects of intellectual vision. Yet like shadows they do have a shape, which may resemble and therefore remind us of the forms of brighter, truer things in the intelligible world that is both within and above the soul. This possibility of reminder, so important to Plato, is taken up by Augustine's semiotics and attached to the notion of signification rather than resemblance, so that a lower thing may direct our attention to a higher thing without being an image or likeness of it. Hence the epistemology of Western Christianity has often centered on the notion of signs and signification, in contrast to that of Eastern Christianity which remains resolutely focused on icons and similitudes. But in its historic rejection of iconoclasm Eastern Orthodoxy too adopted an externalistic piety, which like the Western piety of the sacraments looks to corporeal things to find the grace of God.

Augustine, on the other hand, never gives up on the inward turn, retaining the epistemological as well as ontological priority of the intelligible to the sensible so characteristic of Platonism. For Platonism, what we understand with our minds are not abstractions but more real and substantial than the bodily things we see with our eyes. They are intelligible, in precisely the sense of being objects of the intellect, as visible things are objects of the eye of the body. The difference between sensible and intelligible things is illustrated by the difference between seeing a triangle drawn on a chalkboard and the kind of seeing that is inadequately expressed when someone trying to figure out the Pythagorean theorem suddenly stops figuring and just "gets it."[7] "Aha! Now I see!" she might say, and what she sees is a different kind of being from any triangle drawn in chalk. It is an eternal truth that has always been and will never cease to be: a divine Form, Plato might say, or an Idea in the mind of God, as Augustine put it.[8] It would be absurd to try to understand this divine and eternally real triangle by taking empirical measurements of its resemblance drawn in chalk, which could at best clue you in about how to look for the real triangle with your mind, not give you genuine understanding of it. So sensible things cannot make intelligible things intelligible to us, which means they cannot give us knowledge of what is eternal, most real, divine, and spiritual.

Downward Causality

This conviction about the inadequacy of sensible things to reveal intelligible things is retained in Augustine's semiotics, which helps explains why outward signs can signify divine gifts but not confer them. The full explanation, however, requires us to say a bit more about how causality works in Platonist metaphysics. Just as intelligible things in Platonism are more real than sensible things, they are also more powerful. Thus for example souls move bodies, not the other way round. This is as much as to say: the living move the dead, not vice versa. For in Platonism the body without the soul is a corpse, and it is obviously the soul that gives life and movement to the body, not vice versa.[9] Not even sense perception, for a consistent Platonist like Augustine, is an example of outward, bodily things having the power to cause changes in the soul.[10] This means that Augustine is never threatened by anything like modern anxieties about physical determinism or ancient fears of astrological fate. Nothing external controls the soul (God of course is not external) and corporeal things in fact have no real causal power at all but are governed by more spiritual causes, including the cosmic order established by their Creator. The only efficient causes in the universe are therefore "voluntary causes," Augustine says, by which he means the will of God as well as the wills of angels and souls.[11]

This unfamiliar conception of causality is a consequence of the ontological structure of Augustine's Christian Platonist universe, which consists of three levels: God, souls, and bodies.[12] In this three-tiered hierarchy of being, to be higher is also to be more inward. The inner life of the soul is superior to mere external things at the bottom of the hierarchy, while God at the top of the hierarchy is not only above the soul but within it, being indeed "more inward than my inmost being."[13] Hence at the inmost center of the soul is not emotional depth but intellectual height, like a sun shining within and above us which only the eye of the intellect can see.[14] This is the divine inner Light that gives our souls being and life, understanding and conversion toward the good, "unchangeable, yet changing all things."[15] God is above all things in that he is immutable and impassible, absolutely unchanged and unaffected by what is below him. By contrast, the creatures at the middle level of the hierarchy, angels and souls, are mutable in just one respect: they change in time but are not moved in space. Their thoughts and feelings are altered but not their location. Indeed they do not really have a location in space (it is not even strictly accurate to describe human souls as literally located "in" their bodies)[16] and therefore they afford no handle, as it were, that corporeal things could use to get a grip on them. They can be moved inwardly by God, by his grace and beauty and love, but not by external things, which literally have no power to move souls, no causal efficacy over them. For bodies are at the very bottom of the hierarchy of being, where they can be moved by higher things but not move them. Corporeal things are mutable in two respects, continually changing in both time and in space. This is their distinctive weakness and lowliness.

Mapping relations of power against the background of Augustine's three-tiered hierarchy of being, therefore, it is clear that causal efficacy always flows downward, from God to souls to bodies, never the reverse. God changes all things, souls do not change the immutable God but do govern bodies, and bodies are accordingly governed by the "voluntary causes" found in the will of superior beings, God, angels, and souls. It is because of this Platonist axiom of downward causality (as I shall call it) that no sensible thing could possibly give us knowledge of intelligible things. The world of bodies has literally no causal effect on the soul, much less the effect of giving it knowledge of intelligible truths above it. This is the original ontological background to the Augustinian conviction that external signs are inadequate to express what lies within.

There is, however, a very important sense in which souls are moved by bodies indirectly: souls voluntarily move themselves when they allow their love to be attracted or attached to external things. When this love is rightly ordered—for instance when the soul takes appropriate care of the health of the body or gives alms to the poor—then all is well. But of course there are sinful attachments (called "carnal" not because they derive from our flesh but because they are directed toward fleshly things) and these may be the source of immense misery and grief, as illustrated by Augustine's *Confessions* and many of his ethical writings. Precisely because Augustine believes so strongly in the inward turn and the ascent to higher things, there are few writers who can match him for giving us a sense of the weight of external things and the body itself dragging down the soul, which has the hardest time letting go of carnal attachments once it has made a habit of them.

Mother and Child

To round out this introduction, consider three illustrations of Augustine's expressionist semiotics at work, providing an initial sample of the phenomena of expressionist semiotics whose origin this book seeks to explain. Each illustration situates the familiar concept of outward signs expressing the inner self in the context of Augustine's three-tiered hierarchy of being and the Platonist axiom of downward causality.

The first illustration, occurring early in the *Confessions,* is Augustine's description of his own soul learning to express itself as an infant. It is literally the first thing he tells us about after mother's milk. Having praised God for the goodness of food from the bodies of women who nursed him while a baby, Augustine describes his response:

> At that time I knew how to suck, to rest content when satisfied, to cry when in pain, and nothing more. Later I began to smile, first in sleep, then awake. . . . Then gradually I became aware of where I was, and wanted to show my wants to the people who could satisfy them, but I couldn't—for the wants were internal, but the people were external and could not by any of their senses enter into my soul. So I threw around my limbs and voice as *signs* resembling my wants, as best I could—for they weren't very truthlike.[17]

Even the baby at the breast is not so close to another human being as he appears. She is external but he lives within, in an inner space she cannot enter, where his wants (*voluntates,* literally his "wills") are hidden from her perception. His first task in this mortal life is to find a way to make them known lest he remain alone, isolated in his inner self. The baby searches for means of expression, signs that somehow resemble what he wants in his soul. At first he cries simply because he is in pain and he smiles in his sleep, having no intention to communicate. But eventually he learns to use his cries and smiles and other bodily movements as signs to communicate his wants, expressing the hidden inner will of his soul.

In the process he develops a new kind of will, the intent to communicate: the will to express his will and make it known to others. He has come into this world a soul of inner depth unknown even to the one who carries him in her

bosom, but it is not his will to remain so. Who would be always an infant—
infans in Latin, meaning literally unable to speak? So he tries to express
himself, at first inarticulately:

> By that very mind which you gave me, my God, I wanted to bring
> forth the feelings of my heart by sighs and all sorts of vocaliz-
> ings and bodily movements so that my will might be obeyed, but
> I couldn't—not all I wanted nor to all those whom I wanted.[18]

This bringing forth (*edere*) of the feelings or awareness of the heart (*sensa cordis*)
is the movement we now call "expression," taking what is hidden within and
making it manifest in the outside world by means of perceptible signs.

The great transition is from infancy to childhood, from merely throwing
around one's limbs and voice to mastering articulate speech. In a famous
passage Augustine describes himself learning human language by observing
how his elders speak and move, remembering and making the connection
between bodily motion and the sound of the voice:

> I thought in memory: when they called a thing by name and when in
> accord with that voiced sound [*vocem*] they moved the body toward
> something, I saw and retained that this sound they made [*hoc quod
> sonabant*] is what they called that thing when they wanted to point
> it out. That this was what they wanted was evident from the move-
> ment of their bodies, as it were the natural words of all nations, which
> they made with the face and the wink of the eyes, the action of
> other members and the sound of the voice [*sonitu vocis*] indicating the
> affections of the soul as it sought, possessed, rejected or fled from
> things.[19]

Augustine portrays himself (and by extension all children) coming to understand language by watching how other people give bodily expression to their
will or wants. For Augustine acts of will are always forms of loving, and love is a
desire to be united to what one loves. So the natural expression of our will is to
move toward what we want, gravitating toward it, as it were. When the thing
wanted is named aloud, the child can match the sound of the name to the thing
toward which someone's body moves, and thus learn what the sound signifies.
Then he tries it himself:

> Thus by hearing words properly placed in various sentences, I
> gradually gathered what things they were signs of, and by training
> my mouth to form these signs, I was now able to express my will
> through them. So I came to share with those among whom I lived the

signs by which we express our will and I entered more deeply into the stormy society of human life, in dependence on the authority of my parents and the beck of my elders.[20]

By learning to use words to express his will the child has solved one problem and inherited others. He has entered human society, the community of fallen souls where words deceive and manipulate and thus become instruments of power,[21] where they can be bought and sold (young Augustine will make a living by teaching rhetoric) and where they are so overvalued that he will be beaten by his teachers for not mastering them. Words do not overcome the separation between one soul and another, but build a kind of bridge that traverses the external distance between one inner depth and another, not only establishing connections but also making all sorts of new and more subtle separations and misunderstandings possible. For man born of woman there is no going back to Eden, no unmediated union with other souls this side of death.

Why Lectures Get Boring

But there is always the longing for it, as well as the dissatisfaction with mere words, which are external things unable to express fully our inner depth. This frustration with the inadequacy of words can be seen in a striking remark Augustine makes about the difficulty of teaching Christian doctrine. Since the text is not well known, it is worth reproducing here in full. Augustine is offering counsel to a clergyman who wonders how to give more interesting catechetical lessons. He sympathizes:

> I too am almost always displeased by my own talking. For I am eager
> for something better, which I often enjoy inwardly before begin-
> ning to unfold it in sounding words, and insofar as I fall short of this
> initial impulse I am grieved that my tongue cannot suffice for my
> heart. For my will is that those who hear me may understand all that
> I understand, and I realize that I have not spoken well enough to
> accomplish this, especially as such understanding saturates the mind
> like a quick flash of light, while the speaking is long and drawn-
> out and far different, and as it rolls on, the other has already con-
> cealed itself in its hiding place. Nevertheless there is a sort of trace or
> vestige which is in some wonderful way impressed upon the mem-
> ory, and it lasts through the period of time taken up by the syllables.
> And it is because of such traces that we are able to carry through

to completion the sounding signs which we call Latin or Greek, Hebrew or whatever other language, whether we merely think these signs or actually utter them with the voice. For these traces are neither Latin nor Greek nor Hebrew, and they are not the property of any one people, but act in the mind as the face does in the body. We say "anger" one way in Latin, another way in Greek, and yet another for each different language; but an angry face is neither Latin nor Greek. Hence not all peoples will understand when someone says "iratus sum," but only the Latins; but if the emotion burning in the soul bursts forth in the face and affects the expression on it, everyone realizes that they're looking at someone who's angry. Yet we are not allowed by the sound of our voices to bring forth and as it were spread out before the sense of our hearers these vestiges which understanding impressed upon our memory, in the same way that a face is plain and manifest; for these are within, in the mind, while that is outside in the body. From this one can conclude how far different the sound in our ear is from that stroke of understanding, when it is not even similar to those impressions of the memory.[22]

Why are catechetical lectures boring, even to the person giving them? Because the words coming out of his mouth are already at two removes from what they signify, being the outward expressions of an inward memory of a moment of understanding in which the human mind sees a truth above itself. This passage operates on the epistemological landscape of Augustine's three-tiered Platonist hierarchy, descending from divine truth to human understanding to external words. The understanding was once saturated with divine truth, that moment of insight which is like a flash of light filling our mind but fading, inevitably fading with the passage of time (time is its enemy, since this flash is a moment of contact with eternity) and now all that is left of it is traces (*vestigia*) impressed in memory. And even those traces in our soul are not adequately expressed by the sounding words, which spread out in time the compact memory of that eternal truth. The will to make others understand can only be put into effect through words, and therefore is almost inevitably frustrated.

Shared Vision

There are exceptions, but they too are momentary. This, I think, helps explain one of the most astounding passages in all of Augustine's writings, the vision at Ostia which he shares with his mother in the ninth book of *Confessions*. It has usually been interpreted as a mystical experience, but if so it is unparalleled: two people sharing the same mystical vision simultaneously. I would suggest that it is more like a mutual catechetical lecture that for once is not boring, where by the grace of God the words spoken and heard actually succeed in directing both minds to see with some clarity what they are trying to understand. For throughout the experience, *Augustine and Monica are talking*. They do not cease to speak to one another the whole time, but they cease paying attention to the sound of the external words, so that their own speaking fades from their minds, giving way to vision. The result has the same basic structure as the insight Augustine had following his reading of the books of the Platonists in *Confessions* 7: those too were words which alerted him to turn away from external things, to examine his own mind but then pass beyond it, looking above it to see the light of eternal Wisdom and Truth, which is God.

The implications for Augustine's view of language come in a single long, magnificent sentence in which Augustine describes Monica and himself reflecting on the experience just after it happened. Having ascended beyond all creation (both external things and the contents of their own minds) they have for a brief moment touched eternal Wisdom and then "we returned to the noise of our mouth, where a word has both a beginning and an end."[23] What comes next? Augustine begins with an eloquent verbal silencing of all creatures, including those creatures called words:

> Therefore we said: if for anyone the tumult of the flesh were silenced, silenced the images of earth and water and air, silenced too the poles—and if even the soul itself were silenced and passed beyond, not thinking of itself—silenced the dreams and imaginary revelations, all tongues and all signs, and whatever takes place and passes away—if for anyone these were all wholly silenced (for to anyone who hears, they all say, "we did not make ourselves, but he made us who remains for eternity") if they would say this and then be quiet...[24]

What *then*-clause could follow such *if*-clauses? The whole creation by its mutability tells us that the unchanging Truth we are looking for is not in them but in him who made them, saying in effect, "what you seek is not me, but him who made me."[25] All outward things are to that extent signs, directing attention away from themselves toward their Creator, bidding us turn inward and ascend to him. When used rightly, our words do the same—as Augustine's words in the text are meant to do, describing his and Monica's words as they talk about the silencing of all words and every creature, hoping for a time when words are utterly unnecessary. What would that time be like, when our minds, freed from attending to creatures, permanently grasp eternity?

> ... for the ear would be raised up to Him who made these things, and
> He alone would speak, not through them but through himself, and
> we would hear His Word, not through the tongue of the flesh nor the
> utterance of angels nor a voice from the cloud nor a likeness in a
> glass darkly, but we would hear Him Himself, whom in these things
> we love—we would hear Him without them, just as we now
> reached out and touched in a quick thought the eternal Wisdom
> abiding above all things... [26]

We would hear a different kind of word, one without beginning or end, the Word of eternity, not the sounding temporary words of our mouths and tongues. Insight into eternal Truth would not be a momentary flash of quick thought but our whole way of being, caught up in eternal life. Augustine returns to if-clauses, trying to conceive it:

> ... if this were to continue, and other sights of a far inferior kind were
> taken away and this one sight seized and engrossed and enclosed
> in inward joy the one who saw it, so that life was forever such a
> moment of understanding as that for which we sighed... [27]

The if-clauses thus contain the answer to the question with which the conversation began, about the nature of the life of ultimate blessedness:

> ... would this not be: "enter into the joy of your Lord"? [28]

And so in the last of the narrative books of the *Confessions* we have a mother-and-child reunion, not in the flesh (for her flesh is about to depart from him in death) but in the hope of seeing the same Wisdom they have talked about, longed for, and in a brief moment of understanding, caught sight of and touched together.

For Augustine words are inadequate to express what lies within because what we see most deeply within is God, who is both Wisdom and Truth, visible to the mind but far beyond the power of words to convey. "It can be understood ineffably," he says. [29] Expressionist semiotics is inseparable from some such notion of inner height or depth in which whatever is ultimate can be found. Our inner self is so much greater than its outward expressions because it contains that which transcends the human self. Expressionist semiotics is thus the theory of meaning that goes along with the conviction that we find within ourselves that Other we most love, which is our true happiness. [30] Words are inadequate to express what we want to see, but that is not ultimately a problem, because we do have the ability to see, and redemption means that our mind's eye will be purified so as to see God. Words cannot give us God, but intellectual vision can. That conviction makes the invention of expressionist semiotics possible. For those who do not believe in the vision of the mind's eye, words will have to take on a more indispensable importance.

PART I

Words from Which
We Learn Nothing

I

Before Words Were Signs

Semiotics in Greek Philosophy

Expressionist semiotics includes the twin theses that words are external signs and that they get their significance by expressing things that belong to the deeper ontological level of the soul or inner self. To show that Augustine invented expressionist semiotics requires a survey of ancient theories of signs before Augustine, showing why these two theses are not found there. Most fundamentally, Greek semiotics is a theory of inference, not of communication or expression. Plato, who originates the ontology of the soul that results in Augustinian notions of inner depth, does not develop a semiotic theory of language nor make a sharp ontological distinction between external words and words within the soul, as expressionist semiotics requires. These twin theses are often attributed to the opening chapter Aristotle's On Interpretation *but recent scholarship has argued this is a mistake, which in effect reads Augustinian semiotics into Aristotle's text. The most important precursor to expressionist semiotics in Greek thought is the Aristotelian concept of physiognomics, which uses the form of the body as a sign from which to infer the character of the soul. In the Hellenistic era the Stoics developed a philosophy of language which incorporated a verbal notion of signs, but which did not subsume words under the classification of signs nor treat meaning as a feature of the soul. Semiotics also played an important role in a debate about the nature of empirical knowledge between Stoics and Epicureans, where the ambiguity of "common signs," already noted by Aristotle, becomes a central issue. Philosophical sceptics eventually argued that all signs were ambiguous, "common" to more than one thing signified, and thus unsuitable to be the basis of an empirical science—though useful in daily life as reminders. In Augustine's view of signs, it turns out he is closer to the sceptics than to the philosophers who believed in the possibility of empirical knowledge.*

What makes expressionist semiotics something fundamentally new is its dimension of inner depth. In inventing expresssionist semiotics Augustine was the first to conceive signs as the crucial epistemic link between outer and inner, body and soul, which are literally two different dimensions of being. The external, bodily dimension can be measured in inches, feet, or miles, whereas the internal dimension of the soul is not measurable in spatial terms at all because the soul has a different kind of being from the body and its magnitude is of a different sort.[1] It is this internal dimension of being with its psychological magnitude that we in modern times tend to describe with metaphors of depth—though ancient philosophers preferred metaphors of height. (And the metaphor of depth with which I am beginning this exposition will gradually fall away as we work our way more fully into ancient modes of thought. But "depth" is a good enough metaphor to start with). In any case, the ontological difference between outer and inner results in an epistemic difference. The external dimension, in which signs have their place, is unlike the soul in being perceptible by the senses. It is what Platonists call the sensible world, or modern philosophers the empirical world. Hence the "expression" in expressionist semiotics means bringing something out from the inner depths of the soul and into the visible world for all to see, like taking it out of a private inner closet and bringing it into the open. Of course for Augustine one cannot literally transfer things from the one dimension to the other, for the inner cannot literally be externalized or changed into something external. When we speak, for instance, "what is understood remains inward while what is heard resounds outwardly."[2] That is indeed why the private inner self needs a semiotics, an account of how inner things can be signified by outer things while remaining within. To say that Augustine's expressionist semiotics is new is to point out that signs never had this function before.

Semiotics and Semantics

Semiotics before Augustine meant discussions of the nature of empirical inference. Its task was to articulate epistemological connections within the sensible world rather than to link two different worlds or dimensions of being. That is why it did not occur to Greek philosophers to classify words as a kind of sign (*sēmeion*). For them signs belonged to a process of inference, not a process of expression. They served not to communicate what lies hidden in the soul but to reveal what lies unseen in the world, as for example medical symptoms reveal an underlying condition hidden in the depths of the body or as smoke on the horizon indicates a fire that is somewhere nearby but perhaps not yet seen. Umberto Eco and his colleagues state the contrast thus:

> the semiotics of the Greeks, from the *Corpus Hippocraticum* to the Stoics, made a clear cut distinction between a theory of verbal language and a theory of signs. Signs (*sēmeia*) are natural givens, which today we would call symptoms or indexes, and they entertain with that which they signify, or designate, a relation based on the mechanism of inference: if such a symptom, then such a sickness; if this one has milk, then birth has been given; if smoke, then fire. Words, however, stand in a different relation with the thing they signify, or designate, and this relation is that which is sanctioned by the Aristotelian theory of definition.[3]

The difference between signs and words is, in English as well as Greek, the difference between semiotics and semantics, *sēmeia* and *sēmaina*. The Stoics in particular developed theories of both. Their theory of language made prominent use of semantic vocabulary (*sēmaina* and *sēmainomena*, "things that mean" and "things that are meant") while their theory of inference relied on semiotic vocabulary (*sēmeia*, "signs," and occasionally *sēmeiōta*, "things signified"). These were two different areas of inquiry but it turns out they intersect, and it is not hard to see how later readers could confuse them.

A crucial cause of confusion, from Augustine's day to this, is that Latin has a special vocabulary for semiotics but not for semantics. It has *signa* to translate *sēmeia*, but no word that is an exact equivalent of *sēmaina* or the English word "meaning." Hence in Latinate languages semiotic vocabulary such as "signifier" and "signification" is often used to translate semantic vocabulary in Greek philosophy such as *sēmainon* and *sēmainomenon*. We can see descendants of this Latin usage in the quotation above, where words are said to "signify or designate" things—both terms derived from the Latin vocabulary for signs. This seems to be one reason why Eco and his colleagues, despite noting a "clear cut distinction" between the Greeks' theory of verbal language and their theory of signs, feel free to lump the two together under the heading of "the semiotics of the Greeks."

In my view, this confuses matters. The term "semiotics" is best used simply as a synonym for "theory of signs." Therefore, precisely in the interest of maintaining a clear-cut distinction between theory of signs and theory of language, one should not subsume Greek theories of language under the heading "semiotics." But evidently the authors are thinking that the theory of language is a branch of semiotics because (in their Latinate vocabulary) words *signify* things. These authors are also, of course, heirs of several traditions of European semiotics (associated with Ferdinand de Saussure, C. S. Peirce, John of Poinsot, and various medieval figures going back to Augustine) which do not merely speak in a loose way of words signifying things, but systematically classify words as a kind of sign and thus try to explain linguistic meaning as a species of signification. There is no confusion when such traditions habitually speak of language as one of the concerns of semiotics, and of words as having signification. But it does confuse matters to bring that habit of speech to the study of Greek semiotics, which is about the nature of empirical inference rather than the nature of linguistic meaning.

There is a further problem with this Latinate habit of speech. If one does speak of the *signification* of words, then one must clarify what is distinctive about the signification of *signs*, in the original inferential sense of Greek *sēmeia*. So Eco and his colleagues suggest equating *sēmeia* with "symptoms or indexes." Similar suggestions are made by English and American scholars, who also use the vocabulary of signification to render Greek semantics and therefore find that in order to clarify the distinctive function of *sēmeia* they must use terms like "signal" or "symptom."[4] But I find this unhelpful. "Signals" are communication devices but *sēmeia* are not. And "symptom" and "index" are only two species of sign, for which the Greeks already had specific words like *tekmērion* and *endeixis*. It seems that if one uses the term "signification" for the meaning of words then one will often end up wanting to call *sēmeia* something other than signs, which is cause for more confusion.

I prefer on the contrary to restore the vocabulary of "signification" and its cognates to *sēmeia*, and use other terms such as "meaning" to describe the semantic function of words. So in this book I will restrict my use of semiotic language to signs (Greek *sēmeia* and Latin *signa*) so that the verb "signify" will always be tied to the noun "sign." Signifying is what signs do, and words do it only if they are a species of sign. So I will speak of words *signifying* or having *signification* only when discussing an author who classifies words as a species of sign. There are many such authors in the Western tradition beginning with Augustine, but none among the Greeks. For words are not in general a form of empirical inference, and therefore it did not occur to Greek philosophers to classify them as signs. This is why, if we are attentive to their vocabulary, we will not find them subsuming semantics under semiotics.

Recent studies continue to sharpen the clear-cut distinction between theory of language and theory of signs in Greek thought.[5] Thereby they reverse many centuries of scholarship that tended to run the two together, going back to Boethius's Augustinian reading of Aristotle and Sextus Empiricus's tendency to confuse the Stoics' semantic vocabulary with their semiotic vocabulary.[6] Augustine scholarship in particular should be updated on this score, so as to bring out the novelty of Augustine's expressionist semiotics.[7] To clarify exactly what Augustine did and did not inherit from earlier theories of signs, we need to look first at Plato and Aristotle, then at the Stoics and their rivals. Plato inaugurates the tradition within which expressionist semiotics eventually arose, while Aristotle and the Stoics were central to the very un-Platonist tradition of semiotics before Augustine.

Words Written on Platonic Souls

Expressionist semiotics involves a semiotic triad in which external *words* mean *things* by way of expressing inner *thoughts*. There are various ways of articulating the relations between the three members of this triad, involving various ways of locating the relation of signification. One might expect words to signify things, but sometimes a semiotician will insist that words do not signify things directly but rather signify thoughts in the soul or mind, which in turn signify things. Augustine's own usage is rather free: anything inside or outside the soul can be something signified by words, a *res significata*. However, it is worth noting from the start that Augustine has no notion of signs in the soul. The medieval notion of mental signs is a much later development. Also, Augustine's own notion of the inner word, which he developed rather late in his career,[8] is not linguistic (he insists that it is not in Latin or Greek or any other human tongue) and therefore he does not classify it as a sign. Rather, it is close to what we mean by our term, "concept." So Augustine's "inner word" is not literally a word, and therefore not a sign. The overarching point is that for Augustine signs are always sensible and external, having a different kind of being from the soul and its contents. This ontological gap between soul and signs, inner and outer, belongs to the very essence of language as Augustine conceives it: there is no need of words where there are no inner depths to express.

The philosophy within which to locate the rise of expressionist semiotics is Platonism, the tradition that gave us the notion of inner depth.[9] Plato in this respect is precursor not founder: he originates a tradition in which it later makes sense to develop an expressionist semiotics, but he does not develop one himself. His account of the relationship of words and thoughts tends in fact to leave out the dimension of depth, minimizing the contrast between what is in our souls and what we speak aloud. He tells us, for instance, that "thought [*dianoia*] and discourse [*logos*] are the same thing," the only difference being that the former is "a voiceless inner dialogue of the soul with itself."[10] So thinking is just one form of *logos* or discourse, a dialogue carried on within the soul as it talks to itself, answers its own questions, and so on.[11]

Significantly, there is only one speaker in this inner dialogue. Plato does not go the route of Augustine, who writes a whole inner conversation between himself and another character called Reason in his *Soliloquies*. Plato in fact does not picture the *logos* of thought as resounding in an inner space but as written on the soul. After giving an example of a man thinking and trying to make up his mind about something, which he describes as if the man were silently talking to himself and asking and answering his own questions, Plato proposes that when this happens "our soul resembles a book" and explains: it is as if memory, joined by sense-perception, makes for affections (*pathēmata*) that write words (*logous*) on our souls.[12] This immensely influential metaphor of words written on the soul kept generations of Greek philosophers picturing the contents of their souls in two-dimensional rather than three-dimensional terms.[13] For them the soul is not an inner world but an inner tablet, like the waxed board on which schoolchildren wrote their exercises.

Aristotle is probably working with this Platonic metaphor when he says, in one of the most influential remarks in his logical writings, that "things in the voice are symbols [*symbola*] of affections in the soul, and things written [are symbols] of things in the voice."[14] The puzzling phrase "things in the voice," usually translated "spoken words" (as if Aristotle had written simply *phōnai* rather than *ta en tēi phōnēi*) is easy to understand if Aristotle is thinking of Plato's talk of "the image [*eidōlon*] of thought *in the voice*,"[15] which Plato describes as "imprinted on the stream through the mouth as on a mirror or water."[16] "Things in the voice" are whatever is imprinted on this stream of sound coming through our mouths when we speak; the imprinting itself is the articulation of speech. If with Norman Kretzmann we let the relation between written and spoken words be our guide for interpreting Aristotle's use of the term *symbola*, then being a symbol of something means being a notation for it in a different medium, as writing is a notation for spoken words[17] or a musical score is a notation for musical sounds. Interpreting *symbolon* this way, we get a threefold analogy: there are things impressed on the stream of sound coming through our mouths, there are things literally impressed on wax or papyrus, and there are things that make an impression on the soul—its affections (*pathēmata*). *Logos* can be found in any of these media: voice, wax, soul.

Thus Aristotle's cryptic sentence, which has occasioned an enormous amount of commentary and puzzlement over the centuries, makes good sense, and even its cryptic nature is to be expected, if it is an allusion to a well-known

Platonic metaphor that was too familiar to Aristotle's audience to need explanation (especially in one of Aristotle's logical treatises, which were probably written early in his career while he was still teaching Plato's students at the Academy). This situation of teaching in Plato's school would also explain why the stunning phrase "inner *logos*" appears in another of Aristotle's logical writings, contrasted with "outer *logos*" in a brief remark making a minor point, but is never developed further.[18] The inner word, so important a notion in later Christian thought, is for Aristotle just shorthand for Plato's familiar picture of words written on the soul.

So far we have found neither signs nor inner depth in Plato's view of language. The deepening or enlargement of the soul that begins with Plato's doctrine of recollection[19] and culminates in Augustine's invention of private inner space is not a persistent feature of Plato's own thought. The concept of soul takes a different direction in the writings of his later years as well as in those of his great student Aristotle—a direction away from what is nowadays called "Platonism." On the standard chronology of Plato's writing, the doctrine of recollection, together with much else that belongs to the philosophy of Platonism, is characteristic of his middle period, while the writings in which we have just traced his "two-dimensional" picture of the soul (*Sophist, Theaetetus,* and *Philebus*) come from his late period—probably the twenty years or so in which Aristotle was studying and then teaching at Plato's Academy, during which we must assume Aristotle and Plato were having some of the most influential conversations in the history of Western thought.

On the border between the two periods sits the *Phaedrus*, the first half of which contains Plato's most elaborate account of the preexistent source of the soul's recollections[20] and the second half of which argues that true memory is a form of writing on the soul.[21] It is as if the first half of the dialogue were taking a valedictory look at the past and the second half were turning to the future of Plato's thinking. The first half locates our deepest knowledge in a heavenly vision, the memory of which still lies hidden within us—the sort of vision that makes it possible for Plato to insist, in the Allegory of the Cave, that education cannot be a matter of transferring knowledge from one soul to another, since the power of knowledge is already in us.[22] The second half, by contrast, tells us that the true teacher is the dialectician who accomplishes just such a transference by planting his words of knowledge in the students' souls, resulting in words written on their souls.[23] As we shall see, Augustine's view that the true teacher is found within the soul, requiring a "three-dimensional" picture of the soul as inner space, puts him very much on the side of the Platonism of the Allegory of the Cave, against Plato's later "two-dimensional" picture of words written on the soul.

Not long after the *Phaedrus* Plato writes the great epistemological dialogue *Theaetetus,* where he evidently rejects the doctrine of recollection altogether[24] and speaks of memory only in terms of writing on the soul. In doing so he introduces the metaphor of impressions imprinted on the soul like characters imprinted on wax.[25] In contrast to the doctrine of recollection, this metaphor comports very well with a materialist conception of mind and becomes widespread among the materialist philosophers of the Hellenistic era, beginning a couple of generations after Plato. When Hellenistic philosophers—Stoics, Epicureans, or Academics—speak of a mental "appearance" (*phantasia*) they are thinking of an impression stamped on the soul. This is not the modern notion of an idea seen in the mind like an image viewed within a private inner room.[26] As Plato spells out the metaphor, mental "impressions" are not what the mind looks at but more like the shape of the mind that does the looking. We recognize things outside us by using our mental impressions, the way we recognize a foot by fitting it to a footprint, an impression in the ground.[27] The impression in the mind is the way the mind fits itself to its object; it is the form or shape of the mind's attention to what is outside itself. Thus Plato's metaphor of mental impressions leaves no room in the soul for the depth of inner vision.

Likewise, apart from the recurrent metaphor of the signet ring (whose impression on wax can be called, rather confusingly for our purposes, a *sēmeion* or sign)[28] all this talk of writing words or stamping impressions on our souls is quite different from literal talk of signs and signification, and thus quite far from a semiotic account of language. To show this will take an argument, however. The argument about Aristotle must wait until after we have examined his semiotics. The argument about Plato can begin by noting that he does not *have* a semiotics. This is to be expected since he has no great interest in empirical inference, which is what Greek semiotics is about. (By the same token it is not surprising that the first semiotics in Western philosophy is developed by Aristotle, for whom empirical inference is a matter of great importance.)

What Plato does do, quite simply, is on a couple of occasions call words signs. One occasion is in the *Cratylus,* where we hear of a hypothetical legislator of language who makes letters and syllables into "signs and names for every being."[29] The other occasion is a passage in the *Sophist* where Plato twice describes words as "signs of the voice."[30] On both occasions, the semiotic vocabulary shows up and then is dropped, not developed further. The *Cratylus* is pursuing the thesis that words are vocal imitations of things, and talk of signs evidently does not further that agenda. Indeed, it seems one reason an expressionist semiotics was so long in coming is that talk of signs is not much at home in Platonism, where the key relations that make things intelligible to us are imitation, imagery, reflection, and similarity, not signification. In the *Sophist*, likewise, words are not signs of thought or of anything else in soul but of the things to which they refer. There is no semiotic triad here, much less an expressionist semiotics. Turn a couple of pages and you find the discussion of inner dialogue that we noted above, which is conducted entirely without the vocabulary of signs. What this tells us, I think, is that Plato could have developed a classification of words as a species of signs if he thought it served any useful theoretical purpose, but it didn't. In the context of Greek thought and usage, the notion of a semiotics of language makes too little sense to be a promising line of inquiry. So Plato briefly entertains the notion that spoken words are vocal signs and then does nothing with it.[31]

The Logic of Aristotle's Signs

Semiotics as a philosophical discipline begins with Aristotle, who treats the logic of signs in the last chapter of his *Prior Analytics,* with a parallel treatment in his *Rhetoric.*[32] In both places he compares the concept of sign with the related concept of "the likely" (I translate the term *eikos* here literally, instead of the more usual translation, "probability"). What is *likely* according to *Prior Analytics* is any widely accepted proposition such as "jealous people hate" and "enamored people love."[33] The concept of sign on the other hand is more specific, for a sign is always involved somehow in inference. A sign is a proposition (*protasis*) that may be necessary or merely widely accepted but is in either case supposed to be "demonstrative," in the sense of playing a role in inferences that can be spelled out in some form of syllogism.[34] This inferential role is based on relations that are essential to the nature of the sign. Hence Aristotle defines the concept of sign in terms of relations between objects (things that exist) or relations between events (things that happen):

> A thing [*pragma*] that exists when something [else] exists, or that happens before or after something [else] happens, is a sign of what happens or exists.[35]

Note here a systematic ambiguity (of the kind that a medieval philosopher would call an analogy). The concept of sign is introduced as a type of proposition (*protasis*) but then is described as a type of thing (*pragma*). Signs are thus both linguistic items involved in forms of reasoning and objects or events related to other objects or events. In the ordinary sense, for example, the event of lactation is a sign that a woman has earlier been pregnant (thus fitting the definition as "something . . . that happens . . . after something [else] happens"). But when Aristotle explains the logic of signs he gives examples of *propositions* such as "all women who have milk have been pregnant." This ambiguity in the meaning of "sign" will meet us in another form in Stoic semiotics.[36]

The most important kind of sign, which in his *Rhetoric* Aristotle calls a *tekmērion* and describes as a sure sign of what it signifies (literally a "necessary sign"),[37] supports an inference that can be spelled out in the form of a deductively valid first-figure syllogism. To use the example indicated in *Prior Analytics*:

> All women who have milk have been pregnant (= sign).
> This woman has milk.
> Therefore, this woman has been pregnant.[38]

Aristotle will call this kind of sign "proper" (*idion*) in the sense that lactation is an effect belonging exclusively to pregnancy and to no other underlying condition. Other kinds of signs are not so exclusive and therefore not so sure. For example, paleness can be a sign of pregnancy, but it can be a sign of many other things as well. Consequently, inference from paleness to pregnancy is not at all certain. We can see this from the syllogism that spells out the inference:

> All pregnant women are pale (= sign).
> This woman is pale.
> Therefore, this woman is pregnant.[39]

This (second-figure) syllogism is not valid. Even if we suppose all pregnant woman really are pale, a pale woman may not be pregnant, because something else may be making her pale. So paleness may be listed as one symptom of pregnancy, but it is clearly not sufficient by itself for a diagnosis: it is not a sure sign of pregnancy. In terminology later used by the Stoics and Augustine, Aristotle will call this a "common sign," in the sense that it is common to pregnancy and many other conditions. The difference between common and proper signs is thus illustrated by the fact that a woman can be pale without ever being pregnant, but she cannot be lactating unless she has been pregnant.

The difference between proper and common signs is at the center of much of the semiotic discussion in the history of Greek philosophy. Sound scientific inference requires signs that do not signify many different possibilities. (Similarly today, to infer that x is the cause of y on the basis of a statistical correlation between x and y requires that one eliminate the possibility of y being the result of other causal factors such as z or w. Otherwise y, taken as a sign of the presence of x—for instance in a medical test—will result in a great many "false positives"). In Aristotelian logic, this means that the proposition stating a proper sign will be the converse of the proposition stating the causal relation on which the sign is based. For instance, the relevant causal proposition in our case is "all women who have been pregnant produce milk," which states the causal relation: pregnancy causes lactation. But to use lactation as a proper sign of pregnancy, we also need the converse proposition to be true, the one that appears in the valid syllogism above: "All women who have milk have been pregnant." For this adds the logically decisive point that only women who have been pregnant produce milk, which means that lactation is a sign belonging exclusively to pregnancy and not to any other condition. That is what makes it a "proper sign" of pregnancy, in Aristotle's technical sense. In contrast, paleness is a common rather than proper sign of pregnancy because even if we accept the relevant causal proposition (that pregnancy always makes women pale), its converse (that all pale women have been pregnant) is obviously untrue. Consequently, the major premise in a semiotic inference will be a proper sign only when (in Aristotelian terminology) the middle term of the syllogism is "convertible" with the first term. This means in effect that not only does the thing signified cause this sign (women who have been pregnant produce milk) but also that this sign belongs only to this thing signified (all women with milk have been pregnant, which is logically equivalent to saying that only women who have been pregnant have milk). This convertibility—this ability to move from a causal statement to its converse—is characteristic of proper signs.

Scientific inferences must begin with the converse of a causal statement because inference proceeds from effect to cause, not cause to effect. This is what some medieval philosophers had in mind when they said the order of knowing is the opposite of the order of being. Greek semiotics is about this epistemic order of inference, rather than the ontological order of causality by which signs are produced. So the Greeks did not have anything to say about how the soul expresses itself by producing signs, but did have an interest in how others may infer something about the soul from the signs it produces.

Physiognomic Inferences

The notion that there are signs of the soul long predates expressionist semiotics. From the beginning of ancient semiotics, philosophers were interested in using bodily signs to make inferences about the state of the soul. Thus Aristotle's discussion of signs in the last chapter of *Prior Analytics* is followed by a kind of appendix on physiognomy,[40] where he lays out the logical requirements to be met by a science that would infer the character of a man's soul from the features of his body. Along with two other treatments of physiognomy in the Aristotelian corpus,[41] this text inaugurates the long tradition of Western philosophers looking at the body for signs of the soul. The practice of physiognomy goes back long before Aristotle[42] and evidently tended to use comparisons between human beings and other animals—attributing courage to a man because he has lion-like features, for instance. In proposing a more scientific version of this style of inference, Aristotle obviously needs to impose restrictions on the selection of signs, rather than relying on arbitrary hunches about how someone looks. This is the key methodological issue in all three treatments of physiognomy in the Aristotelian corpus. Since these together comprise the first extended discussion of inference from signs extant in the Western philosophical tradition, it will be worth our while to look at them more closely.

Although the texts do not actually use the word "science" (*epistēmē*) in connection with physiognomy,[43] the discussion is evidently an answer to the question: under what conditions could physiognomy be considered a science? So in the *Prior Analytics,* Aristotle casts physiognomic inferences in the mold of deductively valid syllogisms using bodily features as proper signs of affections of the soul. Adopting the method of comparing human features to the characteristic features of animal species,[44] he assumes for the sake of example that all lions are courageous and have large extremities, and that no other species is like that: individual animals of other species may be courageous or have large extremities, but only in lions do courage as well as large extremities belong to the very nature of the species. So courage is in this sense proper to lions as a species, and moreover having large extremities is proper to courage. Evidently, Aristotle is thinking this makes large extremities a proper sign of courage in individual animals of other species as well. If that is so, then we can construct the valid syllogism:

> All animals with large extremities have courage (= sign).
> This man has large extremities (i.e., is an animal with large extremities).
> Therefore, this man has courage.

This is a valid first-figure syllogism, like the example of lactation as a sign of pregnancy. Once again, the proper sign is a proposition that is the converse of the related causal proposition: "All animals with courage have large extremities." The underlying causal assumption is that courage in the soul produces large extremities in the body.

The terminological contrast between "proper" and "common" signs first enters the written record of ancient philosophy in Aristotelian physiognomics.[45] In the Hellenistic era the contrast becomes central to semiotic debates where, as in Aristotle, what is at stake is whether a given form of inference can be scientific. So Greek semiotics is a discussion about the empirical basis of scientific knowledge, concerned with how scientific knowledge might be extended by inference from things easily observed, like bodily features, to things that cannot be seen directly, like the passions of the soul. Thus the relation of body and soul was a concern of semiotics from the beginning, though the notion of expression was not.

Body Affecting Soul

The Aristotelian project of making a science out of physiognomic inferences might strike us as odd for a number of reasons. It is not just that physiognomy nowadays seems more like folklore than science. (Perhaps it should not surprise us that Aristotle, in the process of inventing the very notion of empirical science, considers some candidates for the status of "science" that we have long since put behind us.) What is perhaps most striking is the project of making scientific inferences about the soul on the basis of the body. The surprise dissipates a bit if we imagine the soul as a material thing, rather than a hidden inner depth belonging to a different dimension of being from the body. We need to be willing to make this leap of imagination because it was the common philosophical view in the period after Aristotle. The Stoics, for instance, were materialists who believed the soul was made of fire and thus was as corporeal as the body. So it is not surprising that they had no qualms about drawing inferences from body to soul.[46] For them this kind of reasoning would be a form of empirical inference not much different from a physician's inference from observable symptoms to underlying causes.

It is all the more interesting, then, that these treatments of the method of physiognomy are found in the corpus of the writings of Aristotle, who is not exactly a materialist but who is a key force in the move away from Platonism (i.e., the philosophy that originates with Plato's middle dialogues and centers on the intelligibility of unchanging Ideas or Forms) and toward the more empiricist philosophies that dominated the Hellenistic era.[47] All three discussions of physiognomy in the Aristotelian corpus begin with the premise that body and soul mutually interact, a premise that suggests they belong at the same level of being. In the most rudimentary formulation body and soul are "co-affected by one another,"[48] while in the most sophisticated and noncommittal formulation (that of *Prior Analytics*) they are merely "changed at the same time."[49] But in the most elaborate formulation of all, we get the rudiments of a biological theory about the necessary relation between body and soul in all living things. This formulation is especially worth noting, as it shows that the sign-inferences used in physiognomy are premised on a view of the relation of soul and body that is profoundly un-Platonist. It would for instance exclude the possibility of transmigration of souls from one species of animal to another, as well as subject the soul to the causal power of the body's affections.

This most fully developed treatment of the mutual influence of body and soul is found in the treatise in the first half of the *Physiognomics*. Here the key premises for a science of physiognomy are not just accepted hypothetically, as in the *Prior Analytics*, but asserted and argued for. The opening claim of the treatise challenges the Platonist propensity to see causal power working only "downward" ontologically from soul to body: "Thought-processes follow bodily features, nor are they in themselves unaffected by the movements of the body."[50] The argument for this claim rests on an observation about how the notion of biological species involves soul as well as body:

> It is especially in things engendered by nature that one can see how soul and body are mutually related in such a shared nature [*symphuōs*] that they become the cause [*aitia*] of most of one another's affections. For no animal that was ever engendered had the form [*eidos*] of one animal and the thought-process of another, but rather body and soul are always of the same [kind of] animal, so that such-and-such a thought-process necessarily follows such-and-such a body.[51]

This biological notion of the soul makes it impossible to imagine human souls being reborn in the bodies of beasts. In addition positing a much tighter fit between body and soul than in Platonists theories of embodiment, this passage also provides an example of the drastic misuse of Platonist vocabulary that abounds in the two treatises of the *Physiognomics*. *Eidos*, Plato's word for intelligible Form, is used to designate bodily structure;[52] *morphē*, another term for Form, is used to designate bodily shape or body type;[53] and a little after the passage just quoted, *idea* is used in the sense of "observable feature"![54] All these usages were unexceptionable in ordinary Greek but run quite counter to Plato's philosophical usage. In the *Physiognomics* the vocabulary that Plato used to talk about the intelligible world is consistently used to describe the bodily side of the body-soul relation.

Now the most fascinating thing about this is that it is inconsistent with Peripatetic usage as well. To associate form and structure (*eidos* and *morphē*) with body *in contrast to* soul is hardly Aristotelian, since for Aristotle the soul is the form of the body.[55] It is not surprising, therefore, to find that the *Physiognomics* is nowadays not counted among Aristotle's genuine works. Yet the many things the two treatises have in common with the appendix to the *Prior Analytics* (viz., the structure of exposition and argument, the basic premise of body-soul parallelism or interaction, the interest in "proper" signs and affections, the ongoing effort to refine one particular method of physiognomic inference, the recurring example of the lion) argue against simply rejecting them as un-Peripatetic. Unless the discussion of physiognomy in the *Prior Analytics* was authored by someone other than Aristotle and appended by a later editor (a possibility for which we have no evidence) its resemblance to the discussions in the *Physiognomics* makes it difficult to dismiss the latter as having nothing to do with Aristotle. The appendix to *Prior Analytics* unmistakably belongs to the same discussion as the methodological sections of the *Physiognomics,* and indeed provides a logically rigorous solution to the problems about the selection of signs raised in the latter. At the same time, the very vocabulary that militates against Aristotelian authorship makes it difficult to locate it anywhere within the Peripatetic school. In fact the one semiotic treatise we have from Aristotle's successors, Theophrastus's *Concerning Weather Signs,* displays no interest whatsoever in the logical status of signs or in their place in a possible science.[56]

How then are we to locate the line of thought in these treatises with respect to the Aristotelian tradition? Who, knowing the thought of either Plato or Aristotle, would identify bodily features as "ideas" (*ideai*)? One could imagine a sort of young Turk coming to study at Plato's Academy, who rejects the notion that intelligible Forms exist separately from sensible things and who deliberately uses the Platonic vocabulary of Form and Idea to promote an empiricist style of thought. But in that case there is no likelier author of these treatises than the young Aristotle himself, at least if we follow one plausible view of his intellectual development.[57] It is not hard to imagine Aristotle, a physician's son[58] who later invented the empirical discipline of biology, borrowing semiotic notions from the physicians and using them to articulate the relation between body and soul in a way analogous to the relation of symptom to underlying state of health. And one could imagine the brilliant young upstart quite consciously emphasizing his departure from the master's teaching by applying the vocabulary of intelligibility and Form precisely to bodily signs. One would not be surprised to see him connecting this with the work he was doing at that time on logic, thinking from the very beginning about how signs might be incorporated into syllogisms to make a science.[59] And one could imagine how it might eventually lead him to the thought that the nature and powers of the soul are not independent of the organization of the living body in which it is found—a thought that plays a major role in his treatise *On the Soul,* where he rejects the theory of transmigration of souls:

Here we come upon another absurdity of this and most other theories
about the soul. They join soul to body and place it therein, without
explaining the cause of this, or the condition of the body. Yet it would
seem that some such explanation is needed, for it is because of the
association between them that the one acts and the other is acted
upon, the one is moved and the other moves it—this is not what
happens with things that have only a haphazard relationship with one
another. But these theories only bother to talk about what the soul
is like, and have no further explanation of the body that is to receive
it—as if it were possible, as in the Pythagorean myths, for any old
soul to enter any old body. But this can't be, for each one evidently
has its own proper form and shape [eidos kai morphē].[60]

On these grounds it seems to me that it would be well to re-open the question
of the authenticity of the treatises in the *Physiognomics*.

But however it may be with the authorship of these treatises—and whatever we make of Aristotle's development—this much is clear: the physiognomic writings in the Aristotelian corpus (meaning both the book titled
Physiognomics and the appendix to the *Prior Analytics*) are the founding documents of philosophical semiotics, and they mark semiotics from the beginning of its history as an essentially un-Platonist line of inquiry. Semiotics
begins with an empiricist bias, for in it the accent of intelligibility is on bodies
rather than on those higher or deeper things that Platonists call "intelligible."
It furthermore implies a view of body and soul in which the two are much
more closely interconnected, much more dependent on one another for their
causal operations and characteristic processes, than in the rather loosely embodied picture of the soul that is so influential in later Platonism and so
determinative for Augustine.[61] Hence it is striking that the concept of sign is
central to the epistemological relation that Augustine wants to establish between body and soul, the outer and inner dimensions of being. One could put it
this way: originally semiotics wanted to say something different from what
Augustine would like to say with it. Hence we shall see that Augustine is in no
position to adopt the concept of signs uncritically, but must approach it with a
great degree of scepticism.

The Semiotics of *On Interpretation*

Something like the physiognomic style of inference, the notion that bodily
things can be signs of the soul, seems to have been what Aristotle had in mind

when he wrote in the opening chapter of his treatise *On Interpretation* that "things in the voice" are signs of affections in the soul.[62] This chapter, "the most influential text in the history of semantics,"[63] gained its influence in part because Aristotle's term "signs" (*sēmeia*) was later interpreted as if he meant what Augustine would have meant by it. That is to say, traditional readings take Aristotle to be offering a semiotic theory of language, in which words get their meaning by being a species of signs that signify the thoughts or intentions in our souls. Such readings have been abetted by translators who use the same word to render this claim as they do to render the quite different claim discussed above, which occurs just a little earlier in the chapter: the claim that things in the voice are symbols (*symbola*) of the affections of the soul.[64] The most influential of the many such translators was undoubtedly Boethius, who uses the same Latin term, *notae* ("marks"), to translate both *symbola* and *sēmeia* in this chapter, "thereby hiding this difference from the view of Western philosophers for seven centuries or more, the centuries during which his translation of *De Interpretatione* was one of the few books which every philosopher discussed."[65]

To overlook the difference between symbols and signs in this text is a serious mistake, because Aristotle uses the two terms to refer to two quite different relations between words and the things in the soul. Aristotle explicitly tells us that written words are symbols (not signs) of spoken words—hence Kretzmann's interpretation, which we followed earlier, that symbols should be understood as a notation for the phenomena of one medium in another medium. This suggests that the way we put words on paper is somehow analogous to the way we form thoughts in our minds—an analogy that does not seem very far-fetched if one is already used to picturing thoughts as words written on the soul. Thus Aristotle's concept of symbol here operates wholly within the realm of articulate language—of *logos* in thought, speech, and script. It is quite a different thing, however, to describe spoken words ("things in the voice") as signs (*sēmeia*) of affections in the soul. This means seeing them as indications or symptoms from which we can draw inferences about what is going on in someone's soul.[66] This is not a property of language alone but includes the way a dog's bark might show us that it is hungry or afraid. So as Aristotle shortly points out, you don't get names (i.e., language or *logos*) until you have symbols, even though "inarticulate noises, like that of beasts, also show something [*dēlousi ti*]."[67] Hence to say that spoken words are signs of affections of the soul is not to say anything about semantics or theory of language. It is merely to point out that the sounds people make can be used as the basis for inferences about how they are feeling or what is on their minds—just as you can infer that a dog is hurt from the way it yelps.[68]

Interpretations of *On Interpretation* will perhaps always be controversial, and Kretzmann's interpretation has generated its share of controversy.[69] The key point I would add in its favor is that if Aristotle intended to give a semiotic account of linguistic meaning then he was making a surprising and radical innovation in Greek semiotics (treating linguistic meaning as if it were a form of inference from signs) and this slender text with its single use of the term *sēmeion*[70] gives no indication of proposing, much less defending, anything so grand and revolutionary. Whereas if on the contrary Aristotle is simply mentioning that vocal utterances like other bodily changes can be signs of affections of the soul, then he is using the notion of sign in a way well established in the semiotics of physiognomy where body and soul change with one another and affect each other. He is not claiming that the way words mean things is somehow generically the same as the way smoke signifies fire or lactation is a sign of pregnancy. Yet Aristotle's text has often been cited in support of philosophies of language that take precisely this route, classifying linguistic meaning as a species of signification because words are outward signs expressing the inner states of the soul. In other words, Aristotle has been misread and used to support a view of language that actually originates with Augustine. Not surprisingly, this misreading was especially common among the philosopher-theologians of the Christian Middle Ages, who were all, directly or indirectly, students of Augustine. Thus for centuries Aristotle's *On Interpretation* was one of the fundamental texts used to support an Augustinian expressionist semiotics.

Stoic Semantics without Depth

The Stoics' philosophy of language was much less influential in the long run than Aristotle's brief remarks in the first chapter of *On Interpretation*. In fact none of their treatises on the subject survive. Yet we do know that in the Hellenistic era the Stoics played a central role in Greek discussions of semiotics. Moreover, the reports that have come down to us suggest that in contrast to Aristotle, they did in fact have a fully developed theory of semantics designed to give an account of the nature of linguistic meaning. That theory was elaborated in the highly technical language for which the Stoics were famous, which included a precise distinction between linguistic meanings and empirical signs, *sēmaina* and *sēmeia*, respectively. As the Kneales explain the difference, "The relation between *sēmainon* and *sēmainomenon* is that between language and what it expresses, while the relation between *sēmeion* and *sēmeiōton* is that between what is known first and what is known through it."[71]

Strikingly, this important distinction has only been rediscovered recently.[72] But any scholar who observes it will be safe from the temptation of thinking that the Stoics classified words as a type of sign.[73]

Unlike Augustine, the Stoics do not subsume semantics under semiotics. If anything it is the reverse. For the Stoics, linguistic meaning is not a kind of signification; rather, signs are a particular kind of linguistic meaning. Signs are used in the process of drawing inferences about the natural world, and for the Stoics this process is linguistic. Thus the distinctively Stoic definition of signs identifies them as a kind of proposition: the antecedent of a true conditional statement which reveals the consequent.[74] A stock example of such a sign is a variation on the example used by Aristotle: "This woman has milk" in the conditional statement, "If this woman has milk, then she has been pregnant." The logical form is different, however, because Aristotle's sign is a whole statement, a premise that can be used in a syllogism, while the Stoics' sign is the antecedent or if-clause in a single conditional statement (i.e., an "if-then" statement). Thus the Stoics articulate the semiotics of inference in terms of the semantics of conditional statements, because in their view "the sign itself has the character: 'if this, then that.' "[75]

This does not quite mean that a sign consists of words. A sign is not a particular set of words but their semantic content or meaning. The antecedent of a conditional statement is in Stoic terms a "proposition" (*axiōma*), which consists not in words but in a *lekton* or "thing said."[76] The idea here is roughly that words say things, and *lekta* are what they say. Hence for the Stoics words are "things that mean" (*sēmaina*) while *lekta*, including signs, are meanings or "things that are meant" (*sēmainomena*).

The notion of *lekta* is central to the Stoic philosophy of language but presents many puzzles to scholars.[77] These puzzles, which provide an instructive contrast to Augustinian semiotics, begin with the ontological status of *lekta*. Words are bodily things, vocal utterances (*phōnai*) that resound in the air and in our ears. But a *lekton* is not a bodily thing; it is incorporeal (*asōmatos*).[78] This is a very surprising claim coming from the Stoics, who are materialists in their ontology. If it was Platonists who said that meanings are incorporeal, we might anticipate what they had in mind: that meanings are ideal objects, belonging to a timeless realm of things understood by the mind like mathematical truths. There is in fact is a modern semantics that develops something like this Platonist line of thought based on Frege's notion of *Sinn* or sense, together with the technical concept of a proposition as a timeless truth-bearer independent of all language (unlike a sentence, which is a corporeal utterance or inscription in some particular language, and which came into being at a particular time).[79] But the Stoics, being materialists, do not believe in the existence of this unchanging realm. For them, "the incorporeal" refers not to a timeless realm of being but to something nonexistent. So then in saying meanings are incorporeal, are they saying they do not exist?

The answer is in one sense yes, in another sense no—in roughly the same way we say that unicorns do not exist, but that there is such a thing as the meaning of the word "unicorn." After all, it seems on the face of it that we *can* talk about things that do not exist, because we can talk about unicorns and there is such a thing as the meaning of such talk. So a philosophy of language must take a stand about the ontological status of such things. One strategy is to reserve the word "exists" for objects in the world (i.e., material objects, for the Stoics) and assign to "meanings" a different ontological status—call them "real" in some sense but do not say that they "exist" in the strict sense. The Stoics can adopt this sort of strategy because their ontology includes a category called "something" (*ti*) which embraces things both existent and nonexistent.[80] Among the latter are all incorporeal things, including categories such as place, time, and void, as well as *lekta*. Each of these categories is "something" but not an existing object (*on*).[81]

This Stoic ontology of *lekta* contrasts with two alternatives that would give meanings a weightier ontological status. One, as we have already seen, is to treat meanings as ideal objects, the way Platonists treat numbers and geo-metrical figures and Forms—unchanging, always existing, never coming into being or passing away, and thus always available for our epistemic use. But that would be the end of Stoic materialism. Another is the expressionist alternative, which would identify meanings with thought processes in our minds or souls. This is the Augustinian view we find in traditional misreadings of Aristotle's *On Interpretation*. We will in fact encounter something very much like this expressionist interpretation of *lekton* in an early treatise of Augustine's, where he introduces the concept of *dicibile*, the "sayable," which could very well be intended as a Latin equivalent of *lekton*.[82] Such an expressionist semantics is something the Stoics could have developed themselves if they wanted to. Unlike modern materialists they believed in the existence of souls; they simply regarded souls as material objects. (This was the common position of most Hellenistic philosophers, who took their view of the soul not from Plato or Aristotle but from earlier Greek traditions that identified the soul with material breath or *pneuma*—the thing that departed from the body with its dying breath.) Hence for the Stoics, our thoughts are dispositions of our souls, which are material things. The Stoics could thus have identified meanings with some material feature of our souls, much as modern materialists might try to identify them with some feature of our brain activity. Yet they did not, for that would have been very much like identifying them with uttered words (*phōnai*).[83]

Both words and thoughts, for the Stoics, are material things that have meanings and hence both belong to the category of *sēmaina*, things that mean, rather than to the category of *sēmainomena*, things that are meant. To identify *lekta* with thoughts would thus be to remove them altogether from the class of meanings and put them instead in the class of things that only *have* meanings.

It is important for anyone who wishes to understand the Stoics to keep these categories (meanings and things that have meaning) distinct. How important can be seen by returning to the Stoic view of signs, where the dangers of this conflation first became clear.[84] In ordinary Greek usage, signs are physical objects or events from which can be inferred other physical objects or events, as from smoke one can infer fire, or from lactation one can infer that a woman has been pregnant. Both the smoke and the milk would in ordinary Greek be called signs, *sēmeia*. But the Stoics, in their technical discussions of the logic of inference, do not talk that way.[85] Strictly speaking, for the Stoics smoke is not a sign, for all signs are meanings. The sign, properly speaking, is not the physical smoke but the incorporeal thing said by the words "if there is smoke." Thus a sign is the meaning or thought-content of such words, which subsists along with them. Similarly, *lekta* in general are not words but what words say or mean, their semantic content. They are not timeless propositions as in Fregean semantics, because they exist only as long as the material things (words or thoughts) that mean or say them. And they are not something in our minds, because unlike our minds they are incorporeal. Nor are they fully real like material objects. Strictly speaking, meanings do not exist but only "subsist along with" the words or thoughts whose meanings they are.[86] But that makes them real enough (or at least so the Stoics evidently thought) to be the basis of a semantic theory.

It is quite possible that Stoic semantics is not ultimately coherent. However that may be, it belongs to a subtle and resourceful attempt to formulate a philosophy of language that is consistent with a thoroughgoing materialism. It is a theory of meaning that resolutely refuses to appeal to a form of being apart from the material world. It is thus a semantics without a dimension of depth. And Stoic semiotics is merely part of that semantics.[87] Stoic signs, unlike Augustine's, do not give expression to an inner dimension of the soul.

Empirical Inference and "Common Signs"

Philosophical semiotics before Augustine, being a theory of empirical inference, had its natural home in the empiricist epistemologies that went along with materialist ontologies such as those of the Stoics and Epicureans. That is to say, semiotics was part of the widespread reaction of philosophy in the Hellenistic period against the dimension of spiritual depth, the other-worldly immaterialism that had been introduced into Greek thought by likes of Plato (with help from Pythagoras and Parmenides). Methods of inference from signs were essential to the way empiricist epistemologies in that period explained the possibility of scientific knowledge (*epistēmē*) without believing in the mind's ability to perceive unchanging immaterial Forms of things—part of an account of the intelligibility of the world that did not rely on the Platonist notion of intelligibility as the visibility of unchanging immaterial essences to the mind's eye.

Sextus Empiricus, the second-century (A.D.) sceptic, writing in Greek, presents a summary and critique of Hellenistic epistemologies, within which he locates the notion of signs. Since the function of signs is to reveal what is nonevident, Sextus takes it as obvious that any project of building an empirical science will need to use inferences from signs to extend knowledge beyond what is evident in immediate sense-impressions.[88] Indeed Sextus counts scientific proof or demonstration (*apodeixis*) as one kind of sign, since it has the sign-function of revealing its conclusion.[89]

Sextus's point can be illustrated by a look at the most extensive discussion of semiotics actually surviving from the Hellenistic period, a debate between Epicureans and their opponents about methods of inference from signs. The treatise by the Epicurean philosopher Philodemus containing this debate bears the title "*On Sēmeiōsis,*" which is commonly translated *De Signis* (On Signs) or "On Methods of Inference."[90] The latter is a reasonable translation, since in this text as in Sextus, the term *sēmeiōsis* and its associated verb are used to describe processes of empirical inference. (Again, think how far this is from expressionist semiotics, where the term *sēmeiōsis* would have to include the signification of words.) The underlying issue in the debate was the Epicureans' atomism, their theory that everything that exists consists of combinations of atoms and the void. Their opponents were convinced that there is no valid method of inference leading to this theoretical conclusion—no observable sign that reveals the nonevident (or as we would now say, microscopic) world of atoms moving in the void. The Epicureans on the contrary defended a method of inductive inference they called "*sēmeiōsis* by similarity,"[91] in which the reasoning is that nonevident things are similar to observed phenomena. Just as we infer that all human beings, even those we have never met, are mortal from the fact that all those we have met are mortal, so we can infer the existence of unseen microscopic bodies moving through the void from the fact that all the things we have seen moving at the macroscopic level, despite their many differences, have in common their movement through some kind of empty space.[92]

The criticism of this Epicurean form of inference, as recorded in Philodemus's treatise, is based on the Stoic conception of the truth of conditional statements, which depends on a necessary connection between antecedent and consequent.[93] The way the Stoics put it is that in a valid conditional statement, if the consequent is eliminated, then the antecedent is thereby "co-eliminated." Since a sign is the antecedent in a valid conditional statement, this is as much as to say: no sign without its signified! In a valid *sēmeiōsis*, there can be no sign ("there is smoke" cannot be true) unless the thing signified exists ("there is fire" is true). And the critics of the Epicureans see no reason to think that the macroscopic movement of bodies is so strictly and necessarily connected with microscopic realities. The logic of this criticism can be summed up in terminology that goes back to Aristotle: no valid inference can be based on a "common sign," one that could signify many different things. Such a sign is compatible with the nonexistence of the thing it is taken to signify. An example of this would be to take wealth as a sign of virtue: "Someone who thinks a man is good because he is rich is ... using an invalid and common sign, since wealth can be found in good men and hideous men as well."[94] Sound *sēmeiōsis*, the critics insist, requires "proper signs," which are inseparable from one particular type of signified, so we can be sure that if we observe it then the hidden thing it signifies also exists.[95] The Epicurean method of inference by similarity, according to this criticism, is vitiated by the fact that it uses common signs rather than proper signs.

The Sceptics' Reminding Signs

Judging by the Stoic definition, which requires that a sign necessarily "reveals the consequent," it would seem that common signs are not really signs at all. One wonders (as one does about other Stoic definitions, such as those of virtue and wisdom) whether this is not a little too restrictive. Even granting the point that scientific inference requires "proper signs," should we really deny that "common signs" are signs at all? Don't we, in everyday life, often use such signs, not for purposes of scientific inference but as warnings or reminders of one of the things they are associated with? To use a modern example: chest pain is not a sure sign of a heart attack, for it could indicate a number of other things as well, but it still may alert me of a danger I had not noticed before and thus serve as a very useful sign.

The sceptic Sextus Empiricus has an interesting way of handling this issue. In the course of his critique of the Epicurean notion of signs he echoes the criticism found in Philodemus's treatise: "If it is common to many things, it will not be a sign. For one thing cannot be grasped by means of something that manifests many things."[96] He even illustrates the point with a similar example: "To go from riches to rags is common to a profligate lifestyle, loss of goods in a shipwreck, and lavishness toward friends—and being common to these many things it can no longer pick out any one of them and disclose it."[97] But this criticism applies only to one kind of sign, which he calls the "indicative sign" (endeiktikon sēmeion) and defines in Stoic terms.[98] For the indicative sign, he says, "is thought to be by nature such as to display what it signifies," so that "it must of necessity be indicative of only one kind of thing."[99] And it is the indicative sign that Sextus is interested in criticizing, so as to undermine claims to scientific certainty made by "dogmatic" philosophers, both Stoic and Epicurean.[100] But he has no objection to a more modest kind of sign, which he calls the "reminding" sign (hypomnēstikon sēmeion).[101] He does not wish to deny that one thing may often make us think of another, and thus serve as a sign of it. This kind of sign is not really a method of inference at all but rather a kind of psychological association. Such a sign "brings us to remembrance" (agei hymas eis hypomnēsin) of something that is presently hidden from our senses but had previously been observed in connection with it.[102] It is no basis for scientific certainty, but it is indispensable for ordinary life. And the sceptics, Sextus insists, are not trying to overthrow ordinary life but only to undermine dogmatic claims to scientific or philosophical knowledge. Thus Sextus has no criticism of the way reminding signs are "believed in ordinary life, as when someone sees smoke fire is signified, and when he observes a scar he says there has been a wound."[103] In fact he paints the sceptic as the champion of ordinary life, defending it against the "dogmatists" who rebel against common opinion by claiming to know "semiotically" (sēmiotikōs, by means of inference from signs) things that are by nature hidden from human perception.[104]

The idea that signs reveal things nature has hidden from us is in fact the focus of Sextus's sceptical attack. He distinguishes indicative signs from reminding signs precisely with reference to how hidden the thing signified is. Reminding signs bring to mind things we have seen before but which are temporarily out of sight. Thus smoke above the horizon can reveal the presence of an unseen fire below it, quite apart from any supposed necessary connection between the two, but simply because we have previously observed the two phenomena so often together.[105] The things signified by reminding signs have the status of "nonevident" but only for the time being, like the way the city of Athens is nonevident to those who live far away from it.[106] The things signified by indicative signs, on the other hand, are nonevident always and by their very nature. As examples, Sextus mentions the infinite void outside the universe (inferred by some philosophers) and microscopic pores in the human body (inferred by some physicians).[107]

It is indeed "dogmatic philosophers" and "rationalist physicians" who devised the concept of indicative signs in the first place, according to Sextus.[108] Both phrases are technical terms, the one referring to the schools of philosophy criticized by the sceptics, the other to a school of medicine rivaling the "empiric" school to which Sextus belonged (his very name means "Sextus the Empiric").[109] The empirics taught physicians to recognize signs like blushing, swelling, and thirst as symptoms to guide treatment,[110] but they rejected the rationalists' notion that manifest symptoms such as these could serve as indications of underlying causes. They were called "empirics" because they relied simply on accumulated medical experience (*empeiria*) to guide them, paying attention to symptoms that had often been observed before rather than indulging in intellectual speculation about what hidden causes these symptoms might indicate. In calling the kind of sign he was criticizing "indicative" (*endeiktikon*) Sextus was no doubt alluding to this debate among physicians about whether it was possible to build medical theories on the basis of indications (*endeixeis*) of underlying causes.[111] Sextus's philosophical criticism of indicative signs is of a piece with the empirics' rejection of medical "indications" in this rationalist sense.[112]

Reminders of Deeper Things

The contentious issue in all the ancient debates about signs is whether something obvious to our senses can reveal something essentially hidden from them. In that regard the physicians' debate about whether bodily manifestations serve to indicate underlying causes is a typical semiotic issue (for of course ancient physicians were not in a good position to observe disease processes in the interior of a living body). We come one step closer to Augustine's expressionist semiotics when we ask whether the soul itself might be one of the hidden or underlying causes indicated by bodily symptoms. In fact, Sextus mentions bodily movements revealing the soul as an example of an indicative sign.[113] This is a form of inference he seeks to undermine, of course, but it does introduce us to the strand of Greek semiotics that most resembles Augustine's. The notion of the body as a sign of the soul is just the sort of concept Augustine needs to solve the problem of how the inner depth of the soul can make its presence felt in the external world—a problem that we should expect to be harder for him to solve than for materialists who believe that the soul, though invisible to the eyes, is as physical as breath or microscopic pores. A notion of inner depth, one would think, needs a semiotics in which the body can reveal the soul.

What is striking is that Augustine, like Sextus, argues against such a semiotics. In his first full-scale treatment of the epistemology of expressive signs, his conclusion is that we do not learn things from signs. In fact, the truth is the exact opposite, according to Augustine's argument in his treatise *On the Teacher*: we learn signs from things, not the other way around, because we must know the thing signified before we can understand the significance of the sign.[114] It is as if the expressionist concept of sign came into being already deconstructed. As Sextus in effect points out, this reversal of epistemic order abolishes the very nature of a sign as it is usually understood: "To say that the sign is grasped after the thing signified, is immediately and manifestly absurd. For how can the sign be revelatory, when what it is supposed to be revelatory of—the thing signified—is grasped before it?"[115] Yet like Sextus, Augustine does not conclude that there are no such things as signs or that they have no use. Rather, signs function as admonitions or reminders.[116] Like Sextus's "reminding" signs, they serve to bring things to mind[117]—as we shall see when we come to examine Augustine's various definitions of the word *signum*. For Augustine a sign is like a finger pointing out what we are searching for, telling us where to look—but we must look for ourselves and know how to see what is there.[118] Thus Augustine's semiotics follows the pattern of Sextus's scepticism about signs: signs do not reveal but only remind.[119]

This is not to say that Augustine learned his semiotics from Sextus. In fact Sextus is one of the many Greek writers with whom he was quite unacquainted. Augustine's conviction that signs remind rather than reveal has more to do with Plato's theory of recollection than with Sextus's theory of signs. The epistemology of signs in Augustine derives ultimately (though probably not directly) from the description of the epistemic value of sensible things in the *Phaedo,* where Plato explains that sensible things may remind us of intelligible things, the way the sight or sound of a lyre may "bring to mind the form of the boy whose lyre it is."[120] Plato does not call such reminders "signs" but Augustine does, and that is what makes him so different from Sextus. According to Augustine signs can remind us of essentially hidden things that we really do know how to see. For Augustine's Platonism adds a new dimension to the previous heritage of Greek semiotics, and with that new dimension comes a new form of knowledge that goes beyond the capacities of empirical inference. Things of the soul are essentially hidden from the senses but not from the mind, which has the power to see intelligible things that will never be seen by the eye of the body. Indeed the new inner dimension is hidden precisely because it is of a nature visible to the mind rather than to the senses—intelligible not sensible. Bodily signs cannot make this dimension known because it would be absurd, on a Platonist reckoning, for a sensible thing to make an intelligible thing intelligible to us.

Hence we cannot expect from Augustine a strong doctrine of Scriptural revelation.[121] For the Scriptures consist of words, which are signs, and signs do not reveal things—especially not divine things, which are seen only by the mind. Thus for Augustine the most fundamental revelation is what occurs when God inwardly reveals the truth to the soul.[122] This is not a form of "special revelation" (a category that would be anachronistic here) but rather God as Truth inwardly enlightening the eye of the mind[123] or (as Augustine puts it in *On the Teacher*) Christ as the Wisdom of God functioning as inner teacher.[124] Revelation is properly speaking a matter of the inner truth becoming visible to the mind, whereas Scripture is a matter of authoritative external teaching.[125] Hence the central concept in Augustine's doctrine of Scripture is not revelation but authority. Scripture does not directly give us knowledge of God but rather tells us where to look to find it, providing exercise, medicine, and purification for half-blind eyes that need to be strengthened for vision of the divine. The relation of Scripture to the knowledge of God is thus like the relation of doctor's orders to healthy vision. The words of Scripture do not embody or give us what we are looking for, but they direct our efforts to learn how to see better.

Thus we come upon a crucial irony of Platonist epistemology, which shall occupy us at length in the next chapter. The Platonists' conviction that our minds have eyes for a deeper dimension of being than our bodies means that their attitude toward empirical knowledge has always been something much like scepticism. The senses at best serve to remind us of what we really want to see, and at worst distract us from the soul's true vision by burdening us with the cares and lusts of the flesh. Convinced that we must turn away from sensible things in order to see intelligible things, a Platonist like Augustine need not be a friend of the semiotics of empirical inference. One does not require signs to mediate knowledge of that which is hidden from the senses if one is able to see the thing directly with the eye of the mind.

2

From Scepticism to Platonism

The Concept of Sign in Augustine's Earliest Writings

The earliest discussion of signs in Augustine's writing does not belong to
his philosophy of language but to his epistemology, his interaction in
Against the Academics *with the Academic scepticism of Cicero. Despite*
the title, Augustine is sympathetic to the Academics' view that no sensi-
ble appearance can function as sure criterion of truth because it may al-
ways have the same kind of ambiguity as a "common sign." Augustine
adopts this sceptical view of empirical knowledge for Platonist reasons: true
knowledge and wisdom are not to be found in the sensible world, where
we cannot perceive the truth but only the truthlike. But whereas the "hor-
izontal" similarity of sensible things to one another undermines all claims
to empirical knowledge, there is another, "vertical" kind of similarity, the
resemblance of the truthlike to the intelligible truth, which points to a higher
and unchanging realm where real certainty can be found. When Augustine
proceeds to develop a distinctively Platonist semiotics, in which sensible
things are able not only to resemble but also to signify intelligible things, this is
a major innovation in Platonist philosophy as well as ancient semiotics.

Augustine is concerned with semiotics from the very beginning of his
career. He discusses signs in his earliest extant writings, the philosophical dialogues he wrote at Cassiciacum in the months prior to
his baptism. This first discussion of signs is also his most Greek, as it
is embedded in his reports of Hellenistic debates about Academic
scepticism. The discussion contains a very puzzling reference to

"common signs," that key term in Hellenistic semiotic debates. Transferring this term from the debates about semiotics to the debates about scepticism may in fact be a simple mistake on Augustine's part—in any case the term plays no role in his mature semiotic theory. Yet because it is the first time he handles the philosophical concept of sign, we need to take note of it and sort through its complexities as well as its implications for the development of his thought. In the process we get a picture of the epistemological context in which his new theory of signs would later emerge.

Plato's Sceptical Successors

To begin with, something must be said about the complex state of the texts. Augustine's odd reference to "common signs" is found in his early treatise *Against the Academics,* which deals with the debate about Academic scepticism reported by Cicero in his philosophical dialogue, *Academica.* Augustine has no independent access to this debate, which stretched through two centuries of the Hellenistic era but ended almost four centuries before he was born. His knowledge of it comes entirely from Cicero,[1] but he sometimes provides information about it that is valuable to modern scholars, because several books of Cicero's work on the subject are lost.[2] Aside from our inferior access to Cicero's writings, we today are in much the same situation as Augustine. The original Greek texts of this Hellenistic debate have not survived, and Cicero is our most important source of information about it. Although writing in Latin, Cicero (106–43 B.C.) is actually closer in time to the debate than any of our Greek sources (such as Sextus Empiricus, who wrote in the second century A.D., and Diogenes Laertius, who wrote later still). In fact Cicero was himself an Academic, having studied at the Academy in Athens at a time when the Academic debate about scepticism was still alive, though entering its final stage. The Academics were named after this Academy, the school founded by Plato, which was at that time still *the* Academy, the only school in the world called by that name.

It is a striking irony that the Academics, intellectual heirs of Plato, took the sceptical side of this debate. The author of *Against the Academics,* whose return to the Catholic church has recently been facilitated by his enthusiastic encounter with Platonism, is acutely aware of this irony, which plays a crucial role in his interpretation of the debate. He knows (because he has read it in Cicero)[3] that the Academy took its turn toward scepticism when Arcesilaus, who was head of the school many decades after Plato, launched an attack on the Stoics and their empiricist epistemology.[4] And he believes that the secret purpose of the Academics' sceptical arguments was to vindicate Platonism against materialistic philosophies such as Stoicism, undermining their empiricist foundations by demonstrating the unreliability of knowledge derived from the senses and thus the need for a higher kind of knowledge.[5] Hence in his first extant letter, Augustine explains that he was not really writing against the Academics[6] but was in fact "imitating rather than attacking them."[7] He is in full sympathy with what he believes are their real motives, which included hiding the teaching of Plato from the curiosity of the vulgar.[8] Thus in the overall treatment of sceptic themes which runs from *Against the Academics* to the *Soliloquies* (and the full purport of Augustine's anti-sceptical arguments cannot be grasped without reading both) Augustine aims not only to repudiate the surface scepticism of the Academics, which stands in the way of his hope of discovering the truth, but also to recover their true but hidden Platonism.

The Grasping Appearance

It is in the context of this sustained inquiry into the purport of sceptical attacks on empiricist epistemology that Augustine raises the problem of "common signs." The central bone of contention in the debate is the existence of the "grasping" or "apprehending" appearance, which Augustine defines as an appearance that "has no signs in common with the false."[9] This peculiar definition is the first technical philosophical usage of the concept of sign in Augustine's writings. It concerns the kind of sense-appearance the Stoics proposed to take as the criterion of truth and the foundation of empirical knowledge. The Academics agreed that a "grasping appearance," such as the Stoics defined it, would make a fine criterion of truth—if only it existed. However, they argued at great length that no such thing exists, and thence drew the sceptical conclusion that there is no sure criterion of truth and therefore no possibility of certain knowledge. Thus battle was joined between Academics and Stoics over the existence of this "grasping appearance," whose original definition is attributed to Zeno himself, the founder of Stoicism. We will need to pay a good deal of attention to what Augustine makes of this definition, for his thinking about it marks the beginning of the development of his epistemology. We will need to pay attention first of all to vocabulary, which in this case is a complicated matter, as we are examining Augustine's reformulations of Cicero's Latin renderings of Zeno's (no longer extant) Greek definition.

But let us begin with the name. What Zeno defines is called the *kataleptikē phantasia*, which I translate as the "grasping appearance." The elusiveness of the term can be highlighted by the fact that it is also very helpful when some of the best commentators on the subject translate it, much less literally, as "cognitive impression."[10] "Impression" captures the pervasive Hellenistic metaphor that a *phantasia* is "impressed" on the soul like a mark or imprint on wax (which as we saw in the last chapter originated with Plato).[11] The Stoics in fact defined *phantasia* as an impression (*typōsis*) on the soul, analogous to the mark (*typos*) made by writing on a wax tablet (we have a vestige of the same vocabulary in terms like "typewriter").[12] But *phantasia* in ordinary Greek does not literally mean impression but rather appearance, as it derives from the verb *phainesthai*, to appear, from which we also get our word "phenomenon." So the word does not have to mean something in the mind: it can simply mean how things appear to someone. And even when it is made into a technical term in philosophy of mind, which evidently happened first in Aristotle, it does not inevitably have to be interpreted as a mental impression or image.[13] So while the Stoic's *phantasia* is indeed an impression on the mind, the word *phantasia* does not simply *mean* "impression." Hence as we proceed to consider this concept at some length, it is useful to keep in mind that in Stoic usage it refers both to an impression imprinted on the mind and to the way things appear to someone.

What *phantasia* does not mean for the Stoics is the way things appear when we look within the soul. For once again, as in Plato, we are not talking about something our mind looks at within itself, but rather the shape of the mind that does the looking.[14] The *impression* is impressed on the mind as on a two-dimensional surface, but the *appearance* is the appearance of external objects. Modern readers can usefully think of the image impressed on the retina by a visible object such as a tree. Without some such image in our eye we cannot see anything, but what we are looking at is not the image inside our eyeball but the tree. This material analogy fits the Stoics' thinking about appearances quite neatly: so long as appearances do not mislead us, looking at the appearance of a tree means seeing the tree itself, not some image of the tree inside the eye or the mind. This is how the grasping appearance serves as the foundation of empirical knowledge: whenever appearances are not deceiving, what we grasp is the thing itself.

Cicero brings this Stoic conceptuality to Augustine by translating the Greek *phantasia* with the Latin *visum* (plural *visa*). This of course suggests a visual appearance. For the most part, in fact, vision served as the paradigm case of appearances in Greek philosophy, though other senses were not in principle excluded. This Ciceronian term recurs in Augustine's later writings because it also plays a role in Stoic theories of motivation, which for many years informed Augustine's thinking about problems of grace and free will.[15] *Visa*, it turns out, are fundamental not only to human knowledge but also to human action, which according to the Stoics is always set in motion by our voluntary assent to some sensible appearance. Both these uses of *visa* will eventually be replaced in Augustine's thinking by a more Platonist approach. However, the replacement of Stoic epistemology is something Augustine has in mind from the beginning, while the need to devise a replacement for Stoic action theory is something he does not decide upon until midway through the Pelagian controversy.

But to continue with vocabulary. What does it mean to say that some appearances are "grasping" or "apprehending"? I use both terms because Cicero translates the Greek *kataleptikē* with the two verbs *percipi* and *conprehendi*—both good renderings except that they are in the passive, which unfortunately suggests that these appearances are grasped or apprehended.[16] The original sense of *kataleptikē*, however, is active: these are grasping or apprehending appearances, in that they afford us a direct grasp or immediate apprehension of what is real, the external object which is their source. To have a grasping appearance is to have clear and certain knowledge of a sensible object that has impressed itself on the mind and left its imprint there. The key questions are: what characteristics must an appearance have in order to afford us such knowledge, and do any of our appearances actually have such characteristics? By now it should be clear why the terms of Zeno's definition are an important matter.

Zeno's Definition

The definition of "grasping appearance" that Cicero attributes to Zeno himself is "an appearance impressed or stamped from that whence it came, in such a way that it could not have been from that whence it did not come."[17] The point is that the grasping appearance cannot mislead us because it could only have come from one place, the sensible thing which is its actual source. As the discussion unfolds, Cicero keeps coming back to this point in different ways. The nonsceptic wants something more certain than "appearances that cannot be distinguished from false ones"[18] or "appearances that are common to the true and the false."[19] These formulations are standard and can be found in other authors.[20] But then come a few paragraphs (*Academica* 2:33–36) where talk of common appearances shifts to talk of common marks, and then to common signs. The overarching point is in each case clear: "proper" implies a firm basis for knowledge, while "common" means something less reliable, even deceptive. For just as (we saw last chapter) a proper sign signifies only one kind of thing,[21] a grasping appearance is the appearance of only one thing—it does not appear like anything else. So the grasping appearance must have characteristic features that could not come from the wrong objects, objects of which it is not the appearance. We could say: it bears all the marks of coming from one thing and one thing only, its true source. So Cicero begins to talk of a mark (*nota*) of the true, saying that the grasping appearance (if there is such a thing) bears "a mark that is proper to the true, not common to the true and the false."[22] The Academics' contention is that there is no such thing, because sensible qualities such as color and taste and sound do not have "a proper mark of truth and certainty that could never be elsewhere."[23]

The talk of common marks then leads to talk of common signs:

> If in this appearance there is something in common with the false, then there will be no criterion [of truth], because what is proper [i.e., to the truth] cannot be marked by a common sign.[24]

This talk of common signs, which we have seen recurring in Augustine, has drawn the attention of modern commentators because it is seriously out of place. Appearances do not function as signs, and grasping appearances in particular are supposed to afford us an immediate apprehension of their objects, not just a sign of their existence. A grasping appearance makes something evident—indeed it *is* something's being evident to the senses, something's appearing to us sensibly—while a sign has the function of revealing what is not evident. Hence in contrast to the knowledge we get from signs, the knowledge a grasping appearance gives us is not inferential but immediate.[25]

Quite a number of explanations can be offered for how this "common signs" formulation got into Cicero and thence into Augustine. The simplest is that Cicero is using the two terms "sign" (*signum*) and "mark" (*nota*) interchangeably, because they are in fact nearly synonymous in ordinary Latin. But one also wonders whether Cicero's *signum* might reflect a usage of *sēmeion* in texts now lost. For instance, could Zeno himself in the early years of Stoicism, long before the development of a formal Stoic semiotics, have used *sēmeion* informally in the sense of "mark," just as Cicero uses *signum* here as equivalent to *nota*?[26] Or could Cicero's usage reflect some lost text where *sēmeion* was used to talk about the grasping appearance in terms of the commonplace metaphor of the impression or mark (*sēmeion*) of a signet ring?[27] But for that matter it could be Cicero himself who is thinking of that very familiar metaphor and using the term *signum*, because it too can mean the mark of a signet ring. Finally, it could just be that Cicero is confusing two different epistemological debates. For there is a parallel between the Stoic-Academic debate we are considering in this chapter and the Stoic-Epicurean debate mentioned in the last chapter:[28] the latter turned on the issue of whether a particular sort of sign was common or proper, the former on whether a particular sort of appearance was common or proper. Cicero likely knew the Stoic-Epicurean debate, as he was a friend of Philodemus, who is our prime source for it.[29] It is certainly possible that the Stoics quite consciously used similar formulations in both debates, and that Cicero's usage either reflects that similarity or gets the differences confused.[30] In any case, the result is that the vocabulary of signs has found its way into a context that is not really semiotic.

It is in that inappropriate context, discussing Zeno's definition of the criterion of truth, that Augustine first uses the term *signum* as a technical term in epistemology. As a result, it is a usage that goes nowhere. Augustine's mature semiotics will proceed from quite a different starting point. Nevertheless, it will be profitable for us to pursue Augustine's treatment of this Hellenistic debate, for although it is not the context for the development of his semiotics it is the context for the initial development his epistemology, which is where we must eventually situate his semiotics. For it turns out that Augustine has something unexpected to say about the Stoic criterion of truth, which has everything to do with why he ends up inventing the first Platonist semiotics.

Augustine gives several formulations of Zeno's definition, all echoing Cicero, though none quite identical with those in Cicero's extant works. When he introduces the grasping appearance he first refers to "the definition of Zeno the Stoic . . . who said, that that truth can be grasped which is impressed upon the soul from that whence it came in such a way that it could not be from that whence it did not come."[31] Then he adds that this "can be said more briefly and plainly thus: truth can be apprehended by signs—those signs which the false cannot have."[32] A little later he formulates the same point in terms of *nota* rather than *signa:* Zeno, he says, introduced the new idea that "nothing can be grasped, except what is true in such a way as to be discernible from the false by dissimilar marks."[33]

Since Augustine is writing a treatise ostensibly against the Academics, one might think that he would favor their opponents, those who (according to him) taught that truth can be apprehended by signs. But that is more than Augustine will ever say about the power of signs. His epistemology is headed in a very different direction. He is not going to agree with Zeno and the Stoics that knowledge can be built on an unambiguous empirical foundation, marked by a sure criterion of truth grasped by the senses. Rather, he will follow up hints that Cicero left about the original teaching of the Academics in Plato's Academy, such as,

> They thought *the mind was the criterion of truth*—it alone was worth believing, because it alone discerned what always is simple, uniform, and of the same sort. They called this an *idea*. . . . [34]

Likewise, Cicero tells us that "Plato thought the whole criterion of truth—and truth itself—belonged to thought itself and the mind, drawn away from opinion and the senses."[35] Augustine drops us a hint along the same lines in the treatise *Against the Academics,* when he admits that he is willing to support the Academics in their arguments against philosophers who put too much stock in the senses:

> For whatever they argue against the senses has no validity against all philosophers. There are those who admit that everything the mind receives from the sense of the body can generate opinion, but deny it can generate knowledge. Rather, they think knowledge can be contained in the intelligence and live in the mind, removed from the senses. And perhaps among them is the wise man whom we seek. But more of that later....[36]

I think we can guess who this wise man is when a few pages later Augustine gives us a thumbnail sketch of the history of the Academy concluding with a reference to Plotinus as Plato *redivivus.*[37]

A few months later Augustine will write an inner dialogue in which Reason itself warns him that he must "absolutely flee from these things of the senses."[38] This is not a man who aims to vindicate the possibility of empirical knowledge! Rather, he is interested in how scepticism about the senses may lead us to a higher kind of knowledge—how it may help us, as his favorite passage from Plotinus puts it, "close your eyes and awaken a different kind of vision."[39] Thus Augustine belongs historically to the reaction against the reaction, the great movement toward Neoplatonism in late antiquity, which reversed the Hellenistic reaction against Platonism by reinstating an epistemology based on intellectual vision and intelligible Form. In this movement the sceptics of the Hellenistic Academy are natural allies, especially for one who thinks of Platonism not merely as a set of doctrines but as a form of inquiry and a way of life.

The Point of Academic Scepticism

Most modern scholars are highly doubtful that the sceptical posture of the Hellenistic Academy was meant to conceal a doctrinaire Platonism.[40] The scepticism of an Arcesilaus certainly does not look much like the Platonism of a Plotinus, which was the kind of philosophy that had set Augustine's mind afire so recently with a burning love for truth and wisdom.[41] Yet neither can the Academic sceptics be thought of as simply abandoning the tradition of

Plato.[42] We do not hear of them attacking the epistemology of what we now call "Platonism" (the view, derived from Plato's middle period, that the human mind is capable of a pure intellectual vision that sees what most truly is, the unchanging and immaterial Forms of things).[43] And we have a good deal of evidence that they thought of themselves as heirs of Socrates, using a method of refutation that could be traced back to the practice of Socratic dialectic recorded in Plato's dialogues.[44] They were operating in an era when the one thing all philosophers agreed on was that a philosophy is not merely a theory but a way of life, whose point is to achieve happiness, the ultimate goal or *telos* of human life (the disagreements were about what exactly makes for happiness and how to achieve it).[45] Hence their scepticism must be understood not as a form of pessimism or despair but as an ideal of human life, a vision of what *eudaimonia* or fulfilled humanity looks like.[46] One way to make sense of the unfamiliar Platonism of the Academic sceptics is to observe that in their view the good life for human beings on this earth consists of unending *inquiry*—the original meaning of *skepsis*. Their motto, in effect, is the famous exhortation to the people of Athens which Plato places in the mouth of Socrates:

> the greatest good for a human being is to spend every day discussing
> virtue and the other things about which you hear me discussing
> and examining myself and others, for the life without such exami-
> nation is no life for a human being.[47]

Who but a dedicated Socratic Platonist could endure a life of such continual "examination," in which one's beliefs and opinions are exposed to the constant danger of refutation? This was not the ideal of life that the other Hellenistic schools had in mind, at any rate. The Stoics in particular were convinced that only the wise man lives a truly good life,[48] and that what makes it good is his unshakeable knowledge of the nature and rationality of the universe—both its *physis* and its *logos*, which are ultimately the same thing.[49] Hence the wise man cannot live a life of continual inquiry, always seeking what he does not yet know and open to refutation of what he thinks he already knows. Rather, he is the consummate dialectician who never gives his assent to an opinion he must retract, who indeed never opines at all, but only *knows*, firmly, irrefutably and infallibly.[50]

Consider in this light Cicero's reconstruction of the origin of the debate with the Stoics in which Academic scepticism took its rise. What is at issue is the kind of knowledge possessed by the wise man.

> This is how one can understand Arcesilaus fighting with Zeno, not
> just to criticize him, but to find the truth. No one before had ever

said, much less theorized that it was possible for a man not to hold
opinions—and that this was not only possible but necessary for the
wise man. This view impressed Arcesilaus as not only true but good
and worthy of the wise man. Perhaps he asked Zeno what would
happen if the wise man did not grasp anything, and yet was not to
hold opinions.

No doubt Zeno replied that he was to hold no opinions, because
there *was* something that could be grasped.

"And what would that be?"

"An appearance."

"What sort of appearance?"

Then he would define it thus: "one impressed and stamped and
imprinted from something which is, exactly as it is [*ex eo quod esset,
sicut esset, impressum et signatum et effictum*]."

Next came the question, whether this was so even if a true appearance was of the same sort as the false.

Here Zeno saw clearly that no appearance could be grasped if it
was from that which is, in the same way it could be from that which is
not [*si id tale esset ab eo quod est cujus modi ab eo quod non est posset esse*].

Arcesilaus rightly accepted this addition to the definition, for
the false cannot be grasped, and neither can the true if it is just like
the false. And he leaned on these arguments to teach that there is
no appearance from the true which could not be in the same way
from the false. This is the very debate that endures to this day.[51]

Cicero leads us into the subtle reformulations of Zeno's definition from a
starting point that is fairly simple, one with which Arcesilaus readily agrees:
that the wise man does not opine—that is, that he does not give his assent to
mere opinions. Zeno meant this to support the conclusion that the wise man
has only firm and irrefutable knowledge, but Arcesilaus goes in the opposite
direction: suppose that there is no basis for firm knowledge—no "grasping"
appearance which comes from its source in such a way that it could not be
mistaken for an appearance that comes from a different source? If so, then
Zeno must agree that there is no basis for firm empirical knowledge. In that
case he would be forced to concede that the wise man, who does not opine,
must give his assent to nothing: that in short the wise man is necessarily a
sceptic, withholding all assent and practicing that suspense of judgment which
the Academics called *epochē*.

The point of the Academic attack, then, is to undermine the Stoic notion
of the wise man as the possessor of firm and unshakeable knowledge—to

question whether it is even possible for such a person to exist. This strikes at the heart of Stoicism, and thus at a leading force in the Hellenistic reaction against Platonism. For as Anthony Long observes, in Stoicism the wise man replaces the Platonist's Forms:

> As the ideal referent of all human excellences the 'wise man' in Stoicism fulfills many of the functions of the Platonic Forms. In rejecting these incorporeal entities Zeno offered the wise man as the goal and standard of a perfectly rational life.[52]

Aristotle had already taken a crucial step in this direction by identifying the judgments of the wise and good man (the *phronimos* or *spoudaios*) as the standard by which to judge right actions.[53] This was perhaps not unrelated to Aristotle's project of bringing the Forms down to earth, as it were, and locating them in the material world of nature. At any rate, Stoicism is built on the correlation between these two concepts: the wise man and Nature. Nature (*physis*) is ordered by an inherent rational principle (*logos*) that the wise man perfectly understands. The great difference from Aristotle is that the Stoics went all the way to a thoroughgoing materialism, describing the teleological rationality of the universe not in terms of intelligible forms but in terms of a material *logos,* which they identified with the divine and creative fire of the heavens that also pervades the earth and constitutes the soul.[54] So the unshakeable knowledge of the Stoic wise man is thoroughly empiricist, derived not from a vision of intelligible forms but from his grasp of sensible appearances.

The Wise Man Needs Depth

It is not quite as trivial as it seems, then, when Augustine proposes to refute scepticism by getting his debating partner to agree that there is such a thing as a wise man, and that the wise man does know wisdom.[55] Modern philosophers tend to be none too impressed by this particular anti-sceptical argument,[56] which Augustine presents as the culmination of the debate in *Against the Academics.* Yet it does get to the root of the central epistemological disagreement of the Hellenistic era, which is about what it means for there to be a wise man. Augustine is going back to the beginning of the Academic tradition in order to move forward from there, along the line not of scepticism or of Stoicism but of Platonism. For in his view what makes the wise man possible is not Zeno's "grasping appearance" but rather the fact that the wise man knows wisdom. What that means is best ascertained by looking at another early dialogue of Augustine's, where he argues that what the wise man must know in order to be truly wise and happy is something immutable and imperishable that cannot be lost.[57] The wisdom possessed by the wise man is thus not based on an appearance derived from the changing sensible world. It is eternal and intelligible Wisdom, which Augustine proceeds to identify with Christ, the Wisdom of God—the identification that lies at the foundation of his Christian Platonist philosophy.[58] To say there is such a thing as a wise man is to say that someone on earth truly knows this divine Wisdom.

Where does that leave Zeno and his grasping appearance? After all, Augustine—like Arcesilaus—does affirm the correctness of "Zeno's definition."[59] But in a somewhat cryptic passage he claims that the whole Academic debate would soon have ended "if only Zeno had woken up sometime and seen that nothing can be grasped except the sort of thing he defined, and that no such thing can be found in bodies."[60] What Augustine is getting at is spelled out more clearly a few years later in a discussion of the question "whether truth can be grasped [percipi] by the senses of the body."[61] In this discussion he contends that because all sensible things are changeable, they cannot be firmly grasped. Consequently, "one cannot expect purity of truth [sinceritas veritati] from the bodily senses." And lest one be impressed by the constancy of the celestial bodies (as the Stoics and Manichaeans both were) he adds that "there is nothing sensible that does not have something similar to the false," and proceeds to buttress his claim with references to stock sceptical arguments about the indistinguishability of images in dreams and hallucinations from actual sense-perception.[62] The conclusion is put in terms that clearly allude to Zeno's criterion of truth:

> Therefore, if there are false images of sensible things which cannot be distinguished by the senses themselves, and if nothing can be grasped unless it can be distinguished from the false, then there is no criterion of truth in the senses.

This does not mean that there is no criterion of truth at all, however. It means we must look for it in an entirely different dimension:

> Thus we are admonished in a salutary way to turn away from this world, which is obviously corporeal and sensible, and to turn with complete eagerness to God, i.e., to the Truth contained by the intellect and the interior mind [veritatem quae intellectu et interiore mente capitur], the Truth which remains forever and in the same way, which has no false image from which it cannot be distinguished.

This salutary admonition in fact signals the direction that Augustine's early thought takes from Against the Academics to Soliloquies, from sceptical arguments to a proof that the soul is immortal by virtue of the presence of unchangeable Truth within it.[63] With the aid of Neoplatonism, he is about to recover the dimension of inner depth that had been missing in the philosophy and theology previously known to him.[64]

The Status of the Truthlike

Augustine's sceptical critique of empiricist epistemology turns on the conviction that the knowledge the wise man possesses, which makes him not only wise but happy, is not empirical but intelligible:[65] it is knowledge of God, who alone is the Truth "which has no false image from which it cannot be distinguished."[66] This is not to say that no such false images exist or that it is easy to distinguish them from God. It is to say that with the right sort of education and mental exercise one can learn to make the distinction—to purify the mind from false images or phantasms which the uneducated mind is apt to mistake for knowledge of God.[67] The Cassiciacum dialogues sketch such a course of education, together with the purification from phantasms or mental images that is essential to it. It is purification in a specifically Platonist sense, based on making a sharp distinction between sensible and intelligible—for example, between merely imagining a geometrical figure and actually seeing the "true figure contained in the intelligence."[68] This is a distinction you can experience for yourself. It is the difference between, say, picturing in your mind a white triangle drawn on a black chalkboard, and the seeing you experience when you suddenly understand why the Pythagorean theorem is true and burst out, "Aha! Now I see it!" The former is an example of "what the Greeks call *phantasia* or phantasm"[69] and what Augustine in a related passage calls "false images of the things we number."[70] For again, there is a great difference between imagining numbers and intellectually "seeing" the unchanging truth of numbers. Thus for Augustine a proper study of the liberal disciplines such as arithmetic and geometry will lead the mind to ascend from sensible numbers and figures to intelligible numbers and figures, leaving imagination and phantasms behind so as to see purely intelligible things.[71] Thus the mind arrives in the end at a vision of God, who is "the immutable Truth containing all that is immutably true."[72]

But this does not mean that the sensible world is to be despised as if it were mere falsehood. That would be a Manichaean conclusion, not a Platonist one—akin to thinking that because God is the one true Good, the material world must be false and evil. On the contrary, Augustine's Platonism offers a third epistemological possibility: that which is neither eternally true nor wholly false (just as the created world is neither incorruptibly good nor pure evil). Augustine's label for this epistemological possibility is "similar to the truth" or "truthlike" (*veri simile*). This label applies to everything in the bodily world, and thus designates the overarching epistemological context in which his notion of signs will eventually be placed.

Yet to understand what Augustine is up to when he uses this label, it is important to realize that it first makes its appearance as a term belonging to the sceptics. *Veri simile* is a technical term in Cicero's exposition of Academic scepticism. Cicero introduces it as equivalent to *probabile,* which he uses to translate the Greek term *pithanos,* the "persuasive" or "convincing." (*Probabile,* of course, is the ancestor of our word "probable," but its sense in Cicero is often closer to "approvable" or "apt to be accepted or approved [*probari*]."[73] *Veri simile* is likewise the ancestor of our "verisimilitude" but also of our "likely.")[74] Cicero uses this pair of terms as a label for what the sceptic wise man will live by, in default of certain knowledge: he will "follow many things that are *probabile,* not apprehended or grasped or assented to, but *veri simile.*"[75] The extant Greek sources concerning the Academics contain no equivalent to the term *veri simile,* and Cicero introduces it in a way that suggests it is his own gloss on the more straightforward translation, *probabile.*[76] But it is likely that Cicero is transferring the term *veri simile* from rhetorical usage,[77] where it was equivalent to the Aristotelian term *eikos* ("the likely") which we encountered early in chapter 1.[78] *Eikos* is also used by Plato, and so could certainly have been present in the writings of the Academics.[79]

This may seem like a lot to say about one term, but Augustine clearly thinks it is a term worth fussing about. At first, he appears to be using it simply to make the same connections as Cicero. Against the objection that anyone who approves (*approbaret*) nothing will be paralyzed by indecision and unable to act, Augustine reports the Academics' claim to follow what is worth approving, the *probabile,* which they also call the "truthlike."[80] But then he proceeds to make this the first point of attack against Academic scepticism. How can you recognize what is *like the truth,* he asks, if you do not already know *the truth* which it is like? It is as if you said a young man looks just like his father, when you have never seen the father.[81] The clear conclusion is that what is *like truth* cannot be known unless *truth* is known.[82] Augustine's debating partner, trying to defend the Academics, wants to shift his ground back to the term *probabile* in order to escape this notion of "likeness"[83] and thus evade Augustine's critique. But Augustine is curiously insistent upon this one word, despite the reminder from another participant in the discussion that Cicero himself disapproved of wrangling about words rather than things (*verba* rather than *res*).[84] Yet Augustine persists: "Do you suppose that Cicero, whose words these are, was so poor at Latin that he would impose inept names on the things he was considering?"[85]

The reason for this odd persistence in hanging on to the one term "truthlike" becomes clear when Augustine recounts the history of the Academy. This history begins with Plato, of course, and it is to him that Augustine traces the notion of the truthlike:

> Plato held that there are two worlds. The one is intelligible and
> Truth itself dwells in it, while this world is sensible and obviously we
> sense it by sight and touch. Thus the one is true, while the other
> is truthlike and made in its image.[86]

This Platonist otherworldliness,[87] in which Truth is assigned to the intelligible world and truthlikeness to "this world," is the hidden doctrine of the Academy, Augustine thinks, a doctrine now finally shining forth with full clarity in Plotinus, a Platonic philosopher so similar to Plato that he is to be regarded as Plato come back to life.[88] Indeed Augustine's account of Plato in this passage probably comes mainly from Plotinus. There is nothing like it in Cicero's extant works, and it hardly seems like something from Plato himself.[89] But Plotinus has a treatise "On Virtues" in which he explains the nature of the virtues in terms of how they make us similar to what is divine and intelligible, and distinguishes civic virtues from higher virtues[90] in a way that seems to have inspired the odd passage with which Augustine concludes his account of Plato:

> Whatever actions are performed in this world by the virtues called
> "civic," which are similar to other true virtues that are unknown to all
> but a few wise men, can only be called truthlike.[91]

Thus Augustine assigns a Platonic pedigree to the Academic sceptics' claim that following the truthlike is sufficient for purposes of action.

He puts this pedigree to use when, after recounting the conflict between Arcesilaus and Zeno, he comes to the high point of Academic scepticism under the brilliant Carneades, who became head of the Academy several decades after Arcesilaus's death. According to Augustine, Carneades used the term "truthlike" not only to answer those who objected that whoever assents to nothing will be paralyzed into inaction, but also to leave hints about the secret truth of Platonic teaching:

> He wisely noticed what kind of actions they approved [*probarent*]
> and, seeing that these were similar to certain true ones, called
> that which is to be followed for the sake of action in this world,

"truthlike." For as an expert he knew that to which it was similar and prudently hid it. He called this by the name "probable" also. For one who beholds the paradigm approves [*probat*] its good image. Now how could a wise man approve or follow what was similar to the truth, when he did not know what the truth itself is? Therefore these men [the Academics] did know, and approved false things in which they observed a laudable imitation of true things.[92]

By this account, Augustine's earlier objection against the Academic notion of the truthlike (that it could not be recognized unless one knew the truth) is actually in conformity with Carneades' deepest intention; it follows up the hint he left for posterity as "a sort of sign [*signum quoddam*] of his viewpoint."[93] That sign is his choice of the word "truthlike," which indicated that he was not ignorant of truth, but served to hide that fact from those who were. Thus the Academics, as Augustine puts it elsewhere, used the word *truthlike* "to hide their views from the slow-witted and to hint [*ad significandam*] at them to those who were more alert."[94] (Here we come for the first time upon a vocabulary of signification that is specifically Latin rather than Greek. More of this in the next chapter. For now, note that Augustine here is not classifying all words as signs, but is simply using the word *significare* in one of its ordinary senses, "to hint." This is a sense that has no equivalent in the semiotic language of Greek philosophy.)

The Two Kinds of Similarity

When Augustine comes to comment on *Against the Academics* many years later in his *Retractations,* he turns to this passage on Carneades and regrets saying that the truthlike, which the Academics approved, was false. For "that which is similar somehow to something true" he explains, "is also true in its own way [*in genere suo et . . . verum est*]."[95] This correction is important, for it bears on the central argument of the last of the Cassiciacum works, the *Soliloquies,* in the second book of which Augustine discusses at length the notion of similarity or likeness and its relations with truth and falsehood. In this book[96] he draws his final implications from Zeno's definition, first in a sceptical direction and then in a Platonist direction. That is to say, in a movement that summarizes the development of Augustine's epistemology thus far, first scepticism corrects empiricism, then Platonism corrects scepticism.

The course of this movement is hard to see because it excruciatingly in-direct. The *Soliloquies* is not only an inner dialogue but a piece of genuinely

Socratic dialectic, full of refutation and puzzlement and the recognition of ignorance. In this text an inner teacher named Reason purifies a character named "Augustine"[97] of his false opinions by questioning him in a way that leads him to see their incoherence and falsehood.[98] Augustine himself draws attention to the fact that the discussion is circuitous and frustrating, full of twists and turns, backtracking, delays and confusions.[99] "Reason" will propose views that look likely, then refute them after "Augustine" (the character, not the author) is foolish enough to give them his assent—and then they must start over. Further complicating matters is the fact that overlying the Socratic ethos of critical questioning and admission of ignorance is the Hellenistic note of shame at rashly assenting to false opinions—the shame that the character "Augustine" repeatedly feels when he is shown up for a fool (as both Stoics and Academics would judge) by his rash yet wavering opinions.[100] He is working to overcome such foolishness, for as Reason reminds him, the purpose of their dialogue is "to give you joy in things wherein you need fear no fall [casum]."[101]

Nowhere is this dialectical circuitousness more prominent than in the first half of *Soliloquies* 2, where the topic of discussion is truth and falsehood in the sensible world and their connection with the concept of similarity.[102] Here the manner fits the matter: repeated refutation and reconsideration is only to be expected when one of the main points under discussion is how the similarity of things in this world makes it difficult to distinguish true from false. This rather extreme dialectical complexity is perhaps why the second book of *Soliloquies* is seldom discussed in the scholarly literature. I cannot here do justice to the subtle and irregular development of the argument, which is not as random as it looks on a superficial reading, but I shall try to pick a way through the complexity of the text by situating my exposition within a brief overview of its structure.

The first argument made in the book is a quick proof that truth always exists (2:2). For (the argument goes) even if the world ceased to be, it would still be *true* that it ceased to be. This notion of an unchanging and imperishable Truth, which Augustine plainly means to identify with God, is taken up in a much more elaborate proof for the immortality of the soul, which occupies the second half of the book, in which the crucial premise is that Truth is inseparably present within the rational soul (2:19–36). Our concern is with the stretch of text that lies between this quick initial proof of eternal Truth and the elaborate proof that locates Truth inseparably in the soul. We can narrow the focus further by skipping over the most intricate and deliberately confusing dialectic of all, in which Reason leads "Augustine" through a series of puzzles designed to reinforce the conclusion that truth is independent of the senses but falsehood is not (2:3–9). My exposition begins with paragraph 10, where Reason

introduces the concept of similarity by alluding to a series of sceptical arguments made by the Academics.

The Academics had used the concept of similarity to show that nothing
available to the senses fits the definition of Zeno's grasping appearance. It is
always possible, they argued, for an appearance to come from something that
is so similar to something else as to be indistinguishable, as for example with
identical twins or a pair of eggs or two different impressions from the same
signet ring.[103] No such appearance is (to use one of Augustine's formulations
of Zeno's definition) "true in such a way as to be discernible from the false by
dissimilar marks."[104] The Academic claim was that we can never guarantee an
appearance is free of such deceptive similarities. Hence "Augustine" is led to
the conclusion that the similarity of sensible things is "the mother of falsehood."[105] The Academics' sceptical arguments also used another set of similarities, more psychological, which later played a central role in modern
scepticism: "for example, a man we see in our dreams is of course not a true
man: he is false precisely because he is similar to a true man."[106] Likewise
the false tree we see in a picture, the false face in the mirror, the false appearance of a bent oar in the water: these are all called false precisely because of
their similarity to the true. Reason thus leads "Augustine" to see truthlikeness
as the source of falsehood.

But then comes refutation and reversal. Reason proceeds to distinguish
two kinds of similarity, which we could think of as "horizontal" and "vertical,"
for the one is a similarity between equals and the other between higher and
lower things.[107] Identical twins and indistinguishable eggs exemplify similarity between equals, while a true thing and its image in a dream or in a
painting exemplify similarity between higher and lower. The latter kind of
similarity is, of course, analogous to the familiar Platonist relation between
paradigm and image, model and copy, substance and shadow, which is always
a hierarchical relation in which the lower gets its form and reality from the
higher. The lower thing is not true reality, but neither is it wholly unreal or
false. It has its own kind of being and truth, precisely by virtue of its similarity
to its model. Hence Reason leads "Augustine" to reverse his previous conclusion: this hierarchical or "vertical" kind of similarity is the mother of truth,
and dissimilarity is the mother of falsehood.[108] Even the similarity between
two eggs shows that they are both true eggs.[109] The sceptical use of similarity
accordingly gives way to the Platonist understanding of sensible reality as
"truthlike" or similar to true reality, and thus true in its own way. After going
through an interlude of dialectical puzzlement over this (2:14–15), "Augustine"
is led to see the hierarchical kind of similarity as a tendency toward true being,
even a desire for true being in the sense that a picture "wants" to be what it

resembles or fiction tries to imitate fact (2:16–18).[110] Then he launches into the second half of the book (2:19–36) by introducing dialectic or logic as the discipline that distinguishes truth from falsehood. But that leads us away from sensible things and into investigations of the mind's relation to intelligible truth.

The first half of Soliloquies 2, for all its dialectical complication and indirection, is important for understanding Augustine's development, because it is his final statement on the legacy of Hellenistic epistemology he inherited from Cicero.[111] It "places" the empiricist epistemologies of the Hellenistic era next to the sceptical questioning of the Academics, which is then transcended by the insights of the Platonists. (Hegelian language is well-nigh irresistible here: the empiricism of the Stoics is negated by the scepticism of the Academics, and both are subsumed by the otherworldly truth of the Platonists). Thus we recover the changing and uncertain truth of the sensible world as a subordinate moment within Augustine's insight into eternal and intelligible Truth. The sceptic denial of this world's uncertain but real truth can be rejected along with the Manichaean denial of its corruptible but real goodness. Young Augustine's insatiable desire for transcendent Truth—so much like the infatuation of Plato's philosophic lovers—is made compatible with an adult adjustment to the ambiguities of the ordinary world.

Even so, he will never be perfectly happy calling sensible things "true," preferring to reserve the noble word truth for what is most truly real.[112] It is only much later that he will explicitly affirm that not only intelligible things but also external utterances can be true[113]—an affirmation which, if it showed up in this text, would rather unsettle the conclusions toward which he is aiming. Modern readers, used to thinking of sentences or statements as the primary "truth-bearers" (i.e., the things to which the predicates "true" or "false" are most properly attached) need to get used to the idea that when Augustine uses the word "true" without qualification he is usually thinking of what is immutably true, that is, of Platonic Ideas in the mind of God (which are themselves no different from God, because everything within God is God) and that when he speaks of the Truth (veritas) he is almost always referring to God (for Truth, like supreme Good and eternal Beauty and true Being, is a name for God).

Augustinian signs do not inhabit the higher realm of truth but rather the ambiguous world of the truthlike. What they add to that lower realm is a new way of relating the two worlds. Augustine's theory of signs enriches Platonist philosophy by articulating the relation of sensible to intelligible, lower to higher, in terms of signification rather than likeness or similarity. In contrast to images, imitations, reflections, and shadows (favorite Platonist metaphors), signs need not bear any similarity in form to the things they signify. Augustine's semiotics thus offers a better foundation for a Platonist theory of language than Plato's own semantics, which treats names as fundamentally imitations (*mimēmata*) of what they name.[114] One can see why the novelty of a Platonist semiotics rapidly came to seem inevitable and even natural. The relation between names and what they name is surely not one of similarity, but it may plausibly be treated as one of signification, in the sense that a sign signifies something by reminding us of it, calling it to mind. This new Platonist semiotics of language, which is the topic of chapter 3, comes to dominate Western Christian thinking about word and sacrament (both of which are signs in the Augustinian view) and creates an important contrast with the theology of Eastern Orthodoxy, which retains the old Platonism of the image (*eikon*, whence our word "icon"). Yet as we shall see in chapter 4, Augustinian signs continue to share with Platonist images and imitations the ontological and epistemic inferiority of sensible things, which are merely "truthlike." There may be a sense in which words and other signs can be true, but this is an inferior truth which we can only recognize for what it is if we first know the real truth, the unchanging inner Truth of which lower and external things should serve as reminders. Like the forms seen by our bodily eyes (on a Platonist reckoning) the words heard by our bodily ears are not the basis of certain knowledge or revelation, but can at best point beyond themselves to something higher, more inward and more intelligible, which must be known first and seen for itself.

3

How Words Became Signs

The Development of Augustine's Expressionist Semiotics

Two innovations come together when Augustine invents expressionist semiotics. First, he treats sensible things as signs of higher things, beginning in his early treatise On Order, *where works of nature and works of art, including human speech, are signs of an underlying Reason. Second, he classifies words as a species of sign, treating linguistic meaning as a form of signification, beginning in his early treatise* On Dialectic. *Combining these two innovations requires a notion of expressive signification absent from Greek semiotics but common in Latin rhetoric, where bodily gestures are said to signify the movements of the soul. The whole package comes together in Augustine's treatise* On Christian Doctrine, *where words are classified as one kind of "given signs," which get their significance by expressing the communicative will of the soul. Not all given signs are conventional, and even words cannot be understood simply in terms of convention, for they are products of human communities either governed by or in rebellion against a higher, unchanging Truth. In fact the rebellion of the Fall infects human language, which would not even be necessary in an unfallen world, where souls could understand each other and see each others' minds without need of words. But as it is, this necessary medium of fallen communication is itself a medium of fallenness, a means of deception and manipulation, as when souls that ought to be moved only by truth allow themselves to be moved by the words of a rhetorician.*

Augustine's concept of signs, like the Platonist concept of similarity, serves to link different dimensions of being, one of which is higher, better, more spiritual than the other. It does this not by becoming the basis of an inference, as in Greek semiotics, but by being a form of communication. Augustine's semiotics is expressionist in that it concerns not merely the epistemic movement from sign to signified, as the mind uses signs to get knowledge of what is hidden from it, but also the expressive movement from signified to sign, as the mind uses signs to give indication of what lies hidden within it. The soul is the higher dimension of being linked to the lower dimension of bodies by its power to use external, bodily things as signs to express its communicative will. In one of the more fateful developments in Western thought, Augustine draws words into this expressionist semiotics, so that for centuries it is taken for granted that language has meaning only because words are signs expressing what lies hidden within the inner self. In this chapter we examine how this conception of the meaning of words came about and how it was originally situated in the hierarchical world of Augustine's Platonist ontology.

Signifying Reason

In Augustine's earliest writings, the higher, more spiritual dimension is often called by the name Reason. What Reason is, exactly, is not quite clear, for the nature of Reason is what Reason itself is trying to find out.[1] Young Augustine wants to know nothing but God and the soul,[2] and he is convinced that Reason is the key to the relationship between the two, for Reason is somehow both a divine power and part of the human soul. However, once he has fully assimilated the Catholic doctrine that the soul is not divine but a creature of God, Augustine will have no more of this unclarity about the nature of Reason. He comes to make a sharp distinction between mutable human reason and the immutable divine Reason (*Logos*) or the reasons (i.e., Platonic Forms) in the mind of God. But in his early philosophical dialogues the divine Reason in the human soul—the human reason that is also somehow divine—is investigated as the key to everything. The means of investigation is a program of studies in the seven liberal disciplines, through which the Reason in us will come to recognize its own immortality and divinity.[3] A good education, in other words, makes us aware that our inner depths are home to something divine. But seeing what lies within us is not easy and requires long, disciplined study. So the education of the soul must begin with things visible to the senses and ascend by gradual steps to the vision of intelligible and unchanging truths.

We begin with the hints our own Reason has left us in sensible things themselves—hints which Augustine calls signs or significations.

In the earliest adumbration of Augustine's new theory of signs, in his treatise *On Order*, he uses semiotic vocabulary (*signa* and *significare*) to describe the relation of the sensible aspect of human arts and sciences to the intelligible Reason that underlies them. He wants us to see the seven liberal disciplines as founded by Reason itself, so he composes an allegorical narrative in which a personified Reason invents human language and then proceeds to invent the linguistic disciplines of grammar, dialectic, and rhetoric. This is followed by Reason's discovery of the mathematical disciplines of music (which in Augustine means the study of poetic meter), geometry, and astrology, and then capped by the invention or discovery of philosophy, in which Reason comes to self-consciousness and recognizes itself in the work of all the other disciplines.[4]

Preceding this narrative and forming its epistemological context, Augustine describes the rationality of human works and words generally in terms that link the sensible to the intelligible: "For I see two things in which the power and strength of reason can be applied even to the senses themselves: human works which are seen and words which are heard."[5] Reason appears in the rationality of things we see and hear, as when in the Latin of Augustine's day one could say that something looks or sounds "rationally," *rationabiliter*.[6] (The other three senses do not participate so much in reason: things do not smell, taste, or feel "rationally"). Reason thus leaves its traces or vestiges (*vestigia rationis*) in the form and rhythm, measure and order that we can enjoy through these two higher senses,[7] as for instance in the sight of a well-designed building, whose very design is called its *ratio* or reason.[8] Thus the human mind perceives traces of divine Reason in the beauty of sensible things. Here Augustine operates within a standard Pythagorean-Platonist framework, thinking of sensible beauty as a resemblance, similarity, or image of the intelligible beauty of unchanging Form and Number. It helps that in Latin one can praise the movement of a dance as *numerosus*, just like the rhythm of poetic meter.[9] To call something "numerous" in this sense is to point out a visible semblance of the beauty of Reason.

Signs then come into the picture as another way for works of human art to be rational: not by similarity but by signification. In understanding signs, the mind does not perceive Reason in the very beauty of sensible things but is led to turn its attention elsewhere. For instance, the gestures of an actor dancing in a pantomime are "signs of things" not because of the pleasing rhythm of the dance itself but because they do a good job "signifying and showing something beyond the pleasure of the senses."[10] As we shall see, the notion of showing something beyond the senses becomes a keynote in Augustine's definition of signs. Whereas we see the traces of reason in the sensible thing itself, the sign is used to show us something we cannot take in with our eyes. Yet the same sensible thing can function in both ways, not only exhibiting the traces of reason but also serving as a sign of something beyond the senses. So a work of art can direct our attention in two quite different ways. In Augustine's example, the actor's graceful pantomime signifies the myth of Venus and Cupid, which Augustine takes to be offensive to the mind. The two different ways of directing attention are brought out in Augustine's remark that the dance does not offend the eyes but the mind, "to which these signs of things are shown."[11] For the eye is pleased by the numerical rhythm of the dance, the mind offended by the lascivious myth it signifies.

Thus in general Augustine wants us to note the difference between what affects a sense directly and what comes to the mind *through the sense:* "beautiful movement soothes the sense, but *through the sense* the beautiful significance in the movement soothes the mind alone."[12] Thus the sound of a line of poetry gladdens the sense of hearing by its numerical rhythm, "but what is well signified through that same sound is related to the mind alone, though by the ears as messenger."[13] As example he quotes a couple of lines of Virgil, in which "we praise the meter [*metra*] in one way, the meaning [*sententiam*] in another."[14] Augustine concludes that we understand the term "rationally" in two different ways when we remark that something "*sounds* rationally" and when we remark that it "*is said* rationally."[15] The one remark concerns the beauty of the sound itself, the other its meaning—or what we can now call its significance. For here, for the first time, linguistic meaning is treated as a form of signification, as if words had meaning because they are signs. At this point words seem to be signs more or less on analogy with bodily gestures, which Latin rhetoricians called *significationes*. But Augustine is about to extend this familiar Latin usage systematically in a new direction.

In the next paragraph he begins the allegory of Reason founding the liberal disciplines. Reason's first step, before founding any of the individual disciplines, is to invent language, the medium in which the liberal disciplines are taught. This requires that "words, i.e., certain significant sounds, be imposed on things."[16] Here the key elements of Augustine's semiotics come together for the first time. Not only are words described as sounds that signify, but they are needed for souls to express themselves to one another. By means of words, rational souls "could use the sense as a kind of go-between to join themselves to one another, because they could not [directly] sense each others' souls."[17] At issue here is not that which is rational in sensible works of art but its source, "that which is rational in us," which cannot be known through the senses. As always in Augustine, this is at root a single, shared rationality, "tightly bound by a certain natural chain in the society of those among whom it is itself the common Reason."[18] Yet the one Reason common to all needs to use language to keep the multitude of human souls in communication with each other, for "human beings could not form a really strong social bond with one another unless they talked together and thus poured, as it were, their thoughts into each others' minds."[19] Here linguistic signification, and hence semiotics, not only forms the basis of education but explains the very possibility of human social life.

If Augustine had died immediately after writing this treatise, so that we never heard any more from him about the function of signs, we might have supposed that in this text "to signify" means "to hint," and that the description of words as "significant sounds" was a nonce-use, an interesting metaphor describing words as a kind of hint—not a suggestion that words be classified as a form of sign. But in fact Augustine lives on and has much more to say about the signification of words. He is planning to fill out his allegorical narrative of Reason as the founder of classical education by writing textbooks on all seven of the liberal disciplines, and in the key discipline of dialectic his introductory discussion will focus on how all words inherently function as signs.

Words That Signify

The first extant text giving a semiotic theory of language is Augustine's early treatise *On Dialectic*.[20] This is the uncompleted first book of a textbook on logic that Augustine was planning to write as part of his ambitious project of producing a curriculum in the liberal disciplines to serve as propaedeutic to a Platonist ascent of the soul. Judging by the one textbook in the series that Augustine completed, the treatise *On Music*, the early books of *On Dialectic* would have been a relatively conventional treatment of the subject matter of this discipline, to be capped by a final book in which the attention of the student was directed away from the corporeal or sensible subject matter and toward rational and unchanging truths, which afford a vision of the unchanging Truth of God.

"Dialectic" here means the formal discipline of logic, not the art of Socratic discussion.[21] This usage is Stoic, like much else in the treatise.[22] Clearly Augustine is dependent on one or more Stoic handbooks on dialectic, although perhaps on a Peripatetic source as well.[23] It would not be surprising if Augustine were following his sources rather closely in this first book of the treatise, where it is not his aim to be original or innovative but to give a solid and reliable treatment of the discipline.[24] So why is it precisely here that we find so major an innovation in Western philosophy of language? In large part, I think, because this is the first extant treatment of logical semantics in Latin. As noted at the beginning of chapter 1, Latin has no specifically semantic vocabulary and therefore has always tended to use semiotic vocabulary like *significatio* to translate Greek notions of meaning or semantics. Thus Varro, an important author for Augustine, talks about what a word "signifies," using the Latin *significare* as equivalent to the Greek verb "to mean" (*sēmainein*).[25] Something similar will almost inevitably happen in any Latin writer dealing with the Stoic theory of language: Greek semantics will become Latin semiotics, *sēmainein* will become *significare*. This in turn suggests almost inevitably that words are a kind of sign. But we have no writings before Augustine's treatise *On Dialectic* which actually develop such a suggestion, much less base a theory of language on it, though something of the sort could conceivably have happened already in Augustine's lost Latin sources.

Augustine begins his treatment of logic by explaining the meaning of words, because dialectic is defined as "the science of arguing well" and we argue in words.[26] The brief first chapter proceeds to use the verb *significare* five times to describe how words mean things, together with three uses of the noun *significatio* for what they mean. To illustrate the usage: Augustine distinguishes between compound and simple words, depending on whether they signify one thing (such as the word "horse") or have a signification that is not so simple (such as "I speak"). Even though the latter is only one word in Latin (*loquor*), "it nonetheless does not have a simple signification [*significationem*], because it also signifies [*significat*] the person who is talking."[27] This use of *significare* to describe the meaning-function of words is an unprecedented piece of theorizing, but it does not seem to have been a novel or outlandish use of Latin vocabulary, as the same usage occurs once without comment in an earlier treatise of Augustine's.[28]

What it means for a word to *signify* something is henceforth a central topic of Augustinian semiotics. Augustine's basic notion about this is revealed by a parallel usage in the first chapter. Pursuing the point that first- and second-person verbs have a complex signification despite being only one word, Augustine remarks:

> Whoever says *ambulo* ("I walk") makes understood [*facit intellegi*] both the walking and himself who is walking, and whoever says *ambulas* ("you walk") similarly signifies [*significat*] both the thing that is done and him who does it.[29]

It seems from this parallel usage that, as far as words are concerned, "to signify" means something very close to "to make understood." This sets up the semiotic triad that will characterize Augustinian semiotics and its descendants for the next millennium and a half: *words* signify *things* by way of their relationship to what is understood by or contained in the *mind*.

The basic elements of the signification of words are elaborated in chapter 5, beginning with a set of definitions:

> A *word* is a sign of any sort of thing that can be understood by a hearer, expressed by a speaker. A *thing* [*res*] is whatever is sensed or understood or hidden. A *sign* is what shows both itself to the sense and something besides itself to the mind. To *speak* is to give a sign through articulate utterance.[30]

Here for the first time words are defined as a type of sign, and speaking is defined as an activity of giving signs. For Augustine words in the proper sense are always spoken, for in writing we have "not a word but the sign of a word."[31] The significance of the word stems from the communicative situation of speech, in which a speaker gives signs to a hearer by making sounds the latter can understand. The possibility of making something understood is thus of the essence of the word, and follows from its nature as a sign—a thing that is not only available to the senses but also shows something other than itself to the mind. Because the word is a sign it serves to make the thing signified, the *res*, understood by the hearer.

To complete the semiotic triad we need, in addition to "word" and "thing" (*verbum* and *res*), a term for the understanding that the word helps generate in the mind. For this Augustine introduces the term *dicibile*, which he defines as "whatever the mind rather than the ears senses from the word, and which is held within that same mind."[32] A little later he characterizes the *dicibile* as "what is understood in the word and contained by the mind."[33] This is clearly meant to be a key term in Augustine's theory of meaning, but we never hear of it again, because he never got to write the part of the treatise that would have discussed it in detail. But it is not as if the concept it designates simply disappears. The semiotic triad in this work consists of *verbum*, *res*, and "the conception of the word in the mind," which is designated by the term *dicibile*;[34] we will hear no more of *dicibile*, but we will hear of words conceived in the mind or heart, which Augustine will call "the inner word."[35]

Dicibile is an outlandish term, like "sayable" in English, and one can hardly avoid the suspicion that it was devised, by Augustine or his Latin source, as an equivalent to the Stoic term *lekton*, discussed in chapter 1.[36] Yet astute commentators have noticed that Augustine's use of the term is quite different from Stoic usage, because the *dicibile* is something in the mind but the *lekton* is not.[37] The difference marks a step in the direction of an expressionist theory of language, where the meaning of words is a psychological state or property, something within the soul. What has not yet happened, however, is for words to be treated as signs of things in the mind or soul. Signification has yet to be seen as a link between soul and body. For that we must move to a more thoroughly Latin understanding of the function of signs. For even before Augustine Latin *significare*, unlike Greek *sēmainon*, had a long history of use to describe expressions of what is in the soul.

A Latin Orator's Signs

The Greeks discussed signs not only in the context of logic, epistemology, and scientific method, but also in treatises on rhetoric. Thus Aristotle treats the nature of signs not only in the logical treatise, *Prior Analytics,* but also in his *Rhetoric.*[38] In both works signs are connected with probability or "the likely" (*to eikos*). From Aristotle the notion of sign as well as its association with probable inference passes into the rhetorical tradition, where it must have become known to a far wider audience than the logical textbooks and epistemological debates in which the philosophical notion of sign was refined.[39]

Thus it is in Cicero's rhetorical treatise *On Invention* that young Augustine, who made his living by teaching rhetoric, is likely to have first encountered a formal definition of the term "sign." The definition occurs in a discussion of evidence in forensic oratory, and it classes signs under the heading of probability (i.e., that which is *probabile*, in Cicero's Latin). A sign, Cicero tells us, is "something that falls under some sense and signifies something that is seen to proceed from itself."[40] Like the Greek philosophical discussions, this rhetoric textbook treats signs both as sensible objects and as forms of inference. Examples of signs include the kind of physical evidence that is relevant for establishing guilt or innocence in court, such as "blood, flight, pallor, dust and things like that."[41] Later, in a discussion of refutation, Cicero will also speak of signs as inferences that can be confirmed or invalidated.[42] But the inferential aspect of signs is not what attracts Augustine's attention. The generic resemblance between this definition and Augustine's definition consists rather in its division into two parts, referring first to the sensible character of the sign and then to something else beyond the sign itself. This bipartite structure was already present in Augustine's definition of sign in *On Dialectic* (above) and it remains in his definition years later in *On Christian Doctrine:* "a sign is a thing which, aside from the appearance it brings to the senses, makes something else come to mind from itself."[43]

The conceptual difference between this definition and Cicero's looks much like the difference between the indicative sign and the reminding sign described by Sextus Empiricus.[44] Whereas Cicero's definition concerns a sensible thing and what logically or causally follows from it, Augustine's concerns a sensible thing and what it makes us think of. The function of signs, for Augustine, lies not in how they ground scientific or forensic inferences but in how they bring things to mind. The home of semiotics is moving from epistemology to psychology, from relations revealed in the world to thoughts arising in our souls. The move is completed in the ensuing discussion in book 2 of *On Christian Doctrine*, which contains Augustine's most systematic treatment of the theory of signs. This is the classic statement of expressionist semiotics for the next millennium and more. Despite its affinities with Sextus (whose work was probably unknown to Augustine) it initiates a form of thought that no Greek would classify under the heading of *sēmeiōsis*. Its nearest antecedents in fact were Latin, a point that calls for further attention before we proceed to examine *On Christian Doctrine* itself.

I have spoken of "Cicero's definition" of signs, and that is certainly how Augustine would have thought of it, but from a historical point of view that is slightly misleading. For although the immense popularity of the treatise *On Invention* for many centuries was due in no small part to the authority of Cicero,[45] the book is in fact highly derivative, consisting of notes from a lecture course Cicero attended as a youth, which he did not even have the opportunity to revise before they slipped out of his hands and into the public's.[46] In the works in which Cicero sets forth his own views on rhetoric, interestingly, the vocabulary of signification undergoes a twofold shift. First of all, the Greek term *sēmeion* no longer gets translated as *signum*. In his treatise *On the Parts of Oratory*, Cicero renders the Aristotelian terms "the likely" and "signs" (*to eikos* and *sēmeia*) with "verisimilitudes and marks" (*verisimilia* and *notae*).[47] Second and more important, by the time we reach Cicero's masterwork on the art of rhetoric, the treatise *On the Orator*, he has detached talk of signification from notions of evidence and inference, and associated it with notions of utterance and expression instead. This must be due in large part to the mature Cicero's greater reliance on his native tongue, as opposed to the Greek tradition of textbook-rhetoric upon which *On Invention* is based. For the Latin terms *significare* and *significatio*, derived from *signum* and *facere* (to make), suggest the active production of signs rather than the drawing of inferences from signs.[48] Hence in Cicero's mature rhetorical treatises the usual meaning of *significatio* is something like "hint," that is, the conveying of a thought by means that are less than explicit or perhaps altogether nonverbal.

This kind of "signification" is not something the Greeks ever had in mind when treating the nature of signs. It does have some affinity to the physiognomic notion of sign, that is, the bodily indication of an affection of the soul.[49] But it also has the tendency to transform that old notion, as we can see in a striking Ciceronian passage that may well have started Augustine thinking about the parallel between bodily gestures and words, which both express what lies within the soul. The passage is found near the end of *On the Orator*, when Cicero comes to consider the importance of gesture and voice, emphasizing especially the role of the face and eyes in helping the orator express his meaning:

> All action proceeds from the soul, and the image of the soul is the face, and the eyes are its indicators [*indices*]. For these are the only part of the body which can fashion significations [*significationes*] and alterations for every movement of the soul.[50]

If this passage were viewed simply from the standpoint of Greek semiotics, it would look like an interesting variant of the physiognomic notion that bodily features can be signs of the soul—interesting but subtly new as well, because the bodily movements in question are voluntary productions (which is precisely why Cicero the rhetorician is advising us how to use them). But there is more. Bodily gestures express what is in the mind in a way similar to linguistic utterances:

> It is through the eyes, whether tense or relaxed, quizzical or cheerful, that we should signify [*significemus*] the movement of our souls [*motus animorum*] in a way suitable to the particular kind of oration. For *action is as it were the discourse of the body* [*Est enim actio quasi sermo corporis*], which ought all the more to be congruent with the mind [*menti*]. For nature gave us eyes to make plain the movements of our souls [*ad motus animorum declarandos*], as it gave mane, tail, and ears to the lion or the horse.[51]

While words are not classified here as signs, it is clear that they too serve to make plain the movements or emotions of the soul, since it is precisely in resembling discourse (*sermo*) that the action of the eyes serves to signify the emotions of the soul. Hence even when the words of a discourse are too fancy and sail over the audience's head without having their intended effect,

> action, which brings the movement of the soul out in the open, moves everyone. For everyone is stirred by the same movements of the mind, which can be recognized in others by the same marks [*notis*] which indicate them in oneself.[52]

This passage as a whole (the three most striking bits of which I have just quoted) contains so much that resembles Augustine's expressionism that it is important to note what it does not contain. The soul/body contrast here is not described using inner/outer vocabulary, nor are words treated as a type of sign, although such treatment is not far off. The crucial semiotic innovation here is rather a kind of reversal of direction, as our attention is focused on a movement from soul to body rather than (as in physiognomic inferences) from body to soul. This is the movement from which expressionist semiotics gets its name—the movement of expression in which the soul takes its thoughts and feelings and "brings them out in the open" (*prae se...fert*) as Cicero says. Instead of following the direction of inference from sign to signified as in physiognomy, Cicero is interested in the direction of expression from signified to sign. For as a rhetorician, his concern is not with inferring the motions of the soul from body but with getting the thoughts and emotions of the soul properly and effectively expressed in the public realm where they are accessible to the senses. Hence when in this passage he speaks of signification—using both the noun *significatio* and the verb *significare*—he has in view not the process of sign-inference, which is what the Greeks meant by *sēmeiōsis*, but the process of making or giving signs. This is a sense of the term that has no precedent in Greek semiotics, and it is this sense that Augustine is interested in when he speaks of signifying as a "giving" of signs.[53]

Giving Signs

Augustine extends the Ciceronian notion of expressive signification to speech. His innovation is the notion that to speak is to give signs.[54] This very un-Greek notion of the voluntary giving of signs is fundamental to his classification of signs in the treatise *On Christian Doctrine*. Augustine divides the genus "signs" exhaustively into two species, which he calls natural and "given."[55] Everything that the Greeks discussed under the heading of *sēmeiōsis* falls under the species of "natural" signs. In fact Augustine's illustrations of natural signs include stock examples from Greek treatments of sign-inference: smoke is a sign of fire, and tracks [*vestigia*] are a sign that an animal has passed nearby. But he also mentions that certain facial movements are involuntary natural signs of emotions such as fear and grief.[56]

"Involuntary" is a crucial qualification here. The kind of signification that interests Cicero and Augustine is a voluntary production. Indeed what distinguishes "given" signs from natural signs in Augustine's classification is precisely the presence of a will or intent (*voluntas*) to signify. Augustine's main interest lies with this second kind of signs, for which Greek philosophy provides no precedent. Hence after devoting three sentences to the interests of the whole prior tradition of semiotics, he disposes of the topic with the remark that "it is not proposed here to discuss any of this kind of sign,"[57] and passes on to discuss "given" signs. And he never looks back. The rest of Augustine's semiotics, in *On Christian Doctrine* as well as later works, is exclusively devoted to the kind of sign that he was the first to classify as such, namely those which are voluntary communicative expressions of what is in the soul.

Communicative intent serves Augustine as the essential distinguishing feature, the differentia according to which the genus "sign" is divided. The natural signs are defined negatively, precisely by the absence of "any will or desire to signify."[58] All "given" signs, on the other hand, are used in communication of one kind or another, which for Augustine means that they serve to give bodily expression to what is in the soul. The foundation of specifically Augustinian semiotics is accordingly an expressionist definition of "given sign" as a means of communication:

> Given signs are those which living beings give one other in order to show [*ad demonstrandos*], as far as they can, the movement of their souls [*motus animi*] or else some meaning or understanding. And we have no other cause or reason for signifying, i.e., giving signs, than to bring out what is borne by the soul giving the sign and transfer it into another soul.[59]

While it is possible that this kind of sign was suggested to him by the remarkable passage in Cicero's *On the Orator* discussed above, it was clearly Augustine who first made it the cornerstone of a philosophy of language, a philosophical anthropology, and a theory of culture. For in the rest of book 2 of the treatise *On Christian Doctrine,* Augustine proceeds to give an account of culture and education that takes the same basic path as the narrative of Reason's invention of the liberal disciplines in *On Order*. Words are the most important kind of sign because all human achievements of culture and learning are dependent on the kind of communication that uses these signifying sounds.

Words, like all the signs that living creatures voluntarily give, serve to share the thoughts or feelings of one soul with another. The operative verbs in the definition of "given" sign above are "to bring out" and "to transfer" into the other soul (*ad depromendum et traiciendum in alterius animum*). The image is of something being taken down and brought out from a storage place and then carried across an intervening space and put in a new place, the suggestion being that meaning is conveyed from one soul into another through the opaque medium of corporeal signs. To adapt an image from another Augustinian context, it is as if given signs were dishes carrying the nourishment of intelligible content from one mind to another.[60] The difference is that what the words carry is something of a different order of being from themselves, something that belongs to the mind rather than to the senses.[61] The great deceptiveness and inadequacy of human speech stems from this difference, which is nothing less than the ontological gulf fixed between body and soul.

The Ontological Ground of Convention

In most translations of *On Christian Doctrine* you will not read anything about given signs, but will instead see the genus "signs" divided into the species "natural" and "conventional."[62] Such is the usual mistranslation of Augustine's classification of signs. Not only is "conventional" a very poor rendering of Augustine's term "given" (*data*), but it obscures the rationale for his classification, which turns on the difference between the inferential *sēmeiōsis* of the Greek tradition and the voluntary *giving* of signs implied by the Latin *significatio*. Evidently the translators, seeing the term "natural," have thought immediately of the contrast-term "conventional," which has a prominent place in the disagreement between Plato and Aristotle about whether the meaning of words is natural or conventional. Making the usual mistake of confusing issues in the theory of language with issues about the significance of signs, they seem to have assumed that the term *signa data* could only be Augustine's odd way of indicating that words have their significance by convention rather than by nature. It is as if the guild of translators had decided to compensate for their Augustinian rendering of Aristotle's vocabulary in *On Interpretation* by introducing an Aristotelian rendering of Augustine's vocabulary in *On Christian Doctrine*. The two sorts of mistranslations, taken together, do in fact tend to harmonize Aristotle and Augustine along lines familiar in medieval semantics and semiotics—a harmonization that distorts both texts but provides the basis for rich new developments. (This is not the only area in which misreading had a good deal to do with the fruitfulness of Augustine's thought, not to mention Aristotle's.)

Unlike *On Christian Doctrine*, the first chapter of *On Interpretation* does not offer anything so ambitious as a general theory of how words get their meaning. Rather, Aristotle's purpose is to provide a brief rebuttal of Plato's view in the *Cratylus* that the meaning of words is natural rather than conventional.[63] Aristotle's argument is based on one simple criterion: if something is natural it is the same for everybody; otherwise it is conventional.

A specifically Aristotelian conception of "nature" is discernible behind this criterion: an attribute X is natural to a species of animal if it follows from the nature of the species—so that any healthy and full-grown member of the species can be expected to be or have X. By this criterion, spoken and written words are conventional precisely in being symbols (*symbola*), dependent on some rule-governed notation that is specific to particular human communities rather than to humanity as such.[64] The words of the Greeks are sensibly different from those of the Romans, and this is enough to show that Greek and Latin words arise not from nature but from convention.

By this same criterion, not all of what Augustine calls "given" signs are conventional—a point obscured by most translations. Rhetorical gestures are voluntary acts of signification and hence "given" signs, yet as we have seen, Cicero explicitly says they are the same for everybody.[65] Likewise, in the portrayal of how children learn language in the first book of the *Confessions,* Augustine draws attention to the human gestures that preverbal children can understand, calling them "as it were the natural words of every nation."[66] These gestures are natural in Aristotle's sense, that is, species-wide rather than dependent on social convention, but they do not belong to the classification of "natural signs" in *On Christian Doctrine,* for they are products of the will to signify, which makes them "given" signs. Likewise, in *On Christian Doctrine* itself Augustine brings up the borderline case of animal communication and wonders whether it should be classified under "given" signs. The criterion is clear: if a bird calling to its mate is doing so with communicative intent, then this is a "given" sign.[67] Convention clearly has nothing to do with it. Though Augustine does not decide the issue, it is plain that he can at least conceive of signs that involve a will or desire to signify (which makes them "given" signs) but are common to a whole species (which makes them "natural" in Aristotle's sense). This is enough to show that his distinction between natural and given signs does not cut up the pie along the same lines as the classical distinction between natural and conventional.

When Augustine does come to discuss the conventionality of language (and of some other given signs, such as stylized pantomime) it is quite a bit later in book 2 of *On Christian Doctrine,* and the context is no longer a classification of signs but a theory of culture. Here Augustine places far more emphasis on convention as *agreement* than Aristotle or Plato ever did. The same written letter, such as "X" (which in Greek stands for "chi"), signifies different things for Greeks than for Latin-speakers "not by nature but by agreement and consensus as to its significance."[68] The point is a general one, extending to spoken words as well:

All these significations move souls [*animos movent*] in accordance with the consensus of their respective societies, and as the consensus differs they move differently. Nor have human beings come to consensus on signs because of the validity or meaning they already had, but rather the signs have their validity or meaning [*valent*] because human beings have come to consensus about them.[69]

The word I have rendered "have validity or meaning" is from the verb *valere*, which can suggest causal efficacy as well as semantic meaning. But here we see that whatever power a "given" sign has to move minds or souls is entirely derived from social consensus, which for Augustine is always an agreement *of wills*—i.e., a unification that occurs at the ontological level of souls. This thought of souls united by agreement of wills later becomes the basis for the social theory of the *City of God*, according to which human societies are bound together by common loves.[70] Thus from the perspective of Augustinian social theory, language and other humanly instituted forms of signification derive their meaning and whatever power they may be said to have from commonalities at a higher ontological level than that of the sensible signs themselves, namely, the middle level between God and sensible things, which is the soul. As he had already suggested in the allegorical narrative in *On Order*, it has everything to do with "that which is rational in us."[71]

In fact when Augustine's expressionist conception of "given" signs is set in the context of his ontology, the resulting theory of linguistic meaning begins to look less like Aristotle's and much more like Plato's. For Augustine convention is neither the first nor the last word in philosophy of language. It is not the first word, because the fact that linguistic signs are not common to all peoples is a result of sin rather than an inherent or necessary feature of language. In a brief passage resonant with intimations of Augustine's deepest thoughts about the nature of the Fall, he identifies this sin as impiety, as the pride signified by the tower of Babel, and as "a certain sin of human dissension, when one [people] seizes rulership for itself."[72] Here the social and political theory of the *City of God* is adumbrated, and we see how the agreement of wills that ought to unite the whole human race is disrupted by the lust for domination. This human dissension is the opposite of the consensus upon which linguistic meaning is founded, and therefore its outward sign is the dissonance of voices and tongues after Babel. Augustine's consensus theory of language thus suggests that the very feature that for Aristotle serves as the criterion of the inherent conventionality of language (viz., that it is not the same for everybody) is in fact a sign of its decay and failure to fulfill its original function as the outward sign of inner unity. Language is conventional only because it is fallen.

Nor is convention the last word on the nature of linguistic meaning. For as the story of the Fall itself suggests, the human agreements upon which various languages are founded have in turn a higher and ultimate measure of their unity and truth. Things instituted by human beings are "a sort of shadow resembling in some way what is natural."[73] Thus behind the undeniably conventional aspects of human language Augustine, like Plato, spies something natural and abiding rather than conventional and arbitrary. For there are things that human beings learn by investigation that ought to be regarded not as merely human, but as divinely instituted.[74] Here Augustine turns again (and for the last time in any systematic way) to the *disciplinae*, the liberal arts.[75] In addition to the facts known to historical and empirical investigation, which are accessible to the senses of the body,[76] there are those things which pertain to "the reason of the mind."[77] These include especially the truths of mathematics and logic. It is abundantly clear that mere human consensus is not the ground of these truths, for "the truth of logical consequences is not itself humanly instituted but merely noticed and marked [*notata*] by human beings so that they may teach or learn it, for it is divinely instituted in the perpetual reason of things."[78] Signs thus serve the purpose of teaching and learning, *docere* and *discere*—hence *doctrina* (the subject of *On Christian Doctrine*) and *disciplina* (the central concern of his early program of education). And since the human mind is changeable, being at one time learned and at another time not, we must recognize that it occupies a middle place "between the immutable Truth above it and other mutable things below it."[79]

Thus we find the familiar three-tiered ontology serving as the basic structural framework for Augustine's expressionist semiotics, and operating also to mitigate the conventionalism and voluntarism that are such striking aspects on the surface of his philosophy of language. Signs, which by definition are sensible, occupy the lowest tier of the ontological hierarchy and are related to the mind or soul above them by the "downward" movement of expression or signification, considered as a voluntary act of souls. Particular souls give particular signs when they speak, but the meaning of these signs is established by communities of souls bound together by agreement in love and understanding—and perhaps sundered from other communities by concupiscence, misunderstanding, pride, and the lust of domination. But above all souls is God, the Truth that all must love and learn if they are to be happy, a Truth that unites souls in the lasting community of happy souls called the city of God. Signs have their theological significance in being the communicative medium through which, as far as possible in this fallen world, one soul may teach or learn this Truth from another. This happens especially through the exposition of Scripture, to the hermeneutics of which the treatise *On Christian Doctrine* is devoted[80]—thus replacing Augustine's early project of instruction in the liberal disciplines, which is criticized here, never to be heard from again.[81]

Fallen Language

The Fall resulted not only in the division and conventionality of human languages, but also in the human need for them as means of communication. In paradise at the beginning of history and in heaven at the end, there is no need of communicative signs because souls have direct access to each other. In his earliest commentary on the book of Genesis, Augustine interprets the tunics of skin that God made for Adam and Eve after their sin as the mortality of bodies that are now opaque to the mind's eye, hiding the thoughts of the soul unlike the heavenly bodies they had in paradise:

> God changed their bodies into this mortality of the flesh, where lying hearts are hidden. For we are not to believe that thoughts could be hidden in those heavenly bodies the way they are in *these* bodies [i.e., our current mortal bodies]. Rather, just as some movements of our souls [*motus animorum*] are apparent in the face and especially the eyes, so in my judgment no movements of the soul are hidden at all in the clarity and simplicity of heavenly bodies.[82]

The bodies of Adam and Eve in Paradise were evidently ethereal, made of heavenly stuff and shot through somehow with a spiritual light that made plain the movements of the soul within. This heavenly lucidity of human bodies is hard for us to imagine now, Augustine acknowledges, but we see a dim approximation of it in the expressiveness of our own eyes, as he suggests in another text written at about the same time. Answering the question of how we will see each others' thoughts in heaven, he draws our attention to the light of the eyes:

> We should take a guess from that part of our bodies that has the most light [viz., the eyes]. For we are to believe that angelic bodies, the kind we hope we will have, are very lucid and ethereal. So if many of the movements of our soul are [even] now recognized in the eye, it is probable that no movement of the soul will be hidden when the whole body will be ethereal, in comparison with which these eyes are [mere] flesh.[83]

The argument is evidently taken from Plotinus, who says that in heaven "every body is pure, each is like an eye, and nothing is hidden."[84]

It is striking that for Augustine our current failure to see each other's thoughts directly is due not to the weakness or depravity of our fallen minds but to the opacity of our fallen bodies. Bodies have no positive power to give minds a vision of the truth, but they can hinder mental vision in a way somehow analogous to bodily opacity blocking the vision of our corporeal eyes. By the same token, the depravity of the minds of the devils does not prevent them from seeing what is going on in our souls, as Augustine explains in the course of his discussion of spiritual (i.e., imaginative) vision in his much later Genesis commentary. The demons can see the spiritual images in human minds, even though we can't:

> How these spiritual likenesses of corporeal things in our minds be-
> come known to spirits, even unclean ones, or what hindrances
> our soul suffers from this earthly body so that we cannot see into
> each others' spirits, is hard to find out and explain.[85]

Seeing the minds of other spirits seems to be a natural power of every spirit, unavailable to us only because we have earthy, mortal bodies.

In Augustine's earliest Genesis commentary, it seems that the first human beings in their happy state had no use for words at all. Before the soul sinned, Augustine suggests, God "watered it by an interior spring speaking to its intellect, so that it did not receive words from outside," in contrast to our present situation when every human being "has need of divine teaching from human words, like rain from the clouds."[86] But in later works, which give a more prominent role to the participation of the body in the happy life, Augustine suggests that the redeemed in heaven, while not needing words to communicate their thoughts to one another, might use them as a way to allow the body itself to join in the enjoyment of God by raising its voice in praise.

> In that city of the saints ... bodily voices will indicate souls that are
> not hidden, because in that divine society no thought will be able
> to be concealed from one's neighbor, but there will be a harmoni-
> ous concord in the praise of God expressed not only by the spirit
> but by the spiritual body.[87]

There is nothing wrong with using words when the inner and outer self, as it were, come together in praising God.

The problem is with fallen souls that are dependent on words, relying on external signs that can easily deceive, like shadows rather than light. Because the thoughts of fallen souls are hidden in opaque bodies, human communication in this mortal life cannot do without words, and Augustine observes that even a dog is a better companion for a man than another man who does not speak his language.[88] Hence every human community relies on words and other external signs to mark its boundaries and its true inner presence. For the nature of human community is fundamentally inner, given being and coherence not by outward signs but by will and love, which can join souls to one another like a kind of inward glue.[89] But who can tell, in our current opaque and miserable condition, what another soul really loves? The signs by which our friends express their love for us are not ultimately reliable, for even a heart that is not deceitful is changeable: love cools and a friend can become an enemy.[90] Likewise even one who presently shares in the inward charity of the church may not persevere and may thus end up outside the community of those bound to God in eternal life.[91] Consequently, external signs are both necessary for the life of a community and woefully insufficient. They are not the inner power that binds souls together in fellowship.

Freedom from the necessity of external signs such as words is thus a characteristic of the truly happy life, when we can see quite clearly the love that binds souls in one. A transparent unity of love belongs to the ultimate blessedness of souls in the city of God.

> There will be one city of many minds who have "one soul and one heart in God," which will be the perfection of our unity after the pilgrimage of this life—a unity where everyone's thoughts are not hidden from one another nor is there any contradiction among them in anything.[92]

The inner world of the unfallen soul is naturally public, not private. Freed from sin, souls are not divided from one another into a multitude of private inner spaces but united in a public space of inner vision.[93] Outward expressions of the inner self give way to direct contemplation of souls in a shared inner world.

Signs Moving Souls

Since signs lie at the bottom of Augustine's three-tiered hierarchy of being, he attributes to them no intrinsic power over souls. As we have seen, they do not create human community but the other way round: all communicative signs get their significance from agreement of will among souls, which is also the power that joins souls in community. Moreover, words do not even have power over individual souls, for nothing at the bottom of the hierarchy has power over things superior to it.

Even sense perception is not an exception to this Platonist axiom of downward-flowing causality,[94] as Augustine makes abundantly clear in his great treatment of the external form of words, the early treatise *On Music*. "Music" here is actually poetic meter, the rhythmic "numbers" (as poetry used to be called, even in English) which give a sensuous form to words that delights the mind. Near the beginning of the treatise's final book, in which Augustine draws Platonist philosophical conclusions from his technical study of Latin meter, he makes a point of giving us a theory of sense perception in which no bodily thing, including words, has a causal effect on the soul.[95] The soul is not directly affected by sensible things but rather moves itself in response to its own awareness of what is happening in the body. Since the soul's job is to animate, govern, and move the body, it must be aware of how the sense organs are affected by external objects. For instance, it has to act differently to govern an ear that is full of moving air than one that is empty, and its awareness of this change in its own activity is the sensation of sound.[96] Thus sense perception is the activity of a soul that is distracted from its native thoughts by the various clamorings of the body and its organs. Therefore, Augustine tells us, "it seems to me that when the soul senses in the body, it is not affected by anything from it but rather acts more attentively upon the latter's passions. . . . The soul, I think, causes things to happen among the passions of the body, but receives none of these passions."[97] Thus in accord with the Platonist axiom of downward causality, the causal interaction between body and soul runs in only one direction, from inner to outer. Sense perception is based on the soul's power to move itself and the body, whereas the body has no power to move the soul. The soul can be moved by external things only indirectly, by way of its own activity and self-movement in response to what it notices in the body.

Much of this activity of the soul governing the body must be largely unconscious, and indeed Augustine agrees here with Plotinus that in a human being who is both healthy and just, the soul acts on the body without paying it much mind, undistracted by illness, pain, or pleasure, so that its attention is free to contemplate higher things.[98] The times when the soul seems captivated by the body (and they are many) are times of disorder, when the soul gives in to the body's clamoring needs, distracted by its pains or pleasures, attracted by desire for bodily things, attached to merely corporeal goods. In this way the body has a kind of power over any soul that, in weakness or ignorance or sin, voluntarily cedes such power by immersing itself in ill-ordered loves. For the Platonist axiom of downward causality always assumes that, since eminence in being is identical with eminence in goodness, the causal power descending from above is the power to do good, not evil, having the effects of light rather than darkness. Hence lower things can blind, distract, seduce, annoy, and deceive us, but cannot bestow on our souls the inward goods they need: intellectual illumination, holy love, inward justice, or divine grace. This is a primary concern of the ethics of purification and ascent pursued in *On Music*, which blames the soul's fall from contemplation of eternal numbers on its being turned away by "love of acting in response to [*agendi adversus*] the successive passions of its own body" and "love of working on bodies" and interest in its own sensible "*phantasias* and phantasms" as well as a mere idle curiosity about sensible things that does not lead to unchanging Truth.[99]

In this context Augustine turns to the way corporeal signs can be used by one fallen soul to move another. Only God acts on souls "through himself and not through bodies," he points out, "but because of the condition of sins, souls are permitted to do [*agere*] something about souls, *moving them by signifying* through some body or other, either by *natural signs* such as a look of the face or a nod of the head, or else by *conventional* [*placitis*] *signs* such as words."[100] This talk of moving other souls is commonplace in the vocabulary of the rhetoricians, and what Augustine is evidently doing here is explaining rhetorical effectiveness as the result of our sinful condition. He obviously understands this permission souls have to move other souls through signs to be compatible with the argument he made earlier in the book that "persuaded us that the soul does [*agere*] things in bodies, rather than being affected [*pati*] by bodies."[101] Evidently we should conceive the situation as something like this: because the soul fallen away from contemplation of higher things loves to busy itself with what is happening in the bodily world, it is possible (because God permits it) for one soul to stir up passions in another by means of bodily things used as communicative signs (whether natural or conventional, both of which are "given" signs in the sense of *On Christian Doctrine*). One soul can manipulate and persuade another by using pretty words as reminders of all the earthly things that fallen souls desire. It is not as if words had direct power over souls, but they can entice, distract, threaten, and confuse.

The upshot is that Augustine can agree with the rhetoricians that we are in a sense moved by words and gestures, even though nothing sensible has direct causal power over our souls. A fallen soul is easily attracted and held by bodily things, not because of their intrinsic power but because of the soul's own perverse love. It is not that bodily things literally move the soul but that the soul moves itself in its desire for them. This explanation, I think, should be taken as underlying Augustine's adoption of the standard rhetorical vocabulary about words that "move" souls in his treatment of the aims of eloquence in later treatises like *On Christian Doctrine*,[102] where the emphasis is not on how our sinful condition makes it possible to move other souls, but on why doing such a thing might even be worth attempting under certain circumstances, such as when sinners who have already been taught what is right must be persuaded actually to do it. Words thus have the double function of teaching souls what is right and true, and moving them to act on it.

However, Augustine does not take either the teaching or the moving to be within the causal power of words or any other form of human communication. Strictly speaking, no soul can move another soul to do the right thing, for according to Augustine's doctrine of grace only God has such power. Likewise, no soul can succeed in teaching another soul, in the sense of causing the other to know the truth, for that too is solely the work of God within us, as we are about to see.

4

Why We Learn Nothing from Words

The Epistemology of Augustine's Semiotics

We do not learn things from words or other signs. That is the thesis of the dialogue On the Teacher, *where Augustine teaches his own son that he has no teacher but Christ present within him. Signs are used to teach, but we cannot understand them without first understanding the things they signify—so we do not learn things from signs, but the other way round. Our understanding or vision of intelligible things does not come from words but from Christ the inner teacher who, unlike Christ in the flesh, is available to be consulted by every virtuous mind. The* On the Teacher *thesis implies that the Scriptures cannot reveal God, but this does not mean we must use rational proof in order to know God, for proofs too are made of words from which we do not learn anything. Nonetheless, words are not simply useless; they serve as admonitions or reminders directing our minds to look for the truth in a more inward and intelligible dimension of being. Also, when we are just beginning to learn and cannot yet see for ourselves we must believe the words of external teachers, putting our trust in their authority rather than in our own reason. This temporal priority of authority to reason is what Augustine has in mind when he insists that "unless you believe, you shall not understand." Augustine's earliest statement of the relationship between Christianity and Platonism affirms the superior authority of Christian "mysteries," which is to say of baptism and its accompanying doctrinal instruction. The great shift in Augustine's later relation to Platonism is his recognition that the authority of Christian teaching is not something Christians ever outgrow in this mortal life.*

A Platonist semiotics is something close to a contradiction in terms, and it says much for Augustine's genius that he could make it fly. In Greek semiotics signs are supposed to make things known, and this is what Platonism cannot allow. While Stoics and Epicureans agreed that things evident to the senses can be signs revealing things hidden from the senses, for a Platonist what is essentially hidden from the senses is seen by the mind directly, without sensible intermediary. On a Platonist reckoning, if signs are to reveal anything of permanent interest they must make known what is intelligible rather than sensible. But that would mean sensible things made intelligible things intelligible to us, which is absurd. It would turn the universe upside down, violating the Platonist axiom of causality, according to which higher things have causal power over lower things but not vice versa. In a Platonist universe we cannot expect bodily things to have power over the soul, and especially not power to give the soul knowledge of intelligible truths, which are higher and more inward than the soul itself.

So Augustine teaches that signs cannot give us true knowledge of things. In particular, we learn nothing from words. Here, as in many other respects, Platonism is allied with scepticism about sensible things. A Platonist semiotics will inevitably be a sceptical semiotics, because signs are corporeal and therefore sensible. When combined with Augustine's new, systematic distinction between inner and outer, the legacy this leaves modernity is our taken-for-granted sense that external things are superficial, incapable of revealing inner depths. Expressionist semiotics is Platonist in exactly this sense: external signs give sensible, bodily expression to things that lie in a deeper, more real and yet more hidden dimension of being (a dimension that Platonists, not Stoics or Epicureans, believe in) but can never really make these inward things known.

A Socratic Dialogue about Teaching

Augustine developed expressionist semiotics as a theoretical underpinning for his early theological project, which centered on a program of liberal education designed to lead to the vision of God.[1] The idea that the liberal arts could teach you to see God was already in Augustine's time a very old notion, found in other church fathers[2] but having its roots in the program of education devised by Plato to lead to a vision of the Good, the First Principle of all things.[3] The very point of the liberal disciplines, from a philosophical perspective, was not their usefulness in training young people for work or public life (for usefulness is the aim of discipline for slaves, not free men) but how they make the soul capable of that which is to be desired for its own sake, the beauty of wisdom and ultimate happiness. This is why Plato thought that those who are truly wise, having seen the Good shining like the sun above them, must be dragged back down into the darkness and forced to rule over others in the dim sha-dowland of human politics.[4] A wise man knows better than to seek what is ultimate and eternal for the sake of what is useful and temporal, and therefore will never seek wisdom for the sake of its political value. He would rather remain above, outside the cave of politics and absorbed in contemplation. So the wise must be *forced* to rule if society is ever to be governed by wisdom, in light of the ultimate Good.

To examine Augustine's own life conformed to this pattern (as did the life of medieval monks who were forced into positions of power, most famously Pope Gregory I): the life of wisdom and contemplation that he sought by his conversion was wrenched from him, and quite against his will he was made a priest and later a bishop. In Platonic terms, he was dragged back down into the cave to teach others where to look to see the eternal light he had glimpsed. So the vision of ultimate Truth toward which his early program of education is directed re-mains the aim of his teaching as a bishop, but the way to this goal is no longer the self-education of reason through the liberal disciplines but the instruction of the heart through Christian doctrine. For as the bishop explicitly teaches, Christianity and Platonism are in agreement that the happiness for which the heart longs is to enjoy God, not as one enjoys a bodily thing or even another person, but as the eye of the mind enjoys the intelligible light.[5] All teaching that deserves the name, indeed all proper human speech, is a means to arrive at this end, which the later Western tradition calls beatific vision, the seeing that makes us eternally happy.

To examine Augustine's early educational program is thus to become acquainted with his view of the goal of life's journey, as well as his earliest reflections on the road he is taking to get there. Though the outward form of this road will change dramatically within a few years, as philosophical dialogue gives way to the exegesis of Scripture as his normal mode of learning and teaching, the fundamental inner structure of any temporal journey in the direction of eternal Truth remains the same. This is an epistemological structure that becomes, as Rudolph Lorenz has shown, the structure of Au-gustine's mature doctrine of grace.[6] The key to this structure is the notion of inner teaching, an education of the soul accomplished directly by God without external means like words, signs and sacraments, or human flesh. Yet all these external things, Augustine is convinced, must be used properly on the journey that prepares the eye of the mind to see God, in the final and irrevocable vision that makes us truly happy. So one of the key questions to ask is about the usefulness of signs, and especially those signs called words.

The treatise in which Augustine addresses this question, containing his most formative statement on the power of external things, is also his major epistemological statement about the nature of education, the dialogue *On the Teacher*. It is an early work, and the form of education it has in view—indeed the form of education it exemplifies in its literary form as a dialogue—is philosophic education in the liberal disciplines, undertaken through the lengthy and circuitous path of Socratic conversation. But like all of his philosophical dialogues (including the one textbook on the liberal disciplines that he actually completed, the six-book treatise *On Music,* which is also written in dialogue form) the aim of the exercise is for reason to arrive in the end at self-understanding: to know itself as that which knows or can know God.[7] However, *On the Teacher* comes late in the process, not only in the sense that it is perhaps the last of Augustine's works to have in view his project of education in the liberal arts, but also in the sense that it is the one that most clearly proposes to examine the nature of education reflectively from the standpoint of its success. Although all Augustine's philosophical dialogues take a very roundabout route to their conclusion, this one is the least aporetic, confronting us in the end not with deeper problems or an agenda of further things to learn, but with a solution that must count as a clear educational success. Thus in the end the treatise can look back on itself as an actual example of the kind of learning it proposes, and reflect on how that actuality was possible.

What makes the difference is the student. Augustine represents himself in this dialogue as playing teacher to his own son, Adeodatus. And he represents Adeodatus as far and away the best learner in any of the dialogues, a better learner than Augustine himself in the *Soliloquies,* where Augustine is Reason's own student. Pressed hard by Socratic questions that constantly probe his position for inconsistencies, Adeodatus is cautious in giving his assent, quick to see the point of an argument, ready to relinquish his opinions when refuted, tenacious in his memory of what he has already learned, and confident in his hope that God will indeed grant him knowledge of the Truth. This is a very promising young man. He is only sixteen years old at the time of the dialogue, but Augustine later calls God himself to witness: "You know that the views I included there in the person of my interlocutor were all his own. I had experience of many more marvelous things in him; his genius left me awestruck."[8]

If it were anyone else speaking, we might say this was a man proud of his son. But pride is a sin, and Augustine is moreover quite convinced he has nothing to be proud of. His account of Adeodatus's genius is a confession of praise to God for His gifts, for which Augustine can claim no credit. For this son of his is not really his own. Conceived outside legitimate marriage, Adeodatus was "born from me carnally, of my sin" so that Augustine must confess "I had nothing in that boy but the fault."[9] The very name "Adeodatus" means "given by God," as if Augustine were reminding himself that everything good in this child is God's doing, or as if he were saying to his own son: "Call no man on earth father, for one is your father who is in heaven" (Matt. 23:9). In fact Augustine portrays himself as saying something very much like this to his son at the conclusion of the dialogue *On the Teacher,* where he clinches his point about learning nothing from words by alluding to the very next verse of the Gospel, which reads, "And be ye not called teachers, for your one teacher is Christ" (Matt. 23:10). But what Augustine actually says conflates the two verses: "the one teacher of all is in heaven,"[10] he tells Adeodatus, using the phrasing of the verse about fathers to make the point of the verse about teachers. On the one hand, Augustine is quite explicitly telling the boy that he has not really learned anything from his earthly father but only from Christ the inner teacher, but on the other hand he is also hinting that the boy's true father is in heaven too, just like his true teacher. Thus the dialogue's conclusion is in effect a gesture of profound renunciation: this wonderful boy, given by God, is nothing Augustine can claim as his own.[11] God made him well, while Augustine's contribution to his making was only sin. Even the boy's education, over which Augustine has taken great pains, is really a gift from heaven, a work of the true teacher within.

This renunciation is all the more poignant because within a very short time—possibly even before Augustine has finished writing the dialogue—Adeodatus is dead. "Soon you took away his life from the earth," says Augustine, remembering this time in the *Confessions.*[12] The gift returns to the Giver, who was always his true father and teacher. In contrast to other great losses of his life, his mother (in *Confessions* 9) and the best friend of his youth (in *Confessions* 4), Augustine gives us no hint of his grief for Adeodatus and can only assure us he now feels no anxiety on the boy's behalf, as his death came soon after baptism. Indeed, to hear Augustine tell it, there was never anything wrong with Adeodatus. Only from hints like these we can begin to imagine how much he loved him, and how profound was his grief.

The *On the Teacher* Thesis

Augustine clearly devoted a great deal of time to teaching his beloved son, and one of the things he taught him was that he taught him nothing. It was one of the most successful and lasting lessons he ever taught, though its most important impact was on Augustine himself and his own teaching. The lesson, to put it precisely, is that we use signs to teach, yet we learn nothing from signs. The first half of the lesson gives us the point of Augustine's semiotics, while the second half, startling though it is, is a fundamental semiotic principle that Augustine never goes back on. I shall call it the *On the Teacher* thesis. As we shall see, it does not mean signs are of no use at all. For Augustine wants the first half of the lesson also to be taken seriously: we do indeed use signs to teach, because it is the very nature of signs (according to the definitions we examined in the previous chapter) to bring something to mind. So whenever we use a sign to communicate (a "given" sign, as defined by *On Christian Doctrine*) we are trying to bring something to someone else's mind. In that sense we are necessarily trying to teach every time we speak to another person. But whether that person actually learns what we are trying to teach is something else altogether. There is a difference between trying and succeeding, and that is why the lesson of *On the Teacher* is not quite as paradoxical as it seems. The first half of the lesson, "we use signs to teach," should be read: whenever we use signs, we are trying to teach something. The second half, the *On the Teacher* thesis that "we learn nothing from signs," tries to teach us that the success of teaching does not depend on anything the teacher says but on something more inward, which Augustine depicts as a teaching by Truth itself, a vision beyond all external words and signification.

Augustine unfolds the first half of the lesson at the beginning of the dialogue by making new connections between semiotics and psychology, the nature of signs and the nature of the soul. The first connection is simple, if a little surprising: whenever we speak, we are teaching, which means that the only use we have for words is to teach something. Even when we simply say what's on our minds, we are teaching people what we think, and when we ask a question we are teaching people what we want to know. A little later Augustine makes this into a semiotic point by getting Adeodatus to agree to classify words as a type of sign (§3). Interestingly, however, the notion of signification has already been introduced in the previous paragraph—and in a strongly theological context. For Adeodatus's big hesitation about accepting the thesis that all speaking is teaching has to do with prayer: he does not like the implication that in speaking to God, we become God's teachers. Augustine agrees this cannot be, and goes on to make the striking claim that in praying we do not really speak at all. For, he says, "Whoever speaks gives a sign of his will externally by an articulated sound," and prayer does not take place in the external space of sounds but rather in "the inner man," the inner temple in the soul where Christ dwells (§2).

So Augustine introduces the concept of sign into the dialogue in close connection with a fundamental psychological conviction underlying his expressionist semiotics: that the inner self which signs express is a sacred space, the true "place" in which to encounter God. By this reckoning even the Christian liturgy, which takes place in an external space such as a church, contains no prayers. What happens in public worship rather is that priests use the sound of words "to signify their minds, not for God but for human beings to hear, agreeing through this reminder to depend on God."[13] Mere words can only be directed horizontally, as it were, from one human being to another. The will of the heart raised inwardly to God is true prayer, and this will says literally nothing. It is turned inward and therefore seeks God free of external things like words. Thus the fundamental relation between the soul and God is not like one person talking to another or hearing another speak or preach but rather (as Augustine will put it much later in the dialogue) like consulting the light of Truth that presides inwardly over the mind itself.

So the beginning of the dialogue sets forth striking images of the inner self that prepare us for the really startling claims to come. But first Augustine's readers must follow Adeodatus through a dialectical discussion with intricate twists and turns and a great deal of close questioning, all of it concerned in some way or other with the relation between sign and thing signified (*signum* and *res*). Augustine would have us attend especially to the intricacies of signs that signify other signs and especially words that signify other words: for example, the kind of words we use when teaching grammar (§§7–20)—or conducting a dialogue about language! The dialogue indeed quickly becomes intensely self-referential, both explicitly and implicitly. So the dialogue partners find it valuable to distinguish between what modern logicians call use and mention: between using a word to signify something else and mentioning the word so as to signify the word itself (§§22–26). For every sign is itself a thing that can be signified—a point that becomes important later on, as the conversation returns to an earlier question about whether we can show things without using signs.

When I tell you about something, I show it to you by using words. Yet even if I just silently point the thing out, I am still using a sign, for the gesture of pointing is also a sign (§5f). So are signs ubiquitous in human knowledge, impossible to escape or get outside of? Do we never show anything to someone without signs? Augustine and Adeodatus discuss examples in which we show something by doing it ourselves. The first example is that I can demonstrate to you what walking is by starting to walk—or, if I am already walking, by walking faster (§6). The problem is that such a demonstration is ambiguous: does my action demonstrate walking, or starting to walk, or walking faster? When they

return to the question later, Adeodatus tells Augustine that he finds this ambiguity insuperable and can think of no clear examples of showing something
without signs except (as it turns out) self-referential ones: perhaps one can
show what it is to speak by speaking, or to teach by teaching (§29). In effect, the
only thing we can show without signs is the very activity of using signs, or the
sign itself considered as a thing signified.

And then in what seems like comic relief from this intensely self-
referential talk about talking, Augustine suggests that a birdcatcher might
teach us what birdcatching is by silently but deliberately practicing his craft in
front of our eyes (§32). Evidently the activity he shows us is so much more
complex than mere walking that we are not likely to get confused and wonder if
he is showing us how to *start* birdcatching or catch birds *faster*. In any case, this
mute example breaks the frame of learned discourse in which the discussion
has been conducted so far, and does so at a key turning point, just after
Augustine has remarked (as he so often does in his dialogues) on how long and
roundabout the course of the dialogue has been (§31), and just before he drops
the dialogue form altogether and presents the *On the Teacher* thesis in a
lengthy set speech (§§33–46). We are not invited to imagine the birdcatcher
saying anything, much less speaking like Augustine and Adeodatus in the
learned language of men trained in liberal disciplines such as grammar and
dialectic. And yet the birdcatcher's wordless art illustrates the same point as the
other, more wordy examples of things taught without signs: in every case, to
show something without a sign is to do it in plain sight, so that the learner can
perceive the thing itself (the *res ipsa*).

It turns out that far from being the exception, this is how all learning really
works: unless you see the thing itself, you have not learned a thing. So now
Augustine is ready to introduce the really memorable thesis of *On the Teacher*,
that we learn nothing from signs. His basic argument for the thesis is startlingly simple:

> When a sign is given to me, and it finds me not knowing the thing
> of which it is the sign, it cannot teach me; but if it finds me know-
> ing the thing of which it is the sign, then what do I learn from
> the sign? (§33)

To understand a sign as sign (and not just to perceive it as a sensible thing, like
a noise ringing in my ears) is to know its significance. This means, Augustine
reasons, that before I understand a sign I must know the thing it signifies. So the
notion that I learn things from signs is entirely backwards. I must know the
thing before the sign, because I can learn the significance of a sign only if I first
know the thing it signifies. This argument shows something about the scope of

the *On the Teacher* thesis, which is not quite as far-reaching as it sounds. Augustine's argument does not require him to deny that I can learn where a fire is from the sight of smoke (to use a favorite example from Stoic semiotics) or from someone who tells me, "there's a fire over there." I can learn from these signs where a fire is, but not *what* a fire is—and it is the latter that I must know before I can understand the sign itself. If I have never seen a fire in my life then I do not know what smoke is a sign of nor what the word "fire" signifies. So for Augustine vision precedes signification and is its epistemic foundation. A thing functions as sign only for those who have already seen the thing signified.

All the examples Augustine uses to defend the *On the Teacher* thesis depend on this priority of vision to signification, and especially the priority of seeing to speech. The key illustration is a line from the biblical book of Daniel about the three boys who were thrown into a fiery furnace yet protected by God so that not even their *sarabarae* were changed. Augustine focuses on this strange word, which is very useful for his purposes because neither he nor anyone else now knows what it means.

> When I read "and their *sarabarae* were not changed" [Daniel 3:27] the
> word does not show me the thing it signifies. For if some sort of
> head-coverings are called by this name, then when I hear it, does
> it teach me what a head is or what coverings are? I knew these things
> before, and knowledge of them came to me *not when they were de-*
> *scribed by others but when they were seen by me.* For example, when
> these two syllables, *caput* [i.e., "head"] first struck my ears, I was as
> ignorant of what they signified as when I first heard or read of *sar-*
> *abarae.* But as the word *caput* was often said, I noted and paid at-
> tention when it was said and found it was the term for a thing which
> was *already well-known to me by sight.* Before I found this out, that
> word to me was nothing but a sound. But I learned it was a sign when
> I discovered what it was a sign of, which I learned (as I said) *not*
> *by its being signified but by its being seen.* (§33)

The famous explanation of how infants learn language in the *Confessions*[14] is a reprise and dramatization of Augustine's point here about how he learned the word *caput.* The focus on the word *sarabarae,* on the other hand, puts all of us in the same position as an infant who hears words without knowing what they signify. If we have any intellectual curiosity at all, we can feel the desire ourselves: what we need in order understand this sign is to see a *sarabara,* whatever that is. And alas, Augustine picked his example all too well: scholars are still not sure what the word means, or even what the correct form of the word is (some biblical manuscripts have *saraballae*).

The insistence on seeing is of course not accidental: throughout the dialogue *On the Teacher,* true learning means seeing things for yourself. You do not have to be a Platonist to believe this, but it helps. For Plato is the one who gave us the metaphor of the vision of the mind's eye to describe an activity of the intellect deeper than mere imagination, which is dependent on the senses. Nowhere is this metaphor more prominent than in the famous Allegory of the Cave which, Plato tells us, is all about education.[15] The moral of the story is that education a not a process in which a teacher puts knowledge into souls that lack it, but one in which souls that already have within them the power of vision are turned in the right direction to see the light.[16] A teacher can at best show you where to look by asking you questions and getting you to rethink your answers until you see the point for yourself—as in the well-known geometry lesson in Plato's *Meno* where Socrates insists (as usual) that he is not really a teacher, because Meno's slave boy already has true opinions about geometry in his soul that Socrates merely stirs up by all his questions.[17] This is not (as many readers have thought) mere pretense, as if Socrates were coyly denying that he is asking leading questions. It is quite obvious, on the contrary, that he very deliberately, even artistically, shows Meno's slave boy how to find the right answer. The point is simply that the boy answered Socrates' questions for himself. To use Augustine's terms, he has seen the thing itself, though Socrates' words have served as reminders or admonitions about where to look for it. The same learning process is illustrated, as Augustine wants us to notice, by the boy Adeodatus.

For both Plato and Augustine the teacher's job is to turn a student's attention in a new direction, to be the occasion of a turning of the soul, which translates into Latin as *conversio,* "conversion." It is a turning at once intellectual and ethical: from shadows to light, from lower to higher, from sensible to intelligible, or, as Augustine tells us is equivalent terminology, from carnal to spiritual (§39). We must get used to this kind of parallel: for the early Augustine what Plato calls "intelligible," the Bible calls "spiritual." Indeed sensible/intelligible, carnal/spiritual, outer/inner, and lower/higher are all ways of stating the same fundamental dichotomy.[18]

The dichotomy Augustine never accepts, it should be emphasized, is the one enshrined in modern talk about the difference between heart and mind. For Augustine soul and body are different kinds of being, but heart and mind are not. Augustine's use of the scriptural term "heart" is wide-ranging, often co-extensive with the term "soul," but sometimes referring specifically to the soul's higher part, the mind or intellect. That is to say, sometimes Augustine says "heart" and means "mind." In this he follows biblical usage, which speaks of the thoughts of the heart and which, in Hebrew, does not even have a separate word for "mind."[19] The heart both loves and understands, and for Augustine the heart's highest love is to see the Truth with the inner eye of the mind. This is an ethical as well as intellectual task; in biblical terms, it is the obligation to love God with the whole heart, mind, soul, and strength.[20] To turn away from outward, sensible things and look toward the light within is an act of the soul or heart or mind (Augustine can use any of these terms here) motivated by love for Truth and resulting in the intellectual vision of God. Such vision made permanent is eternal happiness, which is why the medieval theologians called it beatific vision.

We cannot begin to understand Augustine's theological ethics or his conception of beatitude and grace without grasping this point about intellectual vision, which is the foundation of the whole project of his life. Talking about the intellect as if it had a different job from the heart will distort our understanding of Augustine's theological project. For instance, when Augustine justifies the roundabout process of question and answer in philosophical dialogues by pointing out the need for mental exercise (§21), we must not import a very modern and un-Platonic qualification and call this exercise "*merely* intellectual"—as if what we learned by seeking the intelligible Truth were not a matter of the deepest spiritual importance, the most inward love of the heart, and more important than all inferior attachments, such as those to our fathers and teachers on earth.

Christ the Inner Teacher

The crucial question on Augustine's mind in *On the Teacher* is of course not how we learn about head-coverings but how we learn about spiritual things, which Plato called intelligible things, Forms or Ideas. Like later Platonists, Augustine locates these in the divine mind or intellect.[21] This means they belong to the very substance of God, for there is no difference between what is in God and what is God.[22] Therefore to see intelligible things is to see God, to catch a partial and transitory glimpse of what God is, "the Truth containing all that is immutably true."[23] It is the same God of which Augustine speaks when he says in *On the Teacher* that we catch sight of intelligible things "present in the inner light of Truth" (§40). Here the teacher and the things taught are the same thing, because "for all the things which we understand [*intellegimus*], we do not consult a speaker resounding outwardly but the Truth which presides inwardly over the mind itself" (§38). The Truth we desire to learn is itself our inner teacher, not using words like an external teacher but rather showing itself to the eye of the mind. So the true teacher is the Truth within, which is

Christ dwelling in the inner man as "the eternal Wisdom of God" (ibid.). Readers of *On the Teacher* have been prepared to hear about this inner teacher not only by the earlier reference to Christ in the inner man (§2) but also by the exploration of how it is possible to teach without signs, where to learn is to observe the teacher in action, doing the thing itself. In coming to know intelligible or spiritual things we always learn by watching that inner birdcatcher, which is not like listening to a lecture or any other kind of human speech but is a matter of seeing the thing itself. Therefore despite the auditory metaphor implicit in the notion of consulting or taking counsel (*consulere*), learning from the inner teacher really means seeing for ourselves, not hearing about something—a point Augustine emphasizes by using the odd phrase, "consulting the light" (§§38f).

It may seem we have moved very quickly from Platonic Ideas to Christ, but the connections are essential for Augustine and go a long way back in the Christian tradition. The church fathers made much of Christ as *logos* (John 1:1), a term that means not simply word (*verbum*) but reason (*ratio*), as Augustine points out in his essay on Platonic Ideas, where he suggests that *ratio* would also make a good translation for Plato's term "Idea."[24] Almost equally important for the fathers was the identification of Christ as eternal Wisdom, which derives from their Christological reading of Proverbs 8 as well as from a Pauline passage that is one of the most frequently quoted in Augustine's early writings, "Christ the Virtue of God and the Wisdom of God" (1 Cor. 1:24).[25] Augustine depicts his own boyhood conversion to philosophy as a turning to eternal Wisdom, "whatever that may be," a Wisdom which (he hints very strongly) turns out to be none other than Christ, even though that human name was unknown to the ancient philosophers who taught him to desire this divine Wisdom above all things.[26] Thus to give Christ the philosophical names of Reason, Wisdom, and also Truth (John 14:6) always seemed to Augustine unexceptionably biblical. Moreover, the identification of Christ as divine Wisdom and *Logos* was indispensable to patristic thinking about the Trinity.

But of course Augustine is also doing something new by locating Christ as eternal Wisdom and Truth *within the soul*. In the Pauline passage to which Augustine refers, Christ dwells in the heart *by faith* (Ephesians 3:17)[27] whereas in *On the Teacher* faith is what we are left with when we are in no position "to consult by reason the Truth within" (§39). Christ is our inner teacher not through an act of Christian faith but by virtue of the rational mind that is common to all.[28] Faith in fact is what we need when we are not yet able to know Christ in the deepest and most inward way, the way most befitting the nature of the rational mind: as the divine Truth seen by the intellect. Hence Augustine tells us that "faith is useful so long as one is ignorant" of intelligible things discerned by the mind (§41). Thus his bold picture of Christ the inner teacher reflects not a Pauline notion of the indwelling Christ but a Platonist account of the intellectual vision of intelligible truths. By the same token, Augustine's talk of Christ as inner teacher must not be given the vague label "incarnational." The Christian doctrine of Incarnation is more specific than that: it is about one particular man, not a Truth available to every mind, "which indeed every rational soul consults" (§38).[29] Augustine understands the inner teacher as the very condition of the possibility of rational knowledge and understanding, and thus of the kind of learning that any good student of the liberal disciplines can accomplish. This is an accomplishment for which one need never have heard of the man Jesus Christ, much less believed in him as God incarnate.

Christ the inner teacher is therefore not a Christological notion, in the strict sense having to do with the doctrine of Incarnation. But it is unmistakably a Trinitarian notion, having to do with the deity of the second person of the Trinity, the Son who is the eternal *Logos* and Wisdom of God. Augustinian inwardness originated not from believing in Christ in the flesh (for what is more external than flesh?) but rather from a desire to know nothing but God and the soul.[30] From this desire stems a project of turning away from fleshly things to the soul in order to understand the nature of God, a project carried out most extensively in books 8 to 15 of Augustine's massive treatise *On the Trinity*. One early form this project took was the dramatization of the activity of an inner teacher called Reason (*ratio*), speaking within the soul to a student called "Augustine"—the very same character who says he wants to know nothing but God and the soul. It may be that at the time he wrote this dramatization called *Soliloquies,* Augustine was toying with the idea of identifying this inner teacher with Christ as the *Logos* of God.[31] Certainly, the character called Reason does look divine in some respects: never ignorant, never doubting, never learning new things as human reason does, but instead serenely confident of his ability "to show God to your mind as the sun is shown to the eyes."[32] Yet this is not quite the same inner teacher as the one described in *On the Teacher*. He uses words, asking questions just like a Socratic teacher, and he does not present himself as the Truth the mind desires to see, but seems rather to be in the same position as an external teacher who can only show us where to look to see the Truth for ourselves. As a literary character, in fact, he behaves a great deal like Augustine, the external teacher, as dramatized in *On the Teacher*. If this is the divine *Logos*, then it is not quite at the same level as the God or Truth it aims to show us. So the kind of inner teaching Augustine dramatizes in the *Soliloquies* is actually a dead end for him, since it only makes sense on the basis of a subordinationist theology, where God the Son, the second person of the Trinity, is not quite at the same ontological level as God

the Father, the first person of the Trinity. That I think is why there is no hint of
a divine Reason in *On the Teacher,* where *ratio* is invariably a power of the
human mind that sees intelligible things, not the divine inner teacher showing
us what to see.

A divine inner teacher in orthodox Trinitarianism must be no different in
being from the Truth he teaches. So if a Platonist notion of the divine within us
is to be incorporated into Christian theology after Nicaea, it cannot be anything
like a power of the soul (an idea Augustine had tried early on)[33] but rather must
be the highest God himself, found by turning within the soul but also looking
above it to see the immutable source of its being. The intelligible sun itself
must be the teacher who shows us how to see the Truth. To depict this inner
teacher Augustine retains the terms Wisdom and Truth (reserving "reasons,"
in the plural, for Platonic Ideas, but avoiding "Reason" in the singular as a
designation for God). The name "Wisdom" continues to designate the object of
intellectual longing, invariably feminine (like the Latin *sapientia*), whose
presence is inward yet not private: she can be wholly embraced by all her lovers
without being divided among them,[34] just as she is touched by Augustine and
his mother together in the vision at Ostia.[35] The name "Truth," though designating the same object of desire, is associated specifically with the inner act
of consultation and learning. Instead of the Socratic questioner of the *Soliloquies,* this inner teacher is one who gives answers to our questions, directly
satisfying our inquiries. This inner consulting of Truth is dramatized in the
Confessions, where Augustine is the questioner and Truth itself, when properly
heard, gives a clear answer.[36] Just as all created things mutely reply to Augustine's questions with their transitory appearance and beauty (*species*), saying
in effect "we are not the God whom you seek; he made us,"[37] so the Truth
shows by its changeless intelligible Beauty that it is precisely the Wisdom our
minds seek. The inner experience Augustine dramatizes is thus not like hearing about something in words but rather like seeing it for oneself in a moment
of lucid and indubitable insight, attended by the joy of recognizing a long-
sought truth.

This Augustinian experience has been called by other names: for instance,
mysticism (which obscures its rational character) and illumination (which
obscures the active role of the human mind in seeking and seeing). Later
medieval theologians described it as a fruit of the supernatural gift of faith,
which obscures the point that it is an essential function of every human mind.
I have insisted instead on calling it intellectual vision and comparing it to
experiences of insight. It is indeed intuitive in the old sense, in which intuitive
reasoning (from *intuitus,* seeing) is contrasted to discursive reasoning, the kind
of thinking that requires the discourse of words. The experience of such in-

tuition is neither mystic rapture nor Romantic feeling (as suggested by Schelling, who in effect taught us to identify intuition with feeling) but intellectual fulfillment. The proper domain in which to locate it is not a supernatural mysticism, but a Platonist epistemology and ethics. For the point is that this possibility of being taught by the inner teacher is not dependent on special mystical experiences nor even on Christian faith. It is, however, dependent on virtue, for the inner teacher "only discloses as much as each is capable of receiving, according to his own evil or good will."[38] Faith is for those whose will is not yet wholly good, not yet pure enough in heart to see God. It serves the purposes of purification, understood in the Platonist sense of getting the mind to turn away from sensible things to gaze at intelligible things.

Finding Christ in the sacred inner space of the self thus does not depend on faith in the Incarnation, but it does indicate the dimension in which Augustine locates the operation of grace, which he will depict as the soul being taught inwardly by God[39] and helped by the inner light.[40] So to understand the development of Augustine's theology we must not assume that the inner gift of grace always had for him a necessary connection with Christian faith. Quite the contrary: the conceptual roots of Augustine's distinctive notion of grace lie in the inward help needed by reason, not faith. This is a perfectly Platonist idea, for ever since the Allegory of the Cave Platonist epistemology has made the mind's grasp of intelligible things naturally and radically dependent on the power of the divine light above.[41] So whereas Augustine is always clear that the intellect needs the inner help of God in order to see God, it is only later in his career that mere belief in Christ is also treated as a work of grace in the soul. As his thinking develops, the scope of our need for grace in effect expands outward, beginning with intellectual vision, the highest and inmost function of the soul, and eventually reaching faith, which is concerned with outward things like the words of the Gospel and the temporal dispensation of salvation in Christ.[42]

But even when Augustine becomes convinced that the inward operation of grace superintends the whole process of coming to God from the beginning of faith to the ultimate vision, he does not think of any part of the process as supernatural, in the Thomistic sense of elevating the mind beyond its natural capacities.[43] The mind's dependence on the power of God above it is perfectly natural, built into the very structure of Platonist ontology as well as epistemology. For what is more natural to the mind than to know the Truth? The capacity for such knowledge and such dependence is what makes a mind a mind, and developing that capacity is as natural to us as education, a process in which the mind's eye learns to behold what it was created to see. Grace heals the diseases of the mind's eye, purifies it of its carnal attachments, and assists it to see clearly, all by way of restoring and fulfilling the capacity for intellectual vision that is the essential function of the rational mind, belonging to the very nature of reason. As Augustine develops an increasingly elaborate and nuanced psychology to explain this process of healing and homecoming for the soul, he has many more interesting things to say about how the inner teaching of the light assists not only the soul's vision but also its faith and love. But his approach to the spiritual life remains fundamentally pedagogical, not mystical or supernatural, and thus it is to the educational role of faith that we should turn to see the starting point of the ever-widening scope of Augustine's theology of grace.

Learning Nothing from Scripture and Proof

You might think that belief in the teaching of the Scriptures, at least, would be an exception to the rule that we learn nothing from words. But Augustine deals with precisely that objection by returning to the example of the three boys and their *sarabarae*. What do we learn from this biblical story? We already know what the words signify: what boys are, what a fire is, and so on. We do not learn these things from the Bible but must know them before we understand the biblical story. Of course we don't know what a *sarabara* is, nor do we know Ananias, Azariah, and Misahel, the three boys themselves. We also do not know the events that are narrated, since we have not seen them but can only believe what we are told: "I confess that I believe rather than know that all the things we read in that story happened at the time just the way it is written" (§37).

It turns out that this defense of the *On the Teacher* thesis runs afoul of biblical usage as well as ordinary speech, both of which allow us to say that we know those things we believe on the basis of the testimony of trustworthy witnesses, such as we have in the words of Scripture. As we shall see in the next chapter, later in his career Augustine is willing to accept a wider sense of the word "knowledge" (*scientia*), generous enough to include things that we merely believe without seeing or understanding them for ourselves.[44] The resulting usage is rather like the distinction we make even today between knowing a mathematical theorem and really understanding it. There is a sense in which we can know Gödel's proof is true simply because every competent logician tells us so, even if we don't quite understand it. But in mathematics at least, the fullness of knowledge really is to understand, to see the thing for ourselves, as when we spend hours working over the proof until we finally "get it," and then shout "aha! now I see it!" In this way faith precedes understanding: first we believe what we are told, then we come to see it for ourselves. This contrast between knowledge and understanding in mathematics fits Augustine's conception of all the liberal disciplines, whose purpose is to raise our minds by gradual steps from sensible to intelligible things, that is, to things seen by the intellect alone.[45] In precisely this sense, Augustine's point in *On the Teacher* stands, despite his more generous use of the word "knowledge" in later years: believing in the words of a truthful witness may count as knowledge but it is not the fullness of knowledge, the understanding in which we see the thing itself. We will never understand Ananias, Azariah, and Misahel that way—not in this life, at any rate—nor will we ever understand what a *sarabara* is.

And it is a very important matter for Augustine that the goal of faith is understanding, not just the kind of knowledge we can get secondhand by believing an external teacher. Hence for Augustine the key epistemological problem of faith is not the modern preoccupation with whether it is rational to believe things without proof, but rather the pedagogical question of whether it is useful to believe what cannot be seen by the mind's eye. Proof is never his primary interest, since proofs consist of words, from which we learn nothing. We do not even learn mathematics from proofs, but from the act of mental vision by which we see for ourselves the things the proofs signify. Once a student "gets it," she can keep her insight in memory and reproduce the requisite proofs whenever needed, for that is merely a matter of words. In precisely Augustine's sense, she has learned nothing from her teacher's lectures or the proofs she copied down in her notebook.

Thus even Augustine's elaborate demonstration of the existence of God as immutable Truth in book 2 of *On Free Choice* is not a proof in the classic sense of modern natural theology, but the dramatization of an ascent to vision by way of Platonic dialogue: it culminates not simply in a logical conclusion but in the enjoyment of a momentary glimpse of God. Augustine's dialogue-partner expresses his "aha!" experience in terms that suggest it is a foretaste of eternal beatitude:

> Saturated with an unbelievable gladness that I cannot express to you
> in words, I receive these things and shout that they are certain. But
> I shout with an inward voice, wanting to be heard by Truth itself
> and to cling to it, which I admit is not only a good thing but even the
> supreme and beatific Good.[46]

This dramatization of inquiry and its fulfillment has in fact the same structure as the glimpses of God as Truth and Wisdom in *Confessions*, which are usually described as attempts at mystic ecstasy. All of them involve an inner ascent from the lower powers of the soul to its higher powers, culminating in the intellect, which then looks above itself to see the immutable Truth shining like the sun. In fact the brief passages of Platonist insight in *Confessions* 7 read like summaries of the more elaborate inquiry in *On Free Choice* 2. Yet the latter inquiry is typically categorized as a proof, the former as a mystical experience. We need to see them instead as Augustine does: expressions of an inner experience of intellectual vision that is natural to the soul as it returns to God.

If Augustine's Platonist project of understanding does not fit the modern notion of natural theology, neither does it belong with its modern opposite, the notion of revealed religion. For Scripture, being composed of words, cannot reveal things to us—especially not intelligible or spiritual things. Augustine's understanding of the work of exegesis coheres with his argument for the *On the Teacher* thesis: we must understand the thing signified before we can understand the significance of the sign. We do not learn to understand anything from the Scriptures, least of all about God. Rather, we must first have some intellectual understanding of the nature of God or we are bound to misunderstand scriptural signs. The point is illustrated by the way young Augustine found that "the letter kills" when, believing Manichaean slanders, he supposed that Catholics had to read the Bible literalistically, as if God were a bearded old man sitting on a throne. This was mere carnal imagination, not catholic teaching. From Ambrose he learned a more spiritual way to read Scripture, though he did not really understand what he was reading so long as he was unable to understand the nature of a spiritual substance.[47] So Ambrose was a fit exegete of Scripture for exactly the reason one should expect on the basis of the *On the Teacher* thesis: unlike young Augustine, he understood the words of Scripture properly because he already knew the spiritual things they signify. But of course precisely for that reason we cannot say that the Scriptures revealed these things to him. He had to know the things first, and on that basis alone could he rightly understand and expound the scriptural words that signify them.

So the epistemology of *On the Teacher* remains in place in the theory of exegesis in the *Confessions*. Indeed, in the *Confessions* not even Jesus Christ is an exception to the rule that we learn nothing from the words of external teachers. Although Augustine loves to introduce quotations from the biblical speeches of Christ with startling phrases like "as Truth himself says" or "from the mouth of Truth,"[48] he explains our understanding of them in a way that upholds the *On the Teacher* thesis. For the eternal Word, he says,

> also speaks with us. So he says in the Gospel through the flesh, and this sounds outwardly in human ears in order to be believed *and inwardly sought and found in the eternal Truth, where the one good Teacher teaches all students.* There I hear your voice, Lord. . . .[49]

The proper way to hear the teaching of Christ in the flesh is to believe it and therefore to seek understanding of it inwardly by consulting the Truth within. Such according to Augustine is always the proper movement of the mind as it learns spiritual things: from external to internal, from sensible to intelligible, from Christ in the flesh to Christ the inner teacher, from faith to understanding.

Admonitions to Look Inside

What is the use of words, then? This is tantamount to asking: what are we doing when we try to teach? Words cannot form the mind or make things intelligible to it, for the mind is always active, words passive. According to the Platonist axiom of causality all signs, being external things, are devoid of causal power over higher things like the soul. Yet the mind can notice them, do something with them, be attracted to them or distracted by them, take heed of what they say or signify, use them well or ill, for its own good or harm. So the question is always about usefulness, about how the soul or mind actively uses signs like words. What might the mind find in mere words to help it on the way to understanding? It cannot find what it is looking for in the external signs themselves. There is no place in Augustine's theology for a Lutheran clinging to the external word of the Gospel, an Eastern Orthodox contemplation of icons, or a Roman Catholic devotion to sacramental means of grace. For Augustine sacred signs have precisely the function of directing our attention away from themselves, indeed away from all external things. They are not like Luther's Gospel, a promise that actually gives what it signifies, but rather like a promise of things to come, which we must wait and hope for. Nor are they like an image of the Beloved we might dote on, but rather like instructions telling us where to look if we really want to see him. Indeed the great error Augustine warns us against is to be detained by the beauty of external things when we should be looking in a different dimension altogether. All creation says in effect: "Not me! What you're seeking is not here! Look higher!"[50] Not to heed this admonition is to fall into the unloveliness of soul that Augustine describes in a key moment of penitence in the *Confessions*, addressing God as inward and eternal Beauty:

> Late have I loved You, O Beauty so ancient and so new, late have
> I loved You! And look—You were inside and I outside, and there
> I sought You, rushing about malformed among the well-formed
> things You have made. You were with me but I was not with You.

> These things kept me far from You, which if they did not have their
> being in you, would not be.

The true Beauty we seek is within us, though other than us—we find it by
turning to look within our souls but then also above them, seeking it in quite a
different dimension of being from the external beauty of sensible things.
Augustine wants us to see these things not as icons but as signs: not images in
which to find a reflection of God's eternal Beauty (though they do in a dim way
reflect that Beauty, else they could not exist—since divine Beauty only makes
well-formed things) but as admonitions to look away from themselves and all
outward things, to turn inward to find the unchanging Truth, Wisdom, and
Beauty, which can be seen only there, in the inner space of the soul. Truth itself
"admonishes outwardly, inwardly teaches."[51]

Words are fundamentally admonitions, directing our attention, trying to
get us to turn our hearts in a different direction from before. The verb *admonere*
is in fact Augustine's most characteristic term for the usefulness of words. In
his usage the term does not have the reproachful connotations of the English
word "admonish." To hear an Augustinian admonition is to be alerted, not
scolded—like someone shouting, "Look!" rather than someone yelling "Naughty
boy!" Indeed, in Augustine's semiotics it is as if every sign were saying "look"—
ecce![52] Not that a mere sign can force us to look where it is pointing, of course,
but we can choose to believe the sign and turn in that direction. So the term
"admonish" indicates the aim of signification: to get the mind to turn from
hearing a word to looking for what it signifies, and especially from perceiving an
external sign to seeing the Truth within. For in Augustine's intensely visual
account of the working of the mind there is a *looking* which aims at *seeing*, just as
seeking aims at finding and inquiry aims at knowledge.[53] So although words
cannot give us knowledge or vision of the intelligible truth, they can admonish
us to look in the right direction, and if we believe the admonition we will at least
get started on that inner seeking for truth that is called inquiry.

"Admonition" is thus the central term in Augustine's explanation of why,
despite all appearances to the contrary, we really do not learn things from
words. We can therefore gauge the depth of Augustine's commitment to the
powerlessness of external signs by tracing his use of this term in his defense of
the *On the Teacher* thesis. The term first occurs as he explains how we might
learn about *sarabarae*, if there were anyone who knew what they were. Could
someone like that teach us what *sarabarae* are? Not in words:

> If he saw them while I was there and admonished me, saying,
> "Look, *sarabarae!*" I would learn the thing I didn't know, not by the
> words that were said, but by the sight of it. (§35)

This example from sensible things prepares us for the general point about words: they cannot give us knowledge of what they signify but only alert us where to look.

> To this extent words have value—let me attribute to them as much as possible—they only admonish us to seek the thing, not show it so we can know. (§36)

Next the term appears in a summary of his argument for the *On the Teacher* thesis:

> This reasoning is very true, and very truly is it said: when words are uttered, we either know what they signify or not. If we know it, then they remind us of it rather than teach. If we don't know it, then they don't even remind us, but perhaps admonish us to seek it. (§36)

Admonitions would simply be reminders if all learning were recollection—a Platonic doctrine that Augustine had until very recently defended.[54] In fact Plato's notion of sensible things serving as reminders of intelligible things has the same structure as signs, in Augustine's definition.[55] So to think of signs as reminding rather than revealing, as both Augustine and the sceptic Sextus Empiricus do,[56] makes for a sceptical view of signs but need not lead to an overarching sceptical epistemology, if signs serve to remind us of what we can know already by other means. In fact Augustine does not seem to have given up the Platonist notion of recollection yet, but rather is leaving the question open. Later he will resolutely replace recollection with vision, pointing out that we could not recollect intelligible things unless we had first seen them. And if our minds are capable of such vision, then no theory of recollection (with its related doctrine of transmigration) is needed to explain the possibility of human knowledge.[57] So for Augustine—perhaps in keeping with Plato's own deeper thinking—a Platonist concept of intellectual vision takes center stage away from the Platonist concept of recollection. This in turn means that admonition rather than reminder becomes the key semiotic term for Augustine—the more general and explanatory term, since a reminder functions as one kind of admonition, alerting us to look for something specifically in memory.

Having made the general point about signification as an admonition to seek, Augustine applies it next to the way we learn intelligible things:

> But concerning all the things we understand [*intellegimus*] we do not consult someone who speaks with outward sounds but rather the

> Truth which presides inwardly over the mind itself—perhaps
> admonished by the words to consult. (§38)

This must mean that all instruction in the liberal arts by way of philosophical
dialogue really consists in admonitions. How might that be? Augustine briefly
suggests that the experience of refutation or *elenchus*, in which the student is
prompted by Socratic questions to rethink his position, is also at root an experience of being admonished or alerted to look more carefully at the parts of
a problem that the student cannot yet see clearly as a whole:

> Now it often happens that the person being questioned denies
> something, then is driven by other questions to affirm it. This is
> because of the weakness of the one trying to see, who cannot consult
> the light on the whole of the subject. He is admonished to do this
> piecemeal, when he is asked about the parts of which this whole
> consists, which he is not capable of seeing all of. (§40)

This experience of being driven to change one's mind by more questions is of
course illustrated in *On the Teacher* itself, both by Adeodatus's experience and
presumably by the experience of the reader following the dialogue. The task of
seeing a complex subject as a whole is most difficult (as Adeodatus had earlier
remarked, §31) and it is something a teacher cannot do for his student, except
by alerting him to the problems in his partial view of the matter.[58]

Finally, Augustine offers an error theory, an explanation of how it comes
about that nearly everyone thinks we learn things from the words of external
teachers.

> Human beings make the mistake of calling those "teachers" who re-
> ally are not, because often no interval of time comes between speech
> and knowledge—and since they inwardly learn right after the ad-
> monition of the person who's talking, they judge that they learned
> from someone who [merely] admonished them outwardly. (§45)

In effect, we don't understand how our minds work because they are too good,
too quick and active for us to notice them at work within us while we are paying
attention instead to the slow flow of words outside. This is a specific case of
Augustine's general diagnosis of the disease of carnal, materialistic thinking:
we get so used to looking at external things that we do not notice the working of
our own minds.[59] This is in fact a moral fault, a weakness in the mind's eye
caused by its habit of peering in the darkness of the cave, as it were, at sensible
things until it is terribly unaccustomed to the intelligible light, finds it too
dazzling to take in, and therefore cannot even see itself clearly. Thus it is not an

innocent error when we think that real knowledge comes to us from our teachers on earth.

It is important to see that this point is self-referential. We can believe the *On the Teacher* thesis if we wish, but if it is true we cannot know this until we see it for ourselves. So for Augustine philosophical dialogues are as much a matter of faith as any other set of words. One therefore cannot contrast Scripture with the writings of the philosophers as if the one inspired faith and the other reason. Both are merely believed until you understand the point for yourself. So the verb "admonish" captures the role of words in philosophy as well as theology. In what is perhaps its most famous use, Augustine tells us that he was *admonished* by the books of the Platonists to return to himself, and was led by God into his inmost self, where he was able to look above his mutable mind and catch sight of God himself shining as the light of immutable Truth. All three levels of the ontological hierarchy are here in due order: the external admonition from words, which is least important but comes first in time, followed by the soul's turn to look within itself, which is a necessary step in the right direction but fruitless unless, at the very height of the ontological ladder, "You had become my helper."[60] The lesson applies to Scripture as well as philosophy: the powerlessness of words is part and parcel of a piety of inwardness that finds true power only in the grace of what is highest and inmost.

Authority and Reason

According to the *On the Teacher* thesis words are powerless, but that does not make them useless. They cannot give us the truth they signify, but they do tell us where we must look to find it. By using them properly we can get started on our way to seeing the thing for ourselves. The condition of our souls when we are still on the way, having received a good word but not yet fully understanding the thing it signifies, is faith or belief (Latin makes no distinction between the two, nor shall I). Because learning is a long process, we are often in a situation where we must believe what our external teachers tell us because we cannot yet see the truth for ourselves. This is a pedagogical point familiar in the Platonist tradition, especially prominent in Plotinus[61] but most pithily expressed by Plato's greatest student, who observed that "the learner must take things on faith."[62] Aristotle's verb (*pisteuein*) is the same one that Paul and other New Testament writers use for Christian faith. His pedagogical point is illustrated every time students take notes from a math teacher without quite understanding what they're writing down. Augustine has the same pedagogical point in mind when he quotes Isaiah 7:9, "Unless you believe, you will not understand" in *On the Teacher*.[63] The quotation is found frequently in his writings, especially in the programmatic contexts of his early works.[64]

The same point is made in more explicitly pedagogical terms in Augustine's first extant writings, evidently before he discovered this particularly useful biblical passage. The two ways of making the point in fact nicely reinforce each other, and recur in prominent places throughout his early works. The pedagogical way of putting the point is that there are two approaches to learning: authority and reason.[65] Though sometimes Augustine treats these as two parallel tracks, taken by the unlearned and the learned, respectively, he is also keenly aware that there is a natural progression from one to the other: "Indeed such is the order of nature that *when we learn anything,* authority precedes reason."[66] This illuminates the first half of his lapidary statement: "Authority is prior in time, but reason in reality."[67] He explains the second half by pointing out that the order of doing (*agendo*) is different from the order of desiring (*appetendo*), and in our desiring the end comes first. So reason comes first in reality in that it is concerned with the end, the goal of understanding that initiates all our learning, but authority comes first in time because the words of external teachers are what we start with. In short, if we want to understand the truth we must begin by believing what we are told. In Augustine's mature theology this same means-end relationship remains in place: in our journey toward the vision of God, faith in authoritative teaching is prior in time to reason, as means is prior to end, but reason is prior in reality, because the goal of seeing for ourselves is what sets our hearts in motion.

Augustine's full-scale defense of the usefulness of faith is in effect an argument in favor of employing this same pedagogical order in matters of religion. He combines the authority/reason terminology with the faith/understanding (or faith/sight) terminology in order to undermine the rationalist claims of the Manichaeans, who attacked the Catholics' reliance on authority. Writing to an old friend who is still a Manichaean, he puts it this way:

> My aim is to show you, if I can, that the Manichaeans are rash and irreligious in inveighing against those who, following the *authority* of the catholic *faith,* are fortified by *believing* before they are able to behold the truth *seen* by the pure mind, and thus prepare for God to illuminate them.[68]

Lest we think the correlation of the two pairs of terms here is accidental, he makes it central to his epistemological categories in the same treatise, *On the Usefulness of Believing:* "What we understand, we owe to reason; what we believe, to authority; what we opine, to error."[69] This threefold categorization is designed to distinguish faith in authority from the mere opining that Hellenistic philosophers, both sceptics and Stoics, condemned as rash and unjustified: "I am saying these things so that we may understand that in maintaining faith in things we do not yet comprehend, we are vindicated from the charge of being rashly opinionated."[70] Belief in authority is not rashness but the humility appropriate to one who is just beginning to learn.

It is important to emphasize that in Augustine's usage "authority" is always a pedagogical, not a political term. Rulers do not have authority (*auctoritas*) but rather power (*potestas*) or command (*imperium*). (English translations are almost inevitably misleading about this, regularly translating *potestas* as "authority.") Only teachers have authority, as when we say a scholar is an authority on her subject. This usage remains constant throughout the middle ages, during which a phrase like "the authorities" (*auctoritates*) refers not to kings and princes but to the Bible and Augustine and Aristotle and other authoritative texts of the tradition. So the term "authority," as we meet it in Augustine's writings, should make us think about believing what we're taught rather than obeying orders. But there is of course some overlap, and Augustine will defend the command of authority (*auctoritatis imperium*) as necessary for true religion.[71] Thus he renounces his boyhood resentment that "faith was commanded of us before reason," which had prompted him to believe Manichaean promises to lead him to God "by sheer and simple reason, quite apart from the fear of authority."[72] It is important to bear in mind that the command and even the fear he speaks of here derive not from imperial officials but from the religious teachers of his youth, including most importantly the Catholic clergy who were not learned enough to answer his clever questions.[73]

Authority, though not political, is a social concept: it is about how the young learn from their elders and from the tradition in which they are raised. Augustine realizes he must defend the usefulness of belief in authority because the implication of the *On the Teacher* thesis, as of Augustinian inwardness generally, is that insofar as we are content with this external kind of pedagogy we have not really learned anything at all. This is clearest where the contentious issue of ecclesiastical authority is not in view. For example in his treatise *On Music*, the only textbook on the liberal disciplines that Augustine completed, a teacher leads a student in a dialogue where the aim is to transcend authority. Approaching the question of the length of syllables, which is a key consideration of their inquiry (for in this treatise "music" means, in effect, poetic meter) they realize they are approaching an issue where the grammarians have authority. Yet even though they both in fact began their education by believing what the grammarians teach, they are now intent on going back to the beginning so as to understand the matter by reason. So the teacher (*magister*) addresses the student (*discipulus*):

> First of all, tell me whether you have learned well what the gram-
> marians teach, the distinction between short and long syllables,
> or—whether you know this or not—you prefer us to inquire as if we
> were complete beginners in these matters, so that *reason* may lead
> us to all these things rather than ancient custom or *prejudiced au-
> thority* compelling us.[74]

Just as Gadamer taught us to expect, the authority of a tradition consists in large part of certain legitimate prejudices or prejudgments in which one is educated.[75] The most important of these is the meaning of words themselves which, according the teacher in *De Musica,* are established by authority. He uses here a distinction between name and thing (*nomen* and *res*) that is the precursor to the distinction in *On the Teacher* between sign and thing:

> We cannot answer questions about the *names* belonging to a disci-
> pline the same way we do about the *things*. This is because the things
> are implanted in all minds in common, but the names are im-
> posed as anyone pleases, and their force [*vis*] depends mostly on
> *authority* and custom. That is why there can be diversity of languages
> but not of things, which are constituted by Truth itself.[76]

It turns out that the rational basis of disciplined inquiry into poetic "music" has nothing to do with what words mean but only with the metrical relationships of syllables in poetic feet, which add up to verses in a mathematical way that derives from reason, not authority.[77] This inquiry can thus become the launching-point for a Pythagorean-Platonist ascent from transitory, sensible numbers (such as those you can literally hear in poetic verses, whose meter is called "numbers" in Latin) to intelligible and unchangeable numbers.

Augustine's program of education in the liberal disciplines clearly does not expect students to remain content with putting faith in authority. He makes this especially clear in the case of his own teaching. "Don't depend too much on authority," he tells his dialogue-partner in *On the Quantity of the Soul,* "especially on mine, which is nil. And as Horace says, 'Dare to Know!' Otherwise fear may subjugate you before reason."[78] The same point is dramatized in one of his earliest dialogues by Trygetius, a student of Augustine who refuses to be in-timidated by the authority of Cicero quoted against him by another student. Trygetius announces that "by the liberty in which philosophy promises to defend us, I have shaken off the yoke of authority,"[79] a moment of courage for which Augustine later congratulates him.[80] That the issue here should be Cicero's authority as a philosopher is ironic, not because Cicero has no such authority (it's plain from the discussion that he has) but because Cicero's philosophy is explicitly geared toward making progress by reason, not authority.[81] In fact, Cicero is as likely as anyone to be the literary authority who convinced Augustine that this pedagogical terminology of authority and reason, with its implicit goal of transcending all authority, had a central place in philosophy.

But this is only one side of what is, in Augustine's early writings, a two-sided strategy for explaining the structure of Christian life and learning. In setting forth the pedagogical order of authority first, then reason, Augustine is pointing out both a goal and a necessary means, either of which he may emphasize depending on his purposes in any particular context. In the context of his discussion of the liberal disciplines, he is primarily concerned with the goal of passing beyond authority to reason, which means transcending faith so as to achieve understanding. But in the context of discussions with his old Manichaean friends he emphasizes how useful faith is, and how healthy authority is for eyes not yet ready to see for themselves.[82] Neither side of this two-sided strategy invalidates the other. All of us who learn must begin with authority, because unless we believe we shall not ever understand. But the goal is indeed to understand, so merely believing in the authority of an external teacher is not enough. Even the fact that Christ became an external teacher for our sake does not change this, as we have seen, for by his words he too admonishes us to turn inward to understand the Truth within. This is indeed the very purpose of the Incarnation: "Through human beings a reminder can be made by the signs of words, but one true teacher teaches, the incorruptible Truth itself, the only inner teacher, who also *became external in order to call us back from externals to inward things*."[83] Just as we should expect from the *On the Teacher* thesis, the Incarnation has the aim of all good teaching: admonishing us to turn from outward authority to the inner vision of reason.

Christian Mysteries and Platonist Philosophy

The *locus classicus* for this two-sided strategy of authority and reason is found in the conclusion of one of Augustine's earliest works. Shortly after a sketch of the doctrine of the Trinity in which he describes Christ as the authority of the divine Intellect descending to a human body,[84] he introduces the authority/reason contrast thus:

> There is no doubt we are impelled toward learning by the twin weight
> of authority and reason. For me, however, there is a fixed certainty
> of separating nowhere at all from the authority of Christ, for I find
> none more valid. But as for what is to be pursued by extremely subtle
> reasoning (for I am now moved by the impatient desire to grasp what
> is true, not by believing alone, but also by understanding) I am
> confident that meanwhile I will find in the Platonists what does not
> contradict our sacred rites [sacris].[85]

This statement is both extremely subtle and very specific. The *sacris* to which he
refers are not the Holy Scriptures (this has been a common mistranslation of
the text) but the sacred rites connected with baptism, which Augustine will
undergo on Easter, in a few months. The most important of these apart from
baptism itself is the solemn ceremony of the "handing down of the creed"
(*traditio symboli*) the week before Easter, in which those to be baptized are
formally taught the creed for the first time.[86] This is tradition in a very active
sense of the term, a *traditio* or act of handing down the faith from one generation to another. Augustine comes back to this touchstone of Christian
teaching in his second programmatic statement about authority and reason,
found in the next work he writes, where after another summary of the doctrine
of the Trinity in philosophical terms (where Father, Son, and Spirit are called
Principle, Intellect, and Reason, respectively)[87] he describes the *traditio* which
takes place in the Christian *sacris*:

> All these things are being handed down [*traduntur*] more secretly and
> firmly in the sacred rites [*sacris*] in which we are being initiated,
> in which the life of good people is cleansed more easily by *the au-
> thority of the mysteries* than by *the roundaboutness of disputation*.[88]

This secrecy about the creed, a vestige of the time when Christians were a
persecuted sect who did not want to expose their doctrines to public scrutiny, is
a prime reason why these sacred rites are called mysteries, just like the initiation rites of other ancient religions called mystery cults, where the initiate is
brought into the religious community by being given secret knowledge[89]
(Masonic initiation is very much a "mystery" in this ancient sense). Calling
these rites *mysteria* or *sacramenta* (the Latin translation of this originally Greek
term) bears strong suggestions of hidden meanings that may need special
interpretation.[90] By using the term *mysteria*, in fact, Augustine is echoing a
standard Platonist suggestion, that the secret teaching of various mystery cults
was in harmony with Platonist philosophy, especially with regard to purification and liberation of the soul.[91]

At the center of what he learns in these sacred rites is of course the doctrine of the Trinity, and though he has not yet formally been taught the creed, he has been listening in Milan to the sermons of Ambrose, the bishop who will baptize him, and who was at this time the leading exponent of Nicene Trinitarian orthodoxy in the West. So it is no accident that Augustine associates the doctrine of the Trinity with the authority of the Christian mysteries. But it is also no accident that he presents this doctrine in veiled form, not in the overt language of the creed but in the philosophical language that designates Christ, the second person of the Trinity, as divine Intellect or *Nous*, the mind that contains the whole intelligible world which the other-worldly philosophy of Platonism is all about.[92] He obviously thinks that a Platonist interpretation of the doctrine of the Trinity, the central teaching handed down by Christian authority, will support his desire of moving from mere belief in what is true to understanding it. His notion of Christ the inner teacher in *On the Teacher* is a further development of this harmonizing interpretation, designed to support his whole program of exercising the mind in the liberal disciplines by philosophical dialogue and "extremely subtle reasoning" even though this entails the arduous "roundaboutness of disputation." For he will not separate from the authority of Christ, but neither is he content to remain with authority alone.

Augustine obviously does not want us to think of the way of reason as pure Platonism. He is from the beginning of his extant writings a *Christian* Platonist, confident that the authority of Christ is supreme because it is none other than the authority of the divine Intellect, where all intelligible things are ultimately to be sought. He is not treating Christian authority and Platonist philosophy as two independent forms of knowledge, as in the modern dichotomy of faith and reason. As there is only one intelligible world, so there is only one true understanding of it toward which all reason, indeed all learning, is directed. Moreover, insofar as the Platonists are teachers and writers, they too have authority. That is why he compares them precisely with the authority of the sacred rites, as one authority to another, believing that "meanwhile"— that is, while he is still on the road from faith to understanding—the lesser authority of the Platonists will not contradict the "more valid" (*valentiorem*) authority of Christ. In practice, this means Augustine will persistently interpret Christian doctrine in Platonist ways, while always modifying or even abandoning Platonist beliefs whenever he finds they do contradict what he comes to learn is firm Christian teaching. This weakening of the authority of the philosophers is not alien to philosophy, after all, but inherent to its very purpose, as Augustine has already had the opportunity to learn from Cicero, that student of Plato's Academy, who taught that the purpose of philosophical teaching was to help the student transcend the teacher's authority.

The Great Shift in Augustine's Teaching

The deep problem Augustine must face is that it is not so clear the authority of Christ is meant to be transcended in the same way as the authority of the philosophers. Going beyond the man Jesus Christ is indeed what Augustine means to teach us by insisting that the reason the inner teacher became external (i.e., incarnate) was in order to call us back inside, away from carnal things to the unchanging Truth within.[93] This is a teaching he continues to develop, as we shall see in the next chapter.[94] For Augustine Christ as man is always the Way to Christ as God, and we do not want to stay on the Way forever. Yet as his account of this Way becomes richer and more elaborate in the decade or so after his baptism, a fundamental shift takes place in Augustine's thinking. In educational terms, we can characterize it as a shift from liberal *disciplina* to Christian *doctrina:* he gradually abandons the project of writing textbooks and philosophical dialogues designed to lead to the vision of God and develops instead a new theory and practice of scriptural exegesis that undergirds his work as a bishop. Inseparable from this shift is what Peter Brown memorably calls Augustine's "lost future," his giving up hope of coming to full understanding of divine Wisdom in this life.[95] In effect, we remain under authority all our lives, never graduating to the pure vision of reason.

Brown represents a near consensus of scholarship when he turns to Augustine's reading of Paul to explain how Augustine lost his future,[96] though Brown is more cautious than many when he warns that this cannot be read simply as an abandonment of Platonism. Of course there can be no doubt about the epochal importance of Augustine's engagement with Paul's teaching on sin and grace, which begins in this decade. But I do not think this explains the particular features of the great shift in Augustine's teaching that takes place at this time. Augustine did not need Paul or even Christianity to teach him that our souls are fallen, far from God, and in need of divine help if they are to return. In fact Augustine himself attributes to pagan Platonists the view that so many Augustine scholars say he learned from Paul. Addressing the pagan Porphryry, he says, "following Plato's view, you do not doubt that there is no way for a man to arrive in this life at the perfection of wisdom, but that anything missing in one who lives according to the intellect will be made up for by the providence and grace of God."[97] What the pagan Platonists lack, by Augustine's account, is not the concept of grace but "Jesus Christ our Lord and his Incarnation itself."[98] If we take Augustine's words here as our guide, we will look for an explanation of the great shift in his teaching by turning to the external authority of Christ in the flesh, not the inward effects of grace.

We can best begin by looking not at concepts and doctrines but at Augustine's way of life.[99] For by the end of this decade he is a different kind of teacher from what he was at the beginning. He has been ordained priest and then consecrated bishop. His lifelong task from this point on is to teach the Scriptures and Christian doctrine, not the liberal disciplines. And, as Brown helpfully emphasizes, this is not a task he undertook voluntarily, like the project of education in the liberal disciplines resulting from the famous conversion of will narrated in the eighth book of the *Confessions*. On the contrary, he was press-ganged, grabbed by a crowd of local boosters in the basilica at Hippo and forced to come forward to be ordained quite against his will, an eventuality he had up to this point carefully avoided precisely because he knew it would deprive him the leisure for philosophical inquiry, by which he aimed to become divine.[100] Thus in contrast to his conversion, the consequences of his ordination—his new ecclesiastical mode of life and the form of teaching that went with it—were not sketched out in advance by programmatic statements like those in his earliest writings, but rather grew on him as he settled into a new teaching job he had never planned to take.

The crucial unexpected consequence of his new job, I suggest, had to do not with the ideas of sin and grace but with a much more essential feature of Christian faith. At issue is the inescapable importance for Christian life of Christ incarnate, from whose external teaching we never "graduate" for as long as we live in this mortal flesh. This results in an underlying tension in his classic early statement about authority and reason, which eventually gets resolved in a way he clearly was not anticipating at the time. We can see why he did not anticipate this by examining the contrast between the way of philosophical inquiry he was originally planning to take, driven by his impatient desire to proceed from faith to understanding, and the way of mere faith that is taken by the great majority of Christians, who rely on authority alone. Augustine sees this in typical Platonist terms as a contrast between the few and the many. In his second programmatic statement about authority and reason, Augustine explains the lives of the many within the church as a life of moral virtue rather than of learning:

> As for those who are content with *authority alone,* giving constant
> attention to good morals and right devotion, and either despising the
> best liberal disciplines or incapable of being educated in them—
> I do not see how I can call them happy, so long as they live among
> human beings. Yet I unwaveringly believe that as soon as they
> abandon this body, they will be liberated with greater ease or diffi-
> culty, depending on how much or little they have lived good lives.[101]

This passage describes the form of Christian life that Augustine the convert had *not* chosen; yet the last sentence expresses what he thinks is true of *every* Christian life, including his own, by the time he is a bishop. For Augustine the convert, Christians who live by authority alone (which is to say, by faith alone) are less advanced than those who do not wait until death to find the freedom that philosophy promises; whereas for Augustine the bishop no one is free to see God until after death, because all of the Christian life on earth is lived by faith in the authority of Christ. This does not mean Augustine will ever be content to embrace a formula like "faith alone," which in his theology could only signal the intention of remaining at the beginning of the road of Christian life.[102] He never gives up the goal of understanding God by reason, seeing the Truth for himself, and in his mature theology he thinks that all Christian life involves real progress in this direction, strengthened and gladdened by glimpses of what lies ahead, like one who catches sight of the Promised Land from afar.[103] But he no longer contends that such wisdom and beatitude are possible in this life.

To see why this great shift in Augustine's teaching is well-nigh inevitable once he becomes a bishop, consider how his early view of authority and reason compares to his mature teaching about Christ. Here is another early text, where Augustine explains to his dialogue-partner the view of authority and reason adumbrated more briefly in the better known *locus classicus* above:[104]

> It is one thing to believe with authority, another with reason. To believe with authority is a great shortcut and no work. If that is what delights you, then you can read the many things which great and divine men have said about these matters, which have seemed to them necessary as a kind of healthful hint [*nutu*] for the unlearned.... For them it is exceedingly useful to believe in the very best authority, and to live their lives accordingly. If you think that's safer, then not only will I not stand in the way, but I will greatly approve. But if you cannot restrain the strong desire [*cupiditatem*] persuading you to arrive at Truth by reason, then you must put up with *many long and roundabout paths* so that the only reason leading you is one that really deserves the name, that is, true reason, which is not only true but is so certain that it is *foreign to all similarity to falsehood*.[105]

We are here in the same atmosphere of discussion as in the *Soliloquies* and *Against the Academics*, concerned to get beyond what is merely truthlike and eliminate any appearance that resembles something false, a project that requires the long, circuitous, and wearisome dialectical investigation conducted in Augustine's dialogues. But if you share that impatient desire to move by reason from faith to understanding, mentioned both here and in *the locus classicus,* then there is no alternative to the "roundaboutness of disputation," which can only be avoided by those who, as we saw above, were "cleansed more easily by the authority of the mysteries."[106]

In the same text Augustine explains that precisely as we transcend authority by coming to understand what we believe, we will see by reason that our initial trust in the authority of the church was justified:

> Then we will acknowledge how true were the things we were commanded to believe, how well and healthfully we were nourished by Mother Church, *how useful was the milk* which (the apostle Paul preached) he gave little ones to drink—that this food is very useful to receive when one is being maternally nourished, *shameful when one is grown up;* that to spit it out when it is needed is pitiful; to speak ill of it at any time or hate it is wicked and impious; but to treat and distribute it appropriately is worthy of all praise and love.[107]

Authority is epistemological milk for beginners not yet ready for the solid food of reason. Only impious heretics like the Manichaeans speak ill of it, while honored teachers of the church (Ambrose, for example) distribute it appropriately, like a good household manager taking care of all the servants of the house and their little ones. Even so, its usefulness has limits, because it would be shameful for a grown-up to keep needing mother's milk.

The consequence of Augustine's becoming a bishop—one of those honored teachers of the church—is that he must outgrow this shame and get used to the idea that he remains with the little ones. For the milk of Mother Church is none other than the incarnate Word of God, whose authority we never outgrow in this life. The word was made flesh, Augustine confesses, "so that your Wisdom might provide milk for our infancy."[108] It follows that if we ever ceased to be infants in this life we would cease to need Christ incarnate, and no good bishop can ever teach that. This consequence applies to the bishop himself: "I am a little one," he confesses.[109] Just as the Socratic teacher can never claim to be wise, the Christian teacher can never claim to be a grown-up who needs no more of the milk of authority.

Innumerable passages from the bishop's sermons could be used to illustrate this point. "We can see God with the mind or inward eye of the heart," he says in one of them, "but the eyes that desire to see are crushed, dulled, cast down by weakness,"[110] which means we have this vision as yet only in hope, not in reality. What do we do in the meantime, while we are still on the road to that goal?

In order to get there, *if we cannot yet see the Word as God, let us hear the Word as flesh.* Since we have become fleshly, let us hear the Word that has become flesh. This is why he came, why he took up our infirmity—that you may have the firm speech of the God who bears your infirmity. Truly is this called milk. *He gives milk to little ones, and the food of Wisdom to those who are bigger.* He gives milk patiently, that you may avidly feed. For how did he become milk to feed infants? Was there no food on the table? Yet the infant is not capable of eating the food on the table. What does the mother do? She incarnates the food and makes milk from it. She produces something we are able to have. That's the way the Word became flesh, so that *we little ones* could be nourished by milk.[111]

The mature Augustine speaks to a congregation of little ones as if he were one of them, not a grown-up. Of course no one in Augustine's congregation doubted that their star preacher understood the Scriptures far better than they did. In this very sermon, for example, he spends a great deal of time explaining the incorporeal nature of God, just like the kind of exegete he said Ambrose was: one who has at least some insight into the intelligible truth signified by the words of the Scripture, and therefore can understand them and dispense the milk of the Word appropriately. Nonetheless, Augustine does not present himself as a grown man feeding infants but as one infant among others, all in need of the same milk. He may have caught more glimpses of the eternal Word than his congregation has, but the business of his life on earth is the same as theirs: to hear the Word as flesh.

Yet there can be no doubt that seeing, not hearing, remains the goal of the whole process, the very raison d'être of the incarnation of the Word. Augustine does want to grow up eventually, to see the Truth forever with his own eyes, which he believes is true happiness and eternal life. Augustine always upholds the fundamental implication of *On the Teacher*: though it is useful to believe external teachers in the church, what we really want to know can be learned only from the one inner teacher, who is no one we know on earth, neither father nor preacher, neither friend nor loved one, not even Christ incarnate. For ultimately we do not live by the external authority of words, merely hearing about what we want to know and believing it, but by the direct vision of the mind or heart in which we understand the thing itself. That is why for Augustine Christ as man is not of eternal importance, as we shall see at some length in the next chapter. The Word became external to lead us away from external things, including even the flesh of Christ.

5

Believing Persons

Theological Implications of Augustine's Semiotics

If Augustine's expressionist semiotics and his thesis in On the Teacher *are correct, then the knowledge which our life is all about is not like believing a friend but like seeing with our own eyes. It is only in this life that we must believe what our friends tell us about their hearts rather than see it for ourselves. Of course this means that nearly everything we know about human society and history is in fact based on belief in what we are told. Likewise, to believe the Scriptures is to accept the testimony of witnesses who have seen what we have not. Seeing the Truth to which they bear witness is in fact easier than seeing what is in their hearts, and in that sense God can be known more clearly than other persons. If we want to know who a just man like Paul inwardly is, for instance, we must first understand Justice, which means we must turn inward and look with the mind's eye at the same eternal justice that shaped his heart. The same is true of our knowledge of Christ, which as it grows depends less and less on what we know of his historical particularity, his flesh. Could it be that Augustine does not give enough credit to the way that external things give us knowledge of other persons?*

For Augustine, knowing God is not like knowing another person but like seeing an eternal Form. It could not be otherwise unless the Platonists were wrong about our ultimate happiness—and Augustine affirms quite explicitly in his mature works that the goal of intellectual vision is the crucial point of agreement between Platonism and

Christianity. The final beatitude of the soul, as the Platonists taught, is "not like a friend enjoying a friend but like the eye enjoying the light."[1] Thus in passing from our beginning in faith to our goal in understanding we rise above not only bodies but souls, even the souls of our friends, and then our knowledge is not like the give and take of conversation but like a moment of perfect intellectual vision.

Nonetheless, the ultimate happiness is a social and shared beatitude, the blessedness of the community that Augustine calls the city of God. So friendship itself shall become something more like seeing God: instead of having to believe what is said by those we love, we will see their minds clearly in the vision of God, just as we enjoy them in enjoying God.[2] For there will be no division, dissension, or dishonesty in the heavenly city, no opacity of heart that could result in one thought being hidden from another:

> For there will be but one city out of many minds that have one soul and one heart in God, and the perfection of our unity after this present pilgrimage will be that everyone's thoughts will not be hidden from one another nor in conflict among themselves on any point.[3]

In the end, therefore, all that is mere belief is left behind, even faith in that unique human person Jesus Christ, who is now known only by faith but will then be seen in his eternal deity. In this way the Platonist goal of intellectual vision defines the meaning of Christian faith. For if you believe in inward vision, you will think of belief itself as outward, and that will affect the way you think about the nature of persons in whom you must believe.

Secondhand Knowledge

Because of its roots in Platonist epistemology, expressionist semiotics regularly assumes not only that the inner is superior to the outer, but that seeing is superior to believing. The two pairings run parallel in Augustine, for whom the inner self is the space of intellectual vision and belief is dependent on the authority of an external teacher. To this day, we are Augustinian when phrases like "inner vision," and "external authority" roll easily off our modern tongues. The metaphor of vision is needed to make the Augustinian language of inwardness work, because the epistemological point of conceiving an inner space of the self is to have a dimension in which intelligible things are directly present within the mind, unmediated by external authority—so you can see them for yourself, as the well-nigh irresistible metaphor puts it. Therefore, as

Augustine explains in his treatise *On Seeing God*: "the difference between seeing and believing is that things present are seen, things absent are believed."[4] The *On the Teacher* thesis is in this connection a lesson about presence and absence, about what we do not see but only hear about. In the metaphorical register of Augustine's semiotics seeing is firsthand and hearing secondhand, because the one is about understanding what is directly present within your own mind, the other about merely believing what you're told by another person. Yet faith comes by hearing, as the apostle says, for it is dependent on the word of Christ (Romans 10:17). This means, for an expressionist semiotics, that Christian faith receives outward signs, not inner presence.

But suppose, in a rather un-Augustinian moment, that what we ultimately wanted to know is precisely another person, an external teacher like Christ in the flesh. Surely there is something to be said for external authority, if it is the authority of those who live outside our own hearts to speak for themselves and tell us who they really are. The secondhand structure of hearing, in which our access to the truth depends on what another person says rather than on our ability to see for ourselves, has a peculiar appropriateness when what we want to know is precisely that other person. It is the appropriateness of an Othello who—we could wish—desires no "ocular proof"[5] of his wife's virtue but is wise enough to believe what Desdemona has to say for herself. Othello should have seen through Iago and believed the word of Desdemona, and the difference has everything to do with the fact that the one person is wicked and the other a gem. A Desdemona can give herself to be known in her words because she is faithful and true. To be dependent on her authority is to learn a truth that can be had in no other way—indeed, a truth that one should desire to have in no other way. This is a case where hearing is superior to seeing, and dependence on external authority is better than understanding for yourself. For what more appropriate way is there to know the truth of another person than to be dependent on the other for the truth? In an important sense the truth about herself is a gift that only she can give. The secondhand structure of hearing is profoundly appropriate here because it makes characteristics that only a person has, her truthfulness and self-knowledge as well as her word, inescapably necessary for knowing her. Of course when we are dealing with a liar like Iago it may be necessary to "see through him," as we say, but that is not how we should desire to know someone as trustworthy as Desdemona. Here it is wisdom to recognize that the knowledge we seek is secondhand, dependent not on our ability to understand what we see for ourselves (how ill Othello understands the "ocular proof" that he sees with his own eyes!) but on the virtues of the person we aim to know, who can speak for herself. So it is possible to think that in contrast to mathematics or the other liberal disciplines as Augustine conceives them, when it comes to knowing other persons the appropriate goal—even the ultimate goal—is not to see for ourselves but to live by faith.[6]

Of course Augustine's epistemology would have it otherwise. For a Platonist, beatitude is vision, and what we really want—indeed what we *ought* to want—is to get past the external, fleshly shell of the self and see what lies within. Ultimately to know other persons is to see what is in their hearts with the same inner vision they do, not dependent on their authority to tell us about themselves. Augustine is perhaps the earliest writer to propose this as an eschatological goal, though the thought has its precursor in Plotinus, as we have seen.[7] When we see God we shall also know each other in the deepest possible way, seeing each other's thoughts, "for in that divine society no thought can be hidden from one's neighbor."[8] Yet as his career unfolds and he no longer thinks of the liberal disciplines as the means to seeing God, Augustine has more and more to say about living by faith and is even willing to call it a kind of knowledge, though it is never the ultimate knowledge he longs for. So the mature Augustine both accommodates the fact that faith is an appropriate way of knowing another person and subsumes it under the ultimate Platonist goal of intellectual vision. In friendship, as in Christology, the aim of the Christian life is to get beyond external speaking and hearing so as to see inwardly for ourselves.

Belief in Things Not Seen

According to the *On the Teacher* thesis we learn nothing from words or other external signs, but believing them can be useful for as long as we do not really know what they signify. To return to the biblical example in that text,[9] we know what a king and a furnace and three boys are, but we do not know what the boys' *sarabarae* were nor do we know that the events actually happened as narrated, but can only believe them. Most important, the boys themselves are in the same category as *sarabarae* and long-past events: we can believe them but not see or know them. It would seem that all the figures of the Bible or of any other historical text are in the same boat, people like Moses or Jesus or Paul. But one wonders: should it make a difference that we have written record of these people's words, which signify something of what they had in mind? Beginning about 395 (not long before he starts writing the *Confessions*) the possibility of knowing other persons' minds through their writings becomes an important theme of Augustine's correspondence, especially with Christians he longs to know but will never see.[10] As Augustine's career unfolds, the pressure builds to classify belief in the words of others as a form of knowledge, lest he be forced to say he has no real knowledge of his friends and must indeed remain ignorant of the whole human world extending beyond his immediate vision.

The way this pressure builds can be gauged in the little treatise *On Faith in Things Not Seen,* which he wrote before fully succumbing to the pressure. In this treatise he is once again defending the Catholic faith from rationalist (probably Manichaean) objections against being commanded to believe what they cannot see. His first move is to expand the notion of "things that can be seen" to include not only the objects of bodily sight but things within the mind, including our thoughts and our beliefs themselves.[11] Invisible as these things are to the eye, Augustine says, they are clearly seen by the mind. The underlying picture here is so easily taken for granted by Augustine's modern spiritual descendants that we may need to remind ourselves of what he is expecting his readers to imagine: the kind of inner space of the mind he pictures at length in the *Confessions* (which he was just completing at the time) in which the mind's eye can see things inwardly present in the mind itself.[12] This is of course not literally a space, just as the mind's vision is not literally vision. But it is a dimension of being in which things are present to be known firsthand. With such a picture of the self in view, one can raise a new kind of question about other persons: what access do we have to the inner self of our friends, since we cannot see within their hearts as we do within our own? That of course is the point Augustine urges on his opponent:

> But whoever you are, who do not want to believe anything except
> what you see—look! you see bodily things that are present with
> the eyes of the body, and with the mind itself you see your
> own thoughts and wills present in your mind: but I ask you to tell me
> by what eyes you see the will of your friend toward you?[13]

For a believer in expressionist semiotics, a friend present in the flesh is present only externally. Her inner self is not presented to our bodily or mental sight. We can only infer what is present in her heart from external things like her words and deeds, and the result does not have the firsthand structure of vision but the secondhand structure of faith.

> Perhaps you will say that you see someone else's will through
> their works? That way you will see deeds and hear words, but con-
> cerning your friend's will, what you cannot see or hear you will
> *believe.* For this will is not color and shape, to be brought into the

eyes, nor sound and pitch, to slip into the ears; nor is it your own will, so you could feel it by the emotion of your heart. Unseen, unheard, not inwardly beheld within yourself—all that's left is to believe it, or else your life will be left devoid of all friendship and the love spent on you will not be repaid.[14]

Augustine's final point here is that belief in one's friends is an obligation, a debt owed to anyone who loves us: for our friend's love ought to be returned, which is impossible if we do not believe in it. So the notion of being *commanded* to believe is not so outrageous but belongs to the ethical landscape of friendship, indeed of social bonds generally. For Augustine goes on to point out how much of society depends on such faith: the bonds of marriage and kinship, our awareness of historical events we did not witness and places we have never been, even our confidence that the people who raised us really are, as they tell us, our fathers and mothers.[15] The social world is well-nigh constituted by belief in things not seen.

Testimony about Temporal Things

To read *On Faith in Things Not Seen* immediately after *On the Teacher,* where the lesson is that we do not have true fathers on earth, is to encounter a strikingly enlarged view of the human world. Instead of the simple dichotomy of the earlier text,[16] in which our ethical task is to turn from external sensible things to inner intelligible things, here we encounter things that don't fit neatly in either category but require the richer tripartite ontology of body, soul, and God. For at this point the category of the internal has itself become more complex, with the inner space of the soul sharply distinguished from the inner presence of Truth, even though both can still be called inner and even intelligible.[17] So the things we are to believe require now a different name, referring not solely to the inner Truth of God nor merely to external things. Augustine here calls them temporal things, and his great concern is to show that they too can be something we ought to believe: "So really we ought to believe even some temporal things that we don't see, so that we may merit seeing the eternal things that we believe."[18] All of Augustine's mature soteriology is implicit in this sentence: we need purity of heart to see the eternal God, so we must be purified by faith until we have heart's eyes pure enough to see, and this faith concerns not just the eternal things that we can at present only believe but also temporal things that belong to what Augustine calls the "temporal dispensation" (his rendering of the Greek patristic term *oikonomia,* the divine economy or plan of salvation) whose focal point is the human life of Christ incarnate.[19] Hence the second part of the treatise *On Faith in Things Not Seen* focuses on Old Testament prophecy and New Testament narrative, as well as the present success of the church, which Augustine presents as visible evidence that the prophecies concerning Christ were fulfilled in the past (in his nativity, passion, and resurrection) and will be fulfilled in the future (on Judgment Day), though neither past nor future events can presently be seen. Thus in the temporal dispensation Augustine finds a whole Christological philosophy of history. Yet the priority of the eternal remains: we believe in these unseen temporal things so that we may be purified by faith, eventually meriting the vision of the eternal things of God which only the pure of heart can see.

Just as in the earlier formulations of the inward turn, where we turn away from external, fleshly things in order to see inward, spiritual things, there is still envisioned here a turning from temporal things in order to arrive at eternal things. But the turning is more complex than we might have thought from the simple dichotomies of previous texts like *On the Teacher*. In a brilliant metaphor from one of Augustine's most elaborate and mature discussions of authority and reason, he compares Christians to people who have fallen to earth and must put their weight on the ground in the very act of ascending from it:

> In order to rise one must put weight [*incumbere*] on the very place one has fallen. Therefore we must lean on [*nitendum*] the same fleshly forms by which we are detained, in order to come to knowledge of things flesh does not announce.[20]

Since our movement is upward, we begin by putting our weight on those lower things from which we are turning away, precisely in order to push off from them and leave them behind. So as we begin to learn, we rely on authority, putting our faith in temporal, even fleshly things. We may even temporarily love them, contrary to the central message of Augustine's earliest ethical formulations, which relied in a simple dichotomy between outer and inner, carnal and spiritual. Though the temporal is not to be loved for its own sake, there is a kind of love that consists in properly using temporal things for the sake of enjoying eternal things.[21]

The shift from Augustine's earlier and cruder dichotomies can be summarized in three areas: being, love, and faith. Ontologically, the category of the temporal straddles the divide between external and internal, covering the mutable being of both body and soul—something close to what we now mean by talking about persons, society, and history. Ethically, it is good to love certain temporal things, not seeking to enjoy them for their own sake but using them rightly so as to come to enjoyment of eternal things. And theologically,

Augustine eventually comes to the conclusion (not yet reached in *On Faith in Things Not Seen* but clearly foreshadowed there) that faith in the authority of trustworthy testimony counts as a form of knowledge, even though it is not the longed-for vision of things eternally present to the mind.

"Far be it from us," says Augustine in the last book of his great treatise *On the Trinity*, "to deny that we know [*scire*] what we learn from the testimony of others."[22] The pressure against the *On the Teacher* thesis has become irresistible, and Augustine is plainly affirming the opposite: we do learn things from the words of others and this learning even deserves the name *scientia*, knowledge in a rather strong sense, though still a lesser form of knowledge than *sapientia*, the wisdom that is our ultimate goal. In an important discussion earlier in the treatise, Augustine had compared *scientia* to *sapientia*, as learning about temporal things is compared to vision of eternal things.[23] Here he affirms that this knowledge of temporal things includes belief in trustworthy testimony, lest we remain ignorant (*nescientes*) of famous places and cities where we have never been, the people and events of history, even current events the news of which is brought to us from afar—and most unsettling of all, our own native land and parents, whom we can know to be our real origin only by faith in the testimony of others. Knowledge of the temporal world, it turns out, is to a very large extent secondhand.

It is interesting that the people from whom we learn these temporal things are witnesses rather than teachers. The focus here is not on those who already understand intelligible things and thus can admonish us, telling us where to look to see them for ourselves, but on those who have seen temporal things that we will never see and thus can give us indispensable testimony as eyewitnesses. Augustine had explained this point at length in the treatise *On Seeing God*:

> Things are *believed* which are absent from our senses, when the testimony on their behalf is seen to be adequate; whereas things are *seen* which are present [*praesto*] to our senses, either of body or mind, whence also they are named present things [*praesentia*]. . . . Our knowledge [*scientia*] consists therefore in things seen and things believed. But for things we have seen or are seeing we ourselves are witnesses, whereas for things we believe we are moved to faith by other witnesses, as signs of things we don't see or remember seeing are given in spoken words or writing or other evidence—and *seeing the signs, we believe what we don't see*. Yet it is not undeservedly that we say we know [*scire*] not only what we have seen or are seeing but also what we believe, when moved to it by adequate testimony or witnesses.[24]

There is more here that deserves the name of knowledge than we would have expected from the treatise *On the Teacher,* yet the same semiotics remains in place, as faith relies on present signs of absent things.

It is not as if Augustine has radically reconceived the nature of faith, along the lines of Luther speaking of Christ as "present in the faith itself."[25] Rather, succumbing to the pressure of ordinary usage, which is also biblical usage, he realizes he must use the name "knowledge" in a wider and more generous sense than before. In this wider sense of the term, faith does deserve the name knowledge, as Augustine explains in the *Retractations,* where he explicitly corrects his earlier view:

> Strictly speaking [*proprie . . . cum loquimur*] we only say we *know* that which we comprehend by the mind's firm reason. But when speaking more in accordance with common usage [*cum . . . loquimur verbis consuetudinis aptioribus*], which is how the divine Scriptures also speak, we have no doubt in saying that we know [*scire*] both what we perceive with our bodily senses and what we believe by faith in trustworthy witnesses.[26]

Accepting this more generous usage, Augustine verbally abandons not only the *On the Teacher* thesis but also his earlier sympathy with the Academics' scepticism about the senses, while retaining the substantive point underlying both of them: that the aim of knowledge, strictly speaking, is rational comprehension by the mind. Indeed this more generous epistemology is articulated in our passage from the last book of *On the Trinity* precisely in the conclusion of a refutation of the Academic philosophy, where he affirms that we know not only what we believe on the basis of adequate testimony but also what we learn from the senses:

> Far be it from us to doubt that the things we learn from the senses of the body are true. Through them we learn of heaven and earth, and the things therein that are familiar [*nota*] to us, as much as He who created both them and us willed them to be familiar [*innotescere*] to us.[27]

It is noteworthy that even at this late date Augustine cannot quite bring himself to use the language of scientific knowledge, *scientia,* to describe the epistemic reliability of the senses, but rather uses the weaker language of *notitia*—of things being known to us in the sense of being noted, becoming familiar or entering our awareness. The language is more generous than before, but it is very clear that neither bodily perception nor belief in trustworthy testimony is the sort of knowledge we should ultimately seek.

Nonetheless, in licensing us to say that belief in mere words can give us knowledge of what is in other persons' souls, Augustine makes the strongest positive claims he will ever make on behalf of the epistemic value of signs. In an important though not ultimately adequate sense, we really can get to know people by believing what they say, which means that words, which are external signs, can afford us knowledge of the inner things of the soul. This is the high-water mark of Augustine's semiotics. It puts an expressionist version of the inference from body to soul, which had been an important part of Greek semiotics ever since Aristotelian physiognomics, into permanent circulation in the West as one possible way of accounting for our knowledge of other persons. Strikingly, however, this is not how Augustine accounts for our knowledge of God. It is not as if we could come to know God by believing his word. For the understanding we are to seek, even in the reading of Scripture, is something higher and more inward.

Witnesses to Christ

The shift that takes place in Augustine's thought as it matures—from a stark turning away from external things to a complex using, believing, and loving of temporal things—makes for a great enrichment in his scriptural exegesis. He finds in Scripture more than a simple dichotomy of letter and spirit, where the literal meaning of Scripture is a mere shadow of spiritual, intelligible truths. In place of such reading, which can in a strict technical sense be called allegory, Augustine becomes one of the great practitioners of what Erich Auerbach identified as the distinctively Christian style of figural reading.[28] This allows Augustine to develop a Christological hermeneutics that he applies to both Scripture and history.[29] For the mature Augustine the scriptural narrative has its center in the incarnation of Christ, whose human life is at the heart of the temporal dispensation of history. But of course this temporal dispensation has an eternal goal, the ultimate happiness that consists of what Scripture calls "eternal life."[30] So Augustine insists that we believe everything in the temporal dispensation and use it in love so as to rise from temporal to eternal things.[31] As a consequence, in Augustine's account of Christian faith Christ incarnate is the center but not the end.[32] His human life is at the heart of history, but his divine and eternal life is the goal beyond it. As Augustine often puts it: as man he is our road, as God he is our destination, the homeland to which we are journeying.[33]

This way of making the humanity of Christ both central and subordinate—necessary means rather than ultimate end—has enormous implications for Augustine's reading of Scripture as well as his Christology. We can bring these into focus by examining one of his most important and characteristic statements about the authority of the Scriptures, located at the beginning of Part II of the *City of God*, where he turns from his critique of paganism to give a Christian account of the history of the universe, which will of course draw heavily on the Christian Scriptures. He situates scriptural authority in the context of that characteristically Platonist combination of epistemology and ethics that is so foreign to modern thought.[34] The best and highest thing in us, he tells us, is that which is closest to God, the human mind which can perceive divine Truth directly within itself. But our sins have made this direct perception so rare and difficult that we need to put faith in the Scriptures.

> Because of certain dark, ancient vices the very mind in which reason
> and intelligence are naturally present is *too weak to bear the immu-*
> *table Light*, much less cling to it with enjoyment, until made capa-
> ble of such great felicity through being renewed and healed day
> by day; so it had to be instructed and *purified by faith*.[35]

It is as if we are climbing out of Plato's cave and the Light is too bright for our eyes. To strengthen these weak eyes is the central task of Platonist education and the ethical problem to which Augustine returns again and again.[36] In contrast to the Christian Neoplatonism of the East, represented most powerfully by Pseudo-Dionysius and later adopted by the West, Augustine always blames the inadequacy of our intellect on sin, not nature: the reason we cannot see God is because our mind's eye is impure, weakened by the "dark, ancient vices" stemming from original sin, not because it is by nature incapable of such lofty vision.[37] Hence what we need is instruction and purification, which develop and restore the natural capacity of the intellect rather than elevating it to a supernatural or mystical level.

"Purified by faith" is a biblical phrase (Acts 15:9) interpreted in the context of this Platonist epistemology and ethics. In Platonism only the pure soul is free of bodily attachments (love of carnal or temporal things, in Augustine's terms) that hinder it from seeing the divine Light. One can hardly avoid thinking here of the beatitude promised in the sermon on the mount, "Blessed are the pure of heart, for they shall see God" (Matthew 5:8). Even before Augustine, an African Platonist tradition appears to have suggested this convergence of Platonist and biblical purification in a treatise entitled *On Purifying the Mind to See God*, written by an obscure pagan Platonist named Fonteius of Carthage, who later became a Christian.[38] The treatise introduces a problematic that is fundamental for Augustine's Christology: God is by nature omnipresent, so why can't we see him everywhere? Fonteius's explanation is that

"God, who is absent nowhere, is present in vain to the polluted mind, which in its mental blindness cannot see him."[39] Just this problem is what God confronts by taking up human flesh in the Incarnation, according to Augustine: "While he is everywhere present to the healthy and pure inner eye, for those whose eye is ill and unclean he deigned to appear even to the eyes of their flesh."[40] Add to this linguistic convergence about purification the Platonist view that faith precedes vision in time,[41] and Augustine has a rich philosophical structure in which to situate the necessity of Christian faith for salvation, which also provides the framework for his Christology.

The later Platonist tradition was preoccupied with the problem of mediation, as Augustine explains to us at length in the ninth book of the *City of God*. The need for a mediator, as the Platonists understood it, is the need for an ontological intermediary occupying a position between two conceptual extremes, such as the divine and the human, and establishing a link between them. Immediately after our previous quotation, Augustine brings the resources of orthodox Trinitarian and Christological thought to bear on this Platonist problem, thus explaining why God became human:

> In order that we might walk in this faith more confidently, the Truth
> itself—God, the Son of God—constituted and founded this same
> faith *by assuming a human being, not by consuming God*, so that the
> road [*iter*] of human beings to their God could be the human being
> who is God. For this is "the mediator of God and human beings,
> the human being Christ Jesus." He is mediator as human being,
> and so also the Way [*via*]. For if there is a Way *between* those who
> travel and where they are traveling to, there is hope of arriving. . . . But
> the only Way that is completely safeguarded from all errors is for
> the same one to be himself both God and human: the God *to* whom
> we go, the human *by* whom we go.[42]

In this account of the incarnation, Christ does not come to reveal God to us or give us the gift of eternal life, but to become the Way we travel to reach God and eternal life. His humanity is means not end; we do not find God in it but rather are purified by it so that at the end of the road we can see what is eternal and immutable, quite unlike human flesh.

This does not mean his humanity is temporary or that Christ is anything less than fully God. The latter is the point made by Augustine's wordplay about "assuming" a human being rather than "consuming" God, which is a brief reminder of one of the deepest convictions of orthodox Christology: that the eternal Son is still fully God even after becoming a human being, remaining immutable and impassible even as he takes up our mortality and suffering.[43] That is why he is mediator as human, not as God: for in his divinity he remains eternally equal to the Father,[44] not a lesser and later God as the Arians taught. Since he is not anything less than fully divine, his divinity cannot serve as a conceptual intermediary between the divine and the human. Having ruled out any category in between God and creation, Nicene Trinitarianism can only say "both/and": the only possible mediator is one who is both Creator and creature, fully God and fully human.

Augustine's Christology is thus deeply orthodox but also makes a fateful choice, in which most of Nicene orthodoxy (especially in the East, but also in the West) does not follow him. From the orthodox conviction that Christ is mediator in his humanity, Augustine draws the conclusion that Christ's humanity is means not end, a Way by which we travel but not the destination at which we arrive. Our hearts are purified by faith not to gaze at the glory of God in the human face of Jesus Christ, as in the Eastern Orthodox theology of transfiguration, but to contemplate the eternal Truth prior to all creation and present even apart from the Incarnation to every pure mind. The reason Augustine draws this unnecessary conclusion is perhaps clearest in light of the educational theory in *On the Teacher*. If our aim is to perceive the inner Truth which is God, then we must ultimately outgrow external authority, if not in this life then in the next. This means we must pass beyond the humanity of Christ, which is external and temporal, to behold his pure divinity as eternal Wisdom. Like Christ himself, we are to pass through the road of this temporal life without being detained by love of it, since "the Lord himself, insofar as he deigned to *be* our Way, did not want us to be detained but to pass on, so that we should not cling in weakness to temporal things, even though they were taken up and borne by him for our salvation."[45]

As road rather than destination, Christ's humanity becomes the center of Christian life, the life of the church, the scriptural narrative, and the temporal course of world history. By the same token it is the foundation of all other authority in the church, the teaching of the Scriptures, of prophets and apostles, priests and bishops, whose speech is either a precursor or an extension of Christ's. These outward signs are means of purification and instruction which (as the treatise *On the Teacher* would lead us to expect) do not give us the truth they signify, because they are the basis of faith not vision. Thus Augustine proceeds:

> Hence first by prophets, then by his own self, later by apostles, he
> spoke as much as he judged sufficient, also establishing the Scripture
> which is called canonical, of the highest authority; and we have

faith in it concerning things of which it is not advantageous for us to be ignorant but which we are not capable of knowing by ourselves.[46]

The highest authority belongs to external teachers who have already seen the things signified by the words of Scripture. Indeed in Scripture itself we have external teachers who bear witness to what they have seen:

> Now if those things can be known [*sciri*] by ourselves as witnesses, which are not remote from our senses, whether inward or even outward (from which they are called "present things" [*praesentia*] because we say they are "before the senses" [*prae sensibus*] just as things before the eyes [*prae oculis*] are present to the eyes [*praesto sunt oculis*]) then for those things which *are* remote from our senses, since we cannot know them by our own testimony we need other witnesses, and we believe people from whose senses we believe these things are or were not remote. Therefore just as, for visible things we have not seen, we believe those who have seen them . . . so for things sensed by the soul or mind . . . that is, for invisible things which are remote from our inward sense, we have to believe those who learned these things displayed in that incorporeal light or gaze on them permanently.[47]

This is the secondhand structure of Christian faith, in which Christ is at the temporal center of an array of human witnesses who speak to us of things they have seen but which are remote from our own sight, not present before our inner eyes. All witnesses testify of Christ, and Christ is the road from temporal to eternal things. This is the mature version of Augustine's earlier account of the meaning of the Incarnation in terms of Christ's role as external teacher, where he "became external in order to call us back from externals to inward things."[48] For the inward turn does not simply disappear in Augustine's later works but is the goal and meaning of the temporal dispensation, which is the central thread both in Scripture and in world history. So at the center of this center of all temporal things is a turning away from all temporal things. This is evidently the best explanation of why, in Augustine's vast narrative of universal history in the *City of God*, centering as it does on the advent of Christ in the flesh, his crucifixion and resurrection are barely mentioned.[49] Christ comes in the flesh to direct us away from fleshly things, not to get us clinging to his body—even his body fixed on the cross or freed from the grave. This is surely the central example of those temporal things to which "we should not cling in weakness . . . even though they were taken up and borne by him for our salvation."[50]

Moses and Truth

In Augustine's hermeneutics, all Scripture bears witness to Christ incarnate or else to the same inner Truth to which Christ is witness. So we can approach the question of the significance of Christ in the flesh by looking at the proper use and understanding of Scripture. As we saw in our treatment of the treatise *On the Teacher,* the words of Scripture are signs whose significance is only understood by those who have already seen the things they signify. But as the stark dichotomy of external and internal, sensible and intelligible, that is so prominent in Augustine's early work gives way to the three-tiered ontology of body, soul, and God, more attention is devoted to the middle level of the hierarchy, the contents of the soul. In terms of the semiotics of Scripture, this means that in addition to external signs and the invisible truths they signify, the speaker's communicative will or intent (*voluntas*) becomes a prominent consideration.

"Speaker" is not an inappropriate term, even for the author of a written text. Like other ancient writers, Augustine thinks of words as inherently spoken: "Every word makes a sound. For when it is in writing, it is not a word but the sign of a word."[51] Given the look of ancient books, which had no punctuation or breaks between words, reading a text normally meant, even for those few who were literate, hearing it read aloud by oneself or others. It was more like performing a musical score than like the modern habit of silent reading. So it is not merely metaphor when Augustine writes as if the readers of Scripture were hearing the words of Moses: for them, reading normally meant hearing the words of the author. Nor does Moses' bodily absence make any fundamental difference in the interpretive situation. The death of the author is no big deal if the author has an immortal soul. This is not because his soul remains with us, but because no soul is ever present to our sight. Neither presence nor absence in the flesh affects the fundamental remoteness of the inner contents of the author's soul from our vision. Seeking Moses' meaning is therefore not so different from trying to understand someone speaking right in front of us: in both cases we hear external signs produced by a soul whose communicative will is not visible to us. Understanding the relation between this bodily expression and the soul's inward will is the fundamental task of interpretation, because it is the latter that establishes the significance of communicative or "given" signs, as we saw in the semiotics of *On Christian Doctrine.*[52]

When reading Scripture, therefore, we are concerned with all three levels of Augustine's ontological hierarchy: external words, the inner will of the soul, and the inmost Truth which is God. In the immensely sophisticated discussion of the exegesis of Genesis in the last books of the *Confessions,* Augustine begins to bring the relation between these levels into focus by imagining himself speaking with Moses about the very first words of Genesis:

> Moses wrote this; he wrote and departed . . . nor is he now before me
> [*neque nunc ante me est*]. If he were, I would take hold of him and
> beg him, imploring him by You, to unfold these things to me, and
> would lend the ears of my heart to the sounds issuing out of his
> mouth. And if he spoke Hebrew words, they would beat upon my
> sense in vain nor would anything thence touch my mind; but if Latin,
> I would know [*scirem*] what he said.[53]

The bodily presence of the author would hardly do this particular reader any good, because at the nitty-gritty level of the lowest tier of the ontological hierarchy, Moses' spoken words would be in Hebrew, completely opaque to Augustine's understanding. But even if we imagine Moses answering Augustine in Latin, the questions that concern Augustine most deeply will remain unanswered. For the only important questions are about the truth, not what Moses thought or meant:

> Yet whence would I know whether he said what was *true?* And if
> I knew this, would I know it from *him?* Inwardly, rather, within the
> house of my thought, without the organs of mouth or tongue, without
> the noise of syllables, Hebrew, Greek, Latin or foreign, Truth would
> say, "he says what is true"; and I would at once be certain and would
> confidently say to that man of Yours, "you say what is true."[54]

This is a clear affirmation of the *On the Teacher* thesis: Augustine does not think he could learn the truth from Moses' words, even if Moses were present before him in the flesh speaking Latin. On the contrary, he judges that Moses is saying what is true (*verum*) on the basis of his inward consultation with the divine Truth (*veritas*). The implication for Augustine's view of Scripture is far-reaching: we do not learn the truth from the words of Scripture, no matter how accurately we interpret them, but by seeing it inwardly in our own minds.

A crucial feature of Augustine's mature hermeneutics, in other words, is that the task of interpretation is not so important. For interpretation concerns the significance of words, which is derived from the speaker's communicative will or, as we would put it nowadays, the author's intent. And while it would be useful to know what Moses was thinking as he wrote, what we ultimately want to learn is not what Moses meant but the truth Moses saw. So Augustine is not particularly concerned if his preferred interpretation of the first verse of the

Bible is inaccurate. Perhaps when Moses wrote the Hebrew equivalent of "In the beginning," he did not mean (as Augustine thinks) "In the Word," but that does not make Augustine's understanding of the verse any less true.

> I can say with confidence that in Your immutable Word You created all things visible and invisible, but can I say with the same confidence that Moses had just this in view when he wrote, "in the beginning God made heaven and earth"? For *I do not see in his mind* that this is what he thought when he wrote these words, with such certainty as *I see it is so in Your Truth.*[55]

The source of certainty here is not Scripture but the mind's vision of Truth, just as we should expect from the Platonist epistemology undergirding the *On the Teacher* thesis. Since we can see God much more clearly than we can see inside each other's minds, the search for ultimate Truth is more likely to succeed than the search for a definitive interpretation of Scripture.

This also has implications for how Augustine deals with disputes about interpretation. So long as everyone agrees that whatever Moses says is true, then disagreements about what he meant ought not to injure the charity that binds together lovers of the truth in the fellowship of the church. We should get our priorities straight in terms of the three-tiered hierarchy, where words (which are bodily things) are meaningless apart from the communicative will of the author (which is a matter of the soul), which is of far less importance than the will of God.

> In You, Lord, I join in delight with those who feed on Your Truth in the wide fields of charity, and we approach together *the words of Your books* and seek in them *Your will* through *the will of your servant Moses,* by whose pen you distributed them. But which of us does so well finding this will (among the many truths which in these words, understood this way or that, occur to those who seek) that he can say with as much confidence "this is what Moses meant" or "this is what he willed to be understood in this narration" as he says "this is true, whether he meant this or something else"?[56]

Augustine is not arguing for some form of relativism, where all interpretations are equally valid. On the contrary, when there is disagreement between interpreters, he assumes someone is getting Moses' meaning wrong. The point is, rather, that finding out who got Moses' meaning right is not as important as it would be if interpreting Scripture were how we came to learn the truth about God. Augustine is therefore free to insist that preserving the bond of charity is more important than determining the best interpretation of Scripture.

To bring this point home Augustine imagines another conversation, this time not between Moses and himself but between himself and a rival interpreter with whom he agrees about the truth but disagrees about Moses' meaning:

> This brotherly and peaceful word I relate to him: "if we both see that what *you* say is true, and we both see that what *I* say is true, then *where, I ask, do we see it?* I don't see it in you nor you in me, but both in the same immutable Truth which is above both our minds. Therefore, since we may not contend about the very Light of our Lord God, why are we contending about *the thought of our neighbor which we cannot see as the immutable Truth is seen*—when, if Moses himself appeared to us and said, "This is what I thought" we wouldn't thus *see* it, but *believe?*[57]

The witnesses of Scripture testify to what they have seen, and our ultimate aim is not simply to believe what they say, but to see what they've seen. That is what their testimony is for, just as Christ became external in order to admonish us to see the inner Truth. Precisely because this Platonist vision is our goal, Scripture cannot be the ultimate or fundamental source of our knowledge about God.

The words of Scripture, like the humanity of Christ, are to be used on the road to somewhere else, deeper and clearer, more certain and more lasting. This explains the striking parallel statements about the temporary value of scriptural authority and of Christ's Incarnation toward the end of the first book of *On Christian Doctrine,* written at about the same time as *Confessions.* A thoroughly virtuous human being, Augustine tells us, supported by faith, hope, and charity, "is not in need of the Scriptures except for the sake of instructing others."[58] Similarly, Christ's Incarnation is "the beginning of God's ways," which means that someone who has proceeded far along God's ways "has already gone past the beginning of the ways, that is, he is no longer in need of it."[59] In both cases, our need for the external gifts of God comes to an end, because the usefulness of the temporal dispensation itself is temporary, not eternal. Both statements are grounded in the Platonist epistemology of intellectual vision underlying *On the Teacher* and the educational commitments summed up in that lapidary early formulation: "authority is prior in time, but reason in reality."[60] They are unusual only in retaining so clear a residue of Augustine's "lost future," his erstwhile project of graduating even in this life from belief in external authority to the full understanding of reason, the inner vision of God that belongs to the pure in heart.

Seeing Trinitarian Love

It is reasonable to wonder whether Augustine really thinks that Christians learn so little from Scripture as this argument about Moses suggests. One can concede that it was from the Platonists that Augustine learned such ontological attributes as God's eternal and incorporeal being as supreme Good and eternal Truth, yet insist that the very concrete, not to say peculiar, Christian understanding of God as Father, Son, and Holy Spirit is not something he could have learned apart from the orthodox tradition of Christian doctrine rooted in the Scriptures. Could anyone possibly have thought of such a notion as the Nicene doctrine of the Trinity simply by looking inward?

Imagine how Augustine might reply if he is really serious about the *On the Teacher* thesis.[61] First of all, he would repudiate our notion that he learned anything from the Platonists. For if we learn nothing from words, then the writings of philosophers are surely no better off than the words of Moses: the best they can do is admonish us to look inward and see for ourselves. This is in fact exactly what Augustine says the books of the Platonists told him to do.[62] If he is serious about the *On the Teacher* thesis, we should expect him to do the same thing in response to orthodox teaching on the Trinity: admonished by this Christian doctrine, he should look inward and try to see for himself. And that is exactly what we find him doing in his most distinctive contribution to ancient Christian literature on the subject, the second half of his massive treatise *On the Trinity,* which contains a single elaborate inquiry set in motion by the same kind of problem that the books of the Platonists helped him solve in the *Confessions.* The problem is that mere belief without inner vision will inevitably result in our picturing God in imaginative terms by way of mental "phantasms" (in the philosophical language of *Confessions*)[63] or "feigning," *fingere,* the verb used in book 8 of *On the Trinity* to elicit the kind of worry that modern philosophers might have about knowledge that is merely a human construct. *Fingere* can mean to form or compose, to imagine or think, but also to feign or pretend, and its past participle is *fictus,* from which we get our word "fiction." Hence Augustine's worry is, "we must beware lest our faith be feigned [*ficta*]."[64] Faith alone, belief in external authority without inner vision, is in danger of being nothing but imagination.

Augustine attempts to give his readers a sense of the depth of this problem by returning to the question of what we can know about biblical persons we have never seen, which he had first illustrated by reference to the three boys in the furnace in *On the Teacher.*[65] In book 8 of *On the Trinity* the examples are

Paul and Mary and Jesus.[66] We have never seen their faces, and our feigned mental pictures of how they looked in the flesh are not tied down to any historical reality (evidently Augustine had no experience contemplating icons, traditionally thought to be an accurate representation of the saints they picture) and are no doubt inaccurate. But since it is not their bodies we want to know, this reliance on mere imagination poses no real problem. For we do have the knowledge we need in order to believe what is said about them in Scripture: we know *what* they are (viz., human beings) and we can understand what events like virgin birth and resurrection are because we know what it is to be a virgin, to be born, to die, and to be alive after death. This knowledge is not sufficient to prove that the events narrated in Scripture really happened, of course, but proof is (as usual) not what Augustine is after. The knowledge required is not for something as ambitious as historical proof but for something much more modest: mere linguistic understanding. Without it we do not know what is signified by words like "birth," "death," and "resurrection," and therefore we cannot even *believe* the words of Scripture, never mind prove that they are true.

Thus the *On the Teacher* thesis holds for the scriptural teaching about Paul and Mary and Jesus in the same way as for the story of the three boys in the furnace: we must first know the things signified, at least generically ("by species and genus," as Augustine says repeatedly here)[67] in order to understand the significance of the words of Scripture. This knowledge does not stem from belief in things unseen but is rather a more fundamental kind of seeing that makes belief itself possible. Augustine is even willing to reverse his usual formula and affirm that understanding, in this linguistic sense of seeing what the words signify, comes before faith. Those who hear his sermon about faith and understanding, for instance, "cannot believe it unless they understand what I say."[68] So both are true: we must believe before we understand, but in another sense we must also understand before we believe. The issue in book 8 of *On the Trinity* is about the latter.

The problem is that we have no such generic knowledge about the Trinity as we have about the three young men in the furnace, or about death and resurrection. Leaving the problem unsolved is not an option, for if the only thing we have in mind when we think about the Trinity is imaginary fictions, then we do not even know enough about it to believe it. We should note that Augustine has no use here for the new epistemological move made in the treatise *On Faith in Things Not Seen*. He does not bring up the possibility that by believing persons' words we can learn what they will or think: not that he denies the possibility, but it appears to be irrelevant to his inquiry. Equally unconsidered is the possibility that we might learn the will or thoughts of the Triune God by believing the words of Scripture. For clearly this would not address the problem implied by the *On the Teacher* thesis: that we cannot even understand the significance of the scriptural words about Father, Son, and Holy Spirit, much less believe them, unless we first see what they signify. At least some level of vision is required before faith is even possible.

We should remind ourselves that this is not an obvious or inevitable problem, but a consequence of Augustine's particular brand of Platonism. Those who are not Platonists are free to be content with a knowledge formed by faith alone (placing no confidence in the mind's ability to see but only in God's ability to keep his word) and even within the Christian Platonist tradition the majority of theologians have taught that the Triune God is altogether beyond the capacity of our intellect to see, so that a faith that transcends understanding is precisely what the Trinity calls for. All that is needed is to deny the implication of the *On the Teacher* thesis: that vision of the thing signified must precede linguistic understanding.

So the answer to our question is that Augustine really does not think we learn the truth about the Trinity from Scripture or tradition. If he did, there would be no point to his distinctive inquiry in the second half of *On the Trinity*. What he can say is that Scripture and tradition teach us what to believe about the Trinity, for (to use the formulation of *On the Teacher*) all words do teach, even though we do not learn from them. So even without having learned the thing it signifies, Augustine is able to work very carefully through the logic of Nicene teaching in the first half of *On the Trinity*, books 1 through 7. But the point of the second half of the treatise (the problem that Augustine spends all of book 8 introducing) is that this is not enough, for we have not even begun to believe the truth taught by Nicene doctrine until we have something to see with our mind's eye when we think about the doctrine, beyond merely imaginary mental pictures. It is specifically the doctrine of the Trinity that raises this problem because (according to Augustine) the mind can look within and see God as immutable Truth and supreme Good,[69] but it has no such vision of God as Father, Son, and Holy Spirit.

Not only is an inward vision of the Trinity beyond the range of anyone's experience, but the Nicene tradition had by Augustine's time already forcefully affirmed that the Trinitarian nature of God was incomprehensible. Augustine himself insists on this in a sermon that contains his most important statement about the incomprehensibility of God, leading to a lengthy discussion of the eternal generation of the Son, the doctrine that (I have argued elsewhere) was the original home of the Christian doctrine of divine incomprehensibility.[70] Yet incomprehensibility for Augustine means simply that we will never fully grasp the divine nature, not that it is utterly beyond our mind's ability to see. For the very same sermon includes the flat affirmation of the intelligibility of

God I quoted near the end of chapter 4: "We can see God with the mind or inward eye of the heart."[71] The doctrine of the Trinity is thus no exception to the rule that the knowledge we should seek is the inward intellectual vision of the mind. Indeed Augustine's inward turn is never more fully elaborated than in the second half of the treatise *On the Trinity*, precisely because it cannot be as straightforwardly successful here as the glimpse we can have of God as Truth in earlier texts such as *Confessions*, book 7, and *On Free Choice*, book 2.

Strikingly, the inward turn is also applied to our knowledge of other persons by way of illustration. How is it that we know Paul enough to love him, Augustine asks in book 8 of *On the Trinity*. We believe what Scripture tells us about his virtuous life, but we do not depend on such secondhand information to learn that a virtuous life like Paul's is a thing to be loved.

> That the ministers of God should live in this way is not something
> we believe by hearing it from anyone, but we inwardly see it in
> the Truth within us or rather above us. Therefore *it is from what we see
> that we love him* whom we *believe* to have lived in this way.[72]

We love Paul not simply because of what we have heard and believed, but because of what we see for ourselves, the immutable Form of justice or righteousness, "with which his life...fittingly coincided."[73] Here the vision of intelligible Form is what makes love possible, for "a man who is believed to be just, is loved because of that Form and Truth which the one who loves him sees and understands within himself."[74] Thus the truest kind of love for another person directs our attention inward, not outward, for reasons that stem from the Platonist semiotics of *On the Teacher*. Suppose there were external signs, gestures, a look of the face, or outward actions that we could see with our bodily eyes, indicating that this was a just man. Should this draw our love and attention outward toward the person standing in front of us in the flesh? Not at all, for "justice is a certain beauty of mind"[75] that requires a different kind of vision to see.

> Perhaps signs stand out by way of bodily motions, by which this
> or that man appears to be just. But whence does anyone who is
> entirely ignorant of what a just man is, know these to be signs of a
> just mind? Therefore he must know what a just man is. But
> where does he know that...? If we know something outside us, then
> we know it in a body. But this is not a bodily thing. Therefore *we
> know in ourselves what a just man is.*[76]

It is as if you saw someone acting justly and wondered if that were sufficient to show that he was a just man, and along came someone like Socrates to help you decide, by asking you to tell him what justice is:

> When I seek what to say about this, I don't find it anywhere but in
> myself. And if I ask someone else what is a just man, he finds the
> answer within himself. And whoever can hence answer with the
> truth, finds the answer within himself.[77]

This is a distinctively Augustinian theory about Platonic dialogue, combined
with the inward turn as in the treatise *On the Teacher*. It means that we must
look within our own souls to understand the real depth of the souls of others.
True love requires us above all to direct our attention deep within ourselves. It
is an astonishing move, made overly familiar by modern introspective accounts
of the knowledge of other persons, where we understand other's thoughts and
feelings only because of our firsthand acquaintance with our own. In Augustine's Platonist framework, this introspective account of knowledge of other
persons means that what we really want to know about those we love is not
their individual lives, their thoughts and choices and careers through time, but
their participation in eternal Forms in the mind of God. Just as our overriding
concern in reading Moses' words ought not to be his meaning or thoughts (at
the second level of the ontological hierarchy) but the Truth he saw (in God's
mind, at the highest level of the hierarchy) so also our concern in loving our
neighbors should be above all to see in them the same unchanging Form and
Truth that inwardly defines justice for all of us in common.

Augustine's inward turn, originating in a theory of intellectual vision but
now issuing in a theory of love, means that we must look within the self in
order to love the other. The same inward turn of love is the basis of Augustine's
long inquiry aimed at progressing toward an understanding of the Trinity. For
in loving Paul's just mind we love love itself (since true justice is rightly
ordered love), which is no different from loving God (because that true love
called charity is inseparably the love of neighbor and the love of God, who is
love itself).[78] To see this love inwardly, therefore, is to see the Trinity itself, and
that is what offers us an alternative to feigned imaginary pictures of the Trinity.
This vision of love is the basis of the whole inquiry that follows, and if we don't
believe it, then it is the task of *On the Trinity* to admonish us, that we may look
and see it for ourselves: "*You do indeed see the Trinity if you see charity. But
I will remind you, if I can, so that you may see that you do see.*"[79] This vision is
so inward that we are often unaware of it, but once we see it with reflective
clarity then it too, like the vision of Truth in *Confessions,* is something we can be
more certain of than our knowledge of the thoughts of other persons like
Moses or Paul:

> Let no one say, "I do not know what I love." Let him love his brother,
> and he loves that same love. For he knows the love by which he

loves better than the brother whom he loves. Look! Already you can have God more known to you than your brother—*more clearly known because more present, more known because more inward,* more known because more certain.[80]

The love by which we most truly love, like the justice by which we are truly just, is ultimately none other than the eternal Truth itself, which is also eternal Love. Therefore the inward turn in the end leaves not only bodies but also souls behind in order to gaze at what is more inward than any human thought or will. That seems to be the deep reason why not only the Scriptures but also Christ's humanity are not of lasting importance for Augustine. He came, as Augustine puts it here, to turn people toward "things that are eternal and inward."[81]

Outward Voice and Inner Word

Augustine explains the ultimate unimportance of the humanity of Christ as analogous to the transient importance of external words in his expressionist semiotics.[82] The analogy centers on the most important new concept that he develops to enrich his account of the middle level of the three-part hierarchy: the inner word or word of the heart. This "word," it must be said right away, is not really a word at all in the ordinary sense of the term; it is something higher and more inward. All words are signs, in Augustine's semiotics, and all signs are external. So the word of the heart, which is not external, is not really a sign and not literally a word. Augustine makes this point clear when he emphasizes that the word of the heart does not belong to any human language, not Latin nor Greek nor Hebrew.[83] By the same token, this inner word should not be confused with the act of thinking about such words (Latin or Greek or Hebrew) silently in our minds, which is really a form of imagination; for the inner word is to be understood "not only before it makes a sound, but before the images of its sounds are turned over in our thoughts."[84] We could categorize the inner word not as a sign but as a significance, if we turn to the triadic semiotics Augustine briefly develops in one of his early works where he speaks not just of sign and thing signified but also of significance. The sound of the word "sun" is a sign (*signum*), the sun itself is the thing it signifies (*res quam significat sonus*), and the understanding of the sun (*intellectus solis*) in the mind of those who speak and hear the sound is its significance or meaning (*significatio*).[85] A word consists of both sound and significance, the one external and corporeal, the other present within the mind, so that "the sound is the body, while the

significance is, as it were, the soul of the sound."[86] This analogy is fundamental to all expressionist semiotics, in which meaning belongs to a different
and more inward dimension of being from bodily things.

When Augustine introduces the notion of inner word, it is because he
wants to extend this expressionist analogy to Christology, where Christ is the
eternal Word who comes to us in human flesh like an external sign. (Whenever
Augustine mentions the inner word of the heart, a reference to the eternal
Word is sure to follow.) This means that the inner word, even in the most
ordinary human heart, is not just any old significance, dependent on human
language, sense-perception, or thought in general. For Augustine the inner
word is always true, conceived from real knowledge not from erroneous
thoughts or empty imagination—just as the eternal Son of God is conceived
from the Father, not from any of the changing things in this world.[87] The inner
word of the human heart must originate from Truth in order to be prior,
ontologically and epistemically, to all bodily things including language. For
Augustine, we must not think of the human heart as a realm of meaning and
thought shaped, for instance, by the different ways that languages like Latin or
English or Chinese make sense of the world. The order of things is quite the
reverse: Latin, English, and Chinese are each just one kind of external clothing
in which we who speak can dress up the inner word that existed already, prior
to language, in order to send it forth in visible form to those who cannot see
what is in our hearts. The causal, epistemic, and ontological priority of the
inner to the outer, essential to expressionist semiotics, is the primary point of
Augustine's Christological analogy. It means that the inner word is never
literally externalized or changed into something outward but always remains
inward even as it is communicated outwardly through bodily sounds. The
inner word never leaves its home in the heart, even when it is expressed in
outward speech, just as the Son of God never leaves the bosom of his Father
even when he comes to dwell among us. The omnipresent God does not
literally descend from on high when he deigns to take up mortal flesh as his
own.[88]

The Christological principle here may be unfamiliar, but it is essential to
Nicene orthodoxy. The Arian Christ can become incarnate, suffer, and die
because he is changeable, unlike his Father.[89] But the Nicene Christ is equal to
his Father in deity and therefore is equally eternal and omnipresent. He remains immutably divine, even as he takes up mutable humanity, mortality,
and vulnerability. In the words of the crucial formulation by the Greek church
father, Gregory of Naziansen, "He remained what he was and took up [or
assumed] what he was not."[90] Augustine's sermons often echo this formula
very closely[91] but also expand it in various ways, as for instance: "When he

began to be what he was not, he was made man, remaining God"[92] and "He came to what he was not, he did not lose what he was; he was made son of man but did not cease to be Son of God,"[93] and "Remaining inconvertible, immutable and altogether inviolable in relation to his Father, he was made what you are in relation to you."[94] This is the same lesson we encountered earlier in the brief wordplay in the *City of God* about assuming a human being, not consuming God.[95] He explains the wordplay at greater length in a sermon:

> Let no one believe that the Son of God was converted and changed into the son of man, but rather let us believe both that the divine substance was not consumed and that the human substance was fully assumed—remaining the Son of God, becoming the son of man.[96]

The point is always that the Incarnation involves no descent from the highest level of the ontological hierarchy. Nothing changes in God when God is made man.

Extremely unpopular in recent years, this teaching of the immutability of the incarnate God was universally accepted by the Nicene orthodoxy of late antiquity, but even so required some explaining. And that is the main use Augustine has for his semiotic analogy of the inner word. For in expressionist semiotics the superiority of the inner word to its spoken expression can be taken as a reflection (however distant) of the ontological superiority of Creator to creature, just as in Augustine's three-tiered ontology the superiority of soul to body (level two to level three) reflects the superiority of God to created things (level one to levels two and three).[97] Not that the inner word of the human heart is absolutely immutable like God, but it is (according to Augustine's Platonist axiom of causality) above being affected by external things. So the inner word is not changed or brought into being by anything external, and it is not turned into something external when it is expressed by the outward sign of the voice. It remains unchanged within the heart just as the Son of God remains immutably one with the Father even as he is made human for us.

Augustine formulates the analogy by comparing the inner word and the outward voice, where the term "voice" (*vox*) can mean a vocal sound without significance (like a yell or a giggle) but also an articulate spoken word[98] (which later theologians such as Luther will call "the external word"). Just as the eternal Word of God remains what he was while assuming what he was not, the inner word remains within the heart even as the voice it assumes is heard externally by the ears.

> The word which we bear in our hearts is made voice [*fit vox*] when we bring it out by mouth, yet the one is not changed into the

other but, intact, assumes the other in which it may go forth—so that what is understood may remain within and what is heard may resound without. . . . When the word is thus made voice *it is not changed into a voice* but remains in the light of the mind, and having assumed a voice of flesh it goes forth to the hearer and does not leave the thinker.[99]

The voice is the flesh of the inner word, a word that remains in the light of the mind even as it is expressed in sensible form by the spoken word. So also (we need hardly wait for Augustine to fill out the analogy) the eternal Word remains unchangeably in the intelligible light of God even as it assumes flesh and is made a human being in order to go forth (*procedat*) to us so that we may see him with our bodily eyes. So we have the analogy: spoken word is to inner word as human flesh is to eternal Word. As usual when speaking of the Word made flesh, Augustine takes "flesh" to mean the whole humanity of Christ, soul as well as body. The outward expression of this inner Word of God, as it were, means that he becomes a whole human creature, soul and body together, even while he remains the eternal Creator who made all things, including that same human creature, the man Jesus Christ.

The daring thing about this analogy is not the Christology, which is simply Nicene orthodoxy, but Augustine's use of his distinctive expressionist semiotics to illustrate it. The point regarding which Augustine's Nicene contemporaries might question him is not the immutability of the eternal Word in the Incarnation of Christ, but the irreversible causal superiority of soul to body, which implies that bodies, even Christ's life-giving flesh, can have no effect on souls.[100] Moreover, Augustine is willing to take the further step of drawing his usual epistemological and educational conclusions from this semiotic analogy, including the consequence that the flesh of Christ, like the outward sign of the voice, is a means to be used by the soul to arrive at a deeper and purer intellectual vision of the Word within.

This consequence is spelled out most clearly in a sermon on "the voice and the word," in which Augustine compares outward voice and inner word to John the Baptist and Jesus Christ, respectively. John is "the *voice* of one crying in the wilderness," announcing the "*Word* of the Lord" which "abides forever."[101] He is the last and greatest of all the prophetic voices announcing the coming of that Word in the flesh, each one of whom is a "voice of the Word" (*vox verbi*). As the last and greatest of them, John in his own person symbolizes them all. As Jesus is the Word in person, indeed "the person of the Word," so John is "the person of the voice, in a sacrament" (where "sacrament" has the sense of "symbol with hidden meaning").[102] So here is "a great and marvelous sacrament":

"the person of the voice" has this to say about "the person of the Word": "he must grow while I diminish."[103] What is the hidden meaning here? Certainly not that the eternal Word can grow in size (Augustine explicitly corrects this misimpression) but rather that the understanding of it grows in our minds, while our need for the voice or external words of prophets and apostles, psalms and Gospels diminishes.[104]

And what applies to the voice of other Scriptural witnesses applies also to that "voice" which is Christ's own flesh. Our aim is "to see him as he is," says Augustine (quoting 1 John 3:2). And this means seeing him not in his humanity ("the form of a servant," to use the Pauline terms that Augustine picks up on here) but in his divinity ("the form of God").[105] For our progress toward perfection is, as we have heard already in the *City of God*,[106] a process of purification and education for vision:

> This is the vision promised to us: for this vision we are educated [*erudimur*], for this vision we are purified. For he says, "Blessed are the pure in heart for they shall see God." He showed his flesh, showed it to his servants—but it was the form of a servant. Among the many voices which he sent beforehand he also shows as it were *his own proper voice, his very flesh itself.*[107]

Christ's own flesh is therefore among the voices that must diminish, becoming less and less necessary for us, while Christ the eternal Word grows in us—that is, grows in our knowledge as the light grows not in itself, but in eyes that are being healed and can see more of it.[108] The voice diminishes while the Word grows: this means that our diminishing need for the flesh of Christ gives way to our growing vision of the eternal Word. Once again the parallel between the humanity of Christ and the witnesses of Scripture is exact. This is a Christological hermeneutic of Scripture and history in which the Incarnation of Christ is to be used as a means to arrive at enjoyment of the kind of pure intellectual vision to which the Platonists admonish us to turn.

Words Forming Persons?

The apostle Philip sought this vision, Augustine says in the conclusion of his sermon on "the voice and the word," and in answer to his desire Jesus told him: "Whoever has seen me has seen the Father."[109] In Nicene terms: to see Christ in his divinity, co-equal with the Father, is to see the divinity of the Father as well. From this Augustine draws the conclusion that Philip has not yet truly seen Christ, for he has obviously not seen the Father. The conclusion is reasonable enough, for Christ's answer begins, "So much time I have been with you all, and yet *you have not known me*, Philip?"[110] Philip has seen Christ with his own eyes, but has not yet seen him or known him in such a way as to see the Father. The logical conclusion has to be: he has seen in one sense but not in another. Augustine correlates these two senses of seeing with the two natures of Christ, interpreting the answer to Philip's question in these terms: "You have seen me and not seen me. You have not seen me who made you, but you have seen what I was made for you."[111] That is to say: Philip has not seen Christ the Creator but only Christ the creature—not the divinity of Christ but only his humanity, not the form of God but only the form of a servant. Given Augustine's epistemology, this must mean: he has seen with the eyes of the body but not with the vision of the intellect.[112]

This particular text is one of the best places at which to stop and assess how far an alliance between Christianity and Platonism can go. Is intellectual vision, like rising out of Plato's cave to see the eternal light of Truth, really the goal that Jesus proposes for Philip? This is a fair question to ask, because an alliance with Platonism is not out of the question in this gospel with its notion of a preexistent Word, resembling in many ways the *Logos* theology of Philo of Alexandria, the Jewish Middle Platonist and contemporary of Christ. It is not a stretch when the church fathers interpret the opening of the Gospel of John, "In the beginning was the Word...and the Word was God," to mean that Christ is eternally and immutably divine, in quite a Platonist sense.[113] One cannot avoid the conclusion, if one judges by the Nicene fathers' reading of Scripture, that Plato and his followers were right about a few things. But it is a stretch to suppose that in this gospel the proper aim of the soul is to see God with intellectual vision. In other words, it is far more questionable to find Platonist psychology and epistemology here than Platonist theology. The conviction that the divine is immutably eternal is arguably to be found in the New Testament, which does in places use Platonist language that can be interpreted to that effect,[114] but Augustine's distinctive conviction that the intrinsic goal of our souls is to see God with our intellects is much harder to find there. If we combine the prologue of the Gospel of John with the Allegory of the Cave, for instance, then when the Word is said to become flesh and dwell among us (John 1:14), we must imagine the Sun itself coming down into the cave, full of grace and truth, joining the prisoners there. It would seem anticlimactic if the point of this astounding presence were simply to lead people out of the cave, like any other teacher. Isn't the point rather that the cave is a different place with his glory in the midst of it? A likelier lesson is that we need not ascend to the realm of intellectual vision to see the eternal God, for he is here in the flesh.

If this is so, then there must be a third alternative explaining what it means to know Christ so as to see the Father, a vision belonging neither to the eyes of the body nor to the eye of the mind. Christ's own answer to Philip's question proceeds to suggest (in a passage Augustine does not quote in this sermon) that the alternative might be something like the eye of faith, whose vision consists in believing the word of Christ: "How can you say, 'Show us the Father'? Do you not *believe* that I am in the Father and the Father in me? The words I speak to you I speak not from myself" (John 14:9f). The fourth gospel does not appear to have any conception of intellectual vision, but it does appear to have the notion that believing the word of Christ is tantamount to seeing the Father. The epistemology it calls for evidently supposes that there is no deeper way to know God than to believe his words, as if he were the friend we wished to know in *On Faith in Things Not Seen*.

But if there is no Platonist vision in our future, then our dependence on our friend making himself known in his words looks like a permanent feature of our knowledge of other persons—as if indeed it were a good thing that our knowledge of others depended on others, not just on what they are but on what they have chosen to say about themselves and whether they are true to their word. The suggestion I would make is that knowledge of God is not like seeing an unchanging truth for yourself (so that you henceforth need no external teacher) but rather like coming to know someone present in the flesh, outside your own heart, so that precisely the one you seek to know is always your teacher.[115] The implication is that there is no knowledge of the other that is not ultimately a gracious gift of the other, which we must be glad to receive.[116]

Does this mean, as Augustine fears, that Christian belief is fictive, a product of the imagination? It is a serious question. Of course everything depends on whether Nicene Christology is actually true, but that is not the question Augustine is raising. Nor does he have the modern worry about epistemic foundations, as if we had no right to believe what we cannot prove. The question, rather, is whether secondhand knowledge, hearing without seeing, can really be conducive to beatific union with God. Could believing another person really be something like eternal happiness? Could it be that the peculiar beatitude of the fourth gospel, "Blessed are those who do not see and have believed" (John 20:29), is properly the last word? An epistemology in which believing other persons is fundamental can leave a place for seeing and bearing witness that one's friend has kept his word, but this remains secondary, a matter of confirmation rather than foundation: we will see in the end that Desdemona is trustworthy only if we already have a knowledge of her that comes not from "ocular proof" but from her faithful word. But of course this issue cannot be settled without a much fuller account of the person we aim to know—which is to say, a much more extensive discussion of Christology and in particular the theology of transfiguration, in which the glory of God is seen most properly in the human face of Jesus Christ. It is because he remains what he eternally is even as he assumes what he was not, that to receive this human being in faith is to receive the One who sent him (John 13:20).

It will help us keep these non-Augustinian options open if we recognize that expressionist semiotics, with its preference for vision and its belief in inner presence, is not the only possible explanation of how language and meaning work. We need not be captive to the picture of the soul's inner communicative intent bestowing significance on external words from a position of ontological and epistemological superiority, closer to the inward Truth than bodily things ever get. There are alternative pictures, such as the classical metaphor of the soul being like a wax tablet imprinted by words or biblical talk of words being written on the heart,[117] which suggest that our minds are not causally superior to bodily things but can be formed by the external things they learn. In such a picture, belief in another person's words need not be a temporary substitute for inward vision, but rather the way our hearts are shaped by what someone outside of us wants us to know, including even himself. The suggestion is that to have our hearts shaped by the Word of God is to know the Lord. The parallel between Scripture and Incarnation, on this understanding, is that some external things have the power to grant us everlasting gifts, which can be found by embracing in faith Christ's life-giving flesh.

PART II

Powerless Sacraments

6

Sacred Signs of Inner Unity

Augustine and Medieval Sacramental Theology

Because one enters the Body of Christ by faith not by birth, the Christian church has always had a special need for external marks of its membership. The Western church calls them sacraments, a translation of the New Testament term mystēria, *meaning both sacred rites and their hidden or symbolic meaning. Augustine describes them as sacred signs. One of the things they signify is the grace of God, and the great innovation of medieval sacramental theory is to teach that they can confer the grace they signify, which means they are efficacious external means of grace. Augustine, by contrast, tends to speak as if a sacramental sign and the thing it signifies operate on two parallel tracks, the one given outwardly and the other inwardly. Most fundamentally, for Augustine, the sacraments signify the inner life of the church as a community of souls bound together by love for God. As illustrated by Victorinus's baptism in the eighth book of the* Confessions, *the efficacy of grace is found not in the external signs themselves but in the inner union they signify. Augustine's own conversion in the same book resembles Victorinus's: Augustine must be humbled so as to join the Catholic church, which in his case occurs only when he realizes that he cannot achieve the sexual continence required by the philosophic life without the inward help of membership in this often unphilosophic community. One fruit of this humility is the union of Augustine and his mother in the vision at Ostia, when they both touch eternal Wisdom together. This should be understood not as an exceptional mystical experience but as an enactment of the essential inner unity of the church, which takes place in an inner but public space where divine*

Wisdom is seen, one and the same for all. The same kind of vision takes place whenever preacher and audience share an insight into eternal things as, bound together by love of the same Truth, they participate in common inquiry—a practice exemplified in Augustine's sermons.

Augustine's semiotics provides a conceptual framework for both word and sacrament, resulting in a new theory about how words get their meaning and also a new way of thinking about key Christian rituals. For Augustine sacraments are like words in that they are external signs whose most important use is to signify inner things, sometimes even divine things like the grace of God. Western Christianity has expanded Augustine's theology of the sacraments, treating them not only as signs but as means of grace. In part II we shall see how Augustine gave the West a conception of sacraments as signs of grace without going so far as to conceive of them as means of grace. For in Augustine's semiotics ever since the treatise *On the Teacher* it is clear that outward things can signify an inner thing but cannot cause us to have it. Outward signs cannot communicate an inner gift, in the original sense of the term "communicate": they cannot cause us to share in it as a common good. That sharing or communication must occur at a deeper level, the inward level of the soul, which the outward sign merely signifies and marks. The aim of part II is to show that Augustine remains consistent on this semiotic version of the Platonist axiom of "downward causality" throughout the complex development of his thinking on baptism and the Eucharist, despite leaving behind important formulations that medieval theologians would later use as the basis for their notion that the sacraments are efficacious external means of grace. The pastoral implication of the inefficaciousness and powerlessness of external things is a piety that honors and makes reverent use of sacramental signs but does not cling to them as means by which grace and salvation are given to us. Augustine would rather have us cling (*adhaerere*) to inward things.

Election and Sacraments

Baptism and the Eucharist play the particular roles they do in Christian life in large part because the Christian community conceives itself as chosen by God in a different way from the people of Israel. As a rule, a person is born a Jew according to the ordinary fleshly mode of human birth, as Christ was born of Mary, a Jew from a Jewish mother—so that the choice of who is a Jew is all God's, and easy to see. But a person is Christian by being reborn through faith in Christ, like Abraham "the father of all those who believe" (Rom. 4:11) being justified by faith and given a hope for the future that is beyond the natural capacity of his flesh; here divine choice must operate through human choices, above all the choice to believe the word of God. The new community of those whose life is in Christ, chosen like Israel and precious, is nonetheless constituted in a profoundly different way, called out of many nations by the preaching of Christ heard in faith. Though never so flatly individualistic as some of Augustine's Protestant heirs—as if God simply caused one person to choose salvation rather than another—the ancient church's understanding of divine election did mean that the choices of human individuals mattered in a way they did not for the constitution of Israel as the chosen people. There is room in Christianity for the development of a psychology that makes the heart's act of faith central in a way hardly to be conceived in Judaism. But there is also, consequently, a profound need for bodily marks of the life of this community, not simply the invisible choices of the heart but tangible things like water, bread, and wine.

From its beginning Christian baptism is the new circumcision, a sign of belonging to a different kind of covenant people from fleshly Israel. The people who belong to Christ by faith are buried with him in baptism so as to walk with him in newness of life (Rom. 6:4). Since fleshly birth is not what brings one into this community, baptism becomes the great sign of rebirth, an irreplaceable assurance of belonging to Christ. The Eucharist follows as the meal of the household of God, the reborn family of brothers and sisters in Christ, conceived as a continuation of Jesus' table-fellowship with his disciples and therefore of his presence among the people who are called his Body. Though huge theological disagreements will rage about the meaning and power of these rites over the course of the centuries, the fact that they somehow mark or signify the community of those who live in Christ is never in dispute. Baptism almost inevitably is thought of as a sign serving this purpose like its predecessor circumcision, which is a "sign of the covenant" (Gen. 17:11). One can hardly avoid thinking of both baptism and the Eucharist as external signs if one believes in an ontology of outer and inner, just as one can hardly avoid thinking of them both as signs of grace if one has a theology of grace.

What is not always so clear to later writers as it is to Augustine is that the question of their power is inseparable from the question of their relation to the life of the Christian community. For it will not be as natural for later Augustinian theologians as it is for Augustine to think of the life of a community as fundamentally inner and thus suitable to be the inner gift signified by a sacred sign. Medieval understandings of sacraments as signs of an inner grace make possible a sacramental piety focused on the inner life of the individual—and then with the arrival of modern individualism, when the notion of the inner is firmly cemented to the notion of the private, the life of a community comes to look like something external, in contrast to the private inner life of the individual. At that point the sacraments can be conceived in a way quite impossible for the ancient or medieval church, as external signs of a divine gift meant solely for the individual heart. Yet the Augustinian notion of a "sign of grace" (these are not Augustine's own words but a formulation inconceivable apart from his legacy) does have something to do with this development. For if grace is an inner gift stemming ultimately from divine election, and election is conceived in Augustine's terms as God's choice to save some persons rather others, then to have a sign of grace is to have an external gift that an individual might very well want to hang on to, in order to confirm the inner and more intangible gift of salvation.

The Meaning of "Sacrament"

The word *sacramentum* is one of two Latin terms used to translate the New Testament term *mystērion*.[1] The other, more common translation is *mysterium*, which of course is simply a transliteration from the Greek. Knowing this quite well, Augustine will naturally think of the language of sacrament as biblical (unlike most readers of the English Bible) while also being aware of the underlying Greek term. Like most Latin writers in the patristic period, including Bible translators, he treats the two terms, *mystērium* and *sacramentum*, as interchangeable.[2] He is of course also free from distracting modern associations of the term *mystērion*, such as mystery novels and the aura of the mysterious. The basic sense of *mystērion*, as everyone in the ancient world knew, had to do with the mystery cults and their secret rites of initiation, but by the time of the New Testament the term had acquired a more general use and could simply mean "secret," though usually one with some kind of religious meaning.[3] The Pauline literature is therefore not using the term in a unique way when it calls the preaching of Christ a mystery, in that it was predestined by God from the beginning of the world but kept secret until the time Christ came.[4] To call the Gospel a mystery, in this sense, is to say it is the erstwhile divine secret about Christ that is now proclaimed far and wide.

Of particular importance in this regard is the once-hidden, now-revealed divine intention of reconciling Jew and Gentile by bringing them together in the Body of Christ.[5] The point of the term *mystērion* in this Pauline usage is that although the Gospel of Christ is news to both Jew and Gentile, it was part of God's plan for them all along. Hence it is not surprising that as the Christian

Gospel spreads far and wide in the next few centuries so that its message is no longer startlingly new, and the Christian church becomes more estranged from its Jewish origins, this original usage of "mystery"—the most distinctive sense of the term in the Bible—falls out of use even in the church.

But the term itself remains important for Christians, in part because the New Testament also uses the word in a more general sense to indicate any spiritual secret or obscurity,[6] indeed any hidden meaning. The book of Revelation, for instance, speaks of "the mystery of the seven stars" which John saw in Christ's right hand and "the mystery of the woman and the beast carrying her" (both translated *sacramentum* in the Vulgate) in a way that we could translate simply as "symbol," in the modern literary sense of the term.[7] There is nothing intractably mysterious about mysteries in this symbolic sense: they have a hidden meaning that is intended to be revealed and explained, as the book of Revelation proceeds to do by giving explicit interpretations of the meaning of the seven stars and the woman riding on the beast. This rather ordinary sense of symbolic or hidden meaning remains an important feature also in Augustine's use of the term *sacramentum*.

What *sacramentum* adds to *mysterium* is explicit overtones of something sacred, as in the sacred rites (*sacra*) of a religion. Yet in this regard, too, the two terms continue to run parallel in ecclesiastical usage after the Bible, where both refer to baptism as a sacred rite containing secrets revealed only to initiates.[8] The discipline of secrecy surrounding the Christian rite of initiation was still maintained in Augustine's time, though in Christian Africa it was no longer really needed nor could it be maintained very strictly. Nevertheless, because the discipline was officially still in force, bishop Augustine was obliged every Easter (when most adults were baptized) to explain the sacraments, the sacred secrets of the faith, to the newly baptized as if for the first time. In one of his Easter sermons, for example, Augustine discusses a whole series of *sacramenta*: "the sacrament of the altar" (i.e., the Eucharist), "the sacrament of the creed," "the sacrament of the Lord's Prayer," and "the sacrament of the font" (i.e., baptism).[9] Here the sense of "sacred rite" and "secret" flow together inextricably. But we get a sense of the range of Augustine's usage in either direction if we note, on the one hand, that *sacramentum* can be almost an equivalent of *sacrum* or "sacred rite," as when he uses it to designate the sacrifices of the Old Testament (in effect classifying *sacrificium* as one kind of *sacramentum*) while on the other hand it can simply designate anything with a symbolic or hidden meaning, as frequently in his expositions of Old Testament foreshadowings of Christ. For example, "in the *sacrament* of [Noah's] flood," he says, "by which the just are freed through the wood [of the ark], the future church is foretold, whose king and God, Christ, hangs it above the inundation of this world by the *mystery* of his cross... and gives an example of future judgment as well as foretelling the freeing of the saints by the *mystery* of the wood."[10] Here Augustine uses *sacramentum* and *mysterium* interchangeably to designate biblical symbols having a hidden meaning to be explained in light of Christ. Like the Lord's Prayer and the creed under the discipline of secrecy, they are sacred secrets of the faith whose hidden meaning the bishop explains to those becoming full members of the church for the first time.

Augustine evidently feels no need to make a sharp distinction between various senses of the term *sacramentum*, and often moves freely from one to the other without remarking on the difference. For instance, he moves from the sense of "sacred rite" to the sense of "symbol" in his explanation of how the bread of the Eucharist symbolizes the unity of the church: a multitude of people are gathered like many grains of wheat, ground up into flour through disciplines such as "the sacrament of exorcism," then mixed with the water of baptism to make dough, and finally baked in fire, which signifies the chrism with which the newly baptized are anointed—because oil, which feeds the fire, is "the sacrament of the Holy Spirit."[11] The first-mentioned *sacramentum*, the ritual exorcisms that the catechumens underwent in the weeks before their baptism, is a sacred rite, while the second, the oil that feeds the fire, is a symbol in the most straightforward literary sense, where "sacrament of the Holy Spirit" means simply "symbol of the Holy Spirit." Augustine's doctrine of the sacramental significance of baptism and the Eucharist takes shape within the space between these two meanings of the term *sacramentum*, "sacred rite" and "symbol," neither of which is exactly what later theologians mean by "the sacraments."

In fact this whole range of meaning was available also to later medieval writers, who knew that in Scripture a sacrament could be any "sacred or mystic thing."[12] The great medieval innovation was to propose a strict or technical sense of the term "sacrament," according to which it designates only seven specific rites of the church, distinct from all others in that they not only signify grace but confer it.[13] Peter Lombard, for instance, sets the tone for subsequent medieval theology when he begins his *Sentences* by dividing the subject matter of Christian doctrine into signs and things (*signa* and *res*) as Augustine does at the beginning of his treatise *On Christian Doctrine*, and then adds a new distinction:

> There are some signs whose whole use is in signifying, not justify-
> ing, i.e., which are used merely to signify grace, such as some
> legal sacraments, but others which not only signify but confer what
> inwardly helps, such as the Gospel sacraments.[14]

Later, when it comes time to give a formal definition of *sacramentum,* Lombard focuses not on the whole range of its meaning but on this strict sense of the term:

> A sacrament, properly speaking, is a sign of the grace of God and form of invisible grace, that bears its image and exists as its cause.[15]

Earlier medieval writers, such as Hugh of St. Victor and the anonymous author of the twelfth-century *Summa Sententiarum,* were clearly aware that they were narrowing the sense of the word when they defined it in this strictly "sacramental" sense.[16] Some later writers like Aquinas are still acutely aware that in their sacramental theology "we are now speaking of sacraments in a special sense."[17]

This special sense is precisely that in which medieval theologians are adding something to the Augustinian definition of *sacramentum.* In *City of God* Augustine describes a sacrament as a "sacred sign" (*sacrum signum*),[18] and a variation of this formulation, "sign of a sacred thing" (*sacrae rei signum*), is taken by nearly every medieval theologian to be Augustine's definition of sacrament, becoming the jumping-off point for most medieval discussions of the nature of a sacrament.[19] Lombard for example arrives at his proper "sacramental" sense of the term *sacramentum* by beginning with a discussion of this formulation, as does Hugh before him and Thomas after him.[20] Despite great diversity in their formulations, all medieval theologians from the twelfth century onward make two decisive additions to this Augustinian starting point: first, that the sacred thing signified by the sacraments is grace, and second, that the sacraments of the church confer the grace they signify. This makes the sacraments causes of grace, not in the sense of being the ultimate origin of grace (which of course is God alone) but in the sense of being, as Aquinas clarifies, an instrumental cause that God uses to bestow grace[21]—hence the later designation of sacraments as "means of grace," in the sense of instrumental causes of grace. The question we are investigating in part II of this study can thus be formulated: how genuinely Augustinian are these medieval additions to the Augustinian notion of sacrament?

Signs of Grace?

We need not balk at the medieval misquotation of Augustine's formulation, transforming "sacred sign" into "sign of a sacred thing." For one thing, the notion that every sign has a thing (*res*) that it signifies is perfectly Augustinian. Furthermore, although Augustine does show a decided preference for attaching the adjective "sacred" to the sign rather than the thing signified (emphasizing what in the next chapter we shall designate as the sacrament's *validity*), the sense in which the medieval theologians understand this *res* as sacred is surely not one against which Augustine would have any deep objection.

The difficult questions begin when we consider exactly what this *res* is. Setting aside the very broad sense in which *sacramentum* could refer to almost any hidden meaning (like Noah's ark symbolizing the wood of the cross) and focusing on sacraments as sacred rites, we could begin by noting that the most characteristic feature of Augustine's sacramental semiotics is that it incorporates the key innovation of his expressionist semiotics: it uses the notion of signification to relate the external to the internal. In this Augustine's medieval heirs follow him very closely, describing the sacrament itself as visible, which means that it is an external, bodily thing, while describing the thing it signifies as invisible, which is to say it is an inner good in the soul.

What is not so obvious from Augustine's writings is that the single best word to describe this invisible inner good should be "grace." The sacraments certainly do not express divine grace the way external signs express the inner communicative will of the human soul. Augustine does not talk as if sacraments were a way for God to reveal his gracious inner intent or as if God's will were an inner thing (*res*) that could be expressed in words like the human will. After all, for Augustine, knowing what is in God is not like believing what someone says.[22] So although Augustine's sacramental theology is structured by expressionist concepts of outer and inner, the relation between sacrament and grace cannot be a straightforward example of his expressionist semiotics, except insofar as it relentlessly maintains the priority of the inward as required by the *On the Teacher* thesis: we are in no position to understand or use an outward sign properly unless we first inwardly possess what it signifies.

Although sacraments often do signify grace in Augustine's theology, the connection between sacraments and grace is not nearly so tight as in his medieval successors. In their efforts to forge a tighter connection medieval writers often shifted away from the semiotic language of *signum* and *res* altogether, describing the sacrament rather as a figure or image or (in one of the most important and recurring formulations) "the visible *form* of invisible grace." This too is an Augustinian formulation—again not an exact quote but a phrase derived from Augustine's writings, in this case more than one passage.[23] There is for example the answer Augustine gives to a question about why both Moses and God are said to sanctify the people of Israel in Leviticus:

How is it then that both Moses and the Lord sanctified? It's not
Moses in place of the Lord; rather, Moses sanctified by *visible sacra-*

ments through his ministry, while the Lord sanctified by *invisible grace* through the Holy Spirit, which is also where the whole fruit of the visible sacraments is. For without this sanctification of invisible grace, what is the profit of the visible sacraments?[24]

This passage contains language that was very important for medieval theology, but its argument does not bode well for a doctrine of sacraments as means of grace. Rather than relating sacrament and grace as sign and thing signified, Augustine here puts them as it were on separate tracks: the visible track of sacramental sanctification and the invisible track of spiritual sanctification. The visible and invisible are clearly two different orders of causality and therefore of sanctification, one external and the other inward, and Augustine seems deliberately to avoid saying anything about the interaction between them, least of all suggesting that the visible sanctification of the sacrament might be the cause or means of the invisible sanctification of the Spirit. It is no accident that a later portion of this same chapter is quoted by medieval authors in support of the possibility of a person being inwardly sanctified without external baptism, in a "baptism of desire."[25]

The roots of this two-track approach to the sacrament are ontological—the sharp Platonist distinction between bodily things and things of the soul, together with the Platonist axiom of downward causality according to which the former is powerless to affect the latter—but the immediate occasion is a controversy about the nature of Christian ministry, as we can see in another Augustinian passage that seems to have made a major contribution to medieval sacramental theology:

Grace is always God's, and the sacrament is God's; only the ministry is a man's—who, if he is good, adheres to God and works with God, but if he is evil, God works through him the *visible form* of the sacrament, but *He himself gives the invisible grace.*[26]

This passage is probably the most important single source for the definition of sacrament as "visible form of invisible grace." But here again we have a two-track theory: the visible form of the sacrament (which is another way of saying simply, the sacrament itself as a visible thing) is precisely what does no good apart from the invisible grace that is given inwardly by God. The contrast between good and bad ministers is one insisted on by Augustine's opponents, the Donatists, about whom there will be much more to say in the next chapter. Suffice it to say for now that according to the Donatists, only a holy minister can sanctify those he baptizes, while an evil minister actually does them harm. Augustine, on the contrary, sees no difference between holy and unholy ministers in this regard. The one works with God and the other against him, but both can do just as adequate a job at giving the outward and visible form of a sacrament (for instance, immersing someone in water and saying the right words) while neither has the power to confer the invisible and inward grace, which is God's alone to give.

A richer version of this two-track approach is evident in a passage where Augustine uses the phrase "sacrament of grace," thus implicitly treating grace as the thing signified by the sacrament. In his treatise *On Baptism against the Donatists* he contends that "God gives the *sacrament of grace* even through evil men, but the grace itself only through himself and his saints."[27] What is striking here is the indication that in the giving of his grace God has human partners, whom Augustine identifies not as the ministers or priests of the church but the church itself, that is, "the saints" or holy ones, a term that includes all good Christians. This is our first important clue as to how Augustine thinks of the causal relation between sacraments and grace: it is inextricable from the relation between sacraments and the church, understood as a community of holy people united by love to one another and to God. If Augustine has anything like a concept of means of grace, a sacramental efficacy that is not simply that of God himself, it will be found in this community.

The Invisible Sacrifice

The difficulty of finding a tight or necessary connection between sacrament and grace in Augustine's own writing is illustrated with particular clarity in the very passage where he gives the medieval theologians their Augustinian definition of "sacrament," describing it as a sacred sign. It comes near the end of Part One in the *City of God*, as he is winding up his criticism of pagan religion and contrasting it with the true religion of Christian worship. In this context he takes up the concept of sacrifice, aiming to distinguish Christian worship from both pagan and Jewish sacrifices by arguing that in the Old Testament, "a visible sacrifice is the sacrament, i.e. *the sacred sign*, of an invisible sacrifice."[28] Although the sacraments immediately in view here are Old Testament sacrifices, the same semiotic structure applies to the Eucharist, which he calls "the daily sacrifice of the church."[29] In fact any act of public Christian worship signifies an invisible sacrifice, an inward act of lifting up the heart to God, where "we sacrifice to him fervent offerings of humility and praise on the altar of the heart by the fire of charity."[30] According to this account, the thing signified by a visible sacrament is not the grace of God but the soul's inward act of worship. Augustine has a great many things on his mind in this very complex passage, but a theology of sacramental grace does not seem to be one of them.

Yet a closer look at the complexity of the passage will set the stage for what Augustine does have to say about sacraments and grace elsewhere. His immediate concern here is with pagan Platonists, against whom he makes the same criticism as in his early treatise *On True Religion*: although they were familiar with the invisible and eternal nature of God, they did not refrain from public, visible rites devoted to beings they knew did not deserve worship.[31] For only what can make us truly happy should be worshiped, Augustine argues, and the Platonists knew well enough that true happiness comes only by participation in the intelligible light of the one invisible and eternal God, just as Plotinus taught.[32] Yet they took part in worship of secondary beings, the sun and the moon and various other gods as well as *daemones,* intermediaries between the divine and the human that Christians regarded as demons. One possible excuse for this split between knowledge and practice in pagan Platonism seems to have inspired Augustine's distinction between visible and invisible sacrifice. For he considers the opinion of some unnamed, perhaps hypothetical, pagans who think that "visible sacrifices are suitable for other gods, but the invisible sacrifices for the invisible God—the greater and better sacrifices for the greater and better God—such as the duties of a pure mind and good will."[33] In rejecting this divergence between the objects of worship in visible and invisible sacrifices Augustine points out a parallel between visible sacrifices (i.e., what he has earlier identified as sacraments) and the words used in worship, which can also can be a kind of sacred sign. Both word and sacrament are signs that should be congruent with the inner thing they signify:

> these (visible sacrifices) are signs of those (invisible sacrifices), the way that sounding words [*verba sonantia*] are of things. Therefore, just as in prayer and praise we direct to God significant voices [*significantes voces*] offering in our hearts the things themselves which we thereby signify, so also in making sacrifice we know we are not to offer a visible sacrifice to other beings than him, to whom in our hearts we ought ourselves to be an invisible sacrifice.[34]

Here we can begin to discern the real foundation of Augustine's sacramental theology. The thing signified by all sacred signs, both words and sacraments, is the invisible sacrifice that we ourselves *are* when we offer ourselves to God in our hearts. In effect, every soul ought to be both priest and offering, the heart that offers the sacrifice and the heart that is offered in sacrifice.

The crucial thing to understand about this inward offering of the heart is that it is no less the act of a community than is the visible act of public worship, indeed more so. For in the true invisible sacrifice the soul is joined in unity to Christ together with the whole church of which Christ is Head. The invisible sacrifice takes place in an inner space that is not wholly private. "We are all together God's temple," Augustine writes, "and each of us individually his temples, for he dwells in the harmony of all as well as in individuals."[35] This hint that the inner temple can be a shared space prepares us for a startling identification of the thing signified by the Eucharistic sacrifice: the true invisible sacrifice is the church itself, which is Christ's spiritual Body and the city of God on earth:

> The whole redeemed city itself, the congregation and society of the saints, is offered to God as a universal sacrifice by the great high-priest who also offered himself in suffering for us, that we might be the Body of such a Head.... We are ourselves the whole sacrifice.... This is the sacrifice of Christians: "the many, one Body in Christ." This the church repeats in the sacrament of the altar known to the faithful, where they are shown that in this thing which she offers, she herself is offered.[36]

The whole Body of Christ together with its Head is the thing signified by the sacrament of the altar, the invisible sacrifice that the church not only offers but *is*, so that all the faithful are joined with Christ in being both the priest who offers and the sacrifice that is offered. This is not an act of divine grace but of human worship, as Augustine goes on to stress particularly in the case of Christ, who offers himself "according to the form of a servant," using the term from Philippians 2 to designate Christ's humanity in contrast to "the form of God," which is his divinity.[37] This form of a servant, Augustine continues, "is what he offers; in this he is offered, because according to this he is mediator; in this he is priest and sacrifice."[38] The invisible sacrifice is thus a specifically human act of Christ, joined with his whole human Body that offers itself together with him, and Augustine makes no move to connect it explicitly with the grace of God. Yet grace is not far to seek: the long Pauline passage Augustine quotes to explain the unity of the Body of Christ concludes, "we many are one Body in Christ but individually members of one another, having diverse gifts according to the grace that is given us."[39] Augustine does not pick up on this reference to grace (for the diversity of gifts is not his subject here) but perhaps includes it in the quotation as a way of indicating where he would have us look to find grace. The place to look for something like an instrumental cause of grace is evidently not the external sign itself but the human community it signifies, the inner union of souls with the man Jesus Christ.

Augustine makes his way from the concept of invisible sacrifice to the concept of inner union through a kind of exegetical tour-de-force that is often found in his sermons. This particular tour-de-force is especially complex and indirect, but in outline we can say he moves from sacrifice to mercy to love to union. The first step is to identify true sacrifice with mercy. According to Augustine's argument, when Scripture says God wants "mercy rather than sacrifice," it is not forbidding sacrifice so much as indicating which kind of sacrifice God prefers, "since what everyone calls a sacrifice is actually the sign of the true sacrifice."[40] This true, invisible sacrifice, of which the bloody act usually called sacrifice is but the visible sign, actually consists in mercy, because according to the letter to the Hebrews we are "not to forget to do good and be sharers, for by such sacrifices God is pleased."[41] Augustine is plainly thinking here of alms, Greek *eleēmosynē*, literally "mercifulness," which comes out in Latin as *opera misericordiae*, works of mercy. The African church had a long tradition of treating almsgiving as a kind of propitiation for sins and Augustine endorses this tradition, arguing that "alms assist our prayers" in attaining forgiveness of daily sins,[42] but also hedging it about with qualifications to make it clear that alms cannot be used to buy divine forgiveness. In this passage the key qualification comes when Augustine identifies the true work of mercy as internal rather than pecuniary, the act of having mercy on one's own soul by obeying the divine command of love. So true sacrifice, it turns out, is to love God and neighbor.

The connections here are complex and compressed, set forth in a passage of concentrated exegetical poetry that goes by so fast that if you blink you'll miss them. Just try to keep track of the many identifications of "true sacrifice" in the following quotation, bearing in mind that this is also what the medieval writers would call the *res sacramenti*, the thing signified by the sacrament. I count six.

But furthermore (1) *mercy is the true sacrifice*, which is why it says what I quoted earlier, "by such sacrifices God is pleased." Therefore whatever we read about the many kinds of sacrifices divinely commanded in the ministry of tabernacle or temple is to be related to (2) *the love of God and neighbor, which it signifies*. For "on these two commandments," it is written, "hang all the Law and the prophets." Hence (3) *true sacrifice is every work done to cling to God in holy fellowship*, which is to say, (4) *every work related to the ultimate Good* by which we can be truly happy. Therefore even that mercy by which man is helped [i.e., alms] if it is not done for God's sake, is not a sacrifice... Hence (5) *the sacrifice is the man himself consecrated by the name of God and devoted to God*, insofar as he dies to this world and lives to God. This too belongs to (6) *the mercy which everyone does in himself.* That is why it is written: "Have mercy on your own soul by pleasing God."[43]

The basic connections are clear enough: true sacrifice consists of those inner works of mercy in which one has mercy even on one's own soul by loving God and neighbor. The subtle connection is that this inner sacrifice is impossible without the "holy fellowship" (*sancta societate*) of other souls sharing in the sacrifice, for having mercy on one's own soul requires loving other souls as well. The twofold love command, as Augustine understands it, makes the heart's inner worship of God inescapably social:

> For a man to know how to love himself, a goal is established to which he relates all that he does in order to be happy—for one who loves himself wills nothing other than to be happy. This goal is to cling to God. So when he who knows how to love himself is commanded to love his neighbor as himself, what is he being commanded but to urge him to love God? This is the worship of God, this is true religion and right piety, this alone is the service owed to God.[44]

Here we have what I take to be the fundamental identification of the invisible sacrifice, the inner thing signified by the outward sacrament: it is the common life of souls bound together by love of God and each other, who all love God as their ultimate happiness and urge each other to love God as well. Augustine says nothing about grace in this passage, but it seems clear enough that if efficacious means of grace are to be found anywhere, it is in this nonspatial place, this union of human love directed to God.

Taking Victorinus to Heart

Only by shared love do souls arrive at the ultimate happiness of enjoying God. Since this love is to be directed toward souls and God, what use is there for external signs and sacraments? (Notice how this question resembles the one inevitably raised by the *On the Teacher* thesis: what use is there for words if we learn nothing from them? Augustine has an explanation of the use of sacraments just as he has an explanation for the use of words, even though neither has the power to give us the inner thing it signifies). The sacraments of the church have no power except to signify a good that must come from within, but that does not mean they are useless. As Augustine explains:

> Human beings cannot coalesce in the name of any religion, true or false, unless they are tied together by some partnership [*consortio*]

of visible seals or sacraments. The force [*vis*] of such sacraments means an indescribably great deal [*inenarrabiliter valet plurimum*] and so contempt for them is sacrilegious; for it is impious to contemn that without which it is not [*sine qua non*] possible for piety to be perfected.[45]

A great deal is ascribed here to every kind of sacrament, New Testament, Old Testament, even pagan: in every case a sacrament is indispensable to some religious community or other, literally a *sine qua non* of its piety. This indispensability stems from the need all human communities have, in our fallen and embodied condition, for signs as a medium of communication and sharing of thought.[46] Augustine is not saying that shared external signs create communities—as we shall see, only love does that.[47] But love itself is hidden in the heart, so if we are to recognize who belongs to our community we need to use outward signs such as words and sacraments to mark this inner belonging. Contempt for their meaning or "force" (*vis*, the same term used to designate how words move their hearers in Augustine's early treatise *On Dialectic*)[48] is impious and destructive to the soul, for by such an attitude one puts oneself outside the religious community, separating oneself from the love that is the true power binding it together. So although the outward signs do not have the power to create a community, no one who shares the piety of the community will be contemptuous of them.

Augustine illustrates this point when he tells the story of how he finally decided to become a full member of the church himself. We must bear in mind that long before the famous scene in the garden in Milan narrated in book 8 of the *Confessions*, Augustine was (he tells us quite explicitly) already a believer in Christ as Savior.[49] So what was lacking at that point in his Christian life? The answer is: everything. Although he truly believed in Christ, he did not yet have a Christian life at all, because this is the new life that results when one "is born again through baptism" (*per baptismum regeneretur*).[50] In the language of the *Confessions* one is "not yet a Christian" so long as one is not yet baptized.[51] Lest there be any unclarity on this point, Augustine tells the story of Victorinus, a man of an earlier generation with whom he has a great deal in common. Victorinus was a rhetorician and translator of the books of the Platonists that had just served as such important admonitions for Augustine.[52] His reading had brought him to believe in Christ, but he still hesitated to get baptized, afraid and embarrassed by the ridicule he would have to face from powerful pagan friends. He came to consult the same Milanese priest whom Augustine was consulting on the matter, who turns out to be none other than the addressee (many years later, about the time the *Confessions* was being written) of the treatise *To Simplicianus*. Victorinus tells Simplicianus in secret that he is now a Christian, but Simplicianus says he will not believe it, "nor will I count you among Christians until I see you in the church of Christ." Victorinus laughs and replies, "Is it walls, then, that make Christians?"[53] Victorinus does not appear to understand that there is another and more spiritual way to be "in the church of Christ" than simply to be within the walls of the basilica. Yet it turns out he does have to enter literally within those external walls in order to find himself in the community of souls to which Simplicianus is referring. For that is where he must go to receive baptism.

So this is the story of how Victorinus becomes a Christian, fully incorporated into Christ's spiritual Body, not merely someone who privately believes in Christ. Eventually, with more reading Victorinus overcomes his embarrassment, finding he is more afraid to offend Christ than to displease his pagan friends. He goes to Simplicianus and announces, "Let us go in the church; I want to become a Christian."[54] Within the church he is "steeped in the first sacraments of instruction,"[55] the secret catechetical teaching that Augustine called "the authority of the mysteries" when he was himself preparing for baptism.[56] This means especially the creed, which is "handed over" (*tradi*) to the catechumens in a secret ceremony a few days before Easter when they are to be baptized and must be "given back" (*reddi*) at their baptism by a kind of formal recitation in the church. Victorinus is granted permission to "give back the creed" in private if he wishes, but instead chooses to speak out before the whole congregation, much to their joy:

> He pronounced the true faith with splendid confidence, and they all snatched him up into *their heart*. They snatched him by loving and rejoicing; those were the hands of them that snatched him up.[57]

He must literally enter within the external walls of the church to be baptized by literal water, but the hands by which he is snatched up into the heart of the church are not literal and external but consist in the love and joy of many souls acting as one. It is surely not by accident that Augustine uses the singular to speak of the heart into which Victorinus is snatched, as if within the external walls of the church there is only one inward heart. Walls do not literally make Christians, nor does water or any other external sign, but "those who are to approach Your grace"[58] must literally go there where the baptismal water is, in order to be joined in heart to the spiritual Body of Christ. So although water, walls, and words have no power to change the soul, they can mark the inward place where the power of grace that does change the soul is to be found. If it is appropriate to speak of efficacious "means of grace" in Augustine at all, then the phrase must refer to this community of souls, loving and rejoicing, which takes Victorinus to its heart.

Puzzles in *Confessions* 8

Augustine too hesitates to get baptized, and it is important to see that he ascribes his hesitation to the same root cause as Victorinus's hesitation. In fact, Augustine says, Simplicianus tells Victorinus's story in order to "exhort me to the humility of Christ"[59] and attributes Victorinus's hesitation to his embarrassment at "the sacraments of the humility of Your Word."[60] The latter phrase, with its reference to sacraments in the plural, evidently includes not only baptism but catechesis, which Augustine here calls "the first sacraments of instruction."[61] So both the act of baptism itself and the catechetical instruction by which one is prepared for it signify the humility of the Word incarnate. To be baptized is to imitate the divine humility that the catechumens are to learn from the doctrine of the Incarnation. They are to become more like the eternal Son of God who humbled himself to assume human lowliness, mortality, and suffering. It takes humility for any man "to become a child of your Christ, *an infant of your font,* his neck subjected to the yoke of humility and his conquered brow to the reproach of the cross."[62] Since in ancient Latin church usage the newly baptized are called "infants" (*infantes*) because of their newborn life in Christ, this passage connects the yoke of humility not only to the way of the cross but also to baptism itself, the sacrament of regeneration that is the sacrament of humility as well.

Augustine's explanation of his hesitation to get baptized is summed up in one of the most wonderful sentences he ever wrote: "I did not humbly hold on to my humble God Jesus."[63] This does not mean he refused to believe in Christ but rather points to the moral failing that made it impossible for him to understand the orthodox doctrine of the Incarnation.[64] Like any good Platonist, young Augustine had no trouble believing in the divinity of the Word. But the humility of the Word made flesh is much harder to swallow, especially if your aim is to see God as eternal Truth, far above all temporal things. Augustine compares the pagan Platonists to Moses, glimpsing the promised land from afar while standing on a mountaintop of human intellectual achievement. Their error lay in being unwilling to descend from this eminence to the lowly road (*via*) they must take if they are ever to arrive at the homeland (*patriam*) they have glimpsed.[65] They had indeed caught sight of Christ as the Word of God on high, but they were above joining Christ as man below. Augustine blames himself for sharing this intellectual pride, which in his case means that he hung back from being baptized. For until he was willing to submit to being instructed by the authority of the Christian sacraments, it seems he could not accept the orthodox doctrine that Christ is not just the greatest of wise men but the Word itself in the flesh, nothing less than "Truth in person" (*persona veritatis*).[66] Though already a believer, Augustine had much to learn about Christ that he could not accept until he descended to a road he found beneath him, the path of Christian humility that is taken by Christ's Body, the church.

The narrative in *Confessions* 8 is therefore not about how Augustine decided to believe in Christ for the first time[67] but about how he, like Victorinus, decided to become a fully faithful Christian by joining Christ's Body through baptism. After blaming his own lack of humility at the end of *Confessions* 7, then telling the story of Victorinus learning humility at the beginning of *Confessions* 8, Augustine is preparing us to see the rest of book 8 as the story of how he too learned humility so as to accept baptism. Yet on the face of it the story seems to be all about overcoming lust, not learning humility. This leads to one of the great puzzles in Augustine's autobiography: why is his conversion narrative so tied up with his struggle against sexual indulgence? Must he must give up sex in order to become a Christian? One of his friends, in fact, is unwilling to become a Christian except as a celibate,[68] but Augustine himself knows better and is aware that "the apostle did not forbid me to marry."[69] One does not have to be celibate to be baptized!

This in fact is the key to the puzzle. We must ask: since it is perfectly obvious that celibacy is not required for baptism, what does Augustine actually want celibacy for? As soon as that question comes into focus, the answer is clear enough from the text. The love of eternal Wisdom that burned in his heart ever since reading Cicero's *Hortensius* had always been in conflict with Augustine's worldly ambitions, his desire for wealth, power, and marriage, and nothing held him on this secular path more effectively than his need for a woman.[70] The desire for a life devoted to philosophy, that is, to the pursuit of wisdom,[71] is his overarching motivation, and sheer sexual need is the greatest obstacle to the life he wants. He considers examples of married men who have lived the philosophical life,[72] but even at the time he knows he is deceiving himself: his sexuality is not manageable but incontinent, a vicious disorder in his soul that prevents him from loving Wisdom with his whole heart, mind, and soul. For the true philosopher, being a lover of eternal Wisdom, is as Plato says, a lover of God.[73] Philosophy in this Platonic sense is what Christians call charity, which requires a purity of heart and sexual continence that young Augustine simply does not have.

By Augustine's own account, therefore, he needs celibacy not in order to become a Christian but in order to become a philosopher. What he discovers in book 8 is that he cannot become a philosopher without first becoming a Christian—not just someone who believes in Christ but a full member of Christ's Body through baptism. Perhaps it is less a discovery than the confirmation of a long-dreaded suspicion. If he is ever to make progress on the road to what he had glimpsed from afar in the Platonist inner vision of *Confessions* 7, he needs a different kind of community from the philosophical friendships he had been cultivating so far. He had actually been planning to establish a community of like-minded Christian philosophers, but his need for a woman stood in the way.[74] What becomes clear over the course of the anguished inner struggle in *Confessions* 8 is that he cannot in any effective way engage in the philosophical pursuit of eternal Wisdom apart from the much larger community of the Catholic church, including all the uneducated, hidebound, and authoritarian people like his mother whom he had spent most of his adult life trying to escape. Only in this community will he find grace to refashion the love of his heart so that he not only wishes to put God before his sexual desires but can actually do it.

This is the lesson of the story of Anthony, the desert monk, which weaves in and out of book 8. After hearing how Anthony's story affected others, Augustine turns to his friend Alypius and gives voice to its effect on himself:

> "What's wrong with us? What's this you hear? The unlearned rise up
> and snatch heaven, and we with our learning—look how we wallow
> in flesh and blood! Just because they have gone before us, is it a
> shame to follow—and not a shame not even to follow?"[75]

His learned Christian friends are not enough. He needs to be in the same community as that unlearned man Anthony who is so far ahead of him on the road to the contemplation of divine things. A momentous historical development lies here: the heirs of the ideal of philosophical contemplation articulated so powerfully by Plato, Aristotle, and Plotinus will for many centuries be Christian monks. The inner agonies of Augustine's conversion narrative are poised near the beginning of this historical development, for what he discovers after turning inward to see God (as he is admonished to do by the books of the Platonists in *Confessions* 7) is that he cannot hope to secure this vision without being baptized (as he is admonished to do by the book of Paul in *Confessions* 8). Outside the church there is no possibility of his being freed from sexual incontinence so as to seek eternal Wisdom with his whole heart, mind, and will. Scripture teaches that "no one can be continent unless You give it"[76] and in

Confessions 8 Augustine finally admits to himself that he cannot expect to receive the gift of continence outside the unique community in which splendidly continent men like Anthony are rising up to snatch heaven, the community called the Catholic church.

So it turns out Augustine does not need to be celibate in order to be a baptized, but needs to be baptized in order to be celibate. This humiliating discovery is what finally leads him to the sacrament of the humility of Christ. It is pride not lust that keeps him from baptism, and indeed it is the shamed discovery of the intractability of his lust that finally humiliates him enough to overcome his pride. In *Confessions* 8 he at last gives in to the realization, of which he had been reminding us ever since book 1,[77] that baptism is the cure for sexual incontinence. So the whole of *Confessions* 8 really is about Augustine learning humility, just as we should expect from the end of *Confessions* 7. We ought therefore to read *Confessions* 8 not as a successful attempt to overcome lust before getting baptized, but as an unsuccessful struggle against lust that is resolved only *as a result of* the decision he makes to get baptized, in obedience to the admonition to "put on Christ" which he reads in Paul.

That decision is immediately followed by "a kind of light of security poured into my heart"[78] anticipating the assurance he feels when he is baptized and "the anxiety of the life that was past fled from us."[79] The decision takes the form of a dramatic change of will, not a conversion to faith in Christ but a conversion in the specifically Platonist sense of the heart being turned from temporal to eternal goods: "For You turned [*convertisti*] me to Yourself, so that I sought neither wife nor any other hope of this world, standing on the rule of faith."[80] The rule of faith here is not a newfound belief in Christ but the orthodox teaching of the Catholic church, which like Victorinus he will learn as he is "steeped in the first sacraments of instruction,"[81] the catechetical teaching to which he will commit himself in preparation for baptism. And this in turn will lead to the correction of the doctrinal errors described at the end of *Confessions* 7.

So *Confessions* 8 does not tell of Augustine's coming to faith in Christ (which had happened long before) nor of his being born again as a Christian (which happens afterward, in baptism). It does, however, contain an important moment of conversion, part of the ongoing turn from love of temporal goods to love of God that takes up his whole life but undergoes here the particularly crucial transition from the life under Law (*sub lege*) to the life under grace (*sub gratia*).[82] It is moreover a conversion to God that coincides with a conversion to the church, turning to the one by deciding he must join the other. This inward conversion to the communion of the church, as we shall see, is as necessary to salvation as baptism itself.[83] So it is not surprising that many readers see this moment, rather than his becoming a believer (earlier) or a born-again Christian (later, in baptism), as the decisive turning point in Augustine's life. After all, this story does tell of the deepest change we ever hear about in Augustine's will, the moment when the grace of God most decisively transforms his life from the inside. If inner experience is what makes Christians, then this moment is more important than when he comes to faith or baptism.

But a more accurate account of Augustine's priorities would not put so much emphasis on what happens in one moment.[84] It is better to say that for Augustine conversion, the turning of the will toward God that is the journey of a whole lifetime, is what Christian faith and baptism are for. Since the inner vision of God described by the books of the Platonists is the goal of the Christian life, a Platonist turn toward the eternal Good (as in the Allegory of the Cave) must be the fundamental direction of the whole Christian life, so that Christian faith and baptism have value precisely insofar as they lead us ultimately in that inner direction.[85] The light of eternal Wisdom is the goal, to which the divine humility of the man Jesus Christ is the way.

Two other puzzles remain about book 8 of the *Confessions*. First of all, if the conversion narrated in this book is the transition from life under Law to life under grace, then what new relation to grace is introduced by baptism? In what sense is baptism specifically a sacrament of grace? Here we can be guided again by the story of Victorinus. When Augustine runs to his mother at the end of book 8 to tell her what has happened within him, it is like Victorinus coming to Simplicianus to say: "Let us go in the church; I want to become a Christian." The crucial change of individual will has occurred but not the crucial change of the soul, for the latter is irreducibly social: he must be snatched up by other souls and united with the heart of the church by their love. In his anti-Donatist works, as we shall see, Augustine makes a point of locating the efficacy of grace in this love and unity.[86] The link between the conversion of *Confessions* 8 and the grace of baptism is that his will was able to turn so decisively away from the temporal goods of wife, money, and honors only by giving in and deciding to accept the humble sacrament of baptism, through which alone he enters within the walls of this community so as to be taken to its heart. The life under grace (*sub gratia*) that begins in *Confessions* 8 is not yet life as a baptized Christian, but it is inseparable from the will to begin that life. The content of Augustine's conversion, that *to which* he is converted, cannot be adequately described without mentioning the church and its sacrament of regeneration. The turn to God and the turn to join the church in baptism are one conversion of the will, one charity, one work of grace.

Secondly, there is the puzzle of what Augustine finds so humiliating about baptism. Times have changed since Victorinus's day, and Augustine is not in the position of having to cultivate the patronage of a largely pagan elite. If anything, one suspects that becoming a baptized Catholic at this time would further his career. So what is he ashamed of? Evidently it is the same thing that puts him to shame in Anthony. Until he learns to admire the likes of this unlettered monk, he hesitates to be bound in fellowship with all the ignorant Catholics who have nothing like a good liberal arts education, much less a taste for the sophisticated dialectical inquiries of Platonist philosophy. As the early books of the *Confessions* make clear, he has always known he is smarter than these people—has known it ever since he was a brilliant and intellectually competitive young man who knew how to argue circles around hometown Catholics.[87] He clearly has deep-seated hesitations about submitting his mind to the external authority of what we now call "the institutional church" or what later Augustinians will call the "visible church." That is precisely why the crucial epistemological issue in his earliest writings, just before and after his baptism, is the relation between authority and reason.[88] Judging not by *Confessions* 8 but by the writings he composed around the time of his baptism, the reason he can now submit to becoming "an infant at the font" is because he has figured out how to assign authority a place in the search for understanding of God.

In the years immediately after his baptism he is not in fact as humble about the role of authority as he would later be. The way of reason, he says, is for those eager to find the truth, passing from belief to understanding,[89] whereas the way of authority is for those too busy, too lazy, or simply incapable of taking the way of reason, with its commitment to prolonged and circuitous dialectic.[90] Authority is safer and easier, like staying in the shade rather than risking the dazzling light of truth.[91] Only those who exercise their minds in the liberal disciplines can expect to enjoy the vision of God in this life,[92] whereas those who live "by authority alone" without a liberal education must wait until "they leave this body" in order to be "liberated with greater ease or difficulty depending on how well or badly they have lived."[93] This is the familiar elitist framework of Platonist philosophy, contrasting the educated few and the uneducated many[94] (which of course corresponds quite accurately to the social world of antiquity) now applied to the way the soul comes to God even in the church. But the framework already shows signs of strain in Augustine's earliest writings, where he must make room for the philosophical insights of his unlearned mother.[95] And it will crack altogether when the great shift takes place through which he too becomes one of the many, the "little ones" of Christ who need to be fed with the milk of the Word incarnate.[96]

It seems fair to say that it took some years for the humility of Christ to grow on Augustine even after he was baptized. Indeed in the writings around the time of his baptism, humility is nothing like the prominent theme it is in the *Confessions*. Lack of humility is evidently his later, retrospective explanation of the inner obstacle to his baptism—and hence his mature understanding of what was at stake in his thinking about authority and reason in that earlier time. On the other hand, the early programmatic contrast of authority and reason, though not so prominent later, does persist in Augustine's thought long enough to have an important role in the *Confessions*. It is used explicitly to explain the value of Ambrose's preaching[97] and also (I would suggest) implicitly structures the books that bring the autobiographical portion of the *Confessions* to a close. Book 7 is related to book 8 as reason is to authority: in the one we have the great discovery of reason, the inner vision of God as eternal Truth and Love; in the other we have the crucial surrender to the external authority of the Catholic church. And in book 9 we have a dramatization of the ultimate unity of reason and authority when Augustine and Monica, the man of reason and the woman of authority, catch sight of eternal Wisdom together. The mother-and-child reunion is also the union of authority and reason. They both aim to see the same thing in the end, and for one shared moment at Ostia they join in touching it.

Public Inner Wisdom

How is it that Augustine and his mother can see God together? The question is important because Augustine clearly presents the scene at Ostia as a harbinger of eternal life. The end of the invisible sacrifice of the church is for the whole city of God to cling in holy fellowship (*sancta societate*) to the same divine Wisdom that these two touch together for a moment in this life. At the culmination of the vision Augustine shifts to the metaphor of touch to indicate that this is just a glimpse, a brush of the eye, as it were, against a light too dazzling to bear. (The same shift from visual to tactile metaphor occurs in his description of the insights he aims for in his preaching, when he expects his audience "to arrive at a kind of spiritual contact with the immutable Light, but not to have strength enough to bear the sight of it.")[98] As in other descriptions of intellectual vision in the *Confessions*, what is required is a movement in then up,[99] ascending in the mind "yet more inwardly" (*interius*) beyond earth and heaven and finally above the mind itself so as to "touch the region of unfailing richness" where Truth is the soul's food and Wisdom is life itself, in an eternal plenitude of being that knows no "has been" or "will be" but only "is." And then:

> *while we were speaking* and gaping at her, we *touched her just a little* [*attingimus eam modice*] with the whole strength of the heart; and we

> sighed and left behind the first fruits of the spirit tied there, and we
> returned to the noise of our mouth, where a word has both a be-
> ginning and an end—and what resemblance is that to Your Word,
> our Lord, which "remains in itself" without growing old and yet
> "renews all things"?[100]

The Wisdom they touch here is the eternal Word of God, the second person of
the Trinity, but evidently not the incarnate Christ, who is external and human,
for this is feminine like the Latin *sapientia,* not masculine like the man Jesus.
The feminine beauty of Wisdom we long and sigh for is a keynote of Augustine's concept of the shared vision uniting the city of God.[101]

For it is not as if Monica and Augustine have two private visions of their
own, simultaneously. The vision at Ostia unites them. Only the return of their
attention to the ordinary words coming out of their mouths brings them back
to the separate thoughts they have while in their opaque mortal flesh. In
portraying this united and uniting vision, the author of the *Confessions* clearly
means to hint at the tie that will bind these two forever together with the whole
city of God. It is a foretaste of the eternal union of all the blessed and points
also to a unity that Augustine believes is already present in the hidden depths
of the self, there in the same inward heart to which Victorinus is united in
baptism. Ultimately the inner space where God is seen is the same for everyone, a holy place or temple we all inhabit together.[102] For Augustine this is
not just a striking metaphor or an exceptional mystic experience (the very odd
experience of a mystical vision in tandem) but rather a glimpse of what has
always been present in the soul and of the social beatitude this inner presence
makes possible. Unless we have some such inner dimension in common
Augustine's concept of the church makes no sense, nor therefore his doctrine
of grace and sacraments.

In fact it took some ingenuity for Augustine to invent the now-familiar
idea of a *private* inner space, in contrast to the concept of a shared inner space
that was already available to him in Plotinus. The latter notion follows inevitably from the Plotinian premises underlying Augustine's concept of inner
vision. We can see this in Augustine's most elaborate depiction of the inner
world, which comes in the next book of the *Confessions.* The mind or heart is a
vast inner world containing its own kind of mountains and seas and sky, which
are literally the images of all these things contained in memory (this is the
Augustinian invention: memory as a private inner world into which we can
enter, not just a mental record we can consult).[103] But memory also contains
the intelligible truths of the liberal arts, which are present within our minds
not merely as images but in themselves—as the thing itself, *res ipsa.*[104] Like-

wise God, the Truth which makes all else true, is present himself in human memory, not as a mere image.[105] Unlike our mental pictures of sensible things, where my mental images of sea and sky are clearly something different from yours, each of these eternal things is one and the same for all of us. As there is only one God, there is also only one eternal Truth and Wisdom and Goodness, only one unchanging truth about two plus two equaling four, and so on. To have these things in remembrance is to have within the inner space of the self something common to all souls, not a private individual thought.

In fact the most important literary precursor to the descriptions of inner ascent in the *Confessions* portrays a glimpse of eternal Wisdom taking place in something like a public inner space. Examining this precursor will afford us a clear view of the Platonist psychology underlying Augustine's description of the vision at Ostia.[106] So we turn to the philosophical dialogue between Augustine and his friend Evodius in the second book of *On Free Choice*, completed some five to ten years before the *Confessions*. It is Augustine's first detailed description of a movement in then up, ascending from the lowest powers of the soul to the intellect, and then looking above the mutable intellect to the immutable Truth. Early in the process there is a long investigation of the faculty of the soul which Augustine calls the inner sense but which Aristotle had called the common sense.[107] This is the power of comparing the messages of two different senses such as vision and touch, as for example when we see a square block and then pick it up in our hands and feel that it is square. Despite its name, Augustine does not suggest that the inner sense operates in an inner space of its own. It is a function of the senses, not of reason—a lower faculty that we have in common with other animals. Yet it does include a primitive reflective ability to sense that one is sensing (*se sentire sentiret*)[108] and thus forms the basis of the animal sentience that we share with the irrational souls of the beasts.

The main purpose of Augustine's discussion of the inner sense is to set up the comparison that is his primary interest in the book: between those senses whose objects are shared and public, and those whose objects become a kind of private property. While many different people can see and hear exactly the same thing together, they cannot smell and taste exactly the same thing, because each of them must take in some portion of the object, changing it into something that is part of their own body and therefore cannot be shared with others.[109] The sense of touch is more like seeing and hearing in this regard, because it does not involve consuming the object and because two people can feel the same object together, although not the same part of it at the same time.[110] The basic contrast is between senses that make an object my own, as if it were private property (*proprium . . . et quasi privatum*) and senses that leave the object unchanged as a common possession, available to all and public (*commune . . . et quasi publicum*).[111]

As always for Platonist psychology, the crucial juncture in this investigation is the transition from sense to reason. The key question at this juncture is whether the perception of reason is more like seeing than like tasting, that is, "whether something can be found which all reasoners can see in common by means of reason or mind, since what is seen is present [*praesto*] to all, not changed into what can be used by those to whom it is present like food or drink, but remaining uncorrupted and whole whether they see it or not."[112] The first example that comes to mind is "the reason and truth of number, which is present to all reasoners . . . and common to me and all who think," as Evodius puts it.[113] Everybody sees these truths by the same "inner light,"[114] which consists of "inner rules of truth which we discern in common."[115] The *inner* here is clearly not private, as if it were the exclusive possession of an individual soul. Truth is seen in "a light that is in a marvelous way both hidden and public,"[116] which is to say, it is hidden from our senses but publicly available to all who reason.

Moreover, in the Neopythagorean Platonism that Augustine develops here, the truth of numbers is no trivial thing to have in common, but is consubstantial with Wisdom herself.[117] This means Wisdom too is "present in common to all."[118] It is not as if two different wise men have two different wisdoms. To be wise necessarily means to participate in one and the same divine Wisdom. So perceiving Wisdom is like seeing or hearing, not tasting or smelling:

> None of her food is torn up into parts; you drink nothing of her that I can't. For you don't change anything of hers from something common to something privately yours; what you get from her remains whole for me. . . . For nothing of her ever becomes the property of one or several, but the whole of her is common to all together.[119]

Consequently, Wisdom is both deep within the self and common property, shared by all yet undivided and always whole. For she can only be incorruptibly one, not many.

> So we have what we can all enjoy equally and in common: there is no shortage or deficiency in her. All her lovers can have her without being jealous; she is common to all and chaste for each individual. No one says to anyone else: "Get back so I can get to her" or "Hands off, so I can get a hug too." Everybody can cling to the same one and touch her.[120]

This conception of Wisdom is clearly in back of the shared vision by which Augustine and Monica touch Wisdom together at Ostia. To seek this vision is to be drawn together by a love that cannot be jealous, because it never has to compete or fight over something that is scarce or insufficient or divisible. To use Boethius's famous image, it means being drawn ever closer to the still point at the center of the turning world,[121] and therefore also closer to one another.

But Boethius's image comes much later than Augustine, and it does not explain the most important feature of the peculiar inwardness of *On Free Choice*, book 2. Since this is Augustine, it is not surprising that the eternal Wisdom that is common to all calls our souls away from external things and back into ourselves.[122] The peculiarity is that all of us can turn to look within ourselves and see the same thing. The underlying picture here is not that of the modern private inner self but more like an image found in Plotinus: we should imagine a huge sphere with many faces on the outside, all looking outward. Those faces are our individual souls, divided from one another. But if we turn into the inside and look with the eye of the mind, we will see inner truths that are common to all. And if two souls turn together they can see one and the same thing, and perhaps even touch that which is at the very center of all.[123] Some such Plotinian notion of common inner space must be at the bottom of Augustine's description of a divine Wisdom that is both inner and public.

We can confirm this by thinking through the implications of this Plotinian picture for Augustine's psychology and theology. First of all, if the inner space of the soul is common to all souls, then at root all souls are one. This is Plotinus's explicit teaching, and a consequence that Augustine himself affirms once in an early work, where he says he would find it ridiculous to say without qualification that there are many souls.[124] Some sort of inner unity of souls is a necessary consequence of any serious form of Neoplatonism, and as we shall see in the next chapter, it has theological implications that play an important role in Augustine's conception of original sin (unity in Adam), the church (unity in Christ), and the city of God (ultimate unity of all the blessed, both human and angelic). Yet it is not an accident that he never again explicitly refers to the notion that all souls are ontologically one, and that even in this passage he mentions it only briefly, as a difficult topic about which he is clearly not yet ready to declare his views at any length.[125] We can see the likely source of this hesitation by noting a second implication of the Plotinian picture: the inner space is not only one but divine. If what we see by turning inward is not private images but public truth, then the inner space in which we see it can be nothing less than the unchanging realm of Platonic Forms which Platonists call the intelligible world, all contained (Plotinus insists) in the divine Mind itself, the *Nous* or (to speak Latin) the divine intellect, which is the philo-sophical name Augustine gives to the second person of the Trinity in his early explanations of the Christian mysteries.[126] What we see by turning inward, then, if we are consistent about applying this Plotinian picture to Christian doctrine, is nothing less than the eternal Wisdom that is Christ, who is also the divine Intellect containing all intelligible Forms or (in Augustine's formulation in *On Free Choice*) "the immutable Truth containing all that is immutably true."[127]

The problem is that if the shared inner space of the soul is the divine intellect or intelligible world, then inwardly we are all God. In his very earliest writings, Augustine seems to be toying with some such notion, as if there were an immutable element in the soul so that turning inward and turning to God were really the same thing, just as in Plotinus. We see this for instance in the *first* book of *On Free Choice*, where we are to love eternal things by loving the Good Will in us, which can only mean this Good Will is eternal and divine, equivalent to Christ as the Virtue of God.[128] A similar approach to Christ as the Wisdom of God had been at the heart of his early argument for the immate-riality of the soul in the *Soliloquies* and its immediate sequel, *On the Immortality of the Soul*.[129] But by the time he writes the *second* book of *On Free Choice* things have radically changed. This book makes a sharp, clear distinction between the soul and God, in terms that will ever afterward be characteristic of Augustine: God is immutable, the soul is mutable, and therefore the soul must always look above itself to see God.[130] We see this insistence in the *Confessions* and else-where: Augustine frequently marks the distinction between God and the soul by distinguishing the immutable from the mutable. Later Christian theology will typically think first of the Creator/creature distinction here, and Augustine is quite clear that the two distinctions are equivalent,[131] but it is usually of the immutable/mutable distinction that he thinks first, for he typically arrives at the distinction between God and the soul by thinking not about the doctrine of creation but about the soul's search for happiness, its ascent to Wisdom, which must be accompanied by the realization that the Wisdom sought is immutable, whereas the unhappy soul that seeks it is not.

By insisting that these two distinctions (immutable/mutable and Creator/creature) coincide, Augustine has a powerful Platonist way of affirming one of the great, nonnegotiable commitments of Christian orthodoxy, stemming from the Nicene doctrine of the Trinity itself. The whole point of Nicaea is lost without an exhaustive distinction between Creator and creature, for the point is that the eternal Word belongs on the Creator side of this ontological divide, not in some third category between Creator and creature. None of this is lost on the mature Augustine, which is why he cannot accept Plotinus's picture of a shared inner space without modification. He retains the Plotinian language of inward turn but rejects the implication that the inner space of the soul is divine. This accounts, I think, for the absence in *On Free Choice,* book 2, of any explicit attempt to picture the inner space in which Wisdom is seen. Augustine is convinced that Plotinus is right about things seen by the mind being common to all souls and that our need to turn inward to find them, but he cannot accept the Plotinian picture of a common inner space that is divine. When a picture of inner space does turn up in Augustine, it is his own new invention, the private inner space of memory containing sensible images that are not common property of many souls. Yet within this inner space the soul can also look above itself at what transcends the soul: the eternal Wisdom and Truth of God. The fact that this divine Wisdom above the soul is still common to us all is what Augustine affirms by writing the story of the vision at Ostia.

Shared Insight and Love's Union

"Mystical experience" does not seem the best term to describe the vision at Ostia. This modern term is a label for events of profound, life-changing importance, not episodes that are recorded once but seem to have no other discernible impact on a person's life or thinking. Augustine never wrote about the Ostia experience before or after the *Confessions,* never reflected on it in any of his other writings or built anything on it in any of his other thinking. It has an important role to play in the story he tells about returning to the church of his mother, and that is all. That return is in fact far more important, from an Augustinian perspective, than any "mystical experience" could be. But that leaves us still in need of a label, some category in which to place this odd narrative, as well as some group of similar human experiences with which to compare it.

First of all, of course, we should compare it to the other descriptions of inner ascent in the *Confessions:* the movements "in then up" in book 7 and the more elaborate inner ascent in book 10. Such comparison leads to an interesting discovery about literary genre. The two descriptions of inner ascent in *Confessions* 7 are presented almost as narratives, as if they told of particular events in Augustine's life, whereas *Confessions* 10 is a general description of the structure of the soul and how anyone may ascend: turning away from outward things to look at the soul, moving from lower to higher powers of the soul until one reaches the mind, then using the mind itself to look above the mutable mind and see God as immutable Wisdom, Truth, Love, or Beauty (there are many terms available, and they can be arranged in numerous patterns, most of them trinitarian). This general description of the ascent of the soul was first developed at length in *On Free Choice,* book 2, without an explicit picture of inner space, as we have just seen in the previous section. If we use these general descriptions (in *On Free Choice* 2 and *Confessions* 10) to interpret the more narrative-like descriptions in *Confessions* 7 and 9 (including Ostia) it is possible to suggest that the latter need not portray unique episodes in Augustine's life, as if they were modern "mystical experiences," but rather illustrate what is a recurrent possibility for the human mind in its relation to God, as understood by ancient Platonism.

I have suggested in earlier work that the best modern term to describe this recurrent possibility is simply "insight."[132] If God is, as the second book of *On Free Choice* puts it, "the immutable Truth containing all that is immutably true"[133]—and all the more so if, as the same book puts it, the truth of numbers is consubstantial with eternal Wisdom[134]—then every time we have an insight about some unchanging truth, for example in mathematics, our minds are catching a glimpse of God. In that case it is not so odd that two people could catch sight of God together. This is not a tandem mystical experience but a moment of shared insight, of looking together at the same inner but public truth. This would also explain how it could all happen *while they were talking,* as Augustine explicitly tells us. They do not go into some sort of simultaneous trance; they are having a conversation. Their experience works exactly as we should expect from the semiotics and epistemology of the treatise *On the Teacher.* Their words serve as admonitions directing each other to look more inwardly, away from words and all created things, and by the grace of God they succeed in looking together at the one true Wisdom at the same time, just touching her together with their mental gaze.

The Ostia experience, interpreted in these Augustinian terms, is a conversation about divine Wisdom that brought mother and son together in the joy of shared insight, a foretaste of the ultimate beatitude of beholding divine Truth forever, very much like the philosophical conversation between Augustine and Evodius in *On Free Choice,* where the joy of insight shared by the two friends is explicitly called "the happy life."[135] Augustine could very well have had many such conversations with his mother about the life to come, conversations that were lovely and encouraging but not particularly remarkable, and the narrative in the *Confessions* might not record one specific event but rather conflate a whole series of these conversations, without distorting the essential truth that Augustine is trying to convey. Alternatively, it is certainly possible that Augustine had one particular conversation in mind; the point is that for understanding the narrative in *Confessions* 9 it does not much matter which alternative makes the most accurate history. For if we do interpret the Ostia narrative in light of the treatises *On Free Choice* and *On the Teacher*, as I am suggesting here, then understanding the conceptual structure of the text is much more important than trying to recover the original experience, at least if we want to learn the lesson that Augustine is trying to teach us in his writing. There may not have been any one single originating experience, and the truth of Augustine's text is none the worse for that. For the point of the narrative is not to record a mystical experience but to show us something about how minds can see God together, illustrated by Augustine's life with his mother and confirming his return to the Catholic church as the one social location where such shared inner vision has the prospect of becoming eternal life.

The crucial question for Augustine's theology of grace and sacraments is how this shared vision works if all souls are not one in the robust Plotinian sense of having a single common inner space. I earlier adopted a Boethian image to speak of souls drawing closer to the still center of the turning world, because to love, in Augustine, is to be drawn closer to what is loved, to seek and perhaps to find unity with it. Love is both a force of attraction and a unitive power, like gravity[136] and like glue.[137] Only love can unite souls, producing friendship by making one soul out of two[138] and producing community by joining a multitude of souls in love for the same thing. In contrast to the Plotinian notion of the intrinsic ontological unity of all souls, love seeks a unity that may not yet exist and results in a unity that is dependent on the will of the souls involved. Moreover, loves that are less than good can produce unities of soul that are less than good, cities and communities that are quite other than the city of God.

Augustine's notion of an inner unity of souls that is not an ontological given but an outgrowth of love forms the basis for a new kind of social theory, which he develops at length in *City of God*. By the definition he gives in the *City of God*, to call many persons one people or community is to say they are "a group of many rational beings brought together [*sociatus*] by shared agreement in the things it loves."[139] This social unity involves but is not the same thing as friendship, in which two souls are united by loving one another directly. An analogy Augustine uses elsewhere is a group of people brought together by love for a particular actor (like a modern fan club).[140] Their love for him joins them at heart; they stimulate each other's love, feed and inflame it, and draw in others to share it. The city of God is as it were God's fan club: angels and rational souls brought together by love for God, feeding one another's love and being drawn to each other in the act of being drawn to God. And the church is the human portion of that city, brought together in union with Jesus Christ, who "was made human for us so that he might be the Head of the whole church as of his whole Body."[141]

Words and Common Inquiry

In such a city we should expect to find Ostia experiences happening all the time, and I think if we look at Augustine's life and work through Augustinian eyes, we will see that they do. Consider his sermons.[142] Augustine is the kind of brilliant teacher who can get a large audience to join him in inquiry, luring them into a difficult intellectual problem so that they actively share the excitement of seeking a solution. "We are all to hope that he will open to those who knock," he tells his audience at the beginning of one sermon, adapting a favorite biblical saying ("knock and the door shall be opened," Matt. 7:7) as a metaphor for inquiry, for the heart's knocking at God himself, in effect asking the inner teacher for illumination. "I knock by the attention of my heart [*intentione cordis*] at the Lord God, that he may deign to reveal this mystery to us," he says, then adds, "knock with me . . . by the attention of your hearing [*intentione audiendi*] . . . and the humility of praying for me."[143] Like Plato,[144] Augustine insists on praying before he inquires into divine things, and he therefore asks his audience to pray for the divine help needed by both speaker ("that I may see what to say")[145] and hearers ("God helping the attention of your prayers and the preparation of your hearts").[146] But Augustine also suggests that the very attention of his audience helps him ("if I can say what I want, *with the help of your attention* and your prayers, I think whoever understands will rejoice").[147] Clearly in Augustine's view preacher and audience need each other and owe each other their help. And it is striking that the most powerful expressions of this ethos of common inquiry come in sermons on the most abstruse doctrinal topics, as if the attentive souls of his listeners help Augustine's mind see farther when he labors with a difficult thought.

Perhaps nowhere is this clearer than in a sermon on the Trinity in which Augustine tries out key ideas that he would later use in his great treatise *On the Trinity*.[148] The text of this sermon gives us a particularly vivid sense of his interaction with his audience. Throughout the early portion of the sermon he checks to see that his audience is following him as he sets forth the inquiry (*quaestio*), noting for instance that "the inquiry proposed pleases you; God help that the solution also be pleasing."[149] He is probably responding to audience reaction here, as he clearly is later when he points out to them their own depth of understanding:

You have already cried out, because you have flown on ahead. Having been educated in the school of the heavenly teacher, like those who hear the reading and piously repeat it you're not ignorant of what follows.[150]

The heavenly teacher here is the inner teacher of the treatise *On the Teacher*, present invisibly in their hearts to lead their understanding forward as they fly ahead to see more than Augustine has yet said, like people who already know the next words of a familiar Bible passage being read aloud in church. The analogy is between the external words of the reading and the logical connections made clear by an inner light. Their prayers for the presence of divine help have been answered, as Augustine can tell by hearing their voices:

The Lord has been present [*aderit*] and I see that he is present; from your understanding I understand that he is present. From these voices [*vocibus*] of yours I notice how you have understood and I assume he will keep helping so that you may understand it all.[151]

Because of the presence of this divine inner teaching, Augustine can still affirm the most startling claim of the treatise *On the Teacher*, that we first know the thing signified by words before understanding the words themselves: "See then how confidently I commend to you what you have understood; I'm not inculcating something unknown, but commending once again what has already been grasped."[152] Even when hearing a sermon, the aim is not merely to believe what one is told but to see for oneself. So Augustine exhorts his audience: "I'm not asking you to believe me for what I am about to say. Don't accept it if you don't find it in yourself. So look carefully...."[153]

This heightened attention to audience reaction stems from the fact that this is one of Augustine's most intensely reflective sermons, in that he wants his audience not only to understand the topic but also to understand their own act of understanding. For he is about to suggest that by understanding their own understanding and memory and will, they can find an image of the Trinity itself. But first he must get them to see what a great thing understanding is. So he talks about what happens when they understand the words of his sermon:

And perhaps with my words someone whose mind is dazzled by the flashing radiance of Truth can say these words, "I said in my ecstasy..."[154]

This biblical language of ecstasy has often been the occasion of meditations on mystical or visionary experience, but here it simply refers to the insight of one who hears Augustine's words, understands a little, and is mentally stunned. The experience of understanding even a little about God feels like being beside oneself (the literal meaning of "ecstasy") as if for a moment one has transcended one's own humanity—not only turning away from bodily things but also looking beyond the thoughts of the soul—but then must return to one's own human self.

> And because this was done in ecstasy, snatched away from the senses of the body and snatched up in God, where he is somehow called back from God to man, he says, "I said in my ecstasy. I saw—I don't know what—in ecstasy, which I couldn't bear for long, and returned to mortal members and the many thoughts of mortals from the body that weighs down the soul."[155]

The return, however, is not simply to one's humanity but to fallen humanity subjected to death: to a body with mortal members and a soul plagued by the "thoughts of mortals" coming from "the body that is corrupted" which "weighs down the soul," as one of Augustine's favorite biblical passages puts it.[156] The "many thoughts" of the fallen soul contrast with the unity of vision it experiences in catching sight of divine Wisdom, ever so briefly. The vision is more than our mind's eye can bear because of its "sickness and weakness," as a result of which "the eye of its own mind cannot be adjusted to the light of the Wisdom of God."[157]

Augustine wants to affirm both that intellectual insight means catching sight of God and that for us fallen human beings this sight can only be fleeting and partial. Here is where the metaphor of touch is particularly helpful, allowing him to contrast "just touching" (attingere) God with "grasping fully" (comprehendere, which Augustine interprets literally as "grasping all around"). In a memorable aphorism from his most elaborate discussion of divine incomprehensibility, Augustine says, "Just touching God with the mind is great happiness, but comprehending him is entirely impossible."[158] The warning here, in this sermon on the Trinity, is perhaps even more famous:

> If you can comprehend it, you have comprehended something else instead of God. If it is as if you comprehended, then you have been deceived by your own thoughts. It is not him if you have comprehended, and if it is him then you have not comprehended.[159]

In contrast to the strong notion of divine incomprehensibility developed in the Eastern Orthodox tradition and adopted by the West in the Middle Ages, the idea here is not that God is too bright for the mind's eye to see, but rather that in this mortal life we catch only brief and partial glimpses of God, which we must not confuse with the fullness of vision that will be ours when we have hearts pure enough to gaze straight at God as the intelligible Sun. Once fully healed—which is to say, restored to its natural state—the eye of our minds will see God as naturally as the eyes in our body see bodily things, because "God is for the mind to understand, as a body is for the eyes to see."[160] But just as the eye of the body cannot fully grasp bodies because it is incapable of seeing them from all sides at once, so the eye of the mind cannot wholly wrap itself around God. That is what Augustine tells us he means by saying we cannot comprehend God.[161]

So Augustine's doctrine of divine incomprehensibility implies that it is as natural for us to see God with the mind as to see bodies with our eyes. Seeing God, for Augustine, is not a mystical experience but the normal functioning of the intellect, as he elsewhere explains: "The rational soul understands God. . . . For when the soul understands something which maintains itself always the same way, without doubt it understands God. This is Truth itself, to which the rational soul is joined by understanding it."[162] The soul's natural capacity to see and be united with God follows from the most basic features of Augustine's view of God and intellect: the task of the intellect is to see the truth, and God is "the immutable Truth containing all that is immutably true."[163]

With such a view of the power of the intellect, Augustine must be convinced that something like Ostia happens every time someone in the audience understands the significance of a good sermon. But this particular sermon is especially explicit about this, because he is about to ask his audience to turn inward with him to see their inner selves as an image of the Trinity. This inward turn is a shared inquiry:

> God made the human being in his image and likeness. Seek in
> yourself if maybe the image of the Trinity [i.e., yourself] has some
> vestige of the Trinity. . . . I am seeking—you all seek with me! Not I in
> you, but you in yourselves and I in me. Let us seek in common.[164]

The language here and elsewhere in the sermon is reminiscent of the inward turn in *Confessions* 7, as well as Augustine's amazement that people are not amazed at the inner self in *Confessions* 10[165] and the verbal silencing during the conversation at Ostia in *Confessions* 9 ("Let words be quiet, let tongues cease").[166] And when at the end Augustine sees that this inward turn has been successful, he thanks God:

> He has helped us, both in you and in me. Truly I tell your honors,
> I approached this discussion and suggestions with great trepidation.

I was afraid it might gladden the talented but bore those who were slower. But now I see you have listened attentively and understood quickly, not only grasping what I said but flying ahead to what I was going to say. Thanks be to the Lord![167]

The shared inquiry is itself a work of divine grace, for there is no catching sight of intelligible truths without the help of the inner teacher. What is both portrayed and enacted here is the community of those who are beginning to understand God together, a dramatization of the shared inner space in which God is seen.

The text we have is of course only the external record of this enactment. But even the words as Augustine spoke them were only external signs admonishing his audience to look within, just as we should expect from the treatise *On the Teacher*. They made a sound that promptly passed away, but what they suggested to the minds of those who heard them was something that lasts forever. Augustine wants his audience to be aware of this contrast between the fleeting sound of the voice and the understanding that remains in the mind, which he elsewhere he calls the inner word of the heart. He illustrates the contrast by referring to one of the key terms of the inquiry, spoken by a hypothetical interlocutor or perhaps shouted by a member of the audience (he switches here to "you" in the singular):

> Look, I didn't know what was in your mind; you showed me by saying, "memory" [*memoria*]. This word, this sound, this voice proceeded to my ears from your mind. For what memory is, you were silently thinking about, not saying. It was in you and had not yet come to me. So, in order that what was in you might be brought forth to me, you said this very name, *memoria*. I heard it: I heard the four syllables in the name, *memoria*. This is a name of four syllables, a voice; it sounded, proceeded to my ears, suggested [*insinuavit*] something to the mind. What sounded passed away; what was suggested and whence it was suggested, remained.[168]

External words are sounds that die away, but the inner word of the heart is an insight that lives on forever: so the one grows while the other diminishes, like Christ and John the Baptist in Augustine's sermon on "The Voice and the Word."[169] In Augustine's preaching one does not cling to external words that pass away but to the inward understanding that remains in the heart.

That is why our need for words and sacraments, authoritative teaching, and every other external sign of the life of the church is a kind of humiliation for Augustine. They are not what we are after, and for all their usefulness they are not what we want to be stuck with. The earlier, more Platonist theologians of the High Middle Ages saw this and argued that one of the main purposes of the divine institution of the sacraments was "for the sake of humiliation" (*propter humiliationem*).[170] We are made for an intellectual vision of God that transcends all bodily senses, but because we fell by the senses it is fitting that we also must rise beginning with the senses.[171] In later, more Aristotelian theologians this theme of humiliation is muted, because our need of sensible signs comes to seem natural to the human intellect, not a result of the fall.[172] The naturalness of our souls' need for external things is reinforced by the un-Augustinian notion that it is not natural for the intellect to see God—a notion conveyed to the West together with the robust notion of divine incomprehensibility developed in the writings of the Eastern Orthodox theologian known to the West as Denys (or Pseudo-Dionysius, as modern scholars call him).[173] With God thought to be beyond sight of the intellect, sensible signs take on a new weight and power in the sacramental theology of the Middle Ages, a power attributed later to the scriptural word by Luther and other Protestants. Thus all the great orthodox traditions (Roman Catholics with the sacraments, Protestants with the Scriptures, Eastern Orthodox with icons) make us dependent on the power of external things in a way Augustine thinks is both impossible and unnecessary, because for him the mind's power of vision is not strengthened by outward, sensible things but only by the inner gift of divine grace. For Augustine sensible signs, words and sacraments, like the walls of the church, do not confer this grace but rather are necessary outward marks of the community in which grace is inwardly at work. In that sense, and that sense alone, they are sacred signs of an invisible grace.

7

The Efficacy of the Church's Baptism

Against Donatists and Pelagians

Augustine's most extensive reflections on the sacraments are contained in his writings on baptism against the Donatists. His key weapon in these polemics is a sharp distinction between the validity of the sacrament and its salvific efficacy. The latter is found not in the external sacrament itself but in the inner unity and peace of the church, outside of which is no salvation. Therefore people who accept baptism insincerely or without charity in their hearts, separating themselves from the inner unity of the church, receive a valid, enduring sacred sign and are even born again, but gain no lasting forgiveness or salvation. In the case of infants, the inward power of baptism is the efficacy of the prayers of the church—not merely of the bishop or the child's parents or sponsors, but of the universal fellowship of all God's holy people brought together not in one place but in one charity of heart. Though baptism itself is not efficacious, it is necessary as an outward mark of this inward unity, which is why even infants are damned if they die without it. This becomes a key premise in Augustine's arguments against the Pelagians: all who do not belong to the unity of Christ's Body signified by baptism remain united in the mass of damnation generated by original sin in Adam. Baptized adults cannot be saved without conversion, which means turning in charity to the peace of the church. Moreover, they must persevere in this to the end, which explains why for Augustine baptism saves us only in hope, not in reality. Strikingly, Augustine ascribes no special efficacy to the human soul of Christ in the inner unity of his Body.

If there is anything like a concept of efficacious means of grace in Augustine's theology it is inward rather than external, based on the inner unity of the church rather than on external signs. In Augustine's ontology external things have no efficacy, and in his spirituality they are things we must pass beyond in order to cling to what is more inward, more real, and more lasting. That is why sacred signs signify something inward, pointing us away from themselves to where the real power of salvation is to be found. By Augustine's reckoning, it would defeat the purpose of word and sacrament to cling to them as means of salvation. Our souls cling to things by love, and what we are to love is God and other souls, in the unity of rational souls called the Body of Christ, the church. The grace of Christ, when it uses means at all, comes to us through that inner unity of love, not through external signs.

This is not to say the sacraments of the church may safely be despised. As a bishop Augustine is surrounded by sacred signs whose usefulness, even necessity, he must explain. Above all he must give an account of baptism, the sacrament of spiritual regeneration, the sign of the soul's passing from the death of sin to new life in Christ. Augustine will not attribute regenerating power to the water of baptism, but he does join the church in seeing it as a necessary condition of spiritual regeneration. It is like the door that leads within the walls of the church. The door has no power to open itself and let anyone in: the man outside knocks, and the people within open up and take him in among themselves, and there he is safe. Everything depends on passing through this door, but the door itself has no power to save. The action is in the knocking and in the opening up from within, which is the action of souls not bodies—for the knocking is love, and the taking in is love. In this action the grace of God is found, for without grace the action of love does not even begin, much less come to completion in salvation.

Validity without Efficacy

When Augustine returned to Africa from Italy, his thinking transformed by his encounter with the sophisticated Neoplatonist Christianity of Milan, he had to face a number of problems from which he had fled. Chief among these—and an especially pressing problem once he became bishop—was the Donatist schism. Two rival churches, both confessing the same creed and with virtually the same theology, claimed to be the one true church from which the other was in schism. Augustine belonged to the party that the rest of the church around the world and in posterity recognized as Catholic. Their opponents, the Donatists, had broken with them nearly a century before, regarding them as tainted by collaboration with the last great pagan persecution of the church under the emperor Diocletian in the first decade of the fourth century.[1] The Donatist church was an African phenomenon, and this put it at a disadvantage with regard to its claim to be the one true church, since it was out of communion with the church in the rest of the world. But it also afforded certain advantages insofar as the Donatists and their opponents shared a distinctively African theology to which the Donatists could give more consistent adherence.

In the traditional theology of the African church, the taint of collaboration with the enemies of the church was serious indeed. Until the massive theological intervention of Augustine, African Christians thought of baptism as fundamentally the act of a bishop, who through the act of baptism sanctifies and purifies the children of this world so that they receive new birth and forgiveness of sins in Christ.[2] In this theology the power of baptism depends on the bishop's holiness and purity, which is passed on to those he baptizes. This in turn depends on his belonging to the unity of the true church, a point stressed by Cyprian, the great third-century bishop of Carthage who was revered by Donatists and Catholics alike. It was Cyprian who taught in no uncertain terms that "there is no salvation outside the church,"[3] reflecting the strong sense of social boundaries in African Christianity, together with the danger of impurity contracted by crossing those boundaries.[4] As in most social environments that have inherited nothing from Augustine, impurity could be deadly even when contracted involuntarily—for getting dirty is not a matter of the will but of what you have been in contact with. Cyprian, for example, tells how baptized infants taken by their parents to a pagan festival lose, through no fault of their own, the new birth they gained in baptism.[5] The tale is meant to reinforce a simple and deeply ingrained parallel: purity and salvation are acquired within the church, impurity and damnation outside it. Likewise when a bishop collaborates with enemies of the church, he becomes impure and unholy, incapable of passing on purity and holiness to others. Those baptized by such a bishop remain unholy and un-Christian, not truly baptized at all, and any bishop he consecrates, indeed all his episcopal successors and all those in communion with him, contract the same taint of unholiness and the same inability to make anyone holy.[6]

Augustine brings new conceptual resources to the African Catholics' contention with the Donatists and in fact ends up creating a new theology of the church. With his Platonist inwardness he reconceives the unity of the church and the power of baptism. He needs to do this in order to overcome the disadvantage from which the Catholic practice of baptism suffers in the African debate. Following the bishop of Rome rather than Cyprian, the Catholics admitted repentant heretics and schismatics into the church without requiring them to be rebaptized if they had already received baptism among the heretics or schismatics. The Donatists on the contrary maintained Cyprian's doctrine and policy, which was more consistent with their overriding concern for the purity of the church: anyone baptized outside the true (i.e., Donatist) church has received no true Christian baptism but only impurity and guilt, and so must receive a proper baptism in order to be admitted into the church. This difference in practice put the Catholics at a serious disadvantage in the debate, for they seemed to be recognizing Donatist baptism as valid, which suggested that the power of salvation could be found within the Donatist church—a power the Donatists could quite consistently deny to their rivals. Any African with a serious concern for his salvation was bound to see Donatism as the safer bet.

So the immediate theological challenge for Augustine was to explain why Catholics did not rebaptize people who had received baptism outside the Catholic church, such as repentant Donatists returning to the Catholic fold. To do that he had to reaffirm the Cyprianic understanding of the unity of the church and its salvific power, but on different grounds from Cyprian's. His key move was to treat the unity of the church as inward, but the sacrament itself as outward. As a mere sign, the sacrament has no power of its own to accomplish what it signifies (as in the semiotics of On the Teacher)[7] and gets its significance from the agreement of will among those who use it rightly (as in the semiotics of On Christian Doctrine).[8] Hence when it is found outside the Catholic church it is devoid of salvific power but retains its meaning and holiness, which stem not from its external circumstances but from its ultimate origin in the Catholic communion. Even when performed by heretics and schismatics, Augustine contends, it is really the Catholic church's baptism, not theirs. Therefore he concludes that the Donatists "have legitimate baptism but do not have it legitimately."[9] Like the king's gold in the possession of thieves, it is precious in itself but bound to bring evil rather than good upon its possessors, earning them punishment rather than grace.[10]

What Augustine's use of the inner/outer contrast allows him to do, in effect, is to make a sharp distinction between the validity of the sacrament and its efficacy, or what in Augustine's terms are the sacrament itself, its holiness and legitimacy on the one side, and its inner effect, usefulness, or profit on the other. Being an external thing, the sacrament itself can be misused, stolen and possessed by people who have no right to it, but it is still there, still a sacrament, still holy and precious just like any other sacred external thing that can be stolen from the church. That is the sense in which baptism has validity even when performed by heretics and schismatics: it is still the one true holy baptism. What it does not have apart from the true church is salvific efficacy, and

in this regard Augustine can forcefully reaffirm Cyprian's teaching that there is
no salvation outside the church.[11] A valid sacrament does no good for its
possessor outside the unity of the church, for the profit of the sacrament is
received only by those who live in peace and charity with the true church. The
power of grace is not vested in the external sign but in the charity that brings
souls together in the unity and peace of the Body of Christ.

The Efficacy of Unity

Augustine's anti-Donatist theology explains the striking way he tells the story
of Victorinus's baptism in the *Confessions*, including the hints about the one
heart of the church to which Victorinus is joined.[12] Above all, the power to
forgive sins belongs not to an outward sign but to that one heart, the inner
unity and peace of the church, as Augustine explains in his treatise *On Baptism
against the Donatists:*

> The peace of the church dismisses sins, and alienation from the
> peace of the church retains them, not according to the will of human
> beings but according to the will of God and the prayers of holy
> and spiritual people [*orationes sanctorum spiritualium*], those who
> "judge all things and are judged by no one." The rock retains, the
> rock dismisses; the dove retains, the dove dismisses; unity retains,
> unity dismisses. But the peace of this unity is only in good peo-
> ple, those who are already spiritual or are making progress toward
> spiritual things. . . .[13]

The whole of Augustine's view of sacramental efficacy is packed into the dense
imagery of this passage, which will take some time to unpack. He is commenting on the power to forgive sins given to the disciples in the Gospel of
John, where Jesus says, "Receive the Holy Spirit. If you remit anyone's sins,
they are remitted, if you retain anyone's, they are retained."[14] The similar gift
of the keys to Peter in the Gospel of Matthew was the topic of Augustine's
previous chapter, which is why the image of the rock occurs here: Peter is the
rock on which the church is built, to whom is given the power to bind and loose
sins. According to Augustine he receives this power not simply for himself nor
for the ministers of the church but as a symbol of unity (*in typo unitatis*).[15] So
these two Gospel passages, which in later centuries were taken as instituting
the priest's spiritual power of forgiveness in the sacrament of penance, are
taken by Augustine as the basis for the power of forgiveness in baptism, which
belongs not to any minister or even any appointed group within the church but

to the whole communion of holy ones (i.e., of saints, *sanctorum*), which means to all good Christians together. The whole church forgives sins by its prayers, which Augustine describes as "the groanings of the one dove," using an image Cyprian had used for the purity and uniqueness of the church taken from the Song of Songs: "one is my dove, my perfect one."[16]

Of course none of this means that the ultimate source of forgiveness is other than God. As our passage puts it, it is "*not* according to the will of human beings" that sins are dismissed but "according to the will of God *and* the prayers of holy and spiritual people." The meaning of this *not* is perfectly clear, but what about the *and*? God, not human beings, forgives sin, but he evidently exercises his power of forgiveness through the prayers of his people. Clearly whatever power the church has to forgive is derived from God, yet Augustine insists it is real power: the unity of the church dismisses sins, her peace dismisses them, the one dove dismisses. The efficacy of this human unity is real though derivative, because through it God himself forgives sins. This is precisely what medieval theology meant by an instrumental cause or means of grace, except that it is found not in an external sign but in an inner unity. The unique dove is not anything visible like the ministers of the church (many of whom are unworthy) or the local congregation (which includes many bad Christians). It is not anything that could be called the visible or institutional church. It is all those holy and spiritual people anywhere in the world who are united inwardly by Christian charity, even if they have never seen one another. For "the same Holy Spirit dismisses sins that is given to all the holy ones who cling to one another in charity, whether they are acquainted with one another bodily or not."[17] Only the Holy Spirit forgives sins, through the one heart that took Victorinus to herself and caused him to be born again.

The fact that it is only the prayers of *good* Christians that accomplish this is not some form of chauvinism on Augustine's part, but follows from his ontology. The power that makes the one dove one is the same power that makes good Christians good, the uniting power of charity,[18] which is a desire drawing them not only to God but to each other, thus forming what the apostle calls the "bond of peace." (This phrase from the letter to the Ephesians recurs in many variations in Augustine's anti-Donatist writings: "bond of peace," "bond of charity," and "bond of unity" are all ways of referring to the same power).[19] The fundamental ontological point here is that being and unity are not ultimately distinguishable. "To be is nothing other than to be one thing," Augustine says, adding that "insofar as anything achieves unity, it exists."[20] This makes unity an ontological issue (hardly surprising for a Platonist) and it is already clear that for Augustine love is the source of any social unity, which is necessarily a unity of many souls.[21] To be without charity is therefore not only to be a bad person separated from God; it is to lack the specific kind of love that makes the church one, which is to say, to lack that which gives the church its very being.

It follows that bad Catholics, those who appear to be within the church but lack charity and therefore are in fact "pseudo-Christians,"[22] are no better off than Donatists or people baptized by heretics: they have a valid sacrament but do not really belong to the unity of the Catholic church. Of course, just like any heretic they may repent and be converted, in which case their baptism, "which did not profit them when they received it . . . begins to profit them."[23] The same thing happens when schismatics or heretics, baptized outside the Catholic church, convert and come to her unity, "not in order to begin having the sacrament of baptism which they didn't have, but so that what was useless when they did have it might begin to profit them."[24] In each case, the basic rule is that "without charity, nothing profits."[25] For to be without charity is to be without the church, and outside the church there is no salvation. Conversion here has an inescapably ecclesial meaning: to convert is to turn one's will toward charity, which means toward the unity and peace of the church.

This is a profound recasting of the African theology of the church, with immense practical consequences for the drawing of social boundaries. Nothing can pollute the rightful possessions of the church, even when they are found outside the church. No one is made impure by involuntary contact with anything unholy, for the only thing that really puts one outside the communion of the holy ones is an inner failure of the will, the lack of charity. The true social boundaries of the church are thus not visible to any human being, because they consist in the difference between charity and its absence—and only God who sees the heart knows where this difference lies. The spiritual power of grace, insofar as it uses human means, is a social power found only within these boundaries—only in hearts bound by charity, not in external things, words or sacraments. Individual ministers possess no power to sanctify, regenerate, or forgive sins, nor even in the deepest sense to baptize: all such power really belongs to the whole communion of the church and all its holy ones. Hence the *validity* of the sacrament, which is no one's private property but belongs to the whole church, does not depend on the will of the minister conferring it or of the person receiving it, either of whom can misuse it but not invalidate it. The *efficacy* of the sacrament, however, is a different matter: since unity alone dismisses sins, lack of charity, which puts people outside the unity of the church, renders the possession of a valid sacrament profitless. So the Donatists have a pure and holy Catholic sacrament devoid of spiritual power and grace.

If we bring to this conception of church and sacrament the medieval question of whether the sacraments of the church confer grace, the answer has to be no. Augustine's anti-Donatist theology does not conceive the external sacrament of baptism as an efficacious means of grace. All spiritual efficacy is inward. That does not mean it is immediate or individualistic. The grace of God uses human social means, but these are inward, consisting in the power of charity to form the invisible unity of the church, the inner social location within which alone purity of heart and salvation are to be found and nurtured. Grace, in short, comes to the individual soul not by external means but by a kind of inward channel, descending from God to the inner unity of the church, to which the soul is joined by charity. This inner gift is not conferred but only marked outwardly by the sacred sign of baptism. And since the outward mark can be so easily misused and misappropriated, it is not even a sure sign of grace. As we noted back in chapter 1, Augustine never expects signs to provide certainty.[26]

It is in fact as easy to falsify a sign as it is to lie. Augustine illustrates this point by analogy with the military mark, also called (in Latin) a *character*.[27] This is something like a tattoo given to soldiers as they are inducted into the army (when, incidentally, they also take an oath called a *sacramentum*, the primary secular use of this term). Like baptism, the *character* is an external sign of be-longing to a particular social body and indeed is necessary to becoming a member of that body. But like baptism, the sign itself is causally inert. It is not the tattoo that makes a man a member of his military unit but his will, his intention to share with his comrades in the work and sufferings of the unit— just as baptism does not make anyone a member of the church without that form of goodwill called charity, nor does it save anyone who has no intention of doing good works.[28] Hence it is quite possible, indeed almost inevitable, that a deserter will keep his indelible *character* even while he is separated from the army. This is the sense in which his will falsifies the sign: imprinted on his body is a mark saying, in effect, "I belong to the army," when in heart he is no part of the army at all. Yet the sign is still valid, for if he has a change of heart and returns to the army, he will be punished but will not need to get a new tattoo. Indeed, it would be inappropriate to re-do the sign at precisely the moment when what it signifies ("I belong to the army") becomes true again. In just the same way the Catholic church imposes penitence but does not re-baptize those who deserted it and then return—or even those who receive its sacred sign in schism and come to join it for the first time. For Augustine argues that anyone who gets a counterfeit tattoo (analogous to being baptized by heretics or schismatics) would not need to have it re-done if he were caught and required to join the army for real, just as gold coins with a proper image of the emperor stamped on them by a counterfeiter could go straight into the emperor's treasury after they are confiscated.[29]

This last argument is particularly interesting because it is cited by Aquinas in support of the medieval doctrine of baptismal character.[30] But Aquinas's use of the term *character* is actually quite different from Augustine's. Aquinas is thinking of a kind of indelible mark *on the soul,* which is to say it is not literally a mark but is literally in the soul, and nothing ever removes it. Augustine on the contrary is referring quite literally to a mark on the body, and using it as an analogy to explain the validity of the sacred sign of baptism. The externality of both military *character* and Christian baptism is a crucial feature of the Augustinian analogy, which turns on the fact that an external sign can be possessed even by one who is inwardly alienated from the social body it signifies. Even more illuminating is the difference this implies with regard to sacramental efficacy. For Aquinas the baptismal character, which is productive of spiritual effects, is sealed as it were on the soul of anyone who receives valid baptism. Thus the sign, simply by virtue of its external validity, produces a lasting effect on the soul. This is precisely what does not happen according to Augustine's anti-Donatist theology, where valid sacramental signs can be and often are utterly without spiritual efficacy.

The Immediate Return of Sins

For Augustine the primary conceptual weakness of the African theology of the sacraments was its failure to distinguish validity and efficacy. To put it in his terms, "the sacrament was not distinguished from the use or effect of the sacrament."[31] The medieval theologians were fully aware of the importance of this Augustinian distinction, but they went beyond Augustine in connecting certain kinds of spiritual efficacy to every valid sacrament. This is precisely the kind of connection Augustine must attenuate as far as possible to block the inferences the Donatists want to make, such as this: since the Catholics don't rebaptize Donatists, they must recognize the validity of sacraments in the Donatist church, which means they must acknowledge that the sacraments have salvific effect outside the Catholic church. The validity/efficacy distinction allows Augustine a great deal of flexibility in the range of his responses to this kind of inference, a flexibility that medieval theologians develop even further. Validity does not always imply efficacy, but certain kinds of efficacy (such as an indelible mark on the soul, according to medieval doctrine) do follow inevitably from any valid sacrament. Augustine of course denies that Donatists in possession of valid baptism are thereby granted the gift of salvation, but very strong church traditions require him to make some compromises on this score and say that certain kinds of salvific efficacy inevitably accompany valid baptism. In particular, there is no way he can break the bond between baptism and regeneration;[32] there is simply no room in Catholic or Donatist theology for anyone to deny that all who receive a proper baptism are spiritually born again in Christ. So Augustine must affirm baptismal regeneration while emptying it of spiritual power, in a move that brings him very close in substance to Protestant theologies such as Calvin's, which affirm the practice of infant baptism but explicitly deny baptismal regeneration understood as a power of inward grace conferred on the recipient. This "Protestant" move runs so contrary to the African understanding of the power of baptismal regeneration that it results in one of the strangest arguments Augustine ever made, to which we now turn.

As he begins his analysis of baptismal validity and efficacy in the treatise *On Baptism against the Donatists*, Augustine lays down a fundamental principle about "us" and "them," which will govern the whole discussion to follow:

> In what they agree with us about [*nobiscum sentiunt*], they are with us; but they withdraw from us in what they disagree with us about [*a nobis dissentiunt*]. This kind of approach or departure should not be measured by bodily rather than spiritual movement. For as bodies are joined by continuity of place, so agreement of wills [*consensio voluntatum*] is a kind of contact of souls.[33]

Unlike bodies, the contact of souls (*contactum animorum*) takes place not in the outward dimension of space but in the psychological dimension of will. Since what the will does is love, agreement of wills necessarily means agreement in love. We have here the germ of the view Augustine develops years later in the *City of God*, according to which the very being of a community consists in souls loving the same things. The love that gives being to the church is specifically charity, the love of God and neighbor from which the Donatists (on the Catholic view) exclude themselves by their contempt for the peace of the Catholic church. Yet here Augustine adds a crucial qualification: the Donatists do agree with the Catholics about some things, and to that extent they share some of what is holy and good in the Catholic church. Though they are a different community from the Catholic church, there is some overlap between the two communities in the matter of sacred things, insofar as the will that defines the Donatist community does not wholly dissent from the charity that defines the Catholic community. That is why Donatists can have and even give baptism outside the Catholic church: "in the soundness of the sacrament, since they are not against us, they are for us."[34] As a result, the Donatist party "is separated from the bond of charity and peace, but joined in one baptism."[35]

Clearly this is a very flexible principle, which can be applied to any spiritual gift Augustine is willing to concede to the Donatists. It is so flexible that it gives him room to make a crucial concession of what appears at first to be efficacy, not just validity. Because no one at the time thought spiritual regeneration could possibly be separated from baptism, Augustine has to concede that anyone who receives baptism among the Donatists is also born again in Christ. Otherwise, those who returned from the Donatist schism to the Catholic church would still be unregenerate and would need to be rebaptized. So it must be that since valid baptism is present among the Donatists, spiritual rebirth is there also. But once again, this power of birth is a gift belonging not to the Donatists themselves but to the Catholic communion, which alone is "Mother Church which can give birth to sons and daughters through the baptism of Christ."[36] For the underlying principle is as before:

> There is one church which alone is named Catholic, and whatever she has of her own in separated communities consisting of those who differ from her unity—*through that which she has of her own in them, it is in fact she who gives birth, not they.* For it is not their separateness which gives birth, but what they retained with them from her; if they dismiss this, they do not give birth at all. Thus it is she who gives birth, whose sacraments are still retained, from which such birth can happen anywhere—even though not all to whom she gives birth belong to her unity, which will save those who persevere to the end.[37]

So new birth in Christ, like the baptism that is its sign, belongs to Mother Church, the one that alone deserves to be called Catholic, even when it takes place through someone's being baptized by the Donatists. Its source is the regenerative power of Catholic peace and unity, even when it is found outside the bond of peace and unity.

Most striking of all, insofar as regeneration is attached to the sacrament itself outside the church, even spiritual rebirth in Christ has no salvific power. It is like a riddle: When does efficacy have no efficacy? The answer is: When it is attached to a valid sacrament outside the Catholic church. Augustine's extremely perplexing version of this riddle centers on the question of when sins are forgiven. For having conceded spiritual regeneration to the Donatists, he is faced with a very tough question: since Donatists are born again through Catholic baptism (even though they possess this baptism illegitimately) how can it be denied that their sins also are forgiven? Can one truly become a new creature in Christ and yet still be held guilty of sin? Here Augustine must take a stand and turn back the tide of inferences from validity to efficacy, and especially the inference from baptism to remission of sins, lest every sort of spiritual power end up being conceded to the Donatists. It cannot be that the power of baptism among the Donatists extends as far as full remission of sins. Yet the theological connection between baptism and remission is at least as strong as that between baptism and regeneration.

What Augustine would clearly like to say is that Donatists do not receive forgiveness of sins when they are baptized, but this is not a point on which he can safely lay down the law. So instead he proposes a dilemma, in the technical logical sense of the term. He sets forth two alternatives and insists that the Donatists must choose one, then proceeds to show that whichever alternative they choose, they lose. The dilemma is based on the question: what happens to someone like Simon Magus who comes to receive baptism in deceit, merely pretending to have faith in Christ—are his sins forgiven?[38] If the Donatists say no, then Augustine will apply their answer to themselves—and the connection between baptism and forgiveness of sins is cleanly snapped. If they say yes, then they have to agree that the resulting forgiveness lasts but a moment:

> If they say that in him who comes in deceit, by the holy power of so great a sacrament his sins are indeed dismissed at that very point in time, but because of his deceit they *immediately return* . . . then let them understand that this is what happens also to those who are baptized outside the communion of the church.[39]

This is a very odd picture indeed. The pretender's sins "immediately return" not merely in the sense that he keeps right on sinning as before, but in the sense that he is once again responsible for the *guilt* of sins he had committed before baptism. What sort of forgiveness is this? One moment his sins are all forgiven, their guilt washed away in baptism, and the next moment they are back and he is fully as guilty as before. The conceptual oddity here is that a forgiveness that is conferred and then immediately revoked does not look like forgiveness at all, just as a gift that is reclaimed the very moment it is given does not look like much of a gift.

So it is with good reason that none of Augustine's admirers has ever accepted this picture. The medieval theologians, for instance, noting that Augustine here speaks hypothetically, firmly reject the possibility of "the return of sins."[40] Surely they are right that Augustine could not really have intended this as his actual position. But we should notice the logical consequence of this interpretation of Augustine's intentions: it means that the possibility Augustine really accepts must be the one that cleanly snaps the connection between validity and efficacy, that is, between the sacrament of baptism and the forgiveness of sins. There is no necessary connection between the external sign and the inward spiritual benefit of grace, even among those who are born again in Catholic baptism. If one finds that conclusion unbearable (as many of Augustine's African supporters probably did) then one can always opt for the bizarre possibility of the immediate return of sins which, aside from the infinitesimal interval of forgiveness at the moment of baptism, comes to the same thing in the end. For indeed it is very much Augustine's point that the two possibilities come to the same thing in the end, namely, "the remission of irrevocable sins does not follow from baptism unless . . . baptism is had legitimately."[41]

Unity in Adam

Much of the conceptual work Augustine put into his theology against the Donatists theology was also of use against his later opponents, the Pelagians. In large measure this was because of the deep new ontological foundations Augustine laid for convictions held in common by both Donatists and their opponents, such as the teaching that no one, not even infants, could be saved outside the unity of the church signified by baptism. In Africa this was not merely a theological doctrine but a deep-rooted element of church practice. In what becomes a kind of cliché in his anti-Pelagian sermons and treatises, Augustine describes anxious parents running to church to get their children baptized, and everyone in the audience understands why: for not even infants can be saved from damnation without receiving rebirth and forgiveness through baptism.[42]

There was no controversy about this in Africa until the Pelagians arrived. This was indeed the very beginning of the Pelagian controversy, which arose when Pelagius himself came to Africa in 410. Already famous as a spiritual advisor to aristocratic Roman ascetics, Pelagius was washed along with the tide of wealthy and powerful Italians fleeing the barbarian invasion that swept through Rome itself that year. In one of the great missed opportunities of history, he arrived in Hippo while Augustine was absent,[43] then moved on to Carthage in time for the great conference that officially put an end to the legality of the Donatist church (and thus conveniently marks the conclusion of Augustine's anti-Donatist writings and the beginning of his anti-Pelagian period). Augustine actually caught sight of Pelagius in Carthage but was too busy to speak with him before Pelagius departed for Palestine, leaving behind his friend and advocate Coelestius to carry on the fight for his ideas and become the first Pelagian to be censured by the church.

The key Pelagian theses ascribed to Coelestius and condemned by a council at Carthage in 411 were "that the sin of Adam harmed only himself and not the human race" and "that infants who are born are in the state Adam was in before his transgression."[44] These theses ran smack up against the deep-rooted African conviction about the necessity of infant baptism, which Augustine stressed in his early sermons against the Pelagians.[45] The African church needed little convincing on this score, but the rest of the world needed more explanation of how Adam's sin could harm even infants. For it is important to understand that the Augustinian doctrine of original sin is far stronger than what often goes under that name today. It teaches not merely that we are all born with a corrupt and sinful nature due to the Fall, but that we are quite literally born guilty,[46] deserving to be punished eternally for Adam's sin, so that even babies who have never done anything wrong in their lives[47] deserve nothing less than eternal damnation. The justice of infant damnation is the crucial point of contention. The Pelagian argument that there is no justice in damning a person for another's sins had to be met by an argument showing that Adam's sin belongs in some deep way to the whole human race: it is not merely the sin of another but truly yours and mine, so that there is no injustice in our being punished for it even if we die in infancy before we have done anything blameworthy in our own lives.

The basic approach Augustine will take to this problem is worked out in a letter written sometime after 408, which is to say possibly in the years just before Pelagius's arrival in Africa or in the years immediately after it.[48] The letter contains no reference to Pelagian theology, yet it sets forth conceptions of infant baptism and original sin that Augustine will deploy throughout his subsequent campaign against the Pelagians. The strikingly original feature of the letter is its treatment of the unity of human souls in Adam, which Augustine develops in response to questions from a fellow bishop named Boniface bearing on specifically African concerns about solidarity and social boundaries. Boniface wonders whether Christian parents do harm to their baptized children (as Cyprian seemed to think) by bringing them to pagan rituals for healing when sick.[49] If one denies this, saying that parents' faithlessness can do no spiritual harm to their child without the child's willing consent, then (Boniface asks) how can the parents' faith benefit the child in baptism without the child's willing consent? Augustine realizes that Boniface's question also raises the problem of how it is that infants stand in need of baptism at all. If children do not contract any guilt from parental sin, how then do they contract it from Adam?

Augustine's answer is that sharing in guilt, like sharing in grace, depends on an inner and universal solidarity, not local contact initiated by this or that particular person, even a father or mother. Infants contract guilt not from their parents but from Adam, to whom the great biblical denial of inherited guilt does not apply, for he alone includes the whole human race. Augustine quotes the passage in the book of Ezekiel where God tells the prophet: "Both the soul of the father is mine and the soul of the son is mine. The soul that sins is the one that will die." This passage does not count against our contracting guilt from Adam, Augustine argues, for the soul of the son is other than the soul of the father, but it was not other than the soul of Adam at the time of the first sin:

> This is why he contracted from Adam what is absolved by *the grace of the sacrament:* for he was not yet a soul living separately, that is, an other soul [*anima separatim vivens, i.e., altera anima*] of which it could be said, "both the soul of the father is mine and the soul of the son is mine." Thus when he is already a man existing in himself [*cum homo in seipso est*], having become other [*alter*] than the one who begot him, *he is not held responsible for another's sin without his own consent.* Therefore he does contract guilt [from Adam] because *he was one with him and in him from whom he contracted it,* when what he contracted was committed. But one does not contract it from another [*altero*] when each is already living his own life [*propria vita*], of which it is said: "the soul that sins is the one that will die."[50]

This is an astonishing and radical conception of original human unity. When Adam sinned, each one of our souls was not other than Adam's. There was but one human soul in the beginning, and we all were it. Long before we had separate lives of our own, we were all there in Adam and shared in his sin. When infants are damned for Adam's sin, therefore, they are not being punished for the sin of another.

The key conceptual resources needed to understand this notion of original unity in Adam are those Augustine developed in the second book of *On Free Choice* to describe the Plotinian ascent to the vision of a public inner Wisdom. There he contrasted the inner things souls have in common (*communia*) with the outward things that are their own (*propria*), such as their bodies.[51] Of course the point of Augustine's doctrine of original sin is profoundly un-Plotinian, for it means that what all souls inwardly have in common is not divinity but guilt. Still, distinguishing this radical, inward guilt from the ordinary sins and guilt of human life requires the Plotinian contrast between the life that all souls have inwardly in common and the lives of souls divided from each other after the Fall, when each soul has its own life, its *propria vita*, living separately with its own body, its own will, and therefore its own actual sins for which no one else is responsible.[52] Robert O'Connell has traced the key term, *propria vita*, through Augustine's anti-Pelagian writings, along with the contrasting notion that originally all of us were none other than Adam.[53] "All were that one" (*omnes ille unus fuerunt*) is the key formula occurring, in slight variations, on at least seven different occasions in Augustine's works.[54] This radical concept of original unity makes little sense outside of a Neoplatonist ontology such as Plotinus's, in which all souls are at root one. Augustine's formula echoes one of Plotinus's most memorable explanations of why all souls are one, in which Plotinus describes the Platonic Idea of the human being in the divine Mind as "that Man which we all were then"[55]—before we were diminished and separated from one another by our embodiment. Plotinus's "then" is not a point in time but the ontological center of all souls, for the Plotinian Fall is not an event taking place at some time or other in history but rather a necessary condition of the embodiment of souls throughout time. Hence Augustine's defense of the doctrine of original sin must relocate the primal unity of souls in one man from the timeless realm of intelligible being to the historical realm of Adam and Eve (and must moreover largely ignore Eve, with the result that Augustine has no inclination to lay the blame of the first sin on her).[56]

The un-Plotinian notion that what we all have inwardly in common could include something evil is one Augustine arrived at, implicitly at least, in the treatise *To Simplicianus* written more than a decade earlier.[57] It is a profound departure from Platonism. In any normal Platonist doctrine, such as Plotinus's or Origen's, the crucial moral differentiation between souls occurs as a result of their Fall: some sin more heavily, others more lightly, with the result that they descend to different levels of embodiment. Those which govern celestial bodies, the planets and the stars, are less deeply tainted and therefore less deeply embodied than those which fall into earthly bodies, as Augustine explains in his early exposition of this "fallen soul" theory in the third book of *On Free Choice*.[58] The underlying ontological point is that differentiation and division between souls must be due to defects among them, a falling away from the good of an all-embracing inner unity from which they come. This deep Platonist commitment to the priority of unity over differentiation—to the one being both more real and better than the many[59]—is disrupted by Augustine's encounter with the Pauline doctrine of election, which locates the ultimate cause of moral differentiation in the will of the one God rather than in the diverse choices of many souls. The Fall of the one primal soul therefore does not result in moral differentiation as in Plotinus, but in a stunning original unity in evil—the distinctively Augustinian concept of the mass of damnation. Of course Augustine is never so un-Platonist as to think of the ultimate origin of any real unity as evil: that would violate the Christian doctrine of creation as well as the Platonist doctrine of the Good as first principle. Rather, by relocating the primal unity of all souls in the realm of time Augustine can make sense of a secondary, *historical* unity in evil after the sin of the first man. So a primal unity in goodness (when all souls were created good in Adam) precedes original sin, which results in a historical but universal unity in evil.

Unity in Christ

The historical unity of all souls in evil is the crucial counter-concept to the unity of souls in the church. Together the two unities define the end points of Augustine's soteriology, its *terminus a quo* in Adam and its *terminus ad quem* in Christ. For of course the unity of the church is the unity of the spiritual Body of Christ. Hence Augustine's initial blast in the polemical war against the Pelagian denial of original sin, the first book of the treatise *On the Merits and Forgiveness of Sins,* is structured by the Pauline contrast between the reign of death in Adam and eternal life in Christ, the one originating in Adam's sin and the other initiated by baptismal rebirth. But the end is better than the beginning: we are not simply restored to Eden but brought to heaven. For Adam was created without sin but did not descend from heaven, while Christ who did descend from heaven shall return there, taking with him all who are united in his Body. This is how Augustine understands Jesus' cryptic remark, "No one ascends to heaven except he who has descended from heaven, the Son of man which is in heaven,"[60] which is part of Jesus' reply to the question, How it is possible to be born again? In his divine nature, Christ has always remained in heaven, even while he walks on earth in his human nature. For the Incarnation does not mean that the divine nature literally descends in space to be confined to a body on earth, ceasing to be omnipresent.[61] It is by his unique divine power, therefore, that Christ both descends and ascends, remaining what he was but assuming what he was not—remaining omnipresent while assuming bodily location in the flesh—so that his "descent" into human flesh is his assumption of our humanity and his "ascent" is his raising us up with himself to the life of the children of God. Thus Augustine paraphrases and comments on Christ's words, as if what Jesus said was

> "This is how the spiritual birth takes place, so that human beings may be heavenly from being earthly, which they cannot achieve unless they are made members of me, so that he may ascend who descended, for no one ascends except he who descended"—unless, that is, all who are being changed and lifted up come together in the unity of Christ, so that the same Christ who descended may himself ascend—counting his Body, i.e., his church, as nothing other than himself.[62]

Only one man ever descended from heaven, for Christ is the only human being who is the same person as the Son of God on high. Therefore only one man ever ascends to heaven, in that everyone who goes to heaven is one Christ:

> other human beings, his holy and faithful ones, *become one Christ with the man Christ,* so that when they all ascend through his grace and fellowship [*societatem*] it is the same *one Christ* ascending to heaven who descended from heaven.[63]

Augustine rounds off his point using the same Pauline imagery of the unity of many members in the Body of Christ that he uses to explain the invisible significance of the sacrament in the *City of God:*

> So also the apostle says, "As we have many members in one body, but all the members of the body while they are many, are one body, so also is Christ." He does not say, "so also is *Christ's*" that is, Christ's Body or Christ's members, but "so also is *Christ,*" calling Head and members *one Christ.*[64]

Head and Body together are called one Christ, not simply one in Christ or one Body belonging to Christ. The unity of the church is therefore not simply the unity of all who believe in Christ, but includes Christ himself, the man who gives his name to the whole. Only in this unity can any human being be saved and brought to heavenly life; for as we have seen in Augustine's anti-Donatist writings, it is this unity alone that bears the power of forgiveness and spiritual rebirth. Nothing in Augustine's anti-Pelagian writings changes this inward location of the efficacious means of grace.

Since the contrast between unity in Adam and unity in Christ is so fundamental for Augustine's soteriology, it is important to understand how different these two kinds of unity are. Our unity in Adam is more radical. We are all one in Adam simply by virtue of being human, whereas only a portion of humanity is one in Christ by virtue of the charity that is the church's bond of unity. The church is a social unity of many souls joined in love, whereas our radical unity in Adam is pre-social, quite independent of our willing and loving, as it goes back to a time when none of our souls had a will of its own. By virtue of having been none other than Adam, our souls contract guilt from him, which cannot happen in our relations with anyone else: we are not held guilty of the sins of our father and mother, but only the sin of Adam. For the same reason, Cyprian is wrong about a tainted bishop passing on his impurity to those he baptizes; for each soul in the church has its own will and is therefore responsible for its own sins, not those of another. The communion of the church is thus an inviolable sharing of holiness and grace, never of impurity and guilt. That is why, as Augustine explains to Boniface, infants can share with their parents the grace of baptism but not the sin of idolatry.

The crucial parallel between unity in Adam and unity in Christ is a certain kind of universality in what is shared by those within. Just as one may share Adam's sin with myriads of people about whom one knows nothing, so one may share the grace of Christ with saints throughout the world whom one has never seen or met or even heard of. The unity in Christ that is the means of salvific efficacy for all who believe is therefore not anything like an ordinary social process using outward means of communication. The minister who performs the baptism together with the parents and godparents who bring the infant may all be unholy, not truly belonging to the unity of the church, but the infant is still born again through the prayers and groans of the one dove, which is the true church. Thus the efficacy of baptism lies elsewhere than in the external rite or those who perform it:

> The Spirit who dwells in the holy ones, of whom the one dove of silver is melted together by the fire of love, does what he does even through the ministry . . . of those who are damnably unworthy. That is why infants are offered to receive spiritual grace not so much by those who carry them in their hands (although also by them, if they also are good and faithful) as by the whole fellowship of those who are holy and faithful [*ab universa societate sanctorum atque fidelium*]. For they are rightly understood to be offered by all who are pleased by their being offered, and by whose holy, undivided charity they are helped to share in the Holy Spirit. The whole of Mother Church, who is in the holy ones, does all this, because the whole gives birth to all and to each one.[65]

The efficacy of baptism is all inward, requiring water and the words of the Gospel for its outward sign but not for its power. For when Scripture speaks of being born of water and the Spirit, Augustine explains, that means the one signifies grace while the other brings it about:

> Water making an outward display of the *sacrament of grace* and the Spirit working inwardly the *benefit of grace,* loosing the bond of guilt, reconciling the good of nature, regenerate in *one Christ* a human being who was generated from one Adam.[66]

Mother Church gives birth by the power of the Holy Spirit, in which all good Christians share. So it is she as a whole, the whole Body of the one Christ, who

remits sins and thereby acts as means of grace, the inward channel of the Holy
Spirit's power. She uses the minister performing the rite and the parents
offering the child for baptism as outward means to confer a valid sacrament
but not inward means of spiritual efficacy—except insofar as they too belong
inwardly to her unity. This explains why the souls of infants may share grace
with faithful parents and all the holy ones of the church, but do not share in
their parents' guilt except for what all inherit in common from Adam:

> For guilt is not made common by the will of another
> [*communicatur ... per alterius voluntatem*] the way grace is made
> common by the unity of the Spirit. For one Holy Spirit can be in this
> human being and that one, even though *they do not know about*
> *each other* that grace is common to them both through Him. But the
> *human* spirit cannot be both this one's and that one's, the one sin-
> ning and the other not, yet the guilt be common through it.[67]

The upshot is that even after a soul has its own life or *propria vita* it can share in
the same grace with others, despite no longer being able to share the guilt of
others. For it is no longer one soul with Adam, but it does have one Spirit with
all other souls in the church. Once again, the communion of the holy ones is
not like any visible community, as it is effective even when many of its
members do not know each other. The power of baptism is not the efficacy of
good people working together in what we would nowadays call a social setting,
but something deeper and more inward, a unity of many souls in Christ
profound enough to undo the effects of the unity of all souls in the mass of
damnation in Adam.

Conversion and Perseverance

The effect of infant baptism is the most impressive example of sacramental
efficacy in Augustine's theology. Without any assistance from the infant's own
will, the prayers of the church cause the child to be transferred from Adam to
Christ, from the reign of death to newness of life, from carnal birth to spiritual
rebirth. Above all, the groans of this one dove bring about the remission of sins
(in this case only original sin, since infants have no sin in their own life, their
propria vita). This remission implies also a kind of protection for the child,
because by the same prayers all baptized infants who die before the age of
moral discretion and responsibility are assured a place in the kingdom of
heaven, as Augustine writes to Boniface, explaining why baptism is not repeated once the child is grown up:

When a man begins to have discretion, he will not repeat the sacrament but understand it, adjusting his will in harmony with its truth. Until he can do that, the sacrament avails for his protection against adverse [spiritual] powers—and so much does it avail that if he departs this life before the use of reason, then he is freed by Christian help, the charity of the church commending him through the sacrament, from the condemnation which entered the world through one man.[68]

All three levels of the Platonist ontological hierarchy (God, souls, bodies) are lined up in favor of the baptized child: the "Christian help" of grace itself, acquired by the "charity of the church commending him" by its prayers, a commendation signified and expressed "through the sacrament." Thus the efficacy of grace descends from God through many souls to the soul of the child, marked outwardly by the water and words of baptism.

Strikingly, a similar protection is effectual also for baptized adults who are still unspiritual, living as if under the Old Testament dispensation whose promised rewards were temporal rather than eternal. So long as they are willing to make progress toward spiritual things within the unity of the church, which hopes for eternal goods, they are kept safe even if they die in their unspiritual state: "And if they are taken from this life before they are spiritual, they are guarded by the holiness of the sacrament and counted among the land of the living."[69] Though not fully converted from love of earthly things to love of heavenly things (in the Platonist sense of conversion that is so fundamental to Augustine's ethics)[70] they evidently are already converted to the charity and unity of the church, in the Cyprianic and ecclesial sense of the term "conversion" that is especially prominent in Augustine's anti-Donatist writings. Cyprian employs a very old usage when he speaks of the "conversion" of heretics who give up their heresy and join the Catholic church, a usage Augustine follows throughout his discussion of heretics and schismatics returning to the church.[71] But exactly the same conversion takes place when an unworthy Christian begins to take the Christian life seriously:

Whoever has baptism both within catholic unity and while living a life worthy of it, has legitimate baptism and has it legitimately. But whoever is in the Catholic church itself like chaff mixed in with the wheat, or outside like chaff carried off by the wind, has indeed a legitimate baptism, but not legitimately.... And when he is *converted* either to catholic unity or to a life worthy of so great a sacrament, he does not therefore begin to have a different, legitimate baptism but rather begins to have the same one legitimately.[72]

As throughout the anti-Donatist writings, the baptism of unworthy Catholics here has no more salvific effect than the baptism of schismatics and heretics. Both inside and outside the church there is need for conversion, which means not only joining the unity of the church but living worthy lives, for this is essentially a conversion to charity, which both binds the church in one and makes good lives good.

Hence both baptism and conversion are as a rule necessary for salvation. When Augustine tells Boniface that those who receive baptism as infants must adjust their will in harmony to its truth when they grow up, that means they too must undergo this conversion to ecclesial charity. Until then they have baptism but not yet conversion—but that is sufficient for their spiritual welfare until they are grown. Thus infants are the most important exception to the rule that both baptism and conversion are necessary for salvation. But there is another exception, which goes the opposite way: the thief on the cross, promised salvation by none other than Christ himself, has conversion but not baptism. He stands for all converts who desire baptism but die before having the opportunity for it. Augustine sees the two cases (unbaptized converts and baptized infants) as parallel, in that "God makes up for what was involuntarily missing in the one and in the other."[73] As the baptized infant is received into the kingdom of heaven just like one of the converted, so the thief on the cross is received into the kingdom of heaven just like one of the baptized.

Augustine's teaching that baptism is not sufficient without conversion is another way of saying that "without charity, nothing profits" (1 Cor. 13:3). Baptism is an outward sign of someone being inwardly united to the church, which is effected only by charity—and like the semiotics of *On the Teacher*, Augustine's sacramental semiotics requires that the thing signified be inwardly present before the outward sign is of any real use. In the case of infants, the charity of the church itself is sufficient to effect this invisible inner union, but for adults to receive the profit of baptism they must turn their own hearts to join in the charity of the church, a turning that constitutes "true inward conversion"[74] or "true conversion of heart."[75] Without this inward change the outward sacrament does no good, just like the military mark or *character* imprinted on the body of a soldier who is deserting, which does not get him any legitimate privileges but only punishment.

Precisely for this reason, we cannot say in an unqualified way that adults who were baptized in infancy are saved by their baptism. They have been born again in Christ but as we have seen,[76] this spiritual regeneration can be a kind of efficacy without efficacy, emptied of all spiritual power if the one who receives it is not in charity and unity with the church. In contrast to the Protestant tendency to identify regeneration with salvation, for Augustine it is quite possible to be born again without being saved. Even those who receive baptism after their souls are properly converted to ecclesial charity and unity have no guarantee that they will continue therein. That is precisely why Roman Catholic theology speaks of some sins as mortal: they put an end to the new life acquired by baptismal regeneration, which must be restored by the sacrament of penance if the sinner is to be saved. So when Augustine is faced with the question of whether salvation is found in baptism he gives a carefully qualified answer. We are indeed "saved by the washing of regeneration" as the Apostle says (Titus 3:5), but we are "saved in hope" as the Apostle also says (Rom. 8:24) and Augustine takes this to mean we are not yet saved in reality. This account of baptismal salvation is one of the most important uses of Augustine's famous distinction between what is ours in hope (*in spe*) and in reality (*in re*).[77] Until the day we die we are "not yet saved," Augustine says quite explicitly,[78] because real salvation means being safe forever in an eternal life that cannot be lost, and none of us in this mortal life possesses such salvation.

The reason no mortal is saved in reality is familiar from Augustine's late works on predestination, but first appears in his anti-Donatist theology of baptism: the new birth we receive from Mother Church does not save us in reality because "not all to whom she gives birth belong to her unity, which shall save those who 'persevere even to the end.' "[79] Salvation ultimately requires us not only to join the unity of the church by baptism and conversion but also to persevere in that unity and in the charity that brings it about. And only God knows who will persevere to the end: "For in the ineffable foreknowledge of God many who seem to be outside are within and many who seem to be inside are without."[80] This is an explicitly predestinarian point, because as Augustine says, "the certain number of the saints *predestined* from before the foundation of the world" includes not only spiritual Christians as well as carnal Christians who are making progress, but also those who "still are living wickedly or even lie among heresies or pagan superstitions—but even there 'the Lord knows those who are his.' "[81] This predestinarian point means that the inner unity of the church is universal and invisible in a still deeper sense than we have yet noticed: it includes not only many souls who do not know each other in the flesh, but also many who do not even share as yet in the church's unity but who the Lord knows will be converted in the future. More frighteningly, it also excludes many who presently are living good lives of charity within the church but will not persevere to the end:

> According to the foreknowledge of him who knows whom he has
> *predestined* "before the foundation of the world" to be "conformed to
> the image of his Son," there are many who are openly outside and

called heretics, who are *better than many good Catholics.* For we see what they are today but know not what they will be tomorrow. Whereas for God, with whom things to come are present, *they already are what they will be.*[82]

Divine election, from which flows the predestined gifts of grace, is thus the ultimate root of sacramental efficacy.[83]

As usual, grace and free will should not be seen as competing with one another in Augustine's view, as if divine predestination somehow negated the inner efficacy of the charity and prayers of the church. Neither one blocks or hinders the other, but rather the divine power is the foundation of the human efficacy which it uses as means. For prayer too belongs to the outworking of divine predestination, as Augustine insists already in the *Confessions,* where he portrays himself as rescued from heresy and converted to the Catholic church by the predestined prayers of his mother. In a famous scene, a Catholic priest assures Monica, who was weeping for her heretical adolescent son as if he were spiritually dead, that "it cannot be that the son of these tears should perish."[84] Augustine later explains why: Monica's tears are outward signs of the grief-stricken prayers of her inmost heart, and it cannot be that God should deny the prayers of this pious woman, whose prayers and tears and piety are all his own gracious gift. Consequently, "You were present and heard her and did all things in the order that You had *predestined* them to be done."[85] The order of predestined grace includes both Monica's prayers and Augustine's conversion, and the reason the son of her tears could not perish is that nothing can ever happen contrary to divine predestination. Hence if we ask whether Augustine was converted by God's grace or by Monica's prayers, the proper Augustinian answer is clearly "both"—the one working by means of the other, predestined grace as ultimate cause and the tearful prayers of a loving heart as instrumental cause.[86]

The efficacy of baptism, in which divine grace works by means of "the groans of the one dove," is a specific form of the power of prayer operating within the order of divine predestination. It is the efficacy of the prayers of the whole church on behalf of her newborn children. This is not the only time the whole church prays for grace. She also prays for the conversion of unbelievers, especially those who persecute her.[87] This practice of prayer, built into the church's liturgy, is one of Augustine's most powerful arguments for the pre-venience of grace. Anything we can pray for is something God can give, so if the church prays for the conversion of those most deeply unwilling to believe, then the beginning of faith must be a gift of divine grace. In the same breath Augustine will mention the church's prayers for the perseverance of believers as well.[88] This shows the gratuity of grace for everyone, even the best of Christians, since perseverance is a gift that all must pray to receive from God's grace, not earn by their merits. As Augustine presents them, these two gifts, conversion and perseverance, are not themselves effects of baptism but necessary conditions of its efficacy: without conversion baptism profits no one except infants, and without perseverance there is no salvation for any adult. The efficacy of baptism in adults, in other words, is dependent on prior and subsequent acts of their will, which are in turn dependent on a divine grace that the church prays for but cannot confer. Hence it is only in the case of infants that Augustine gives us a really strong doctrine of baptismal efficacy, one that does not look like the semiotics of *On the Teacher*. For only in their case can we be quite sure that baptism marks a real bestowal of grace, the remission of sins by the groans of the one dove. In all other cases—unless we insist on the strange possibility of the immediate return of sins—there can be no sure connection between outward sacrament and inward grace.

The Soul of Christ

In Augustine's anti-Donatist works as well as his anti-Pelagian works the crucial causal connection in the doctrine of grace is between the human prayer for grace and the divine bestowal of grace, and except when infants are baptized that connection is never certain. To pray for grace is to ask for a gift we do not deserve, and there is no guarantee we will receive it. So infant baptism is a fascinating and important exception: why in this one case are the church's prayers sure to be answered? What makes the difference? I have not found any text in which Augustine answers this question. So far as I can tell, the connection is there simply because the church of his time, Catholic as well as Donatist, Italian as well as African, was so utterly unanimous in its belief that baptism saved infants from spiritual harm.

This is not to say that no answer could be given. Luther will (as always in his need for certainty) speak of the promise of God, which for him does not merely refer in Augustinian fashion to the promise of eternal life for the righteous but also to a divine assurance of sacramental efficacy. We can be sure of the forgiveness of sins in baptism because God has promised it, which means to be unsure or to deny it is to call God a liar.[89] But the concept of an efficacious word of promise is not available to Augustine.[90] Another possible answer is prominent in Calvin, who does not believe in baptismal regeneration but does believe baptized children who die in infancy are kept safe by a covenanted grace, and who refers the gift of predestined grace to the intercession of the risen Christ at God's right hand, which is to say, to the prayers of the one human being whose prayers absolutely deserve to be answered.[91] Of course Augustine is well aware of the biblical theme of Christ's intercession, but he does not deploy it as an explanation of sacramental efficacy. Here we might let this theme point to a larger question in Augustine's theology: whether the humanity of Christ, and specifically his human soul, has a distinctive role to play in the inner unity of the church and its efficacy.

I have suggested that the notion of "means of grace" should make us think (in Augustine) of a kind of inner channel of grace, flowing from God through the unity of souls in the church to individual souls, and marked outwardly by the sacraments. One wonders exactly what role the soul of Christ plays in this inner unity of souls. Could we picture the channel reaching down from God the Father to the Son as incarnate, human Head of the church, and thence to all the members of his Body? It is an attractive picture, and I know of nothing Augustine says that would exclude it but also nothing that presses it upon us for acceptance. Augustine often treats the humanity of Christ as exemplary of the activity of the whole church, but not as the source of its efficacy. For example, in the sacramental theology of the *City of God* noted in the last chapter, Christ belongs to the invisible sacrifice of the church (which is the inner thing or *res* signified by the sacrament of the Eucharist) in fundamentally the same way as every other member of the Body. There is nothing unique in Christ's being inwardly both priest and sacrifice, for example, because every Christian soul offers itself in works of mercy and love to God, and in its self-offering is inwardly both the priest that makes the offering and the sacrifice that is offered.[92] There appears to be no sharp distinction here between Christ's invisible sacrifice and that of everyone else in the church. Hence Augustine can describe the visible Eucharist ("the daily sacrifice of the church") as a sacrament signifying Christ's self-offering, then identify "the true sacrifice" with the Church's invisible self-offering as the Body of Christ, of which the many and various sacrifices of the Old Testament were figurative signs.[93] The Church indeed "learns through him to offer herself,"[94] but this makes Christ a teacher and an example rather than a means of grace.

It is not easy to be sure that a concept is absent from the whole corpus of Augustine's writing, but another way of testing this negative conclusion (that the soul of Christ is not a distinctive means of grace) is to examine a sampling of the most important passages devoted to the famous theme of the "whole Christ" (*totus Christus*), which is closely related to the theme of the "one Christ" (*unus Christus*) which, as we have just seen, is central to the soteriology of the anti-Pelagian treatise *On the Merits and Forgiveness of Sins*. Both phrases serve to point out that Head and Body are one community, to which Christ as a human being belongs. Augustine's meditations on the unity of the whole Christ are therefore the perfect occasion for him to show that Christ's human soul is the channel of grace for his whole Body, if that is what Augustine wants to teach.

But in fact he uses this theme to teach something quite different: Augustine refers to the oneness of the whole Christ to explain why the Head gives utterance to the sins and sufferings of the Body when they are not literally his. For example, Christ is not forsaken by his Father on the cross[95] but gives voice to our sinful sense of forsakenness when we lose the objects of our carnal desire, including our bodily lives.[96] The same figurative transfer occurs, Augustine explains, when Christ speaks from heaven to Paul on the Damascus Road, saying "Saul, Saul, why do you persecute *me*?"[97] The risen Christ in heaven is far above all the wounds of persecution but his Body on earth is not, and therefore he speaks as if he were persecuted himself—for he is indeed persecuted in his Body, since Head and Body together are one and speak with one voice. Thus an ontological unity grounds a figurative transfer of terms: the Head speaks as if the suffering and even the sins of the Body are his own, which in a sense they are. Yet Augustine insists on this figure of speech precisely in order to make clear that Christ himself does not sin, nor even suffer in his soul the kinds of emotional affliction (especially fear) that is the inevitable result of souls being too attached to temporal things that can be lost. The relation between real ontological unity and figurative transfer of terms is admirably captured by an analogy: when you step on someone's foot, it is the tongue that says, "you stepped on me!" because there is a real unity of the body to which both tongue and foot belong. Nonetheless it is not literally the tongue that was stepped on.[98] In the same way, it is not literally Christ who is forsaken, terrified, anguished, or repentant when (as happens often in the Psalms, in Augustine's Christological reading) he speaks of these experiences as his own. The point is to make clear that Christ is not really suffering what he figuratively transfers to himself by speaking for his whole Body.

The "whole Christ" theme in Augustine is about the sharing of suffering, not the communication of grace. How Christ's own bodily suffering is related to the gift of grace is a topic to which we shall turn in our next chapter.[99] But for now let us note one more thing about Christ's soul, which is that Augustine himself tends to say very little about it. Of course he regularly affirms with the rest of patristic orthodoxy that Christ, being fully human, has a human soul. But Augustine's soteriology does not seem to have a distinctive role for the concept of Christ's soul to play. Perhaps Augustine is wary about doing too much with this concept because his distinctive doctrine of original sin creates enough problems for it already. In a more straightforward version of the

Platonist doctrine of the Fall, such as that of the Origenists, Christ's soul could be distinguished from all others as the only one that did not sin in its preexistent life. But that view of the Fall is incompatible with Augustine's mature doctrine of election, according to which the Fall makes no difference between souls but lumps them all together in a common mass of damnation in which everyone shares equally in the one sin of Adam.[100] One consequence of this new conception of unity in Adam would seem to be that the soul of Christ also, having originated in Adam with all the rest of us, must have been tainted by the guilt of Adam's sin.

Early in his anti-Pelagian period Augustine even seems to countenance this possibility, suggesting that when the eternal Son of God assumed Christ's human soul in the Incarnation, "he cleansed it in taking it up so as to be born of a virgin, coming to us without any sin at all, either perpetrated [himself] or contracted [from Adam]."[101] But evidently he soon realized it was a serious mistake to allow, even as possibility, that Christ's soul needed any kind of cleansing. So within a few years we find him teaching, "It is not permissible to doubt that the soul of the mediator contracted no sin from Adam."[102] Christ the savior has no need of being saved from any kind of sin. Hence he never received any taint of guilt from Adam, which means that if his soul could not have been in Adam without contracting original sin then his soul was never in Adam. Thus the logical bottom line about Christ's innocent soul is: "if he cannot come from there [i.e., from Adam] without guilt, then he is not from there."[103]

One might want to raise all sorts of questions at this point, most pointedly: if Christ's soul was not in Adam in the beginning with all the rest of us, in what sense is it truly human? But Augustine does not deal with such questions and does not have to, because he never takes a particular position about how all our souls got to us from Adam (whether they are passed along through bodily procreation or not). There are huge questions in this area concerning the transmission of human souls which Augustine never resolved, which means he never committed himself to a particular theory and its particular problems. Hence one reason the concept of Christ's soul plays no particular role in Augustine's soteriology is that these questions would have to be resolved first, and Augustine never finds himself in a position to resolve them.[104]

8

New Testament Sacraments and the Flesh of Christ

The medieval theology of sacramental efficacy made a sharp distinction between the sacraments of the Old Law and of the New Law, teaching that it was only the latter which confer grace. Calvin collapsed this distinction, contending that no external sign confers grace, whereas Luther collapsed the distinction in the opposite direction, affirming that both could function like the Gospel as signs that give what they signify. In this respect Augustine belongs with Calvin, not with Luther and medieval theology. For Augustine the coming of Christ makes believers less dependent on external signs, not more, like a young man who graduates from fearful subjection under a disciplinarian to love of truth under a good teacher. By Augustine's reckoning the difference between fear and love, between literal subjection to external observances and spiritually understanding their inward meaning, is also the difference between Jews and Christians. It was easy for the medieval theologians to miss this turn away from the power of external things because Augustine sometimes spoke of "the virtue of the sacrament" in ways which suggested he was attributing spiritual efficacy to the external sign of the sacrament. But a close examination of Augustine's most important treatment of the relation between the Old and New Testaments, in the treatise Against Faustus the Manichaean, *shows that the phrase refers to human virtues, not to the power of divine grace. The incarnate Christ fulfills the promises of the Old Testament not because his flesh is the effective means of salvation but because it is the first example of salvation and eternal life. In Augustine's doctrine of atonement the power of Christ's blood lies in its powerlessness, the human weakness and mortality that the Son of God took on for our sake, which is overcome by divine power in his resurrection. There is no room in Augustine's thought for a concept of Christ's life-giving flesh, and hence even though he sometimes speaks in his sermons as if Christ's literal body is present in the Eucharist, he does not urge his congregation to find their salvation there.*

What a theologian says about the sacraments is doubly important because it parallels what he says about Christ in the flesh. If there is no external efficacy in the one, there is none in the other. This has terribly important consequences for piety and pastoral care: it means the attention of those who long for life in Christ must be directed to some more inward dimension, to something more spiritual than Christ incarnate. This is the great reason to be critical of any inward turn in Christianity and to be grateful for medieval accounts of sacraments as efficacious external means of grace.

Sacraments Old and New

The medieval theologians arguing for the efficacy of the church's sacraments made a sharp distinction between the sacraments of the Old Law and those of the New Law, the former merely signifying grace and the later both signifying and conferring it.[1] Peter Lombard, in whose *Sentences* this distinction first took shape, seems to have tried various ways of formulating it before settling on the contrast between Old Law and New Law. His initial formulation distinguishes the sacraments of the Law (*sacramenta legalia*) from those of the Gospel (*evangelica sacramenta*).[2] A formulation later in the *Sentences* also relies on the contrast of Law and Gospel:

> The *letter of the Gospel* is distinct from *the letter of the Law* because
> the promises are different: the latter promises things of earth, the
> former things of heaven. The sacraments are also different, because
> the latter only signify, the former confer grace.[3]

The striking phrase "letter of the Gospel" (*evangelii littera*) evidently results from Lombard's combining Augustine's letter/Spirit distinction with the Law/Gospel distinction and recognizing that the two are not parallel. Letter contrasts with Spirit as outward to inward, whereas both Law and Gospel are outward, together with their promises and sacraments. For Lombard, therefore, the distinction between spiritual power and mere signification cannot run parallel to the distinction between inner and outer, as it does for Augustine. He needs a new, hybrid concept, combining spiritual efficacy with externality, locating the grace of the Gospel in the letter of word and sacrament. This is precisely the concept of efficacious external means of grace that characterizes the medieval doctrine of the church's sacraments, which Lombard later in the *Sentences* designates with the term "the sacraments of the New Law."[4] If he had stuck with phrases like "Gospel sacraments" or "letter of the Gospel," the conceptual continuity between medieval sacraments and Lutheran Gospel would have been that much clearer.

Like any medieval or Reformation theologian, Lombard wants to explain his departure from Augustine in Augustinian terms. So after giving his definition of "sacrament" and explaining that the sacrifices and ceremonies of the Old Law are not sacraments in the strict sense because "they were instituted merely to signify grace,"[5] he calls on Augustine to distinguish the sacraments (loosely so called) of the Old Law from the sacraments (properly so called) of the New Law.

> It remains to see what the distinction is between the old and the new sacraments, as we may call "sacraments" what in ancient times signified sacred things, such as sacrifices and oblations and so forth. Augustine briefly indicates the difference between them, saying that "the former merely *promised*" and signified, "but the latter *give* salvation."[6]

Lombard's quotation is not exact, but it does accurately reflect a characteristic passage on the sacraments from Augustine's sermons on the Psalms, which includes one piece of rather uncharacteristic language. The passage is a commentary on the difference between the Old Testament and the New Testament, including the difference in their sacraments:

> The sacraments are not the same, because on the one hand there are sacraments giving salvation, on the other hand sacraments promising a Savior. *The sacraments of the New Testament give salvation, the sacraments of the Old Testament promised a Savior.* Therefore, since now you possess the things promised—already having the Savior—why do you seek the things that make the promises?[7]

Except for the uncharacteristic verb "to give," this passage could be a summary of Augustine's long discussion of the Old Testament and its sacraments in book 19 of *Against Faustus the Manichaean*, which we will examine in detail below.[8] Lombard is clearly reading Augustine's sermon as if his point were that the sacraments of the New Testaments are signs that not only promise and signify salvation but effectually give it.

But this reading, where all the weight lies on the uncharacteristic verb "give," runs counter to the Augustinian text it appears to be summarizing as well as to other, related texts, as John Calvin points out in his critique of medieval sacramental theology. After quoting from the same text as Lombard, Calvin argues that Augustine's language in this text is figurative and hyperbolic. In saying that the sacraments of the New Testament "give salvation," Calvin argues,

> Augustine meant nothing else here than what he wrote elsewhere, "The sacraments of the Mosaic Law foretold [*praenuntiasse*] Christ, ours announce [*annuntiare*] him." And against Faustus: "those were promises of things to be accomplished, these are indications of things already accomplished." It is as if he said: those are figures of [*figurasse*] him who was still awaited, but ours display as present him who has already come.[9]

The main point of this book could be summed up by saying that Calvin is right about Augustine, even if he is wrong about the sacraments. The difference between Old Testament and New Testament sacraments for Augustine is not between signifying grace and also conferring it, but simply between two kinds of signification, one looking forward to the future and the other proclaiming what has already happened. The difference is neatly captured, as Calvin notes, in Augustine's frequent verbal contrast between *praenuntiare* and *annuntiare*, foretelling what is yet to come and announcing what has already arrived, which makes for a change in the outward form of the sacrament just as it requires a change in the tense of the verb, from a savior who *will come* to one who *has come*.[10] In short, what is signified is the same but how it is signified differs, so that the only change is in the outward sign, not in its inward meaning or efficacy. The uncharacteristic verb "give" is simply a vivid sermonic replacement for Augustine's more usual verb, "announce": the New Testament sacraments give salvation only in the sense that they announce a Savior who has already come, so that in that sense we already have salvation. They certainly do not give salvation in the sense of eternal life, as Augustine himself proceeds to clarify: "I say, 'you possess the things promised,' not because we have already received eternal life but because Christ has already come, who was foretold by the prophets."[11] If he had wanted to dwell on this point, he could have spoken in his usual fashion of the salvation we have in hope (*in spe*) but not yet in reality (*in re*). Neither by announcing nor by promising do sacraments literally give the salvation they signify.

When Promising Is Giving

Well before Calvin, Luther also undermined the medieval distinction between sacraments of the Old Law and the New in his extremely influential treatise on *The Babylonian Captivity of the Church* (1520) which was well known to Calvin. In this relatively early work, however, it is not always clear how different Luther's view of the sacraments would turn out to be from the teaching later developed by Calvin and other Reformed theologians in Switzerland. Read in light of his later writings, in fact, Luther's point is clearly the opposite of Calvin's: not only do New Testament sacraments give salvation, but so do Old Testament sacraments. The point is explicit, though perhaps easily overlooked:

> It is an error to hold that the sacraments of the New Law differ from those of the Old Law in the effectiveness of their signs. For in this respect they are the same. The same God who now saves us by baptism and the bread, saved Abel by his sacrifice, Noah by the rainbow, Abraham by circumcision, and all the others by their respective signs.[12]

Underlying this breakdown of the distinction between the two kinds of sacraments is Luther's non-Augustinian notion of the promise of God, which is the foundation both of his sacramental theology in *The Babylonian Captivity* and of his doctrine of justification in the epochal treatise *On the Freedom of a Christian* written in the same year. In Luther's theology Lombard's distinction between the old sacraments *promising* a Savior and the new sacraments *giving* salvation breaks down, because God's promises give what they signify. These efficacious promises are precisely what Luther means by Gospel, "divine promises in which God promises, offers and gives us all his possessions and benefits in Christ."[13] That is why Luther can transform Augustine's prayer for grace, "Give what you command, and command what you will"[14] into instructions about how to find grace in the external word of the Gospel: "*The promises of God give* what the commands of God require."[15] Through faith in the promise of Christ one receives nothing less than the Savior himself, and with him grace, salvation, justification, holiness, and all that is his.[16]

Yet of course Calvin was not simply wrong to see in Luther's writings a critique of medieval notions of sacramental efficacy. The immediate purpose of *The Babylonian Captivity* was to rein in extravagant claims for the efficacy of the sacraments made by the late medieval church, where a whole economy had grown up in which the mass could be bought and sold as an efficacious ritual acquiring grace that was applicable to needy souls such as those in Purgatory, who were in no position to receive the sacrament themselves.[17] Of this kind of sacramental efficacy Luther was a resolute enemy, just like Calvin. And his fundamental criticism was an Augustinian point that Calvin shared: the sacraments do no good at all except to those who receive them in faith. The question that eventually divided Luther from Reformed theologians like Calvin was what good the external sacraments themselves actually do to those who receive them in faith.

Luther made his argument against the extravagant late medieval version of sacramental efficacy by rejecting one medieval principle and endorsing another. It is not true, he insisted, that the sacraments of the New Law have such efficacy that, as the one principle had it, they confer grace on anyone "who puts no obstacle in the way."[18] In practice this principle meant that anyone who does not actively intend to commit a mortal sin could go ahead and buy a mass or an indulgence and count on it working. Luther's doctrine of justification by faith alone, by contrast, is marked by his endorsement of a different principle, which he elsewhere calls "the common saying among our teachers,"[19] the principle that "it is not the sacrament but the faith of the sacrament that justifies."[20] These principles are in effect two different ways of understanding the crucial qualification of sacramental efficacy established in the canonical statement of medieval sacramental theology in the Council of Florence in 1439:

> The sacraments of the New Law . . . are very different from the
> sacraments of the Old Law. The latter do not cause grace but are only
> figures of [figurant] grace to be given by the passion of Christ; ours,
> however, both contain grace and confer it *on those who worthily
> receive.*[21]

Conceptually what was at issue between Luther and his opponents was the nature of this worthy reception. Luther held that faith alone constitutes worthy reception of the sacrament, because the power of the sacrament lies in the promise of God that establishes it and the proper way to receive a promise is simply to believe it. The principle about not putting obstacles in the way, on the other hand, served to legitimize the late medieval economy of sacraments that worked as if by magic (merely by virtue of being performed, as "a work done" or *opus operatum,* according to another principle that Luther rejected) so long as the purchaser was not in a state of mortal sin. Luther's point was an Augustinian one, accepted by most Catholic theologians, medieval and modern, namely, that a sacrament is not efficacious for those who do not receive it in faith. Indeed, he thinks of the "common saying" about justification through faith in the sacrament as "taken from the teachings of St. Augustine,"[22] though he seems aware that it is not a quotation from Augustine but a comment on a key passage (to be discussed below) in which Augustine says that the sacrament is effective not because it is performed but "because it is believed."[23] He explains the principle in a way that must have appealed to Calvin, apparently locating salvific efficacy not in the mere performance of the sacrament itself but in the faith that receives it. Yet the wording of the principle points ultimately in a different direction from Reformed theology, in that what justifies sinners is precisely faith *in the sacrament*.[24]

We arrive here at a subtle conceptual distinction that has immense pastoral implications, for it makes a great difference in how believers are taught to direct their attention. To take as seriously as Luther does the notion that we are justified by believing the sacrament is to direct our attention to external signs in a kind of outward turn. To sum the issue up in a crucial Augustinian metaphor, the question is whether we should ever cling to external things. Whereas Calvin warns that we must not "cling too tightly to the external sign,"[25] Luther insists that not to "cling to the outward signs by which God has revealed Himself in Christ . . . is to lose Christ altogether."[26] For Luther, what Christian faith does is precisely to cling to external things, the sacraments and the external word of the Gospel, as for instance in baptism: "faith clings to the water and believes it to be baptism in which there is sheer salvation and life, not through the water . . . but through its incorporation with God's word."[27] The difference is between finding grace and salvation in the external sign itself (as that which both contains and confers grace, to use the medieval formulations) and taking the sign rather as an admonition to seek something that must be found elsewhere, in a more spiritual dimension. These are not just two different conceptions of sacraments but two different conceptions of faith. Does Christian faith find its Savior in external, bodily things present before our senses or does it turn its attention in some more inward, spiritual, or experiential direction? The difference, in short, is between medieval sacramental theology and the semiotics of Augustine's treatise *On the Teacher*. Calvin and Reformed theology follow Augustine in the latter while Luther follows Lombard and Aquinas in the former (with the proviso that for Luther the Old Testament sacraments too were efficacious insofar as they promised to give a Savior, just like the Gospel, which is a word that effectually gives what it promises).

The Education of the Human Race

For Augustine the sacraments of the Old Testament and of the New are not distinguished by their efficacy, except in a negative way: outward signs have a greater hold over the minds of a carnal people. The fundamental difference between the Old Testament and the New is that they are concerned with two different kinds of people, Jews and Christians, one carnal and the other spiritual, one bound by fear because they desire temporal rewards and the other freed by grace to love eternal goods.[28] Indeed for Augustine all of history turns on this difference, for Christ came when the human race was ready to make the transition from servitude and fear to freedom and love, which is the transition from life under Law to life under grace.[29] It is no accident that this is the key transition both for the order of salvation (*ordo salutis*) in the psychology of grace and for the history of humanity as a whole. Augustine develops the parallel between the ages of individual human beings and the ages of the human race precisely for the purpose of expounding the great Pauline theme of the meaning of Christ's advent for the Jewish people. What are believers in Christ (whom Augustine, unlike Paul, takes for granted are Gentile) to make of these older brothers, the ancient people of Israel, with their strange religious life, their animal sacrifices and outdated observances that were nonetheless commanded by God? Augustine finds he must make sense of the coming of Christ not only as the founding of Christianity but as the undoing of Jewish religion. Yet there must be continuity as well as transition, because Old Testament rites were performed in obedience to the same God whom Christians worship. Augustine's semiotic theory gives him a simple and lucid new way of stating both the difference and the continuity between Old and New Testaments: the signs have changed but the thing they signify is the same.

The key ontological problem lurking behind Augustine's discussions of the difference between Old and New Testament sacraments is a Platonist question about the relation between eternity and time: why does the one unchanging Truth result in so many changing signs, so many differences between the Testaments in laws, promises, and sacraments? Augustine tackles this question near the beginning of his career by distinguishing between the one unchanging eternal Law and the many changing temporal laws, the latter being derived from the former (which is none other than "highest Reason") and justly changed only in accordance with it.[30] Later he uses a similar distinction in the *Confessions* to defend Old Testament mores (such as polygamy) against Manichaean criticism, arguing that because times change, the same eternal Justice will treat one time differently from another, just as one kind of work is permitted in the morning and another in the afternoon, or one kind of armor is made for the hand and another for the foot. "Does this means justice is variable and changing?" he asks, and answers in the negative, adding, "yet the times over which justice presides are not all equal, for they are times."[31] It is hard to put it more simply than that: times change, for they are times. That means one time differs from another, and an unchanging Justice will necessarily treat differently what is in fact different. Just as it treats the innocent differently from the guilty, so it may need to treat morning differently from afternoon and ancient Jews differently from contemporary Christians. To treat unequal things unequally is precisely the equity of divine Justice.

Since the coming of Christ in the flesh marks a huge difference in how divine Wisdom treats the times of human history, Augustine needs to give an account of what exactly makes the times so different. We know why morning is different from afternoon and hand from foot, but why were the times of the Old Testament so different from those of the New Testament: why are prophets and prefigurations appropriate for the one, but the Son of God in the flesh for the other? The fundamental difference, Augustine keeps saying, is between two kinds of people, one less mature and spiritual than the other. Augustine introduces the parallel between the ages of humanity and the ages of individual human beings precisely in order to make this point: to argue that in the times before Christ, humanity as a whole was not yet grown up enough to make the transition from servitude under the Law to freedom under grace.

This is clear from the way the parallel is developed in a series of questions answered early in the collection *On Eighty-Three Different Questions*, which is one of the most helpful sources in understanding the early development of Augustine's theology. The questions begin with the most fundamental issue of all, which is "why the Son of God appeared in a human being . . . ?"[32] Au-Augustine answers: "Because he came to demonstrate an example of living for human beings." He came in this visible form for the same reason the Holy Spirit appeared in the form of a dove: "Each was made in a visible way for the sake of carnal people, to transfer them through stages of sacraments [*sacramentorum gradibus*] from things discerned by bodily eyes to things understood by the mind." Here the concept of sacraments is drawn into an analogue of Augustine's notion of education, progressing from corporeal to intelligible vision by gradual steps or stages (*gradibus*), which are a keynote of his early curriculum in the liberal disciplines.[33] Just as a semiotic theory of words undergirded his project of liberal education for individual souls, a semiotic conception of sacraments is now on hand to describe the education of the human race, where sacred rites are changed but not their significance, just like changing words that signify unchanging things: "For words resound and pass away, but the things signified by words, when something divine and eternal is being expounded in a discussion, do not similarly pass away."[34] Like the very word "God," which passes away before you know it, the sacraments also may change and pass away with no change in what they signify.[35]

The next question is pivotal. Augustine must account for the particular historical location of Christ's coming in the flesh. The question is: "Why does the Lord Jesus Christ come so long afterwards and not in the beginning of human sin?"[36] The problem is that Christ incarnate, coming in the midst of human history rather than immediately after Adam's sin, is not equally available to all people at all times like the inward presence of unchanging Wisdom and Justice. This calls for a theory of universal history, and here Augustine begins the conceptual work required to produce one. He points out that times themselves are ordered in a beautiful way by divine Beauty, as we can see in the succession of ages in a human life from infancy to old age—what we today call a life cycle. Human history too has such an order and beauty, a progression of ages that makes some forms of moral education appropriate at some times and not at others. There is no point in a teacher being divinely sent early in history when only a few people, not the human race as a whole, were ready to learn from him to love eternal things. Therefore—picking up on a key metaphor from Paul but developing it much more ambitiously—Augustine suggests that people were "kept under the guardianship of the Law, like little children under a disciplinarian [*paedogogus*]."[37] Like a good teacher waiting until children reach the opportune age of young adulthood (*juvenilem aetatem*), the divine Truth that illuminates all those who ever arrive at wisdom waited for the human race itself to reach the time of young adulthood (*tempore juventutis*) before taking up human form as an example of the best way to live, so that a whole people might come to wisdom.[38]

A little later Augustine deals specifically with Old Testament rites, addressing the question, "Why did the children of Israel visibly sacrifice offerings of livestock?"[39] Evidently Augustine is already thinking in terms of a contrast between visible and invisible sacrifice.[40] Animal sacrifices are "images which it behooved a carnal people to celebrate so there would be a prefiguration of the new people in the servitude of the old."[41] Here Israel is placed in the context of the education of the human race, resulting in a set of themes that remain fundamental for Augustine's thinking about the sacraments of the Old Testament and the New: not just the idea of prefiguration but also that of Israel's carnality and servitude, which will be undone by the "grace of the Liberator," a key phrase in Augustine's early writing about the advent of Christ.[42]

It seems to me that we can discern here a conceptual adumbration of the genteel anti-Semitism characteristic of progressive theories of history, which regularly treat the Jews as backward, tribal, authoritarian, and illiberal, so that one of the most crucial features of the Incarnation in liberal theology must be that Christ is not in spirit a Jew but represents an altogether different kind of consciousness, freer, more spiritual, more universal, and less particularistic, less captive to externals, a harbinger of Western liberalism itself.[43] All these motifs are present *in nuce* in the Platonist critique of the Jews built into

Augustine's progressive view of history. The "new people" whom Christ frees from Jewish servitude have reached the age of maturity analogous to young adulthood, when "it is no longer necessary to think carnally but one can turn voluntarily [*converti voluntate*] to spiritual things and be inwardly reborn." (At this early stage in his career Augustine has no notion of grace as inner help for the will:[44] here he treats the capacity for conversion of will and regeneration as resulting from the maturity of the human race brought about by divine providence in history, not a special inward gift of grace to individuals.) The point is explicitly educational, as Augustine introduces the great idea underlying the modern Enlightenment theory of progress, the education of the human race: "What takes place in one well-educated human being by the order of nature and discipline happens analogously [*proportione*] in the whole human race by divine providence, and is accomplished very beautifully."[45] This education is moral as well as intellectual, as is especially clear in a later question about why Israel was allowed to deceive the Egyptians and make off with their gold and silver in the Exodus: the Egyptians deserved it and the level of moral maturity in Israel, at that stage of human history, meant it was an appropriate act of justice for them to perform.[46] Human history, in short, is progressive precisely because the human race is maturing, becoming more capable of an education suitable for adult minds. From that perspective the Jews are a throwback to an earlier and more immature age, legitimate for their time (contrary to Manichaean criticisms of Old Testament mores) but no longer appropriate for the world of today.

Fewer and Less Burdensome

For Augustine the Old Testament sacraments, with their requirement of visible animal sacrifice, were an onerous form of servitude suitable for a carnal people, from which Christians are freed by "the grace of the Liberator" in the coming of Christ. The advantage of the New Testament sacraments is not that they confer grace (an idea that does not occur to Augustine) but that they are fewer and less burdensome. So he argues in his earliest statement on New Testament sacramental theology, in the treatise *On True Religion*:

> But now, since piety begins in fear and is perfected in charity, the
> people were burdened by many sacraments [*sacramenta*] in the Old
> Law, bound by fear during the time of their servitude. This was useful
> for such people, getting them to desire the grace of God which the
> prophets predicted would come. When it did come, the Wisdom of

God itself, having assumed a man by whom we were called to freedom, established a few very salutary sacraments which were to
keep together [*continerent*] the society of Christian people, i.e., the
multitude who are free under the one God. But the many sacraments that had been imposed on the Hebrew people, i.e., the multitude shackled under the same one God, were taken out of action and
remain for belief and interpretation. That way they do not tie people up in servitude but exercise the mind in freedom.[47]

The paragraph from which this is quoted completes a description of Christ's
human life as an education for human beings. Expounding "the rule of rational
discipline," the paragraph distinguishes between what is taught in an obvious
or literal way (*apertissime*) from what is taught in a hidden or symbolic way
(*similitudinibus*) in words, deeds, and sacraments. The hermeneutical principle
for the latter is that "the exposition of mysteries [*mysteria*] is directed toward
things said in an obvious way."[48] *Mysteria* here has the broad sense of "hidden
meaning," while *sacramenta* in the long quotation above has the narrow sense
of "sacred rites." But the latter is a subspecies of the former: sacred rites are
sacraments precisely because they are mysteries having hidden meaning.

Hence the principle of interpreting symbolic or hidden meanings in light
of what is taught in an obvious way applies also to the sacraments, especially
those of the Old Testament, which are no longer actually performed but whose
significance still needs to be interpreted. This offers opportunities for mental
exercise that Augustine finds attractive, because for him scriptural exegesis is a
form of intellectual love that delights in passing from obscurity to clarity, from
sensible figures to intelligible signification, as we can see in the gusto with
which his sermons focus not on the plain meaning of the text but on its
cruxes.[49] The obscurity of the sacraments of the Old Law in signifying spiritual
truth would not be so onerous a servitude were there not the added burden of
actually performing them—a burden done away with now that the grace of the
Liberator has set us free. Christ comes, in other words, not as a good Jew but as
one who puts an end to Jewish religion and its servitude to a multitude of
burdensome observances.

Augustine does not say in this text why he associates Jewish servitude with
fear, but in a related text from about the same time he explains the difference
between the Old Testament and the New as that between a disciplinarian
(*paedagogus*) and a real teacher (*magister*): in the Law God gave to humanity "a
disciplinarian whom they would fear" but in Christ he gave them "a teacher
whom they would love."[50] Moreover, the next treatment of Old Testament sacraments we shall examine suggests that this fear arose from a lack of under-

standing, like the experience of a child who must take orders from an intim-
idating disciplinarian rather than be led by a teacher to see the true significance
of words like "justice." Not knowing the hidden meaning of their visible rites,
the Jews were required simply to do what they were told, afraid of how they
might be punished if they didn't.

I would suggest that, as often happens in the anti-Jewish strands of
Christian theology, the real targets of this critique are fellow Christians who are
found to be embarrassingly primitive, literalistic, or authoritarian, keen on the
external observance of familiar rituals but not on understanding their deeper
meaning. In other words, the fearful Jewish servitude described by Augustine
is probably not so different from that of his more hidebound and simple-
minded brethren in the African Church, which he fled as a youth. Now that he
has returned to Africa and been made a teacher he is determined to turn their
attention to a more spiritual, Platonist understanding, which in Italy he
learned can be combined with a solid Christian orthodoxy. In any case, it is
clear enough in this passage from *On True Religion* that the last thing Augustine wants to do is ascribe to the external signs and sacraments of the New
Testament an efficacy greater than the Old, as if Christians should be more
dependent on external observances than the Jews.

The same basic themes and underlying motivation are evident some five
years later in the much more elaborate treatment of the sacraments in the
treatise *On Christian Doctrine,* where Augustine explicitly brings the concept of
sacrament into the framework of the new semiotic theory he has just con-
structed in the treatise's second book.[51] In book 3 he proceeds to connect this
semiotic theory to the letter/Spirit hermeneutics at the beginning of a long
discussion of figurative language, the first examples of which are Old Testament ordinances that Christians are not to take literally. Augustine can now
explain the carnal thinking behind literalism in semiotic terms: to take something literally (*ad litteram accipere*) is to take the sign for the things signified
(*signum pro rebus accipere*).[52] This means taking a metaphor in the ordinary
sense of the words without relating that ordinary signification to anything
further. Augustine gives the example of hearing the word "Sabbath" and understanding nothing but the seventh day of the week, or hearing the word
"sacrifice" and thinking of nothing but offerings of crops and livestock. The
apostle aptly calls this "the letter that kills," Augustine says, for it is like killing
the soul when we subject our understanding, the part of the soul by which we
are superior to beasts, to the flesh.[53] Literalism, in other words, is carnal because it means failing to think like a Platonist: "It is precisely the most wretched
servitude of the soul to take signs for things and be unable to raise the eye of the
mind above the eye of the corporeal creature to drink in the eternal light."[54]

Jewish servitude, in this text, means being subject to signs that must be performed and venerated without understanding what they signify. Nonetheless they are "useful signs instituted by God"[55] because although the Jews "observed signs of spiritual things in place of the things themselves, not knowing what they should relate them to, nonetheless they had this instilled in them: that by such servitude they pleased the one God, whom they did not see."[56] This was certainly better than pagan worship, in which vain and useless signs are venerated.[57] "Christian liberty," however, frees both pagans and Jews from their respective servitude.[58] It frees Jews by interpreting the signs to which they were subject and raising their minds up to the things signified, and it frees Gentiles from slavery to idols, without requiring them to undergo such Jewish ceremonies as circumcision. The result is a new kind of signs, the sacraments of the New Testament:

> But in the time after our Lord's resurrection the most manifest in-
> dication of our freedom came to light. Nor indeed are we burdened by
> the trouble of performing those signs, which we now understand;
> rather, the Lord himself and the apostolic teaching handed down just
> a few in place of the many—very easy to perform, very lofty when
> understood, very pure and chaste in performance, such as the sac-
> rament of baptism and the celebration of the Lord's body and blood.
> Whoever receives them, instructed in that to which they refer, rec-
> ognizes that they are to be venerated in spiritual freedom rather than
> in carnal servitude.[59]

Whether in the Old Testament or the New, the sacraments are related to the things they signify as letter is to Spirit. The New Testament sacraments are better not because they have more intrinsic power but because they are fewer and less burdensome to perform, so that those who understand them may more easily turn their attention to the invisible and spiritual things they signify. In this context a doctrine of sacraments as efficacious external means of grace would defeat Augustine's purpose, returning us to a Jewish, literalistic servitude—as if the things our souls most inwardly seek could be found by clinging to external signs.

The Virtue of the Sacraments

One Augustinian turn of phrase that often suggests to the medieval theologians that he has a doctrine of external sacramental efficacy is his speaking of the virtue (*virtus*) of the sacraments. The Latin term, like its English equivalent until recently, can mean either power or ethical virtue. Augustine shows a decided preference for the latter meaning, usually using *potentia* or *potestas* for the former. This preference has important consequences, as for instance when Augustine reads Paul's phrase "Christ the *virtus* of God and the wisdom of God" (1 Cor. 1:24) as if it were a statement about Christ as divine Virtue being the foundation of ethics.[60] On the other hand, if one has Augustine's less-preferred meaning in mind, so that *virtus* means power, then his remarks about "the virtue of the sacrament" have very much the look of statements about sacramental efficacy.

An influential passage in this regard comes from a sermon in which Augustine distinguishes validity and efficacy by contrasting the Old Testament sacraments and "the grace which is the virtue of the sacraments."[61] These sacraments, including the mysteries (*mysteria*) or prefigurations whose hidden signification was Christ, were shared in common by the whole people of Israel, but grace was not. As usual, in discussing the efficacy of the sacraments Augustine emphasizes the continuity between Old and New Testaments, pointing out that exactly the same thing is true of the sacrament of baptism in his own day.

> The washing of regeneration is common to all who are baptized in the name of the Father, Son and Holy Spirit, but *the grace itself of which these are the sacraments,* by which they are regenerated as members of the Body of Christ together with its Head, is not common to all. For heretics also have the same baptism, as well as false brethren sharing the name of Catholics.[62]

Clearly this passage aims to make the usual distinction between validity and efficacy that Augustine deploys against the Donatists. However, the unusually clear focus on the relation between sacrament and grace, which is governed by the gulf between outward sign and inward efficacy, almost leads him outside the bounds of the traditional theology of baptismal regeneration altogether. For if heretics and false brethren have a valid sacrament but not the grace of regeneration, as Augustine's wording here implies, it would seem they are not regenerated at all, which means they would have to be baptized again upon true conversion to the Catholic church. To reconcile this incautiously phrased sermon with the sacramental theology of *On Baptism against the Donatists,* we must suppose that it is possible (indeed quite common) for regeneration to occur without the grace of regeneration, as if baptismal regeneration were simply another name for valid baptism itself, which can be devoid of grace and spiritual efficacy. Something quite close to this is Augustine's actual position, as we have seen.[63]

Quite apart from this piece of incautious wording, the sermon is important for later sacramental theology because it identifies grace as both the virtue of the sacraments and that of which they are sacraments, leading medieval theologians to equate the two terms, "the virtue of the sacrament" (*virtus sacramenti*) and "the thing signified by the sacrament" (*res sacramenti*).[64] As a result, this sermon is one of the strongest textual supports in Augustine for the medieval view that grace is the thing that sacraments are signs of.[65] However, the sermon does not provide any account of sacraments as efficacious external means of grace but rather assumes the two-track sort of efficacy that is pervasive in Augustine's anti-Donatist works:[66] on the one hand is the visible sacrament of baptism conferred by a minister and common to all in the community, and on the other is the invisible grace that some have and others don't. Augustine offers not the slightest hint that the sacrament itself gives the grace. The virtue of the sacrament that he mentions here is not a power of conferring grace but another way of referring to the *res sacramenti*, the thing signified by the sacrament,[67] which may or may not be present along with the outward form of the sacrament, depending on whether the recipient is inwardly united in charity with the people of God.

Many of the passages cited by medieval theologians on sacramental efficacy come from Augustine's most elaborate discussion of the virtue of the sacraments, contained in book 19 of the lengthy polemic *Against Faustus the Manichaean*, written not long after *On Christian Doctrine*. This is the book in which Augustine explains why the piety of every religious group requires visible seals or sacraments.[68] He goes on to emphasize, however, that these are necessary but not sufficient. The case of Simon Magus, for instance, shows us that "the visible sacraments of piety can be present even in the impious."[69] Such people are described by the apostle as "having the *form* of piety, but denying the *virtue* thereof."[70] This quotation introduces a distinction that is of great importance in the next few paragraphs: between the visible form of a sacrament (or simply "the visible sacrament") and its invisible virtue in the soul. This language, which appears in several other Augustinian texts, leads eventually to one of the most important medieval definitions of a sacrament: "the visible form of an invisible grace."[71] But the quotation from which this formula originates shows why, at least in *Against Faustus the Manichaean*, "the virtue of the sacrament" cannot simply be identified with the divine power of grace, despite the identification in the previously quoted sermon. Augustine is very clear when he introduces this terminology in *Against Faustus the Manichaean* that the virtue he has in mind is piety, because the visible sacrament itself is the outward "form of piety." Augustine takes piety to include both love and faith, defining it in biblical terms as "*charity* from a pure heart and good

conscience and *faith* unfeigned,"[72] so as to tie together the traditional designation of the sacrament of baptism as "the sacrament of *faith*"[73] with his
hermeneutical rule of *charity,* according to which the meaning of all external
signs of the faith is to be expounded in terms of Christian love.[74] In *Against
Faustus the Manichaean,* therefore, the distinction between the sacrament's
visible form and its invisible virtue reflects the great ontological divide between
bodily things and things of the soul. To have the form of piety without the
virtue thereof is to have an outward bodily sign without possessing inwardly, in
the soul, the piety it signifies.

When Augustine proceeds to discuss the difference between the sacraments of the Old Testament and those of the New he applies the distinction
between the visible sacrament and its virtue to both. The Old Testament sacraments and sacrifices are no longer performed precisely because they are
fulfilled, and in their place

> others are instituted, *greater in virtue* [*virtute majora*] and better in
> usefulness, easier to do and fewer in number; for now that the
> righteousness of faith is revealed and the children of God are called
> to liberty, the yoke of servitude is removed, which was appropri-
> ate to a hard and carnal people.[75]

We have seen all this before, except for the phrase I have italicized. A medieval
reader, identifying "the virtue of the sacrament" with the divine power of grace,
would naturally interpret this passage to mean that New Testament sacraments
have more efficacy as means of grace than those of the Old Testament.[76] But in
context it is quite clear that the virtue to which Augustine refers is, as before,
human piety rather than divine grace. This virtue is greater in the New Testament because the virtue of faith by which people are justified is openly revealed
and proclaimed rather than signified in obscure and figurative language.[77]

This identification of the virtue of the sacrament with piety or faith must
be borne in mind as we turn to a passage that had a great influence on medieval
accounts of sacramental efficacy. Augustine proceeds to phrase his contention
against Faustus in his own distinctive semiotic terms. His claim is that "signs
and sacraments" may change without any change in the *res ipsas,* the things
they signify. "The prophetic rite foretold [*praenuntiavit*] as promised" exactly
the same things that "the Gospel rite announced [*annuntiavit*] as fulfilled."[78]
The change in sacraments is analogous to the change in the form of words
used (i.e., the change in verb tense) when the same thing is first foretold as what
will happen and later announced as what has happened. After all, Augustine
adds, introducing a phrase that will have a long history, what are the sacraments if not something like visible words? The same consideration applies

therefore to both words and sacraments—and knowing Augustine's semiotics, we could add that this is because both words and sacraments belong to the same genus, signs. Here then is the crucial passage:

> For what else are these corporeal sacraments but as it were visible words [*quasi verba visibilia*], sacrosanct indeed but nonetheless mutable and temporal? For God is eternal, but the water and the whole corporeal action that is performed when we baptize, which is done and passes away [*et fit et transit*], is not eternal; and the same is true of the syllables which resound and pass away so quickly when the word "God" is said, syllables which must be spoken if the sacrament is to be consecrated. All these things are done and pass away, resound and pass away, but *the virtue that works through them remains continually* and the spiritual gift that is insinuated through them is eternal.[79]

The clause I have italicized is quoted by Thomas Aquinas in support of his teaching that the sacraments are instrumental causes of grace. This is a very reasonable conclusion if the virtue of which Augustine speaks is the divine power of grace; for as Thomas remarks, "that through which someone works is properly speaking an instrument."[80] But as we have seen, the context of *Against Faustus the Manichaean*, book 19, makes it clear that what Augustine has in mind is not divine grace but human virtue. It is specifically the virtue of piety, including faith and especially love, which according to Paul "remains forever."[81] In a similar vein, the eternal spiritual gift insinuated by the sacrament is not a grace conferred by the sacrament but the eternal life it signifies, much as something eternal is "insinuated," that is, signified but not conferred, by the word "God."[82]

The language of "the virtue of the sacrament" appears in one more important passage, perhaps the most frequently quoted of all Augustinian texts on the sacraments. It comes from a sermon on the Gospel of John, where shortly after washing his disciples' feet (which Augustine interprets as a kind of baptism) Christ announces, "Now you are clean because of the word which I have spoken to you." Augustine proceeds to inquire:

> Why does he not say, "you are clean because of the baptism with which you have been washed" but rather "because of the word which I have spoken"—unless it was because even in the water it is the word that cleanses? Take away the word, and what is water but water? *Let the word come to the element, and it becomes a sacrament,* which is itself a sort of visible word.[83]

The oft-quoted clause in italics is not about the efficacy of the sacrament but its validity. Without the words of consecration (viz., "I baptize you in the name of the Father, the Son, and the Holy Spirit") there is no sacrament at all, but just an ordinary washing with water. However, Augustine does proceed to say something about efficacy, which he locates not in the water but in the word, and not really in the external word but in the faith of the heart.

He begins his explanation of baptismal efficacy with another oft-quoted sentence: "Whence does water have such *great virtue, that it touches the body and cleans the heart,* unless *it is the word that does it,* not because it is said, but *because it is believed?*"[84] Aquinas takes the first italicized clause as the key Augustinian support for the external efficacy of the sacraments,[85] while the second is the sort of thing Luther loves to say about the power of the word,[86] but for Augustine himself the key to efficacy is actually in the third, the virtue of faith. The point of Augustine's rhetorical question is that water has no power to cleanse the heart at all, but only to touch the body. And the external word too does nothing in our hearts that is not done by our own faith. In contrast to the word that comes to the element to make it a sacrament, which is an external word resulting in a valid sacrament simply because it is spoken aloud over the water, the word that cleanses the heart has no effect except insofar as it is believed. Hence in the next sentence he distinguishes the outward utterance of the word from the inward virtue it signifies, using the language we have already seen in the treatise *Against Faustus the Manichaean:* "For even in the word itself, the sound that passes away is one thing and the virtue that remains is another."[87] Augustine proceeds to enlist a series of biblical quotations in support of this point, showing that faith belongs in the heart and describing the efficacious "word of faith" in terms that assimilate it to his concept of the inner word.[88] "The word does it all," he concludes, but it seems clear that the word to which he refers is not an external sign, a sound that passes away, but an inner conception of the heart that is formed when (in accordance with the definition of faith he gives elsewhere) the heart consents to what is said.[89] Thus the abiding virtue in this passage, as in *Against Faustus the Manichaean,* is not grace itself but the piety that results from grace. And nothing suggests that this piety is given to us by the external word that sounds and passes away, any more than by the water that merely touches the body. It is not the word that brings about faith, but rather the abiding inward virtue of faith that puts the word into effect.

Sacraments Promising Christ

What does not happen in Augustine's theology is that an external thing becomes the efficacious means by which an inward gift of God is bestowed on the soul. For this would violate the Platonist axiom of downward causality, which is to say that for Augustine it would violate the ontological order of things and their causes, giving lower and external things power over higher and inward things.[90] Aquinas and Luther too have an acute sense that this breaks the rules of nature, but they both think these rules were already broken in a more fundamental way when the flesh of Christ became the means of our redemption. Following Lombard, Aquinas's concept of external sacramental efficacy is explicitly based on the power of Christ's passion, his suffering and death in the flesh,[91] and Luther's notion that an external word can save us is likewise rooted in his Christology, in his conviction that the New Testament Gospel is a promise that gives us nothing less than Christ in the flesh and all that is his, much as a wedding vow gives a bride her bridegroom.[92] Always what theologians make of the sacraments depends on what they think of the power of Christ's flesh and blood. For Augustine too the sacraments cannot be understood apart from the coming of Christ in the flesh, for this is precisely why there is a difference between the sacraments of the Old Testament and of the New. To bring into focus the difference between Augustine's view of the relation between sacraments and flesh, and the medieval view found in Aquinas and Luther, we can turn again to book 19 of the treatise *Against Faustus the Manichaean*, which includes one of Augustine's most important hermeneutical statements about the relation of the Old Testament and the New, especially with regard to the sacraments.

Book 19 has the task of explaining why the Old Testament has authority in the church of Christ despite the fact that many of its rites and ordinances are no longer observed. Like every good Manichaean, Faustus was disgusted with the Jewish Law (especially circumcision, "that obscene little sign")[93] and was relieved to find that Manichaeanism, which he came to regard as true Christianity, rejected the Old Testament altogether.[94] His challenge to Augustine on this score is simple: if the Law of Moses really is the Law of God then why don't Catholics observe it? Why do they treat the ordinances, ceremonies, and sacraments of the Jews as if they were no longer binding, indeed no longer permitted? In fact, does not Catholic practice agree with Manichaean theory in rejecting the Law of Moses?[95]

Augustine's response is one of the most profound vindications of the Old Testament in the Christian tradition. Christ himself said he came not to destroy the Law and the Prophets but to fulfill them (Matt. 5:17), and he did so in two different ways, Augustine says, on the basis of an unusual construal of John 1:17: "For the Law came through Moses, but it became grace and truth through Jesus Christ."[96] This suggests to Augustine that there are two different kinds of fulfillment of the Old Testament in the New: through Christ, the Law became grace and the Prophets became truth. The former fulfillment is familiar from his Pauline exegesis: moral precepts such as those contained in the Decalogue are fulfilled in the sense that they are observed more fully by the grace of the New Testament than by the servitude of the Old Testament, which only makes sin abound until grace is received by faith.[97] The latter fulfillment means that the prophets' predictions come true with the advent of Christ.[98] Hence in contrast to the fulfillment of the Law, which improves the observance of the Old Testament, the fulfillment of the Prophets means that the Old Testament sacraments that prophesied the coming of Christ are no longer observed at all—precisely because they are fulfilled.

Augustine uses a variety of verbs to describe that aspect of the Old Testament which, because it is fulfilled, is no longer observed: its job is to prophesy (*prophetare*), promise (*promittere*), foretell (*praenuntiare*), prefigure (*praefigurare*), and signify (*significare*) what is to come in the New Testament.[99] The complexity of his notion of Old Testament *promises* is particularly interesting. Though in some contexts he emphasizes the contrast between Old Testament promises of earthly, temporal rewards with New Testament promises of eternal life,[100] there are other contexts where he insists on their continuity; for like the Old Testament sacraments and prefigurations, the Old Testament promises signify the same eternal goods as the New Testament, but in a veiled way.

> The same things are in the Old and the New Testaments—there
> overshadowed [*obumbrata*], here unveiled [*revelata*], there prefigured,
> here manifest. For not only are the sacraments different but also
> the promises. There temporal things seem to be set forth, but here it
> is most manifest that spiritual and eternal things are promised.[101]

As Augustine goes on to illustrate, in the one Testament the promised land is a place flowing with milk and honey, in the other it is the kingdom of heaven. But the earthly promised land is itself a figure signifying the eternal kingdom proclaimed openly in the New Testament. Hence he can describe the continuity and difference between the testaments in terms of the same thing being signified in two different ways, first veiled and then unveiled: "The sacrament of the kingdom of heaven is in fact veiled in the Old Testament, which in the fullness of time is unveiled [*revelatur*] in the New Testament."[102] In the anti-Pelagian writings it is the righteousness of God (by which we are made righteous) or grace itself that is veiled in the Old Testament but unveiled in the New.[103]

This insistence on the promise of an eternal good even in the Old Testament creates a certain tension and ambiguity in Augustine's notion of the thing signified by the Old Testament sacraments. On the one hand they promise (in their veiled and figurative way) eternal goods, but on the other they prefigure the coming of Christ in the flesh, which is a temporal event. The way Augustine resolves the tension explains why he often shifts freely (and usually unnoticed) from one signification to the other. The promises and prefigurations of the Old Testament are fulfilled by the coming of Christ in the flesh even when the things they signify, such as eternal life, are not exactly the same thing as Christ in the flesh. Consider for instance Augustine's explanation of the change from the Old Testament sacrament of circumcision to the New Testament sacrament of baptism:

> The Christian now is not circumcised, because the very thing which was prophesied by circumcision, Christ fulfills. For the stripping off of carnal generation, which was figured [*figurabatur*] by actually doing circumcisions, is now fulfilled by the resurrection of Christ.[104]

The nature of this fulfillment by Christ is the crucial point to observe. Augustine proceeds to speak of the bodily resurrection of Christ not as the *cause* of new life in us, but as an *example* of what will happen to us in the future. The fact that eternal life is still to come for everyone but Christ explains why there is still need for a sacrament of new life, even though its outward form has changed from circumcision to washing with water:

> And what is to come in our resurrection is commended by the sacrament of baptism. For the sacrament of new life should not be wholly done away with, because the resurrection of the dead remains for us in the future; but it should be changed for the better in the baptism which succeeds it, because what had not happened then has happened now: we are presented with *an example of the future eternal life* in the resurrection of Christ.[105]

Christ's coming in the flesh, in other words, fulfills the prophesies of the Old Testament sacraments by affording an example of the eternal life they promised. The epochal significance of the presence of God in the flesh, dividing the times of human history in two, is that he already has the gift we are promised to have in the future.

Two things are striking about this conception of the relation of the sacraments to Christ in the flesh. The most important, which we shall consider in the remainder of this book, is that Christ's flesh exemplifies the spiritual and eternal gift we are to seek but does not give or confer it. The second, less important but worth noting at this point, is that Augustine assumes what is promised by the sacraments is something that has not yet been given, as if only something that is not yet present could be the object of a promise. The two points are related: Augustine has nothing like Luther's notion that the promises of the Gospel effectually give us the salvation of Christ, because for Augustine Christ as man, which is to say Christ the mediator, exemplifies rather than effects what we long for. Augustine states the point in more general terms a little later in *Against Faustus the Manichaean:*

> What is still promised to the Church, i.e., to the Body of Christ, is both preached in its manifestation and is now indeed accomplished in that same Head of the Body, the Savior, i.e., "the one mediator between God and man, the man Jesus Christ." *For what is promised but life eternal* by the resurrection from the dead? This is now *accomplished in that flesh,* because "the Word became flesh and dwelt among us."[106]

As before, it is not simply Christ that is promised in the Old Testament sacraments but rather the eternal life of which he is the first example. The fact that this example was not yet manifested and proclaimed then but only prefigured and promised explains why the Old Testament veils what the New Testament reveals:

> Therefore faith also was hidden then, for all the just and holy people even of that time believed and hoped in the same things, promised by all those sacraments and all the ritual of sacred things.[107]

What was promised is fulfilled, insofar as eternal life is now no longer foretold but preached as something that has actually happened with Christ in the flesh. To say he fulfilled the Old Testament in his own flesh is therefore precisely to say he is an example of what is still promised to us in the New Testament as something yet to come:

> But now faith is unveiled [*revelata*] in which the people were shut up when they were under the guardianship of the Law, and what is promised to the faithful in the Judgment is now *accomplished in example* by him who came not to destroy the Law and the Prophets but to fulfill them.[108]

What is accomplished in the flesh of Christ is accomplished as an example for the rest of us. So far as this account goes, the New Testament does not offer Christ incarnate to us as anything more than an example. Augustine does not suggest that the flesh of Christ accomplishes or changes anything in us but rather that the power of God changes his flesh just as it will change ours, raising it from death to immortality. Thus even the flesh of Christ is not an instance of external efficacy.

Powerless Blood

Augustine has many ways of answering the question of why God became flesh, but one of the most characteristic is to refer to Christ as an example who teaches us humility and to live rightly by loving eternal things more than temporal things.[109] In one particularly fascinating and influential chapter in his great treatise *On the Trinity,* he enriches this answer by describing Christ in the flesh as both an example and a sacrament for us, because his one death and resurrection corresponds to a double death and resurrection in us.[110] Unlike Christ, sinners are dead in soul as well as body and therefore need a spiritual as well as bodily resurrection and renovation. Consequently, since Christ is not an example of the soul's death in sin nor therefore of its inner resurrection, in this respect he is a sacrament instead—not exemplifying but signifying the death and renewal of the inner man. Augustine therefore presents Christ's death and resurrection in the flesh as "an example for the outer man," because he undergoes what we shall all undergo in our own flesh, and also as "a sacrament for the inner man," an external sign of an inner transformation in us that he does not undergo himself. What is striking, again, is that in neither respect does Christ's flesh itself accomplish anything: it exemplifies the resurrection of our bodies rather than causes it, and signifies our inner renewal rather than confers it. Quite contrary to the medieval expectations of a theologian like Luther, who preaches that Christ is not just an example of righteousness like any other good man but a sacrament capable of giving us righteousness,[111] for Augustine Christ is a sacrament that does not effect what it signifies.

Thus the ontological powerlessness of external things in Augustine's thought extends not just to word and sacrament but to Christ, which is to say: even the flesh of Christ cannot be an external sign that gives what it signifies. Hence in contrast to Aquinas, the power of Christ's passion does not ground a theory of sacramental efficacy, because both Christ's passion and the sacraments are in themselves (i.e., apart from the virtues of faith and love instilled in us by the grace of the Holy Spirit) powerless. Consider for instance one of Augustine's most important and characteristic discussions of the atonement, which comes later in the treatise *On the Trinity.* Leading up to the discussion is the question of the power of Christ's blood: "What is 'justified in his blood'? What is the force [*vis*] of his blood, I ask, that those who believe in it are justified?"[112] The force of Christ's blood, it turns out, is a kind of powerlessness. In the course of explaining how the death of the sinless Christ paid the debt for us sinners and redeemed us from the bondage of the devil, Augustine deals specifically with the issue of power. God could of course have conquered the devil by sheer power (*potentia*), but instead chose to overcome him first by justice and then by power; for it belongs to the devil, not God, to seek conquest by power without justice. Therefore Christ willingly holds back his divine power, becoming man so that he could give himself over to the humiliation of death. In this way he suffers a death which he not only could have avoided by his divine power, but which as a sinless man he did not justly owe. This undeserved death is the key to our redemption, that is, to the freedom he won for us from the devil, who unjustly killed him and thus does not deserve to keep him or anyone who believes in him. This is how God conquered the devil first by justice and then by power, first allowing his Son to die an unjust death and then raising him from the dead by divine power. The blood of Christ figures in this story not as power but as powerlessness, as vulnerability to humiliation, injustice, and death. The "force of blood," it turns out, is not the power to give life but the ability to die, to pour out one's lifeblood upon the ground. This is not a strength but a weakness; it is precisely the mortal infirmity taken up by the immortal Son of God in his great humility.

The whole structure of Augustine's doctrine of Christ as mediator thus points in the direction of Christ's flesh and blood as forms of weakness and mortality, not life-giving power. As we have seen,[113] Christ is mediator in his human mortality, weakness, and humiliation, not his divine power, which is no different from the power of God the Father and therefore cannot mediate between God and his creatures. The mediator is therefore Jesus the man, because the eternal Son of God, remaining what he was (i.e., immortal, impassible, and almighty God) takes up what he was not (i.e., a human being, with human mortality, weakness, vulnerability, and powerlessness). For Christ to assume flesh and blood is therefore precisely to take up the weakness of mortality, the powerless ability to die.

In this account of the mediator Augustine follows the deep marrow of Nicene Christology as it developed in the fourth century among the Greek church fathers, especially Gregory of Naziansen,[114] but he does not quite arrive at the next conceptual step, taken in the fifth century by Cyril of Alexandria, which Augustine may never have heard of and which in any case only becomes official church teaching in the year after his death. For in addition to involving God in true human weakness and mortality (without making him any less God), the flesh of Christ means that a particular human body became a unique site of divine power (without making his flesh any less human). God, being immutable, was not changed by the Incarnation (so Nicene orthodoxy taught) but humanity, being God's mutable creature, was changed for the better, glorified and divinized by being taken up by the second person of the Trinity. Therefore Christ's flesh is God's own flesh and has unique salvific power. It is "life-giving flesh," to use

Cyril's formula, derived from John 6:51 ("the bread I will give is my flesh, for the life of the world") and accepted in A.D. 431 by the council of Ephesus (the third ecumenical council as it is counted by both East and West, though not nearly so well known in the West as the fourth ecumenical council, held in Chalcedon twenty years later).[115] What Augustine's consistent adherence to the Platonist axiom of downward causality and the consequent powerlessness of external things means for his Christology is that he never got to the point of making room in his thinking for a conception of Christ's literal body as life-giving flesh.

Spiritual Eating

Not surprisingly, the phrase "life-giving flesh" became central to subsequent eucharistic piety and theology. Without some such concept, debates about how Christ's body is present (or not) in the Eucharist have little point. The fact that Augustine's theology is indeed without such a concept goes a long way toward explaining why his many scattered observations on the Eucharist prove to be an unhelpful bone of contention in these later debates of the Western theological tradition. The debates have led many theologians to wonder whether Augustine was a sacramental realist, that is, someone who believes Christ's body and blood are really present in the Eucharist. Typically, as we have already seen,[116] what Augustine identifies as the thing signified by this sacrament is not Christ's literal body but his spiritual Body, the church. The heart of Augustine's eucharistic piety is expressed in the many exhortations in his sermons urging the congregation to *be* the Body that they eat in the sacrament, that is, to be members of the invisible church, which is the thing signified by this visible sign. But given the evidence of the texts, especially his sermons, it would be perilous to conclude that Augustine is not a sacramental realist. Rather, the proper conclusion to draw, I think, is that whether or not he is a sacramental realist makes no great difference, because his sacramental piety is centered on Christ's spiritual Body rather than his flesh.

This can be seen most clearly in precisely those passages that go furthest toward supporting sacramental realism, where Augustine affirms the presence of Christ's flesh and blood and then turns immediately toward his real interest, which is the unity of the church as Christ's Body.[117] For instance, in one of his sermons to the newly baptized he points to the eucharistic bread and cup and explains:

> This bread which you see on the altar, sanctified by the word of God, *is the body of Christ*. The cup (or rather what the cup has in it)

sanctified by the word of God, *is the blood of Christ*. Through them the Lord Christ wanted *to commend his body and blood*, which he poured out for the remission of our sins. If you receive them well, *you are what you receive*. For the Apostle says, "We who are many are one bread, one Body." So the sacrament of the Lord's table is set forth: we who are many are one bread, one Body. Commended to you in this bread is how you are to love unity.[118]

Those who deny Augustine is a sacramental realist must read the opening lines of this passage as symbolic, parallel to the way they read the Gospel word that sanctifies the elements, "This is my body" and "This is the cup of my blood." It would follow that what Augustine means by saying in the first two sentences that the bread and wine sanctified by these words are the body and blood of Christ, is revealed by the third sentence: through them (i.e., on this reading, through the bread and wine) the Lord meant to commend his body on the cross and the blood he shed there.

But suppose we try the alternative reading: following what he could only have regarded as the universal tradition of the church (as he always does even when he does not yet know how to understand it) Augustine affirms that what is visible on the altar is literally the body and blood of Christ. What is striking on this reading is that he says nothing about such an astounding bodily presence. Rather, he tells us that the body and blood of Christ that are present on the altar commend to us what happened elsewhere: the shedding of blood from his body on the cross. And then Augustine immediately changes the subject to dwell on a theme much more in keeping with his usual concern with the virtue of the sacrament: those who receive these things well—which clearly means in faith and charity—*are* what they have received, which is to say, they are the Body of Christ, the church. It is as if, for the purposes of piety at least, the flesh of Christ has suddenly dissolved into an inner unity. This can be taken as evidence against sacramental realism in Augustine, or else—precisely on the assumption that Augustine is a sacramental realist—as evidence that he simply has no piety devoted to Christ's flesh, no notion of what to think or do about the external presence of Christ's literal body and blood. Quite clearly, for Augustine the Eucharist is about the unity of the church, not the fleshly presence of Christ—even if Christ's flesh actually is present. Only this can explain why Augustine is so quick to direct the attention of his listeners away from what stands before them on the altar to consider instead what it signifies, which is the inner unity they themselves *are* when they rightly receive the sacrament in faith and love. This sharp redirection of attention is the eucharistic version of Augustine's inward turn.

That Augustine's piety has no place for a concept of Christ's life-giving flesh can be seen in one of the most characteristic and influential sermons he ever preached, an examination of which will serve to sum up the theological import of the whole inquiry of this book. During the course of this exegesis of the passage in the Gospel of John where Christ explains what he means by calling himself "the bread which came down from heaven," Augustine sets forth many of the themes we have been examining throughout this book. He begins with a doctrine of the grace of justification rooted in the doctrine of the Trinity, proceeds to expound the doctrine of Incarnation, then discusses the virtue of the sacrament of the Lord's body and blood, and concludes by re-turning to the doctrine of the Trinity.[119] To follow his exposition in order will afford us a summary of how Augustine relates the inner gift of grace to the external sign of the sacrament.

To say that Christ is bread that descends from heaven, Augustine begins, is to say that he is the justice or righteousness of God (*justitia Dei*). This is not the justice by which God punishes sin but the justice he bestows on human beings so that through him they may be just or righteous.[120] This conception of the justice or righteousness of God, so important for Luther's doctrine of justification,[121] is fundamentally Platonist: divine justice is the eternal Form or essence of Justice by participation in which justice in this changing world is possible. As he puts it in his conclusion, we become better by participation in God the Son.[122] Here at the beginning, as in his treatise *On the Grace of the New Testament*, Augustine uses this Platonist conception of participation in the Good in opposition to those who would rather trust in their own strength and virtue.[123] True justice is received from above, by the help of grace, which means it is the charity poured into our hearts by the Holy Spirit in Romans 5:5. To receive this heavenly Justice is to eat the bread of heaven, which is Christ, in whom one must believe. Thus emerges in the first paragraph the theme of the sermon as a whole: "he who believes, eats." In the terms used by the medieval theologians to interpret Augustine on this point, true *spiritual eating* is faith, whereby one eats the bread of heaven (i.e., receives the justice of God) in contrast to the merely *sacramental eating*, whereby one literally chews and swallows the sacrament.[124] Once again we have an inner/outer distinction: spiritual eating is done inwardly with heart and mind, sacramental eating outwardly with teeth and mouth.

Augustine now devotes a long discussion to what it really means to eat this spiritual bread, building on the passage that marks his mature doctrine of prevenient grace: "No one can come to me unless the Father who has sent me draw him."[125] Here it is not yet clear that grace is fully prevenient, for one can pray for it ("Have you not yet been drawn? Pray that you may be drawn"[126]), which means that there is already some kind of goodwill before one is inwardly drawn. Aside from that, the next few paragraphs lay down the conceptual framework for the treatment of grace as an inner teaching of delight in *On the Grace of Christ*. Clarifying the ambiguity of the verb "to draw" (*trahere*) which could easily mean "to drag," Augustine explains that we come to Christ inwardly not outwardly, "not by walking but by believing—not by a motion of the body but by the will of the heart," using his old favorite Plotinian theme of a journey not for the feet but for the will.[127]

To understand how this inner movement works in Augustine, we must ignore the modern dichotomy between mind and heart, as if truth was the business of the mind but not the love of our heart.[128] For Augustine the heart desires to understand truth, and this desire is a form of love that is the deepest motivation of the mind, which explains why the inward drawing of grace is not coercion: "Don't think you are drawn unwillingly," he tells his congregation, "for the mind is drawn also by love."[129] He proceeds to explain this intellectual drawing by a series of allusions to his favorite pagan authors. As Virgil says, each person "is drawn by his own pleasure."[130] For the mind no less than the body is drawn by pleasure, whenever a human being "delights in Truth, in Happiness, in Justice, in everlasting life, all of which Christ is."[131] Here Augustine appeals to experience, saying, "Give me a lover and he feels what I say," a memorable line that comes not directly from his experience but from his reading of Plotinus.[132] Above all, we must be the kind of lovers who experience the love of truth, as Cicero expresses in eloquent, very Augustinian terms: "There is nothing sweeter to the human mind than the light of truth."[133] This Ciceronian sentiment is echoed here by Augustine saying, "What does the soul desire more strongly than truth?"[134] To feel these things about the human mind is to understand why grace can draw the heart without coercion, by the sweetness of inner teaching that reveals Truth within. For revelation as Augustine understands it here is not anything external like the Bible but rather is a name for the inward work of grace itself: "this revelation is the drawing itself," as he says.[135] To be drawn by the Father is to be "teachable by God," to be attracted to one who "delights by teaching."[136] If you don't understand how grace can draw the heart willingly, by a love awoken in the depths of our minds—Augustine is suggesting—then you have forgotten what Virgil and Plotinus and Cicero knew, the experience of falling in love with truth and therefore being delighted by the drawing of the inner teacher, which is divine grace.

Once again we are moving in the realm of the Platonic epistemology of Augustine's treatise *On the Teacher*. To be taught by God is not the same as to hear the sound of external words, even if at the same time you do literally hear from human beings. For everyone who belongs to the kingdom of God "will be teachable by God, not hearing human beings. And if they do hear from human beings, nonetheless what they understand is given inwardly, inwardly shines, is inwardly revealed."[137] Christ incarnate is no exception to this rule. When he preached, "the Son spoke but the Father taught."[138] Precisely because the Son in his divine being is one with the Father, hearing his human words with our ears is not the same as hearing the inner and divine Word with our minds. No one but "he who comes from God" sees the Father, Christ says, and Augustine's paraphrase has him explaining this in terms of the analogy between inner word and eternal Word, both of which remain within the heart of the speaker: "I know the Father, I am from him, but in the way a word is from him whose word it is: not what sounds and passes away, but what remains with the speaker and draws the hearer."[139] Divine grace means we are drawn not by the sound of an external word, "a voice of flesh" as Augustine elsewhere calls it,[140] but by the power of the inner Word in the very heart of the Triune God. This is the Word we must hear if we are to believe and have eternal life, and this is the Word that Augustine has in mind when he has Christ explain what faith accomplishes: "Whoever believes in me, has me."[141]

The literal, sacramental eating of the Eucharist signifies this inner, spiritual eating of faith. In this regard, once again, there is no difference in efficacy between the sacraments of the Old Testament and of the New. Outwardly they are different, but inwardly the same: "for in the signs they are different, but in the thing which is signified they are equal."[142] In this sermon, too, the *res sacramenti* is equivalent to the *virtus sacramenti*. So Augustine can explain the difference between the spiritual drink which Christians have in the Eucharist and which ancient Jews had in the rock that symbolized Christ: "theirs is one, ours another—but only in visible form [*specie*], which nonetheless signified what was the same in spiritual virtue."[143] Likewise spiritual eating meant the same thing then as now: it has always been true that whoever eats the bread that descends from heaven has life, that is, "that which belongs to the virtue of the sacrament, not that which belongs to the visible sacrament: whoever eats inwardly, not outwardly—whoever eats in the heart, not whoever presses with the teeth."[144] As he says in an oft-quoted line from the previous sermon, "Why are you preparing your teeth and stomach? Believe, and you have eaten."[145]

Given this account of inward eating, it would be very surprising if Augustine regarded Christ's flesh, an external thing, as the source of our eternal life.[146] And indeed he proceeds to explain precisely why there can be no such thing as life-giving flesh even in Christ. The flesh that Christ gives for the life of the world (John 6:51) is not the literal flesh that anyone can see with their eyes. Rather, "that is called flesh which flesh does not grasp, and all the more can flesh not grasp it, because it is called flesh."[147] In contrast to Christ's literal flesh, which could be seen and grasped even by those who came to crucify him, the true life-giving flesh is grasped by the intellect alone, for it must be understood with the mind rather than seen with the eyes:

> Understand [intellegite], brethren, what I am about to say. You are human, you have a spirit and a body. I speak of spirit, which is called the soul, which constitutes what a human being is: for you are constituted of soul and body. You have therefore an invisible spirit, a visible body. Tell me what you live by: does your spirit live by your body or your body by your spirit? Anyone who lives answers (for I don't know anyone living who can't answer this)—what does anyone who lives answer? "Of course my body lives by my spirit."[148]

Augustine here shows us why anyone in the ancient world would have found the notion of "life-giving flesh" deeply paradoxical: surely everyone knows that spirit gives life to flesh, soul to body—not the other way round! This commonplace of ancient thought is fundamental to the way Augustine relates soul to body in his three-tiered ontology. The soul is superior to the body precisely because "everything that gives life [vivificat] is better than everything that is given life, and no one disputes that the body is given life by the soul, not the soul by the body"[149] By the same token, bodily things are at the bottom of the ontological hierarchy precisely because "nothing is given life by a body."[150] Evidently, life-giving flesh is an ontological impossibility.

Our spiritual lives, for Augustine, are no exception to this ontological rule. We live not by the flesh of Christ but by his Spirit. Hence the flesh we must eat spiritually in order to have eternal life is his spiritual Body, the church, which we eat by *being* what we eat:

> Do you want also to live by the Spirit of Christ? *Be in the Body of Christ.* Now does *my* body live by *your* spirit? Mine lives by my spirit, yours by your spirit. The Body of Christ cannot live except by the Spirit of Christ. Hence comes what the apostle Paul says, expounding this bread: "We who are many are one bread, one Body."[151]

We have arrived here at the heart of Augustine's eucharistic piety, and indeed the heart of his soteriology, of his doctrine of grace and of justification. At this point he can proceed only by breaking forth into exclamation and peroration:

> O sacrament of piety! O sign of unity! O bond of charity! Whoever wants to live, has here a place to live, a place from which to live. Come, believe, be incorporated that you may be made to live.[152]

The life-giving flesh of Christ is not his literal body hanging on the cross or consumed by mouth in the Eucharist, but the church, the inner unity of the many in the one Body of Christ. As Augustine sums it up: "we are made better by participation in the Son through the unity of his Body and blood, which this eating and drinking signifies."[153] This is the inward channel of grace described earlier, descending from God to souls to bodies, that is, from the eternal Son of God to the inner unity of souls in his spiritual Body, marked outwardly by the literal eating and drinking of the sacrament.[154] The visible sacramental eating signifies the invisible spiritual eating, which is fundamentally the action of a whole community of souls bound in unity by love and made better by participating in the divine Good. The significance of the sacrament is to turn our attention away from external things like sacraments and flesh, and direct it to the invisible inner unity in which the Spirit of Christ is to be found, and thus ultimately to what is inmost and highest. The concept of Christ's life-giving flesh could only disrupt this Augustinian piety.

Conclusion

To investigate Augustine's Platonism is to inquire into a crucial moment in the ongoing alliance between Christian faith and classical thought that has, ever since the New Testament, been one of the major concerns of Christian theology. We will not be done with such inquiries until we are done with theology itself. So we inquire: what ought we to make of Augustine's monumental and lasting effort to show that the God of the Bible is not other than the God of the philosophers, and that we are a Platonic soul longing for that God as for the Truth that is its dearest love? It will not do to label some part of Augustine's thought philosophical or "Greek," as if that meant it was unbiblical, and then dismiss it. For even though they are not authorities for the Christian faith, Plato and his followers were right about a few things. Sorting through the rights and wrongs here calls for critical acumen but also a willingness to learn from someone who remains a father of Christian doctrine, as he learns both from the Bible and from the philosophical tradition of the West. I hope this book will help in the work of sorting. To say how I hope it will help is a good way to present its conclusions.

I think it is possible to be a critic of Augustinian inwardness without rejecting classical philosophic theism. That is to say, a piety that does not turn inward to find God but clings to the flesh of Christ is compatible with worshiping God as Augustine does, praising him as eternal Truth, supreme Good, Beauty of all things beautiful, the immutable, impassible, and perfect Being that is the source of all beings that arise and pass away. We should not be intimidated by one major wing of contemporary philosophy into shying away from this "ontotheology," as Heidegger calls it. It is so much better argued and more beautiful a concept of God than Heidegger's that I still fail to understand why anyone would be convinced by Heidegger's unargued critique of it.[1] Above all, it is time to put to rest the absurd idea that this "God of the philosophers" cannot be worshiped, which is obviously, even empirically, false.

The problem on the contrary is the spiritual attractiveness of the Platonist vision of God that lies at the heart of Augustine's inwardness, suggesting that what we ultimately want to see for eternity is something other than Christ in the flesh. The great corrective to this suggestion is one of the crucial implications of the council of Nicaea: that to see Jesus Christ is to see the one true God in the flesh. The culmination of this correction is the Eastern Orthodox piety of the transfiguration, with its conviction that the truly beatific vision means not turning inward but looking outward at the uncreated glory of God in the human face of Jesus Christ. Or as the Western visionary Julian of Norwich put it, "I wanted no heaven but Jesus."[2] She knew well enough that there is indeed no other heaven to be had. The eternal Truth, Supreme Good, Beauty of all things beautiful, the immutable, impassible, and perfect Being that is the source of all beings that arise and pass away *is* this one man, crucified under Pontius Pilate and raised from the dead by God his Father. For remaining what he was, he took up what he was not: remaining immutable and impassible he became the crucified king of the Jews. There on Golgotha we find the Truth and Goodness and Beauty at the heart of all things.

But there is a way the church had to travel from Nicaea to this culmination, and Augustine's lifetime is spent along that way, not quite arriving. Thoroughly Nicene, Augustine does not quite get to the step taken by the church at Ephesus in the year after his death, devoting itself explicitly to Christ's life-giving flesh. His inward turn admonishes us to look in another direction to find ultimate Truth and eternal life, and Augustine reads Christ's flesh and voice, his human life and external words, not as efficacious means of grace but as the most important example of that admonition. Thus Augustine gives us the most important alternative within the Nicene tradition to the piety that finds God in the flesh of Christ. This is not to say that Augustine denies the Incarnation of God in Christ—far from it—but rather that he treats the man Jesus Christ as the way not the goal, as if the purpose of God's coming to us in the flesh were to show us how to get somewhere else, like Socrates leading us up out of Plato's cave.[3]

As in all matters of piety, the crucial issue here is where we are to direct our attention: do we cling to external things as if they gave us God in the flesh or do we take them to be admonitions directing our attention elsewhere? The inward turn, I believe, directs our attention in the wrong way. Medieval sacramental theology, Luther's doctrine of the Gospel and the Eastern Orthodox piety of the transfiguration direct us in the right way, requiring of us an outward turn, turning our attention to find God himself, together with the life-giving power of his grace, in particular external things beginning with the flesh of Christ.

One might get at this point by asking another kind of question: how is it possible to think of the God of classical philosophic theism as a person? Eternal Truth, immutable and impassible, does not look much like *someone*. And yet Nicaea, together with the doctrine of Incarnation that follows from it, says precisely that: eternal Truth, remaining what it was, became a particular someone in human history. The impassible Being at the source of all being became a man who died on a cross. Being both God and man, God is both impassible and passible, immortal and mortal, beyond the vicissitudes of what we normally call personhood (particular actions and passions, feelings, and vulnerabilities) and yet also a person literally just like us. That is why we need a piety of the hearing of God's word that goes beyond Augustine's semiotics with its notion that words only admonish us to look at something deeper and more inward. Because God is a person—is this person, Jesus Christ, the second hypostasis of the Trinity who is a person in exactly the same sense that we are—his word is not just an admonition to look elsewhere but the efficacious means by which he gives himself to us. We should take hold of his external word just as we cling to the sacraments and to the flesh of Christ itself. For it is through their words that persons give themselves to be known[4]—not by expressing what lies within them but by making promises and keeping them. The truth of the word, as for instance in a covenant or a wedding vow, depends not on how well it expresses an inner depth but on whether the one who gives it is true to it by doing what it says. By keeping his word, being true to it, one person can give to another nothing less than himself.

Augustine originates a different view of what it ultimately means to know another person, which I think has had a baleful influence on Western thought. In this view real knowledge is a matter of seeing not hearing, intellectual vision not trusting someone else's word, so that what we ultimately want is to see other persons' thoughts, penetrating through the outer shell of their words and bodies, and looking into the inner depth of their minds. Here persons ultimately dissolve into ideas, things of the soul seen with the mind's eye like Platonic Forms. But that is nothing to be surprised at if, as I have previously argued, the inner self was invented by Augustine as a kind of image of the intelligible world of divine Ideas. At the heart of the baleful notion of inner self, I have argued, is the Platonist notion of intellectual vision.[5] This, I would suggest, is the deep thing that Plato and his followers got wrong: not the notion of an impassible deity with eternal Ideas but rather the notion that the human mind is like an eye designed to see them. Plato's theology, in other words, is better than his psychology, and it is in the realm of psychology that we should be most critical of Augustine's Platonism. If we are unconvinced by the notion of intellectual vision we should also be unconvinced by the inner self and the inward turn.

Of course the notion of inwardness has had a history that goes beyond Augustinian Platonism. The modern inner self, though heir of the inner self Augustine invented, is a different world, filled not with intellectual light but its own private thoughts—private not because of its Fall from the light but because of a kind of inherent right of privacy, as if we were meant to be locked away within ourselves—and eventually it becomes a realm characterized more by inexpressible feeling than private thought. Through a historical process that is deeply revealing of the dynamics of modernity, the Augustinian inner self is secularized (as in John Locke) yet still made the site of ultimate religious concern (as in the Romantics), so that the liberal theologians of the nineteenth and twentieth centuries could turn to the inner world as if it were a universal or neutral phenomenon of the human self and find there (as if Augustine had not put it there in the first place) the deep clues to the nature of God and the experience of faith.

Modernity did indeed involve a movement of secularization, but the result was always secularized *Christendom,* a phenomenon of the heart as much as of social life and institutions, so that liberal theology and other versions of the turn to inner experience could always look into the depths of the supposedly secular modern self and claim to find Christian truth hidden there, deep within. For the secular modern self has always been, unbeknownst to itself, really a descendant of the Augustinian soul, so that to look deep within it was to see not a universal truth but part of the historical residue of Christendom. This dynamic of finding Christian truth buried in the experiential heart of modern secularity will soon cease to carry conviction if our culture is becoming genuinely postmodern, for any postmodernity deserving of the name will be, unlike modernity, genuinely post-Christian. So it may be that we stand at the end of Christendom as Augustine did at its beginning. Now more than ever, we cannot do without his guidance as the most articulate and profound exponent of Nicene theology among the Western fathers. But we do need to learn another set of lessons from him than those of the inward turn.

We also need to learn some lessons that he is not the one to teach us. We need to learn the power of particular external things such as Gospel and sacrament to change our hearts, turn us into Christians, and give us Christ our bridegroom. Christian experience has always arisen from these external sources, even when people believed the theologians who taught that outward things merely give expression to a prior experience of the divine within them. From such teaching we learn to misunderstand the nature and sources of our own experience. To understand the power of external things to form our hearts and experience we need to become familiar with alternatives to expressionist semiotics and its ingrained conviction of the inadequacy of external signs. God is of course always beyond our reach, but he does reach us through the external means of grace that he has chosen. If we choose to find God elsewhere, an increasingly postmodern culture will not support us much longer in the illusion that the result is really Christian faith.

Outward signs can form our hearts because they form our life together. Communities do not use outward signs simply to mark their boundaries but are in large part constituted by their shared use of signs, words, and other means of communication. Thus the word of the Gospel gives Christ to individual hearts precisely by giving him to the whole church as head of the Body. For in Pauline terms, we have Christ in us because we are in Christ: Christ dwells in our hearts by faith precisely as we are members of his spiritual Body, the church.

Yet there are a number of ways to miss this connection between the formation of the community and the formation of the heart. The modern way is to make the inner realm primary, as if human experience rose from within rather than from our life together in the world, and then to make human community a secondary phenomenon, a joining of inner selves through outward expressions, including various social contracts and conventions such as language itself. So social life is formed by external means of communication precisely because it is more superficial than the inner depths of the individual. Augustine misses the connection in a different and more interesting way. More radically inward than modernity, he sees the inner space of the soul as fundamentally public, constituted not by external signs but by shared inner objects of love. The roots of community lie within the soul, which is not by nature a private world but the image of the intelligible world of eternal Truth and Beauty which all souls have in common. Sin disrupts this inner community and privatizes the inner space of the soul,[6] but redemption restores it. Indeed the inner unity of love in the spiritual Body of Christ is the focus of Augustine's soteriology and the point at which we should locate his version of the concept of efficacious means of grace, as we have seen in chapters 6 and 7.

To give up Augustine's Platonism at this point is to see that the presence of God in the human heart is radically dependent on the church's faithfulness to the authority of the external word of the Gospel. For the church is constituted by this word as a marriage is constituted by wedding vows. Without this set of external signs she has no being, and no Bridegroom or God to offer to the world. Of course, how she is to be faithful at this moment in her historical life is a matter for contention—as always. For that is precisely the ongoing argument that is the tradition of Christian theology. To continue participating in this argument is an act of hope in the Holy Spirit leading Christ's Body always toward her fulfillment and the blessing of all nations in the house of our Father.

Abbreviations

WORKS OF AUGUSTINE

C. Acad.	Against the Academics
C. Cresc.	Against Cresconius
C. Duas Ep. Pel.	Against Two Letters of the Pelagians
C. Ep. Fund.	Against the Letter of Mani called "Fundamental"
C. Ep. Parm.	Against the Letter of Parmenian
C. Faust. Man.	Against Faustus the Manichaean
C. Jul. Op. Imp.	Against Julian, an Unfinished Work
C. Max. Arian.	Against Maximinus the Arian
Civ. Dei	City of God
Conf.	Confessions
De Bapt. c. Donat.	On Baptism against the Donatists
De Bono Conjug.	On the Good of Marriage
De Cat. Rud.	On Catechizing the Unlearned
De Cons. Evang.	On the Harmony of the Gospels
De Dial.	On Dialectic
De Div. QQs 83	On Eighty-Three Different Questions
De Doct. Christ.	On Christian Doctrine
De Dono Pers.	On the Gift of Perseverance
De Duab. Anim.	On Two Souls, against the Manichaeans
De Fide et Oper.	On Faith and Works
De Fide et Symb.	On Faith and the Creed
De Fide Rerum Invis.	On Faith in Things Not Seen
De Gen. ad Litt.	On Genesis according to the Letter
De Gen. c. Man.	On Genesis against the Manichaeans
De Gest. Pelag.	On the Proceedings of Pelagius
De Grat. Christi	On the Grace of Christ and on Original Sin
De Grat. et Lib. Arb.	On Grace and Free Will
De Immort. Anim.	On the Immortality of the Soul
De Lib. Arb.	On Free Choice
De Mag.	On the Teacher
De Mend.	On Lying
De Mor. Eccl.	On the Morals of the Catholic Church
De Mor. Man.	On the Morals of the Manichaeans
De Nat. Boni	On the Nature of the Good
De Nupt. et Concup.	On Marriage and Concupiscence
De Ord.	On Order

De Pecc. Mer.	On the Merits and Forgiveness of Sins, and Infant Baptism
De Praedest. Sanct.	On the Predestination of the Saints
De Sp. et Litt.	On the Spirit and the Letter
De Trin.	On the Trinity
De Quant. Anim.	On the Quantity of the Soul
De Util. Cred.	On the Usefulness of Believing
De Vera Rel.	On True Religion
Enarr. in Pss.	Expositions of the Psalms
Ench.	Enchiridion on Faith, Hope and Charity
In Joh. Evang.	Tractates on the Gospel of John
QQs in Hept.	Questions on the Heptateuch
Retract.	Retractations
Sol.	Soliloquies

OTHER PRIMARY LITERATURE

Acad.	Cicero, *Academica*
Ad Herr.	Cicero, *Rhetorica Ad Herrenium*
Adv. Math.	Sextus Empiricus, *Against the Mathematicians*
Anal. Post.	Aristotle, *Posterior Analytics*
Anal. Pr.	Aristotle, *Prior Analytics*
De Anim.	Aristotle, *On the Soul*
De Fin.	Cicero, *On Ends*
De Interp.	Aristotle, *On Interpretation*
De Inv.	Cicero, *On Invention*
De Mem.	Aristotle, *On Memory*
De Nat. Deor.	Cicero, *On the Nature of the Gods*
De Orat.	Cicero, *On the Orator*
De Part. Orat.	Cicero, *On the Parts of Oratory*
Inst.	Calvin, *Institutes*
N. Eth.	Aristotle, *Nicomachean Ethics*
Parad. Stoic.	Cicero, *The Paradoxes of the Stoics*
PH	Sextus Empiricus, *Outlines of Pyrrhonism*
	(= *Pyrrhōneiōn Hypotypōseis*)
Rhet.	Aristotle, *Rhetoric*
Sent.	Peter Lombard, *Sentences*
Soph. Elench.	Aristotle, *Sophistical Refutations*
Summa Sent.	Anonymous, *Summa Sententiarum*
Tusc.	Cicero, *Tusculan Disputations*
ST	Aquinas, *Summa Theologiae*

Notes

PREFACE

1. From Luther's sermon on Chrismas Day, 1519, in WA 9:440.

2. At least so I argue in Cary, "Why Luther Is Not Quite Protestant." The crucial scholarly work on this point has been done by Oswald Bayer in *Promissio*.

3. Calvin, *Inst.* 4:14.12.

4. Here I quote again a passage from Augustine with which I concluded the preface to *Augustine's Invention*: "To be sure, in all my writings I desire not only a pious reader but a free corrector. . . . But as I want my readers not to be bound down to me, so I want my correctors not to be bound down to themselves. Let not the reader love me more than the Catholic faith, and let not the correctors love themselves more than the Catholic Truth" (*De Trin.* 3:2).

5. For an argument to this effect, see Cary, "Believing the Word."

6. Consider Barth's massive use of Luther's writings against liberal Protestant theology throughout the first volume of his *Church Dogmatics*, the rationale for which is perhaps most succinctly stated in II/i,18, where Barth observes that for Luther it was "no less than a principal rule of all knowledge of God . . . [that] we must seek Him where He Himself has sought us—in those veils and under those signs of His Godhead. Elsewhere He is not to be found."

7. The *locus classicus* for Derrida's project of a "deconstruction of presence" is *Of Grammatology*, pp. 70–71. His focus on speech as presence leads him to downplay the importance of vision as the locus of presence in "Plato's Pharmacy," *Dissemination*, pp. 82–83 and 166–165, which I think results in a very partial and skewed reading of Platonism.

8. See chapter 5, "Secondhand Knowledge."

9. Milton, *Paradise Lost*, 4:53. The words are Satan's, describing what he finds hateful about the interminable debt of thanksgiving. But Satan is a fool, and the words are lovely.

10. Duchrow, *Sprachverständnis*, p. 241.

INTRODUCTION

1. *Conf.* 10:9.

2. Ibid. 10:11.

3. Cary, *Augustine's Invention*, pp. 50–51 and 60.

4. *De Trin.* 4:6. See chapter 8, "Powerless Blood."

5. See Mackey for an explicitly deconstructive reading of *De Mag.*, and Rowan Williams for an implicitly Derridean reading of *De Doct. Christ.*, arguing that the failure of sacred language to deliver sacred presence has the great value of endlessly deferring the closure of desire. Williams's essay contrasts interestingly with the immediately following essay by Louth, who is much more traditional in his attempt to rescue Augustine from the deconstructive implications of his own semiotics. For why one might welcome endless deconstructive deferral, see Caputo, esp. chapter 10.

6. For an account of the nature of meaning that does not rely on anything like the expression of an inner depth of the soul but does insist on an essential connection between language and truth, see Davidson. For a promising example of the theological uses of such a philosophy of language, see Marshall.

7. For this kind of mathematical illustration, see *Sol.* 1:34f.

8. *De Div. QQs 83*, 46.2.

9. Ibid. 54. See chapter 8, "Spiritual Eating" (near the end).

10. *De Musica* 6:10–15. See chapter 3, "Signs Moving Souls."

11. *Civ. Dei* 5:9.

12. The key statement of this three-tiered hierarchy of being is very brief, Ep. 18:2. A more elaborate statement, drawing out the ethical consequences, is *De Musica* 6:13–41, while the causal implications are elaborated more fully in *De Gen. ad Litt.* 8:39. In *De Vera Rel.* 3, the three-tiered hierarchy is attributed to Plato and in *Civ. Dei* 8:6 it is attributed to the Platonist philosophers in general. These and related passages are examined in Bourke. For what is distinctively Augustinian about this Platonist ontological hierarchy, see Cary, *Augustine's Invention*, pp. 55–56 and 116–117.

13. *Conf.* 3:11, *interior intimo meo.*

14. Cf. ibid. 7:16.

15. Ibid. 1:4.

16. Augustine argues that souls literally have no location in space in *De Quant. Anim.* 60–61. That they are not confined within their bodies is a point made explicit in Ep. 137:5, where it is used as an analogy for the fact that Christ's deity is not confined to his flesh. For the Plotinian roots of this conception of the soul's non-spatiality see Cary, *Augustine's Invention*, pp. 103 and 130–132.

17. *Conf.* 1:7–8.

18. *Conf.* 1:13. Once again "want," both noun and verb, renders the notion of will, *voluntas* or *velle*.

19. Ibid.

20. Ibid.

21. See chapter 3, "Fallen Language."

22. *De Cat. Rud.* 3. The angry face is a "natural sign" in the classification of *De Doct. Christ.* 2:3 (see chapter 3, "Giving Signs"), while the trace or vestige that understanding impresses on memory is what Augustine later calls an "inner word" (see chapter 5, "Outward Voice and Inner Word").

23. *Conf.* 9:24. For the content of this vision, which is deeply Platonist especially in being shared, see chapter 6, "Public Inner Wisdom."

24. Ibid. 9:25.

25. Cf. Ibid. 10:9.

26. Ibid. 9:25.

27. Ibid.

28. Ibid., quoting Matt. 25:21.

29. Sermon 117:5, *ineffabiliter potest intellegi.* Cf. Sermon 52:15, *ineffabiliter intellegatur.*

30. This finding of the Other in the self is my prime objection to Augustine's inward turn; see Cary, *Augustine's Invention,* p. 141.

CHAPTER I

1. For the soul as alternative dimension with its own magnitude, see Augustine's *De Quant. Anim,* discussed in Cary, *Augustine's Invention,* pp. 134–137. The inner world is the dimension in which the soul takes a journey that is "not for the feet," according to Plotinus, *Ennead* 1:6.8 (this is Augustine's favorite passage from Plotinus, echoed in *Conf.* 1:28 and 8:19; cf. Cary, *Augustine's Invention,* p. 37).

2. Augustine, Sermon 187:3. See the discussion of this point in chapter 5, "Outward Voice and Inner Word."

3. Eco et al., "On Animal Language in the Medieval Classification of Signs," p. 4.

4. Long, in his important article on Stoic semantics, "Language and Thought in Stoicism," uses "signal," following Mates. Kretzmann, in his crucial article on Aristotle's *De Interp.,* uses "symptom."

5. See Manetti, *Theories of Signs in Classical Antiquity,* and his summary of the results of this investigation in his introduction to the volume he edited, *Knowledge through Signs.*

6. Kneale and Kneale note the confusion on p. 142. Sextus will often use the verb *sēmainein* in place of *sēmeioin* to describe the function of signs (e.g., *Adv. Math.* 8:264, 279, *PH* 2:101, 130). This is like talking about what signs "mean" rather than what they "signify": in common Greek usage it is unexceptionable (note such a usage also in Aristotle, *Physiognomics* 805b20, a text discussed below), but in technical contexts of Stoic semiotics it is highly misleading.

7. Two very valuable and informative pieces of scholarship, both gathered in the volume of critical essays edited by R. A. Markus, continue to shape English-language scholarship on Augustine's semiotics but do not take the full measure of Augustine's originality in inventing expressionist semiotics. In the first, Markus recognizes that ancient semiotics is a theory of inference rather than of language, yet cannot quite believe the consequences of his own recognition, because he finds it impossible to doubt that words are signs. Thus he notes that in the Hellenistic, Roman, and early Christian contexts, "the theory of signs is conceived primarily as a theory of inference. Language is hardly mentioned in this context, and when it is explicitly recognized as relevant—since words *signify* and are therefore inescapably signs—the linguistic interest is only incidental" (p. 65, emphasis in original). If we keep semiotic and semantic vocabulary separate, however, then words do not have to *signify* and therefore are not inescapably signs. B. D. Jackson takes issue with Markus (p. 136), arguing that Augustine was doing nothing new when he systematically incorporated theory of language into sign-theory, because Aristotle and the Stoics had already done the same thing. As we shall see, recent scholarship questions Jackson's crucial assumption that in *De Interp.*, "Aristotle uses *symbolon* and *sēmeion* synonymously" (p. 130). As for the Stoics, the claim that they regarded words as signs can only be doubted, Jackson argues, if one is extraordinarily picky about terminology: "Only if one insists that *to sēmainon* does not denote a sign, can one say that the Stoics did not apply a theory of signs to language" (p. 136). This is exactly right. The key evidence that the Stoics did not apply a theory of signs to language is precisely that they never confused *sēmainon* with *sēmeion*. They were in fact known for being picky about technical terminology (see Cicero, *De Fin.* 3:10 and 15, and the systematic discussion in Atherton, pp. 116–125).

8. See chapter 5, "Outward Voice and Inner Word."

9. See Cary, *Augustine's Invention*, chapters 1–3.

10. Plato, *Sophist* 263e.

11. Plato, *Theaetetus* 189e.

12. Plato, *Philebus* 38c–39a.

13. I argue in *Augustine's Invention*, chapter 10, that it was Augustine who made the decisive transition from a two-dimensional picture of the individual soul to a three-dimensional picture.

14. Aristotle, *De Interp.* 1, 16a3; my insertions added for clarification.

15. Plato, *Theaetetus* 208c.

16. Ibid., 206d. The image of the stream through the mouth connects this passage with *Sophist* 263e, where *logos* is described as "the stream coming from the soul through the mouth with sound."

17. Kretzmann, pp. 5–6.

18. Aristotle, *Anal. Post.* 1:10, 76b25–27. Here is the whole extent of the remark: "Demonstration is not addressed to the external argument [*ton exō logon*]—and neither is syllogism—but to the one in the soul. For there is always objecting to the external argument but not always to the inner argument [*ton esō logon*]."

19. See Cary, *Augustine's Invention*, pp. 13–15.

20. Plato, *Phaedrus* 245c–256e.

21. Ibid. 276a–278a.

22. Plato, *Republic* 7:518b.

23. Plato, *Phaedrus* 276e and 278a.

24. Plato, *Theaetetus* 197e.

25. Ibid. 191cd.

26. Something like this picture of ideas as images seen in an inner room is assumed by Descartes but first made explicit by Locke. See my *Augustine's Invention,* p. 123. Recent studies of the very complex history of *phantasia* in Greek thought, though disagreeing about much else, tend to avoid this picture. See for example the books by Barnouw and Watson, as well as the groundbreaking work on Aristotle's notion of *phantasia* by Schofield, "Aristotle on the Imagination," and Nussbaum, *Aristotle's* De Motu Animalium, essay 5. For further discussion of *phantasia,* see chapter 2, "The Grasping Appearance."

27. Plato, *Theaetetus* 193c.

28. E.g. ibid. 191d and 193c; also Aristotle, *De Anim.* 2:12,424a20.

29. Plato, *Cratylus* 427c.

30. Plato, *Sophist* 262a and d.

31. Scholars who attribute to Plato a semiotics of language (e.g., Lozano-Miralles and Manetti) must build their case on much more than Plato's meager use of the word *sēmeion.* Even the verb *sēmainein,* which in Plato can often reasonably be translated "send a sign" (Manetti, *Theories of the Sign,* p. 53) does not occur very often in discussions of linguistic meaning (e.g., *Cratylus* 393d, 394b, and 437a). Far and away Plato's most common verb to describe linguistic meaning is *dēloun,* to show or manifest. Given the preponderance of this term, it does not seem likely that Plato is trying to develop a semiotic view of language, but rather that he sometimes uses semiotic vocabulary as an alternate way of talking about what words show or manifest.

32. Aristotle, *Anal. Pr.* 2:27 and *Rhet.* 1:2,1357b1–20.

33. *Anal. Pr.* 2:27,70a6. The definitions and classifications in the *Rhetoric* are slightly different. Since the concern of this chapter is the logical basis of semiotics I follow *Prior Analytics* here except for the account of *tekmērion,* where the *Rhetoric* is both simpler and more influential.

34. *Anal. Pr.* 2:27,70a7: a sign is *protasis apodeiktikē anankaia ē endoxos.*

35. Ibid., 70a8–10; my insertions added for clarification.

36. For fuller exploration of this ambiguity see Burnyeat's richly detailed discussion in "The Origins of Non-deductive Inference," pp. 193–206.

37. Aristotle, *Rhet.* 1:2, 1357b4. In *Anal. Pr.* 2:27,70b1–6 Aristotle identifies the *tekmērion* with the middle term in these signs or alternatively with the first figure inference itself (because that is where the middle term is validly deployed). Then he adds that only the inferences that are not deductively valid (i.e., those in the second and third figures) are properly called signs. This is not a helpful classification and nobody including Aristotle actually follows it. It makes much better sense to classify the *tekmērion* as one species of sign than to treat it as something other than a sign.

38. *Anal. Pr.* 2:27,70a13–15.

39. Ibid. 70a20–24.

40. Discussion of signs, *Anal. Pr.* 2:27,70a3–70b6; discussion of physiognomy, ibid., 2:27,70b7–38.

41. Aristotle, *Physiognomics.* The attribution to Aristotle is contested by modern scholars. What is relatively certain is that there are two treatises collected under this one title (chapters 1–3 and chapters 4–6), each of which begins with a methodological section on the selection of signs to be used in physiognomic inferences (805a1–806b3 and 808b11–809a25).

42. See Smith's edition and commentary on *Anal. Pr.*, p. 227.

43. Throughout the Aristotelian corpus the practice of physiognomy is consistently designated by the verb "to physiognomize" (*physiognōmein*). It is not called a science (*epistēmē*). However, at one point in the *Physiognomics* (806a16) it is accorded the status of an art (*technē*).

44. Other methods of physiognomizing had been tried, as is pointed out in the treatise in the first half of the *Physiognomics* (805a19–34), but this one gets the most attention in the Aristotelian corpus. A crude version of it, based on classifying animals into male or female types, is proposed in the treatise in the second half of the *Physiognomics* (809a26–810a14), which I take to be the earliest of the three treatments (for it is certainly the crudest). The lion, with its large extremities and other masculine features—including an unhurried gait reminiscent of the man of great soul or magnanimity in *N. Eth.* (1125a12)!—is taken to be the animal typifying courage (809b32). This approach comes in for criticism and revision in the treatise in the first half of the *Physiognomics* (805b10–27), then is reformulated in a logically rigorous way in *Anal. Pr.* 2:27.

45. Aristotle, *Physiognomics* 805b17.

46. Zeno, the founder of Stoicism, is said to have been convinced that character (*ēthos*) can be gathered from features (*eidous*), in Diogenes Laertius, 7:173. And Chrysippus, according to Plutarch ("On Stoic Self-Contradictions" 1042e) wrote that "the affections, such as pain and fear and the like, are perceptible together with features [*eidesin*]." Finally, there is an interesting fragment from Aetius: "The Stoics hold that the wise man is graspable by sense-perception from his appearance [*eidous*] in the manner of a symptom [*tekmēriōdōs*]," SVF 1:204. Though none of these texts specifically mention signs (*sēmeia*), their reasoning does seem to be physiognomic in roughly Aristotle's sense of the term. Sextus Empiricus may be reporting an explicitly semiotic version of this kind of Stoic inference from body to soul in *PH* 2:101 and *Adv. Math.* 8:155, discussed below in "Reminders of Deeper Things."

47. By "empiricism" I mean any epistemology that takes sense-perception to be the basis of knowledge. By "materialism" I mean any ontology according to which all that exists is corporeal. Both are inimical to Platonism and both predominated in the Hellenistic era.

48. *sympathein allēlois, Physiognomics* 808b12. This evidently implies not just that bodily affections run parallel to those of the soul, but that the two interact, as the explanation of the claim proceeds: "When the disposition [*hexis*] of the soul is altered,

it alters with it the form [*morphē*] of the body; and again when the form of the body is altered, it alters with it the disposition of the soul."

49. *hama metaballein*, *Anal. Pr.* 2:27,70b8.

50. *Physiognomics* 808a1–3. The "thought-processes" are *dianoiai*, which this treatise attributes to nonrational animals as well as to human beings.

51. Ibid., 805a8–15.

52. Again in *Physiognomics* 805a22, the *eidos* of a kind of animal is coupled to its thought-process or *dianoia*, as body is to soul. (Neither of these terms plays a role in the treatise in the second half of the *Physiognomics*.)

53. This term is confined to the treatise in the second half of the *Physiognomics*, where it can designate features like pallor (809a13) or be used synonymously with *idea* to designate the shape and type of body, masculine or feminine (809a29, 809b10). The phrase "*morphē* of the body" is especially common (808b13,14,18,25 808b25, 809b10). If this is actually an early treatise of Aristotle's, then there are hints of thoughts to come in the consideration that "the forms [*morphai*] in bodies come to resemble the powers [*dynamesi*] of the soul" (808b28).

54. *Physiognomics* 805a16. The word frequently occurs in this sense in the treatise in the second half of the *Physiognomics*, where both male and female "types" and their bodily structure are referred to as *ideai* (e.g., 809b16, 810a10, 814a5). Cf. also the phrase "the *idea* of the body" in 810a7 and the use of *ideai* at 809a7 to designate the same things as "visible features" (*horōmena*, 809a4) and "surface manifestations" (*epiphainomena*, 809a8). It is hard to imagine a more blatantly un-Platonist use of a key technical term of Platonism. The treatise in the first half seems to signal the fact that it is referring to the treatise in the second half by using the term *idea* in the same way, meaning "bodily type" (805b12).

55. Aristotle, *De Anim.* 2:1, 412a20

56. The index to Wehrli's collection of Peripatetic fragments lists no occurrences of the term *sēmeion*. Theophrastus's treatise *Concerning Weather Signs* contains no methodological discussion whatsoever. All it serves to show us about the semiotics of the Peripatetics is that the notion of inference from signs was familiar to them. The term *sēmeion* also turns up occasionally in Theophrastus's botanical works, where it is used in the inferential sense—a usage so common that it could have come from the pen of someone who knew nothing whatsoever of the definitions of *sēmeion* in the Aristotelian corpus (see, e.g., his *Enquiry into Plants* 1:1.3 and 8:8.7). By contrast, Aristotle's interest in the role sign-inference plays in a science is systematic and pervasive; cf. Barnouw, pp. 131–142.

57. In a portrait of Aristotle's intellectual development that is almost diametrically opposed to Jaeger's more famous work, Ingmar Düring sees Aristotle as a critic of the theory of transcendent Ideas from the very beginning, who becomes more rather than less "Platonistic" as he matures. Emblematic of this development is the movement from Aristotle's early logical works, including the near-nominalism of the *Categories*, to the ontology of substantial Form in *Metaphysics* 7 (see Graham on this movement). Düring pictures Aristotle as a young Turk, describing his attitude during the first half of his twenty years at the Academy thus: "He begins his course of

instruction; he makes a big point of asserting his own viewpoint; he is oppositional and spoiling for a fight. He discusses and rejects the theory of Ideas ..." *Aristoteles*, p. 50. This picture of a *streitlustig* Aristotle has ancient attestation: see esp. Fr. 10 of Aristotle's "On Philosophy" (Ross). Evidently such behavior would not make Aristotle unwelcome in the Academy: in Düring's portrait Plato's school is unlike later Hellenistic schools in having no standard of orthodoxy and harboring a large variety of conflicting views (p. 5).

58. Aristotle's father Nicomachus was a physician according to Diogenes Laertius, 5:1.

59. This seems to be what is meant by a rather obscure passage, "And in the selection of signs, adding the appropriate things to what is already at hand for the syllogism that must be used, when one turns out to be needed ..." *Physiognomics* 809a19–21. This is from the cruder, and thus presumably the earlier, of the two treatises in the *Physiognomics*.

60. Aristotle, *De Anim.* 1:3, 407b13–25.

61. For the rather loose coupling between soul and body in Plotinian Platonism and the importance of this for Augustine, see Cary, *Augustine's Invention*, pp. 117–122.

62. Aristotle, *De Interp.* 1,16a6.

63. Kretzmann, p. 3.

64. Aristotle, *De Interp.* 1,16a3. See above, "Words Written on Platonic Souls."

65. Kretzmann, p. 5.

66. There is a weighty moral difference between interpreting someone's words as *logos* (and therefore as a possible bearer of truth) and merely taking them as signs of their inner states, which I argue has a great deal to do with what it means to know another person in Cary, "Believing the Word."

67. Aristotle, *De Interp.* 2,16a27–29.

68. Cf. Eco, *Semiotics*, whose interpretation of Aristotle on this point is parallel to Kretzmann's. Pointing out that by the time Aristotle was writing, the term "sign" or *sēmeion* had already acquired the technical sense of "symptom" in the Hippocratic medical literature, he concludes, "when Aristotle incidentally uses the term *sign* for words, he is simply stressing that even words can be taken as symptoms" (p. 28). Sedley interprets the use of *sēmeion* in this passage similarly in "Aristotle's *De Interpretatione* and Ancient Semantics," pp. 91–92.

69. For some indication of the extent of the debate see Polansky and Kuczewski, Weidemann, Whitaker, pp. 17–25, and Toom, pp. 119–128. In my judgment Kretzmann's insistence on distinguishing *symbola* and *sēmeia* comes off rather well in this debate, especially when supported by a clear distinction between semantic and semiotic vocabulary.

70. Two chapters later the term *sēmeion* turns up again, used three times in connection with Aristotle's discussion of verbs (*De Interp.* 3,16b7,10 and 24). The term seems to occur here because Aristotle is taking issue with the passage from Plato mentioned above, in which words are twice described as "signs of the voice" in the course of explaining the relation of nouns and verbs (*Sophist* 262). Like Plato, Aristotle

makes no further use of the notion of words as signs and certainly develops no semiotic theory of language on this basis.

71. Kneale and Kneale, p. 142.

72. Mates (p. 13) makes what seems to have been at the time the novel suggestion of distinguishing *sēmainon* from *sēmeion* as a hypothesis for solving a serious difficulty related to the status of signs as *lekta*, which we will deal with shortly.

73. See, for example, Eco, *Semiotics and the Philosophy of Language*, p. 32.

74. The definition is preserved in Sextus Empiricus, *PH* 2:104; the example follows in 106. The whole passage is anthologized in L&S 35C, where the translations are more up to date in logical vocabulary (and thus more illuminating philosophically) than the Loeb editions. The same definition and example are given in parallel passages in Sextus, *Adv. Math.* 8:245 and 252 (not in L&S).

75. Sextus Empiricus, *Adv. Math.* 8:276 (= L&S 53T).

76. L&S translates *lekton* as "sayable," reasonably enough. For key passages on the semantics of *lekta* see Sextus Empiricus, *Adv. Math.* 8:11–12 and 8:70, as well as Diogenes Laertius, 7:55–57 (collected, together with other important testimonies to Stoic semantics as well as valuable commentary, in L&S 33).

77. On this issue see especially Long, "Language and Thought in Stoicism," to which I am much indebted in what follows.

78. Sextus Empiricus, *Adv. Math.* 8:12 (= L&S 33B). See also *Adv. Math.* 10:218 (= L&S 27D).

79. The comparison with Fregean semantics has often proved irresistible. See the comparison between the Stoic concept of *lekton* and Frege's concept of *Sinn* developed by Mates, 19–26, and the comparison between Stoic *axiōmata* and Fregean "propositions" in Kneale and Kneale, pp. 153–158. For the reasons against this Fregean interpretation of Stoic semantics see Annas, p. 76, and Graeser, "The Stoic Theory of Meaning," pp. 94–97.

80. See L&S 27B.

81. Sextus Empiricus, *Adv. Math.* 10:218 (= L&S 27D).

82. See chapter 3, "Words That Signify."

83. For the difficulty of distinguishing in Stoicism between words and thoughts, both of which are "things that mean," see Long: "In Stoicism . . . the processes of thought and the processes of linguistic communication are essentially the same" ("Language and Thought in Stoicism," p. 82).

84. This is closely related to the problem noticed by Mates, p. 13.

85. Burnyeat, emphasizing the distinction between technical and nontechnical usage, mounts a subtle argument for the thesis that the Stoics did not mean to "imprison signs within the conditional form of expression" ("The Origins of Nondeductive Inference," pp. 210–211). This is an attractive suggestion that I believe works for Aristotle (see above, "The Logic of Aristotle's Signs") but not for the Stoics, who are notorious for insisting that their technical definitions indicate the correct way to think, even at the expense of ordinary usage and common sense.

86. Such is the solution to this problem developed by Long in "Language and Thought in Stoicism;" see esp. pp. 96–98. On the crucial distinction that *lekta* can be

said to subsist (*huphistasthai*) but not to exist (*huparchein*) except in the sense of "be true," see pp. 89–90.

87. See the useful summary in Long, "Stoic Psychology and the Elucidation of Language," p. 110.

88. Sextus Empiricus, *PH* 2:95–96, *Adv. Math.* 8:140.

89. Sextus Empiricus, *Adv. Math.* 8:180. The classification of proof or demonstration (*apodeixis*) under the genus of sign is oft repeated (ibid. 8:278,289,299; *PH* 2:96,122,131,134)—once with the added explanation that "it is by participation in this [i.e., sign] that proof becomes revelatory of its conclusion," *Adv. Math.* 8:140.

90. The title is incomplete, as the treatise comes to us in the form of a single damaged scroll found at Herculaneum under the ashes of Mt. Vesuvius. For details see the edition by the DeLaceys, p. 12.

91. Philodemus, *De Signis* 52 (in L&S 18G).

92. Philodemus, *De Signis* 53 (in L&S 18G).

93. Philodemus's opponents seem to be relying on the Stoic Chrysippus's analysis of the conditional in terms of a strong necessary "cohesion" between antecedent and consequent (Sextus Empiricus, *PH* 2:111) rather than on the Philonian analysis in terms closely resembling what modern logicians call a "material conditional" (ibid. 2:110). See L&S 35. The actual opponents to whom Philodemus is responding, however, may not be Stoics but Academics using the Stoic conception of sign; see Asmis, "Epicurean Semiotics."

94. Philodemus, *De Signis* 2 (in L&S 42G).

95. Ibid.

96. Sextus Empiricus, *Adv. Math.* 8:201.

97. Ibid.

98. The Stoic definition of sign reported by Sextus at *PH* 2:104 and discussed above, is verbally identical with his earlier definition of "indicative sign" at *PH* 2:101.

99. Sextus Empiricus, *Adv. Math.* 8:201.

100. Sextus Empiricus, *PH* 2:102, *Adv. Math.* 8:156.

101. The distinction between indicative and reminding signs is introduced in *PH* 2:100–102 and *Adv. Math.* 8:151–158, and discussed at length in ibid. 8:192–202. For discussion of the reminding sign in the context of Sextus's writings (where, like many of Sextus's key concepts, it serves shifting purposes) see Glidden. For a careful historical account of the two kinds of sign, see Barnouw, chapter 5.

102. See the definitions of *hypomnēstikon sēmeion* at *PH* 2:100 and *Adv. Math.* 8:152.

103. Sextus Empiricus, *PH* 2:102. See the parallel passage in *Adv. Math.* 8:157.

104. Sextus Empiricus, *Adv. Math.* 8:158. For a moving defense of this sceptic claim to be on the side of ordinary life (against the dogmatic philosophies that would undermine ordinary life by attempting to establish a higher form of knowledge as the epistemological standard) see Frede's reconstruction of the sceptic position in "The Sceptic's Two Kinds of Assent" and "The Sceptic's Beliefs."

105. Sextus Empiricus, *Adv. Math.* 8:152. The resemblance to Hume's account of causality in terms of psychological association (see Hume, *Enquiry,* section VII, part II) is doubtless no accident. Hume knew his ancient sceptics.

106. Sextus Empiricus, *Adv. Math.* 8:145. In similar contexts Augustine uses the city of Alexandria, which he has never seen, to illustrate one class of things that must be believed rather than seen (*C. Faust. Man.* 20:7, *De Trin.* 8:9 and 9:10; in Ep. 120:10 it's Antioch; and see *C. Acad.* 1:11–12, where Alexandria is the unknown goal of a lifelong journey). Augustine's example may come from the medical literature, as Alexandria turns up in a text of Galen to illustrate how we believe well-attested phenomena we have not seen for ourselves ("On Medical Experience," 126).

107. Sextus Empiricus, *Adv. Math.* 8:146.

108. Ibid. 8:156.

109. On the rival schools of medicine, see Galen "On the Sects for Beginners." For the close relation between school of Pyrrhonist scepticism and the school of empiric physicians, see especially Diogenes Laertius, 9:116. For a fine historical introduction to the philosophical issues raised by ancient medicine, see Frede, "Philosophy and Medicine in Antiquity." For how different schools of medicine endorsed different types of sign, see Barnouw, pp. 245–263.

110. Sextus Empiricus, *Adv. Math.* 8:204.

111. For "indication" (*endeixis*) as a central issue in the debate between rival schools of medicine, see Galen, "On the Sects for Beginners," chapters 3 and 4. Note especially this contrast: "For, in the case of the same manifest bodily symptoms, the dogmatics [i.e., the rationalist school] derive from them an indication of the cause, and, on the basis of this cause, they find a treatment, whereas the empiricist [i.e., the empiric school] are reminded by them of what they have observed often to happen in the same way" (trans. Walzer and Frede, p. 7). On the likely connection between the physicians' concept of indication and Sextus's indicative signs see Frede, "The Method of the So-Called Methodical School of Medicine," p. 264.

112. For insight into the alliance between Pyrrhonist scepticism and Empiric medicine, see Frede, "The Ancient Empiricists," esp. pp. 253–256.

113. "So for example the soul is among the things which are non-evident [*adēlon*] by nature, for it can never naturally come to be self-evident [*enargeian*] to us. Being such, it is pointed out indicatively by movements of the body. For we reckon that some power residing in the body endows it with such movement." Sextus Empiricus, *Adv. Math.* 8:155. See likewise *PH* 2:101.

114. *De Mag.* 33–36; see chapter 4, "The *On the Teacher* Thesis."

115. Sextus Empiricus, *Adv. Math.* 8:167.

116. *De Mag.* 35. The term Augustine uses here and in similar contexts is *admonitio,* which is roughly equivalent to Sextus's term *hypomnēsis.* It is closer in meaning to the English "reminder" than to "admonishment."

117. Glidden (pp. 222–223), looking at the semiotics of *De Doct. Christ.* rather than *De Mag.,* sees a strong resemblance between Sextus's reminding signs and Augustine's category of natural signs. But when he compares Sextus's indicative signs with Augustine's other category of signs, the new category of "given"

or communicative signs that express an intent to communicate, Glidden finds—not surprisingly—that they do not match up well.

118. See *De Doct. Christ.*, prologue, 3.

119. The similarity between Augustine's semiotics and Sextus's scepticism about signs has been noted before. See Duchrow, *Sprachverständnis*, p. 70, who adds the point that we shall be pursuing in chapter 2: "It is particularly interesting to see how Augustine, with sceptical arguments, arrives at a Platonist result."

120. Plato, *Phaedo* 73d.

121. For more detailed discussion of why Augustine would not say Scripture reveals God, see chapter 4, "Learning Nothing from Scripture and Proof" and chapter 5, "Moses and Truth."

122. See esp. *In Joh. Evang.* 26:5–8, discussed in chapter 8, "Spiritual Eating."

123. On the inner vision of intelligible Truth, which Augustine treats as a natural function of the human mind and makes central to his epistemology, see Cary, *Augustine's Invention*, chapter 5.

124. *De Mag.* 38. See chapter 4, "Christ the Inner Teacher."

125. On authority as the key epistemological concept for Augustine's view of Scripture and all Christian teaching, see chapter 4, "Authority and Reason" and "Christian Mysteries and Platonist Philosophy."

CHAPTER 2

1. For the extent of Augustine's dependence on Cicero's *Academica*, see Hagendahl, pp. 52–70 and 498–503, as well as Testard, 1:1–7, and O'Meara's introduction to his translation of *Against the Academics*, pp. 14–15.

2. The textual legacy of Cicero's *Academica* is complex. Cicero produced two editions of the dialogue, first the two-book *Academica priora* then the four-book *Academica posteriora*. Of the former we have only book 2, often called *Lucullus* after its main speaker. Of the latter we have only the first book, in which Varro is the main speaker. References to "*Acad.* 2" are thus to the second book of the first edition of the treatise, which is also the book known as *Lucullus*. Hagendahl's judgment is that "[l]ike other writers of late Latinity, Augustine seems only to have known the *Academica posteriora* ... there is nothing to suggest that *Lucullus* was ever known to Augustine" (p. 498).

3. Cicero, *Acad.* 1:44–45 (= L&S 68A). See also *Acad.* 2:76–77, quoted at length in the next section, "The Grasping Appearance."

4. *C. Acad.* 2:14.

5. Ibid. 3:38–39; see also Ep. 118:16–17, 33. Augustine is not the only ancient writer to ascribe an esoteric Platonist teaching to the Academy. Sextus Empiricus reports the tradition that Arcesilaus tested his companions "aporetically," i.e., by dialectical puzzles, to determine whether they were suitable to be taught the doctrines of Plato (*PH* 1:234). Cicero does not report any such tradition in his extant works, but does describe himself as following the Academic practice of concealing one's own opinions while refuting those of others, a practice he traces back to Socrates (*Tusc.*

5:11, *De Nat Deor.* 1:11, *De Orat.* 1:84 and 3:67). Augustine, reporting this Academic practice from Cicero, ventures to suggest that the opinions the Academics are thus concealing are Platonist, but he presents this simply as a guess (*C. Acad.* 3:43). If he has any definite source for this suggestion, he does not tell us.

6. It is worth noting that even the title *"Against the Academics"* (*Contra Academicos*) is questionable, as the treatise often comes to us instead under the title "On the Academics" (*De Academicis*). See O'Meara's introduction to his translation of *Against the Academics*, p. 16. In *Retract.* 1:1.1 Augustine describes himself as writing "against the Academics or about the Academics." In the treatise itself Augustine is careful to say that his anti-sceptical arguments are directed not against the Academics but against "those who believed the Academics are opposed to finding the truth," *C. Acad.* 2:24. See the similar phrasing in ibid. 3:14, where Augustine proposes to criticize those who think the arguments of the Academics "are opposed to the truth."

7. *Ep.* 1:1.

8. Ibid.

9. *C. Acad.* 3:18: *cum falso non haberet signa communia.* Cf. the phrase *communia signa cum falso,* which occurs in a discussion of this criterion of truth in 3:21.

10. See L&S 1:239–241 and 249–253.

11. See chapter 1, "Words Written on Platonic Souls." Plato uses the wax-impression metaphor in a passage specifically describing memory (*Theaetetus* 191cd). Aristotle treats the appearance or *phantasma* in memory as an impression (*typos*) in *De Mem.* 450a30–32, and compares forms in the senses to the impression of a signet-ring on wax in *De Anim.* 2:12,424a18–32.

12. Diogenes Laertius, 7:46. Cf. also 7:50 (= L&S 39A), where Chrysippus warns against taking the metaphor too literally, as if the mind could have only one impression at a time. Sextus gives a thorough critique of the metaphor of impression using Stoic sources in *Adv. Math.* 7:227–241.

13. On Aristotelian *phantasia* as appearance rather than inner mental impression, see the important article by Schofield, "Aristotle on the Imagination."

14. See chapter 1, "Words Written on Platonic Souls."

15. For the role of *visa* in Augustine's action theory see Cary, *Inner Grace*, chapter 2, "Assent or Delight?" For his need to replace this action theory with something more Platonist see ibid., chapter 3, "Augustine's Evasiveness" and "Taught by God."

16. Cicero may be following the view of Antiochus, one of his teachers at the Academy, who according to Sextus says that in seeing we perceive (*antilambanometha*) both the *phantasia* and the visible object (Sextus Empiricus, *Adv. Math.* 7:162).

17. Cicero, *Acad.* 2:18: *visum . . . impressum effictumque ex eo unde esset, quale esse non posset ex eo unde non esset.* For the Greek formulations underlying Cicero's, see Sextus Empiricus, *Adv. Math.* 7:248 (in L&S 40E), and Diogenes Laertius, 7:46 and 7:54 (L&S 40C and 40A).

18. Cicero, *Acad.* 2:20. The main speaker in the first half of *Acad.* 2 is Lucullus, Cicero's debating partner. However, since Zeno's definition is not a point upon which the two disagree, all formulations of it can safely be attributed to Cicero the author.

276 NOTES TO PAGES 49–52

19. Ibid. 2:33.

20. Cf. Sextus Empiricus, *Adv. Math.* 7:164, which mentions "a *phantasia* that is common to the true and the false."

21. See chapter 1, "Empirical Inference and 'Common Signs.'"

22. Cicero, *Acad.* 2:33.

23. Ibid. 2:103.

24. Ibid. 2:34.

25. This contrast between the immediacy of grasping appearances and the inferential mediacy of signs comes across much more clearly in Sextus's exposition than in Cicero's. Sextus makes a clear division between discussion of the proposals for a foundational criterion of truth such as the grasping appearance (*Adv. Math.* 7:46–446 and *PH* 2:14–96) and the discussion of signs, which concerns empirical inference (*Adv. Math.* 8:141–299 and *PH* 2:97–133), and he does not use semiotic language in the former discussion.

26. See Graeser, *Zenon*, pp. 55–60.

27. The mark of a signet ring could be called a *typos* (impression) or a *sēmeion* (sign). The Stoics evidently preferred the former term (cf. Diogenes Laertius, 7:45 and 50) but Plato and Aristotle both use the latter in contexts where they are introducing the wax-impression model of the mind (*Theaetetus* 191d and 193c; *De Anim.* 2:12424a20).

28. See chapter 1, "Empirical Inference and 'Common Signs.'"

29. Cicero, *De Fin.* 2:119.

30. Cf. Sedley's suggestion that the phrase "common to A and B" may have been a piece of technical terminology used by the Stoics, not strictly confined to the notion of common *signs*, in "On Signs," pp. 243–244.

31. *C. Acad.* 2:11.

32. Ibid.

33. Ibid. 2:14. For the sake of completeness, I add the one other formulation of "Zeno's definition" in Augustine, which contains neither *signum* nor *nota*. According to *C. Acad.* 3:21, Zeno said "that appearance [*visum*] can be apprehended which appears [*appareret*] such as the false cannot appear"

34. Ibid. 1:30.

35. Cicero, *Acad.* 2:142.

36. *C. Acad.* 3:26.

37. Ibid. 3:42.

38. *Sol.* 1:24.

39. Plotinus, *Ennead* 1:6.8. Note the influence of this passage on *Conf.* 7:20 ("I closed my eyes lest they see vanity . . . and I awoke in You and saw. . . ."). For the influence of *Ennead* 1:6.8 in general see Cary, *Augustine's Invention*, p. 37.

40. See Glucker, *Antiochus*, pp. 296–306, and L&S 1:445, as well as the judgment of O'Meara in the introduction and notes to his translation of *Against the Academics* (pp. 17f, p. 158 n. 73, and p. 191 n. 48).

41. Cf. *De Beata Vita* 4 and *C. Acad.* 2:5.

42. That Arcesilaus, the founder of Academic scepticism, regarded himself as rightful heir to Plato (and accordingly read Plato's writings as exercises in scepticism) is tolerably clear from the ancient sources. See Glucker, *Antiochus*, pp. 35–40. Cicero seems to represent the standard Academic reading of Plato when he says that "in his books nothing is affirmed and there is a lot of arguing on both sides, inquiring about everything, saying nothing for certain" (*Acad.* 1:46).

43. The philosophy of the sceptical Academy was primarily a reaction against Stoicism (see Couissin). In contrast to the Academics' extensively documented criticism of Stoic epistemology, their attitude toward the epistemology of Plato is not well attested. Glucker, *Antiochus*, pp. 40–47, suggests they might have endorsed the critique of "Platonism" contained in Plato's own later dialogues, especially the *Parmenides*. This would explain how Arcesilaus could, according to Cicero's report, "take from the various books of Plato and discussions of Socrates especially the view that nothing is certain that can be grasped by the senses or *the mind*" (*De Orat.* 3:67).

44. See Cicero, *De Fin.* 2:2, *De Nat. Deor.* 1:11, *Acad.* 2:74. For a rich and nuanced discussion of the Platonism of the Hellenistic Academy see Tarrant. For the "Socratism" of Arcesilaus in particular see Sedley, "The Motivation of Greek Scepticism," p. 10: "Arcesilaus saw himself as a true Platonist, and his method of concluding '*epochē* about all things' was in essence borrowed from Plato's early Socratic dialogues." For Cicero's reports on the sceptical practice of "arguing both sides of a question," cf. Long, "Cicero's Plato and Aristotle."

45. See Cary, *Inner Grace*, chapter 1, "Wisdom and Virtue."

46. See Sedley, "The Motivation of Greek Scepticism."

47. Plato, *Apology* 38a.

48. On this peculiarly Stoic thesis, see Cary, *Inner Grace*, chapter 1, "Wisdom and Virtue." With hesitation and regret I translate the term *sophos* and its Latin equivalent *sapiens* with the phrase "wise man" rather than "sage," because it will be important in my exposition of Augustine on this topic to keep before the reader the verbal connection between the wise person and wisdom. Nothing in theory prevents the wise person from being female, but unfortunately the traditional term "wise man" accurately reflects how these philosophers actually thought about the subject, imagined it, and illustrated it.

49. Here I follow the work of Anthony Long, especially his "Dialectic and the Stoic Sage" and "The Logical Basis of Stoic Ethics."

50. See Diogenes Laertius, 7:46–48 (= L&S 31B) and Cicero, *Acad.* 2:23–24; also compare *C. Acad.* 1:19.

51. Cicero, *Acad.* 2:76–78 (= L&S 68O and 40D).

52. Long, "Dialectic and the Stoic Sage," p. 103.

53. The step was first taken in Aristotle's *Protrepticus*: "what standard, what determinant, of what is good have we, other than the man of practical wisdom? The things that such a man would choose if his choice followed his knowledge are good, and their contraries evil," Fragment 5 (Ross). See likewise *N. Eth.* 2:6,1107a2,

3:3,1113a33, 9:4,1166a11, 10:5,1176b16 and Düring, "Aristotle on Ultimate Principles,"
p. 38.

54. For the role of divine fire in Stoic cosmology see L&S, chapter 46, and the
informative study of Stoic cosmology by Lapidge.

55. *C. Acad.* 3:5–10.

56. It is ignored, for instance, by Kirwan. And for good reason. Kirwan is a
contemporary analytic philosopher interested in philosophic refutations of scepticism,
and this argument hardly counts.

57. *De Beata Vita* 10–11 and 26–28.

58. Ibid. 33–34. The identification of Christ as the Wisdom sought by philosophy
lies at the foundation of Augustine's Christian Platonism; see Cary, *Inner Grace,*
chapter 1, "Wisdom and Virtue."

59. *C. Acad.* 3:21.

60. Ibid. 3:39.

61. The quotations in the rest of this paragraph are from *De Div. QQs 83,* 9,
a widely overlooked passage that holds the key to interpreting much of *Contra
Academicos* as well as the first half of *Soliloquies,* book 2, as we shall see by the end
of this chapter.

62. *nihil esse sensibile quod non habeat simile falso.* These stock sceptical arguments, which long precede Descartes, are aired at some length in *Sol.* 2:10–11,
which is discussed below, in "The Two Kinds of Similarity."

63. For this proof of the immortality of the soul, which occupies the second
half of *Sol.* 2 and the first half of *De Immort. Anim.,* see Cary, *Augustine's Invention,*
chapter 7.

64. In *Augustine's Invention,* pp. 80–85, I portrayed Augustine's early development as a movement from Cicero to Neoplatonism. There I focused on how Augustine Platonized Cicero's materialist view of the soul (an inheritance from the
Stoics). Here I focus on how he Platonizes Cicero's scepticism (an inheritance from
the Academics).

65. This is made abundantly clear in Ep. 3, written probably while Augustine was
still at Cassiciacum.

66. *De Div. QQs 83,* 9.

67. On purification from phantasms as an ethical issue, see *De Musica* 6:32
and 51–52, *De Vera Rel.* 18, *Conf.* 7:1–2, and *De Trin.* 10:11.

68. *Sol.* 2:34. For the centrality of the Platonist sensible/intelligible contrast
to Augustine's early thinking see his correspondence with Nebridius, especially Ep. 4.
For the ethical meaning of purification, which cannot be separated from this epistemological distinction in Augustine's thought, see Cary, *Inner Grace,* chapter 1,
"Conversion and Purification."

69. *Sol.* 2:34.

70. *De Ord.* 2:43.

71. This ascent from sensible to intelligible is exemplified in the one treatise on
the liberal disciplines he completed, *De Musica* 6:2–6 (distinguishing the different
kinds of numbers), and 6:32–33 (learning to resist phantasms so as to gain "a restored

delight in reason's numbers," which are perceived by the intellect alone—and thereby to have "our whole life converted to God"). Notice that the movement in *Conf.* 7:1–16 follows the same trajectory: turning away from phantasms (7:1) in order to see intelligible Truth, which is God (7:16). On Augustine's early notion that a program of education in the liberal arts is the best way to come to a vision of God, see Cary, *Augustine's Invention*, pp. 75–75, 89–91.

72. *De Lib. Arb.* 2:33. See Ep. 4:2, where intelligible things are eternal and "most truly true" (*verissime vera*).

73. See Cicero, *De Fin.* 5:76 "How can anyone not approve [*probare*] the things that seem to him approvable [*probabilia*]?" and similar usage in *Parad. Stoic.* 1–2. Augustine makes the same connection between what is *probabile* and what is approved (*probatur*) in *De Util. Cred.* 25. The modern notion of probability as a mathematical calculation of chances did not arise until much later, as Hacking shows. A medieval version of Ciceronian usage, where "probable" means "approved by respected authorities," remained in use in English until the eighteenth century (Hacking, chapter 3) but was supplanted by the modern usage originating with the Port Royal *Logic* in 1660 (ibid., chapter 9).

74. See Locke, 4:15.3, where "probability" is defined as "likeliness to be true," in phrasing that conforms with modern English usage but also reads like a literal translation of Cicero's two terms—which is quite possibly what Locke intended it to be.

75. Cicero, *Acad.* 2:99.

76. Ibid. 2:32: the Academics "want there to be something probable and, so to say [*quasi*], truthlike."

77. Cicero uses *veri simile* in defining the rhetorical term "invention" as "coming up with true things and things like the truth, which make the case probable" (*excogitatio rerum verarum aut veri similium quae causam probabilem reddant*), in *De Inv.* 1:9. This definition is found in exactly the same words in the non-Ciceronian rhetorical treatise *Ad Herr.* 1:3, which suggests that the equivalence of *probabile* and *veri simile* was already a matter of common usage.

78. See chapter 1, "The Logic of Aristotle's Signs." Aristotle's usage was picked up by the Latin rhetorical tradition, as we can see when Quintilian explicitly contrasts the Greek terms *eikos* and *tekmērion* (*Institutio Oratoria* 5:9.3–8; cf. the same vocabulary, though a slightly different classification, in Aristotle *Rhet.* 1:2,1357a35–1357b5). Cicero renders what looks like the same contrast with the terms *verisimile* and *nota propria* (*De Part. Orat.*, 10:34), the former evidently a translation of *eikos* and the latter a translation of *sēmeion idion*. For the history of usage of both *veri simile* and *eikos*, see Glucker, "Probabile, Veri Simile and Related Terms."

79. Tarrant (p. 39) suggests the inspiration of Cicero's *veri simile* may be Plato's usage of the term *eikos*, especially in *Phaedrus*, where *eikos* is equated with *pithanos* (272de) and explained in terms of likeness to truth (*homoiotēta tou alēthous*) (273d). Tarrant mentions as well the usage of *eikos* at *Theaetetus* 162e, where it is contrasted to "proof and necessity." I would also point to *Timaeus* 29c, where Plato says our words (*logous*) about the sensible world need only be *eikos*, likely but not irrefutable, since they concern a world that is only an image or likeness (*eikōn*) of the unchanging

intelligible world. See also the contrast between *eoikos* and *alēthinon* in *Sophist* 240b. Perhaps any of these Platonic usages could have influenced Cicero's decision to transfer the equivalence of *veri simile* and *eikos* from his translations of rhetorical terms to his translations of philosophical terms.

80. *C. Acad.* 2:12. See also 3:33.

81. Ibid. 2:16.

82. Augustine's reasoning here closely parallels Plato's argument for the existence of Forms in *Phaedo* 74de. Cf. also *Phaedrus* 262b and *Sophist* 267b.

83. *C. Acad.* 2:20.

84. The reminder comes in *C. Acad.* 2:24 and is repeated in 2:25. Augustine himself agrees with the point at 3:29, where he states it as a fundamental principle of dialectic that "there should be no disputing about words [*verbis*] when there is agreement about the thing [*re*] for the sake of which the words are said." See his appeal to this principle in *De Ord.* 2:4 and 2:21.

85. *C. Acad.* 2:26 (end). See also 2:24, where Augustine first introduces this point, though without explicit reference to Cicero: "In my judgment, these were not men who were ignorant of how to give names to things."

86. *C. Acad.* 3:37.

87. Many years later Augustine acknowledges that this Platonic otherworldliness differs from biblical otherworldliness, which turns on the eschatological contrast between "this world" and the next (*Retract.* 1:3.2). Plato's intelligible world, rather, is the eternal Reason (*ratio*) by which God made the created world. *Ratio* is Augustine's translation both for *logos* and for Platonic Idea (see Augustine's essay "On Ideas," *De Div. QQs 83*, 46.2). Hence the implication is that Plato's intelligible world is none other than the pre-incarnate Christ, the eternal Logos, Wisdom, and Truth of God (for these names of Christ, which are crucial for all patristic theology, see John 1:1, 1 Cor. 1:24, and John 14:6, respectively). See Cary, *Augustine's Invention*, pp. 51–55.

88. *C. Acad.* 3:41. Note also the close linking of Plato and Plotinus in *Sol.* 1:9. Augustine continues to see Plotinus as the culmination of the Platonist tradition in later works, e.g., *Ep.* 118:33 and *Civ. Dei* 9:10.

89. One possible source in Plato himself should be considered. In *Timaeus* 29c, after describing how the universe of becoming is an image (*eikōn*) of an intelligible and unchanging paradigm (29a), Plato argues that our words or theories (*logous*) should match the character of what they are about: unchanging and irrefutable when they are about the unchanging paradigm, likely (*eikotas*) when they are about its image (*eikonos*). He then sums up this analogy between worlds and words in a saying that became very important for Augustine: "As being is to becoming, so truth is to faith." (Augustine quotes this twice in his writings, *De Trin.* 4:24 and *De Cons. Evang.* 1:53; on its significance for him cf. Teske, "The Link between Faith and Time in St. Augustine.") The *Timaeus*, which Augustine read in Cicero's translation, is in fact the only treatise of Plato with which Augustine shows extensive familiarity (cf. Courcelle, *Late Latin Writers*, pp. 168–177). There is no other evidence that he read it this early in his career. See Hagendahl, pp. 131–138 and 535–554,

who dates Augustine's earliest quotation of this text to c. 400 (p. 530). However, if it is true that Augustine is already familiar with this Platonic passage (and it is the Platonic passage he quotes earliest), then that might help explain what he says next in our passage from *C. Acad.* 3:37: "And thus from the former [i.e., the intelligible world] truth is as it were polished and shined in the soul that knows itself, while from the latter [i.e., the sensible world] in the minds of the unwise is generated opinion, not knowledge."

90. Plotinus, *Enneads* 1:2.1–3. For another point at which this treatise seems to have influenced Augustine's thinking, see Cary, *Augustine's Invention*, p. 166 n. 57.

91. *C. Acad.* 3:37

92. Ibid. 3:40.

93. Ibid.

94. Ibid. 2:24.

95. *Retract.* 1:1.4. Note also the explicit rejection of Academic scepticism in *De Trin.* 15:21: "Far be it from us to doubt that what we learn from the senses is true." For the more generous epistemology of Augustine's later works, see chapter 5, "Testimony about Temporal Things."

96. I distinguish "book" and "treatise" in the ancient manner. Thus the *Soliloquies* is not a book but a treatise consisting of two books; hence my reference to "this book," here as well as below, is specifically to *Sol.* 2.

97. I will put "Augustine" in quotation marks when referring to this character in contradistinction to the dialogue's author. The distinction is important because the latter, not the former, is the source of the words of Reason in *Sol.*

98. For "purification" as the purpose of the dialogue see *Sol.* 2:34, and compare *C. Acad.* 2:9, where Augustine describes his activity at Cassiciacum as "nothing but cleansing myself of empty and destructive opinions."

99. For remarks on delay see Sol 2:8 (end), 2:13 (beginning), 2:24 ("Augustine's" second speech), 2:25 (early in "Augustine's" speech). For expressions of confusion (i.e., what is called in the Platonic dialogues, *aporia*) see the end of 2:8 and the beginning of 2:9, as well as 2:15.

100. See, e.g., *Sol.* 2:2 (Reason's first speech warns "Augustine" to answer "cautiously and firmly"), 2:9 (in his third speech, "Augustine" announces his confidence that he has not given his assent rashly), 2:13 (at the end of the paragraph "Augustine" admits with shame that he has given his assent rashly), 2:20 (in his second speech "Augustine" is cautious about assenting rashly), 2:24 (in Augustine's second speech, he recalls making no unwary concessions), 2:27 (which concludes with an exchange in which Reason warns "Augustine" against incautious assent and Augustine promises to guard "against that infirmity").

101. *Sol.* 1:9.

102. This rather extreme dialectical complexity is perhaps why the first half of *Sol.* 2 is seldom discussed in the Augustine literature. I shall be unable to do justice to the subtle development of the argument, which is not as random as it looks on

a superficial reading, but shall be forced simply to pick out the particular themes that are relevant to my current purpose. I discuss the second half of the book (where Augustine considers the notion of truth in the soul) at greater length in *Augustine's Invention*, pp. 95–100.

103. *Sol.* 2:10. Cicero discusses these examples in *Acad.* 2:54–58; for the general Academic argument about indistinguishability between sensible things, see *Acad.* 2:83–86.

104. *C. Acad.* 2:14.

105. *Sol.* 2:10. Plato had reached similar conclusions long before, in *Phaedrus* 261e–262b and *Sophist* 240b.

106. *Sol.* 2:10.

107. Ibid. 2:11

108. Ibid. 2:13.

109. Ibid.

110. The notion that sensible things in some fashion desire to be like Forms originates with Plato himself, e.g., *Phaedo* 74d.

111. This is not to say we never hear of these issues again in the form of reports and summary criticisms, as in Ep. 118 and *Civ. Dei*. But this is the last time Augustine engages Hellenistic epistemology on its own terms.

112. In the *Soliloquies* itself (2:32) Augustine is still willing to say that all bodily things are false, in the sense of "not truly true" (*non . . . vere verum*). A body is "a kind of image of the truth" (*quaedam imago veritatis*) but does not have "true form and beauty" (*vera . . . forma et species*). Hence, even though a body is "true by a sort of imitation" (*imitatione aliqua verum*) Augustine insists that "truth is not in it" (*non in eo sit veritas*)—a claim that he needs to make in order to support the key premise of his argument for the immortality of the soul (viz., that Truth cannot exist outside of the soul). In preparing the ground for this argument Augustine makes the bald statement that "nothing is true except what is immortal" (1:29). But this argument turns out to be more Manichaean than Platonist, as it implies that God, who is Truth, is necessarily absent from the bodily world rather than omnipresent. Hence Augustine does not long maintain this flat denial of truth in bodily things. Cf. Cary, *Augustine's Invention*, p. 104.

113. E.g., *De Mend.* 40.

114. Plato, *Cratylus* 423b.

CHAPTER 3

1. For this characterization of the inquiry driving the Cassiciacum dialogues, see Cary, *Augustine's Invention*, pp. 77–80.

2. *Sol.* 1:7. God and the soul are also identified as the two basic topics of philosophy in *De Ord.* 2:47.

3. For fuller discussion of the place of this program of education in Augustine's early thought see Cary, *Augustine's Invention*, pp. 89–91.

4. *De Ord.* 2:35–44. For fuller analysis of this narrative of Reason's founding of the liberal arts, see Cary, *Augustine's Invention*, pp. 91–94.

5. *De Ord.* 2:32.

6. Ibid.

7. Ibid. 2:33.

8. Ibid. 2:34.

9. Poetic meter is *numerosus* in ibid., 2:33, and dancing is *numerosus* in 2:34. Poetic meter itself is called "number" (*numerus*) not only in Latin (as Augustine points out in 2:40) but also in English up through the eighteenth century.

10. Ibid. 2:34: *gestus illi omnes signa sint rerum ... quod bene aliquid significet et ostendat, excepta sensuum voluptate.*

11. Ibid.: *animum, cui rerum signa illa monstrantur.*

12. Ibid.: *nam sensum mulcet pulcher motus, per sensum autem animum solum pulchra in motu significatio.*

13. Ibid.

14. Ibid.

15. Ibid. *rationabiliter sonat* as opposed to *rationabiliter dictum est.*

16. Ibid. 2:35: *esse imponenda rebus vocabula, id est, significantes quosdam sonos.*

17. Ibid.: *ut, quoniam sentire animos suos non poterant, ad eos sibi copulandos sensu quasi interprete uterentur.* An *interpres* can be almost any kind of "go-between," such as a mediator in a dispute, as well as a translator or interpreter.

18. Ibid.: *illud quod in nobis est rationale ... naturali quodam vinculo in eorum societate astringebatur, cum quibus ille erat ratio ipsa communis.*

19. Ibid.: *nec homini homo firmissime sociari posset, nisi conloquerentur, atque ita sibi mentes suas cogitationesque quasi refunderent.*

20. The Maurists, the seventeenth-century Benedictines who produced what is still the only complete printed edition of Augustine's works (reprinted by Migne in PL) regarded *De Dialectica* as spurious. But the scholarship of the last century and a half has been solidly on the side of authenticity. See Jackson's introduction to his edition of the text for a brief history of the scholarship (pp. 26–30) and Pépin, *Saint Augustin et la Dialectique*, pp. 21–60, for an extended rebuttal of the Maurists' arguments.

21. On the history of the term "dialectic," with an interesting and plausible account of how its meaning evolved from Plato's notion of Socratic conversation to the Stoics' notion of formal logic—an evolution closely connected with the emergence of the Stoic conception of the wise man's unshakeable wisdom—see Long, "Dialectic and the Stoic Sage," pp. 102–113.

22. For the extent of Augustine's debts to Stoic logic in *De Dial.*, see Jackson's notes to his edition of the text, Ruef's commentary, and Pépin's examination of possible sources, *Saint Augustin et la Dialectique*, pp. 72–98 (note also the likelihood that even the Peripatetic concepts came to Augustine in Stoic garb, ibid., pp. 70–72). Note also Anthony Long's judgment that the semantics of *De Dial.* 5 is "thoroughly Stoic or at least largely Stoic in ultimate inspiration" in "Stoic linguistics," p. 50, as well as Mayer's judgment in *Die Zeichen*, Part I, p. 236f.

23. The simplest hypothesis, for which Pépin argues in *Saint Augustin et la Dialectique*, pp. 99–132, is that Augustine used Varro's treatise *On Dialectic* from the latter's *Nine Books on the Disciplines*, a lost work that would have presented Stoic logic (supplemented occasionally by elements of Peripatetic logic) in Latin. We know Varro's work on the disciplines was very much on Augustine's mind at Cassiciacum; see Cary, "Varro," and Pacioni, "Liberal Arts."

24. Pépin, *Saint Augustin et la Dialectique*, pp. 24–29, points to the incompleteness of *De Dial.* and its purpose as a school text to explain its rather low level of originality (by comparison to Augustine's other writings).

25. This is particularly clear in *De Lingua Latina* 5:1–2, where after introducing the disciplines of etymology and semantics (which he designates in Greek: *etymologian* and *peri sēmainomenon*) Varro proceeds to discuss what words signify. He evidently understands *significare* to be equivalent to *sēmainein*. And this is not the only place in the treatise where words "signify" (cf. ibid. 8:3 and 9:7).

26. The opening words of the treatise: *Dialectica est bene disputandi scientia. Disputamus autem utique verbis* (*De Dial.* 1).

27. Ibid.

28. In *Sol.* 1:27, Augustine asks whether the same thing (*res*) is signified (*significari*) by the two words *veritas* and *verum*.

29. *De Dial.* 1.

30. Ibid., 5.: *Verbum est uniuscuiusque rei signum, quod ab audiente possit intellegi, a loquente prolatum. Res est quidquid vel sentitur vel intellegitur vel latet. Signum est quod et se ipsum sensui et praeter se aliquid animo ostendit. Loqui est articulata voce signum dare.*

31. Ibid.

32. Ibid.: *quidquid autem ex verbo non aures sed animus sentit et ipso animo tenetur inclusum.*

33. Ibid.: *quod in verbo intellegitur et animo continetur.*

34. Ibid.: *res autem ipsa, quae iam verbum non est neque verbi in mente conceptio . . . nihil aliud quam res vocatur proprio iam nomine.*

35. See chapter 5, "Outward Voice and Inner Word."

36. Commentators for centuries have noticed the similarity; see Jackson's edition, p. 126, notes 7 and 9, and Long's judgment: "I see no reason to doubt that it refers to the Stoic *lekton*" in "Stoic linguistics," p. 52. For the Stoic *lekton*, see chapter 1, "Stoic Semantics without Depth."

37. See Ruef, pp. 108–111.

38. Aristotle, *Rhet.* 1:2, 1357a32–1357b24.

39. On the role of signs in ancient theories of probable inference, see Burnyeat, "The Origins of Non-deductive Inference."

40. Cicero, *De Inv.* 1:48: *signum est quod sub sensum aliquem cadit, et quiddam significat, quod ex ipso profectum videtur.*

41. Ibid.

42. Ibid. 1:81.

43. *De Doct. Christ.* 2:1: *signum est enim res praeter speciem, quam ingerit sensibus, aliud aliquid ex se faciens in cognitionem venire.* The phrase *ex se* is perhaps a vestige of *ex ipso* in the Ciceronian definition.

44. See chapter 1, "The Sceptics' Reminding Signs."

45. The authority of *De Inv.* was quite extensive. Aquinas, for instance, cites *De Inv.* 2:161 over and over again in support of his classification of the cardinal virtues (*ST* II–II, 49:1,2, and 6, 101:1, 102:1, 106:1, 108:2). The use of this text in moral theology goes back at least to Augustine, *De Div. QQs 83*, 31.

46. Cicero himself tells us this, and judges the work unworthy of himself, especially in light of what he has since learned in his experience as a successful orator, *De Orat.* 1:5.

47. *De Part. Orat.* 34. We have already seen the rationale for such translations in chapter 2, "Zeno's Definition" (for *notae*) and "The Status of the Truthlike" (for *verisimilia*).

48. Augustine points out this etymology in *De Mag.* 7.

49. See chapter 1, "Physiognomic Inferences."

50. *De Orat.* 3:221.

51. Ibid. 3:222–223.

52. Ibid. 3:223.

53. *De Doct. Christ.* 2:3: *significandi, id est signi dandi.*

54. The notion first appears in the definition of "to speak" in *De Dial.* (see above, "Words That Signify"), and becomes important a few years later in *De Mag.* 3: "I believe that in speaking [*loquendo*] with me now, you are not emitting sounds in vain, but in everything that emerges from your mouth you are giving me a sign so that I might understand something [*signum mihi das ut intelligam aliquid*]."

55. *Signa* are either *naturalia* or *data*, *De Doct. Christ.* 2:2.

56. Here too Augustine may have Greek precedent, if Sextus is reporting a long-standing philosophical tradition when he says that bodily movements are signs of the soul in *PH* 2:101 (cf. *Adv. Math.* 8:155). See chapter 1, "Reminders of Deeper Things."

57. *De Doct. Christ.* 2:2.

58. Ibid.

59. Ibid. 2:3. Note the similarities with Cicero, *De Orat.* 3:223. Augustine's *ad demonstrandos* is probably a reminiscence of Cicero's *ad declarandos*; and the phrase *motus animi* seems to be taken directly from Cicero and then supplemented with Augustine's own addition, *vel sensa aut intellecta quaelibet.*

60. This is the governing metaphor in the critique of Manichaean verbiage in *Conf.* 3:10.

61. See likewise *De Fide et Symb.* 4: "There is a great difference between our mind and our words, by which we try to make this same mind manifest.... This is what we are trying to do when we speak, if we would carefully consider the desire of our will: for what are we trying so hard to do, but to bring our very mind itself, if this could be done, into the mind of our hearer to be known and observed...?"

62. Of the English translations of *De Doct. Christ.* known to me, only Green's recent *On Christian Teaching* translates *signa data* as "given signs" rather than as

"conventional signs." Likewise, the scholarly French series, *Bibliothèque Augustinienne*, has "signes conventionnels" in its first edition of *De Doct. Christ*. The second edition however has "signes intentionnels," not an exact translation but one that does properly emphasize the essential feature of *signa data*, which is that they derive from a will to communicate.

63. See Kretzmann, p. 10.

64. Aristotle, *De Interp*. 2,16a27. See chapter 1, "The Semiotics of *On Interpretation*."

65. *De Orat*. 3:222f; see above, "A Latin Orator's Signs."

66. *Conf*. 1:13.

67. *De Doct. Christ*. 2:3.

68. *De Doct. Christ*. 2:37: *non natura sed placito et consensione significandi*.

69. Ibid. The suggestion that signs can move souls is common rhetorical usage, which Augustine does not take literally, as we shall see below, "Signs Moving Souls."

70. *Civ. Dei* 19:24. See chapter 6, "Shared Insight and Love's Union" (end) and for fuller discussion, Cary, "United Inwardly by Love."

71. *De Ord*. 2:35. See above, "Signifying Reason."

72. *De Doct. Christ*. 2:5. On pride as the reason we use words, see also Duchrow, "*Signum* und *superbia*."

73. *De Doct. Christ*. 2:40.

74. Ibid. 2:41.

75. It is significant that Augustine begins the presentation of his theory of culture here (*De Doct. Christ*. 2:27) with a reference to Varro, the author of the *libri disciplinarum* which were the basis of Augustine's own program of education in the liberal disciplines (see Cary, "Varro"). All the disciplines which Augustine includes in his early program are at least alluded to, and some discussed extensively, in the last half of *De Doct. Christ*. 2.

76. *De Doct. Christ*. 2:41–47. It is worth noting the strong claims Augustine makes for historical truth, which are backed up by a very strong version of the doctrine of Providence: "Although historical narratives tell of human institutions of the past, history itself should not be counted among human institutions, since the things that have passed and cannot be undone belong to the order of the ages [*ordine temporum*] whose author and administrator is God" (*De Doct. Christ*. 2:44).

77. Ibid. 2:41.

78. Ibid. 2:50.

79. Ibid. 2:57.

80. The opening line announces the treatise's subject matter: "rules for treating the Scriptures." See Gerald Press's convincing account of the subject and structure of the treatise.

81. Ibid. 2:58. In the great execution of the project of inward turn in *Conf*. 10 the liberal arts are mentioned once (10:16), but no educational project is proposed. About ten years later, in 409, bishop Augustine can look upon the spiritual value of a liberal education with disdain and can scarcely locate his own former

writings on the subject, in which he had once vested such high hopes (Ep. 101). On the meaning of this striking change in Augustine's intellectual project, see chapter 4, "The Great Shift in Augustine's Teaching."

82. *De Gen. c. Man.* 2:32.

83. *De Div. QQs 83,* 47.

84. Plotinus, *Ennead* 4:3.18. Cf. O'Connell, *Early Theory,* pp. 162–166, for the importance of this chapter of Plotinus in Augustine's early thinking. For the place of this kind of vision in Augustine's eschatology, see the opening paragraphs of chapter 5, below, as well as the following section, "Secondhand Knowledge."

85. *De Gen. ad Litt.* 12:34. Cf. ibid. 12:48, where Augustine says that angels "see our thoughts, not of course with eyes, because they see in spirit not in body." For the notion of spiritual (i.e., imaginative) vision, see Cary, *Inner Grace,* chapter 3, "Taught by God." Augustine's use of the terms "spiritual" and "spirit" in these passages, at least in relation to human beings, must be understood as referring to imagination, not intellect.

86. *De Gen. c. Man.* 2:5f (here I use Teske's translation). Augustine is commenting on Gen. 2:6, where Paradise is watered not by rain but by springs from the ground.

87. Ep. 95:8.

88. *Civ. Dei* 19:7.

89. See chapter 6, "Shared Insight and Love's Union."

90. The unreliability of friendship is a central instance in a long list of the miseries of fallen social life, most of which stem from our inability to discern one another's hearts, in *Civ. Dei* 19:5–8.

91. This is one of the more unsettling conclusions of Augustine's anti-Donatist theology. See chapter 7, "Conversion and Perseverance."

92. *De Bono Conjug.* 21, quoting Acts 4:32.

93. See chapter 6, "Public Inner Wisdom," as well as Cary, *Augustine's Invention,* chapter 9, "Inner Privacy and Fallen Embodiment."

94. See Introduction, "Downward Causality."

95. *De Musica* 6:10–15. See the helpful exposition in Gilson, I,iv.

96. *De Musica* 6:11. Cf. the theory of sense-perception in Plotinus, *Ennead* 4:4.23, which also preserves the soul's freedom from being affected by external things by insisting that sensible objects make a direct impression on the body's sense organs, not on the soul itself. The general point that the soul is causally superior to the body and unaffected by it would have been familiar to Augustine already from Cicero; cf. Cary, *Augustine's Invention,* pp. 84–85.

97. *De Musica* 6:10. The Latin relies on the commonplace but untranslatable connection Augustine sees between the verb "to be affected" (*pati*) and the noun "passion" (*passio*), both of which are used to underline the point that the body is at the passive, receiving end of causal relations. Its motions are effects rather than causes, so it is described as affected and passive, hence full of affections or passions: *Videtur mihi anima cum sentit in corpore, non ab illo aliquid pati, sed in ejus*

passionibus attentius agere.... Has operationes passionibus corporis puto animam exhibere cum sentit, non easdem passiones accipere.

98. *De Musica* 6:13 and 6:49. Cf. Plotinus, *Enneads* 4:8.2–4 and 5:8.11.

99. *De Musica* 6:39.

100. Ibid. 6:41. The crucial causal language is: *permittantur animae de animis aliquid agere, significando eas moventes per alterutra corpora.*

101. Ibid. 6:31.

102. See, e.g., *De Doct. Christ.* 2:54, 4:6, 4:27, as well as 2:37 (discussed above, "The Ontological Ground of Convention").

CHAPTER 4

1. For this aspect of Augustine's early project see Cary, *Augustine's Invention,* pp. 73–76 and 89–94.

2. The idea that the liberal arts could help one understand God is found in Justin Martyr (*Dialogue with Trypho* 2), Clement of Alexandria (see Lilla, pp. 169–173), and Gregory of Nyssa (*On Infants' Early Deaths,* PG 46:181C = NPNF ed., p. 378). Cf. also its earliest appearance in the Judeao-Christian tradition in Philo of Alexandria's *On Mating with the Preliminary Studies* (*De Congressu Quaerendae Eruditionis Gratia*).

3. Plato, *Republic,* book 7.

4. Ibid. 7:519b–521b.

5. *Civ. Dei* 8:8. That Platonist intellectual vision is the goal of the Christian life is also clear, I think, in *Conf.* 7 (see Cary, "Book 7: Inner Vision as the Goal of Augustine's Life"). The same goal is stated near the beginning of Augustine's career in *Sol.* 1:12, where an inner voice named Reason tells Augustine: "Reason ... promises to show God to your mind just as the sun is shown to the eyes."

6. See esp. Lorenz, pp. 95–98.

7. For the self-understanding of Reason as the goal of philosophical education in Augustine's early project, see especially *De Ord.* 2:43 and 48–51, as well as the discussion in Cary, *Augustine's Invention* 91–94.

8. *Conf.* 9:14.

9. Ibid.

10. *De Mag.* 46.: *unus omnium magister in caelis sit.* Compare the verses in Matthew as rendered by the Vulgate (which my translation in the text closely follows): (9) *Et patrem nolite vocare vobis super terram; unus enim est Pater vester qui in caelis est.* (10) *Nec vocemini magistri, quia magister vester unus est Christus.*

11. This profound act of renunciation may have stemmed from Augustine's belief at the time that it was wrong to love Adeodatus as his own son instead of simply as a human soul. Cf. *De Ver. Rel.* 88f: "One human being is not to be loved by another as brothers of the flesh are loved, or children or spouses or any relatives, kindred or fellow citizens. For this love is temporal.... Nor should this seem inhuman to anyone. For it is more inhuman to love in a human what is a son, not what is human. For this is to love in him what belongs to oneself rather than what belongs to God."

12. *Conf.* 9:14.

13. *De Mag.* 2. The notion that prayer is not essentially a matter of speaking but of the inward movement of the heart remains in Augustine's later writings, as for instance in his long letter on prayer addressed to Proba, where he says, "in faith, hope and charity we are always praying by continual desire, but at certain intervals of time we also petition God with words, *in order to admonish ourselves by these signs of things,* to acquaint ourselves with how much we have progressed in this desire, and stir ourselves up more keenly to grow in it," Ep. 130:18. The words are for ourselves, not God. The theory of prayer here is fundamentally Neoplatonist, as in Plotinus who speaks of "calling upon God himself, not by word aloud but by stretching our soul into prayer toward him" (*Ennead.* 5:1.6).

14. *Conf.* 1:13. See Introduction, "Mother and Child."

15. Plato, *Republic,* 514a (the first sentence of book 7). The older translation by Jowett renders *paideia* misleadingly as "enlightenment."

16. Ibid., 518bc. The central point of the Allegory of the Cave is that education is the art of conversion. Cf. Cary, *Inner Grace,* chapter 1, "Conversion and Purification."

17. Plato, *Meno* 84d–85c.

18. *De Duab. Anim.* 19. Augustine later enriches his picture of the mind by distinguishing between the spiritual and intellectual in his mature classification of three kinds of vision (*De Gen. ad Litt.* 12:15–21). But in this classification intellectuality is not put below spirituality but above it, since "spiritual vision" (in the technical sense given to it in *De Gen. ad Litt.*) has to do with imagination, dreams and visions, and thus is lower and less valuable than intellectual vision, by which alone we see God. See Cary, *Inner Grace,* chapter 3, "Taught by God."

19. For the Hebrew "heart" as site of understanding and reason as well as feeling, see Wolff, pp. 46–51 (citing such passages as Deut. 29:4, 1 Kings 3:9, Prov. 15:14, Psalm 90:12). New Testament usage is similar, as when Jesus perceives the thoughts in his opponents' *hearts* (e.g., Mark 2:6).

20. These four terms (heart, mind, soul, and strength) appear in the New Testament formulations (Matt. 22:37, Mark 12:30, and Luke 10:27). The original Old Testament formulation (Deut. 6:5) does not include "mind," because the ancient Hebrew word for "mind" is "heart."

21. *De Div. QQs 83,* 46.2, Augustine's very influential little essay "On Ideas."

22. Everything in God is God, according to Augustine's doctrine of divine simplicity in *Civ. Dei* 11:10, which he traces back to the Platonists in ibid. 8:6.

23. *De Lib. Arb.* 2:33. On these partial glimpses of God, which are essential to Augustine's account of the working of the rational mind, cf. Cary, *Augustine's Invention,* pp. 54 and 66–67.

24. *De Div. QQs 83,* 46.2.

25. See the note on this Pauline passage in Cary, *Inner Grace,* chapter 1, "Wisdom and Virtue."

26. *Conf.* 3:7f. See discussion in Cary, *Augustine's Invention,* chapter 4, "Wisdom by Another Name."

27. For this passage, as well as the "inner man" language in the Pauline corpus generally, together with its sources and its influence on Augustine, see Cary, *Augustine's Invention*, chapter 4, " 'Inner Man' Language" and "Christ in the Heart."

28. The point is stressed by Ratzinger, p. 37–38, and is central to his criticism of the "purely metaphysical" conception of the inner teacher in Augustine's early work (p. 35).

29. As Augustine explains more fully many years later, Christ incarnate brought teaching (*magisterium*) to human beings so that truths taught by the holy prophets "but also by the philosophers and even the poets" might be confirmed by "his authority presented in the flesh. . . . for the sake of those who could not see or discern them in the inward light of Truth itself—that Truth which was also present to all who could participate in it before it assumed a human being [i.e., before it was incarnate]," Ep. 137:12.

30. *Sol.* 1:7.

31. It is possible that Augustine was also toying with the idea of identifying Reason with the Holy Spirit, especially in light of the description of Father, Son, and Holy Spirit as Principle, Wisdom, and Reason, respectively, in *De Ord.* 2:26. The same subordinationist consequences would follow, however. In a fully Nicene trinitarianism, a divine inner teacher must be no different in being from the ultimate Truth that is taught, and that is the crucial difference between the inner teacher in *Soliloquies* and the inner teacher in *On the Teacher*.

32. *Sol.* 1:12.

33. For the intrinsic divine power of the soul in Augustine's earliest writings, as well as the reasons, both Christian and Platonist, for his abandoning this idea, see Cary, *Augustine's Invention*, chapters 7 and 8.

34. *De Lib. Arb.* 2:37; see the similar imagery in *Sol.* 1:22 and for a discussion of the ontology underlying this imagery see Cary, "United Inwardly by Love."

35. *Conf.* 9:24. See chapter 6, "Public Inner Wisdom."

36. E.g., *Conf.* 10:10, 10:65, 11:5, 11:10, 12:10–12.

37. Ibid. 10:9.

38. *De Mag.* 38.

39. E.g., *De Grat. Christi* 14 and *De Praedest. Sanct.* 13. See Cary, *Inner Grace*, chapter 3, "Taught by God."

40. See esp. *De Pecc. Mer.* 1:37 and 2:5.

41. For this Platonist epistemological dependence of the mind as the context for Augustine's doctrine of grace, see especially Burns, "Grace."

42. See Cary, *Inner Grace*, chapter 1, "The Widening Scope of Inner Help."

43. The contrast between Augustine's doctrine of grace and Aquinas's illuminates what is distinctively Augustinian about Augustine, but implies that he is not quite a good Roman Catholic (see Cary, *Augustine's Invention*, pp. 67–71). It also helps explain why Thomas needed to develop his distinctive concept of the supernatural in the first place (see Cary, "The Incomprehensibility of God and the Origin of the Thomistic Concept of the Supernatural").

44. See chapter 5, "Testimony about Temporal Things."

45. See Augustine's characterization of his program of studies in the liberal disciplines in *Retract.* 1:3.1 and 1:6 (in some editions 1:5.3) and 1:11 (in some editions 1:10).

46. *De Lib. Arb.* 2:39. Cf. the similar outburst of joy in ibid. 1:29, which Augustine explicitly confirms is the joy of ultimate beatitude, the happy life.

47. *Conf.* 5:24f and 6:4

48. Just a few examples from two well-known works: *Conf.* 6:17, 8:2, 11:1, and 12:1, *Civ Dei* 1:12, 11:13, and 22:20.

49. *Conf.* 11:10.

50. *Conf.* 10:9. Cf. also the admonition in *Conf.* 4:18: "Seek what you seek, but it is not where you seek it. You seek happy life in the region of death. It is not there."

51. *De Lib. Arb.* 2:38.

52. See *De Mag.* 34 and 35.

53. See *Sol.* 1:13 and *De Quant. Anim.* 53.

54. *Ep.* 7:2; see also *Sol.* 2:35, *De Immort. Anim.* 6 and *De Quant. Anim.* 34.

55. Plato's concept of reminder in *Phaedo* 73c and 76a has the same structure as Augustine's definitions of sign, discussed in chapter 3: a sensible thing brings to mind something intelligible.

56. See chapter 1, "The Sceptics' Reminding Signs."

57. *De Trin.* 12:24. See discussion in Cary, *Augustine's Invention*, pp. 13–17.

58. Burnyeat's essay, "Wittgenstein and Augustine *De Magistro*," is particularly illuminating on this point.

59. This is the diagnosis of our problem given in *Conf.* 7:1f, though the diagnosis originates with Plotinus: cf., e.g., *Ennead* 1:6.8 (the need to close one's eyes and notice another kind of vision that has always been going on in us, unnoticed), 4:8.8, 5:1.12, and 5:8.11.

60. *Conf.* 7:16.

61. See Plotinus, *Enneads* 1:3.1–3, 5:8.11, and 6:9.4, as well as the discussion in Cary, *Augustine's Invention*, pp. 40–44. O'Connell first brought attention to the priority of faith to understanding in Plotinus in his *Early Theory*, pp. 223–225.

62. Aristotle, *Soph. Elench.* 2,165b2 (quoted in Aquinas, *ST* II–II, 2.3).

63. *De Mag.* 37. Augustine's Latin, *nisi credideritis, non intellegetis*, is a translation of the Septuagint rather than the Hebrew.

64. See, for example, *De Lib. Arb.* 1:4 and 2:6 (quoted at the beginning of philosophical inquiries), *De Fide et Symb.* 1 (at the beginning of an exposition of the creed), and *De Trin.* 7:12 (the last words of book 7, serving as a hinge on which Augustine turns from the first half of the treatise to the second). For major developments of the theme of believing so as to understand, see Sermons 43 and 118, *In Joh. Evang.* 29, and *Ep.* 120.

65. The most important passages for the authority/reason contrast are *C. Acad.* 3:43, *De Ord.* 2:16 and 2:26, *De Mor. Eccl.* 3, *De Util. Cred.* 2, *De Quant. Anim.* 12, and *De Vera Rel.* 45. The fact that this is a pedagogical distinction, i.e., that it is about

learning (*ad discendum*), is explicit in *C. Acad.* 3:43 and *De Ord.* 2:26, though this is obscured in many translations.

66. *De Mor. Eccl.* 3: *naturae quidem ordo ita se habet, ut cum aliquid discimus, rationem praecedat auctoritas.*

67. *De Ord.* 2:26: *Tempora auctoritas, re autem ratio prior est.*

68. *De Util Cred.* 2.

69. Ibid. 25. Cf. similarly *De Vera Rel.* 45: "Authority demands faith, and prepares a human being for reason. Reason leads to understanding and knowledge."

70. *De Util Cred.* 25. For the Stoic and sceptic agreement that the wise man does not opine, see chapter 2, "The Point of Academic Scepticism."

71. *De Util. Cred.* 21.

72. Ibid. 2.

73. *Conf.* 3:21.

74. *De Musica* 2:1. The aim of the inquiry is stated in the final clause: *ut ad omnia nos ratio potius perducat quam inveterata consuetudo aut praejudicata cogat auctoritas.*

75. Gadamer, Second Part, II,1,b,i.

76. *De Musica* 3:3.

77. Ibid. 2:14.

78. *De Quant. Anim.* 41.

79. *C. Acad.* 1:9.

80. Ibid. 1:24.

81. See for example Cicero, *Acad.* 2:60, *De Nat. Deor.* 1:10 and 3:9, all of which explicitly contrast authority and reason, as well as *Acad.* 2:8–9 and *Tusc.* 5:83, which deprecate philosophical schools that rely on authority.

82. *De Mor. Eccl.* 3, *De Util Cred.* 21, *De Quan. Anim.* 76, *De Musica* 6:1, *De Vera Rel.* 45.

83. *C. Ep. Fund.* 41. Cf. *Conf.* 11:10, quoted above, at the end of "Learning Nothing from Scripture and Proof."

84. *C. Acad.* 3:42.

85. *C. Acad.* 3:43.

86. We have an example of such a *traditio symboli* under the title *Explanatio Symboli*, probably by Ambrose and just possibly a transcript from the very year of Augustine's baptism. See D. Botte's edition for the text and a fine introduction arguing for Ambrose's authorship of the text. (Incidentally, the term *symboli* here is simply Latin for "of the creed," and has no overtones of "symbolic meaning" in the modern literary sense.)

87. *De Ord.* 2:16.

88. Ibid. 2:27.

89. See the entry on *Mystērion* in Kittel for details.

90. See chapter 6, "The Meaning of 'Sacrament.' "

91. E.g., Plato, *Phaedo* 62b, 69c, 81a (cf. *Meno* 81a–b), Plotinus *Ennead* 1:6.6 and 4:8.1. The philosophical meaning of the mysteries is reinforced in another way when the language of mystic initiation is used metaphorically to describe the

philosophical transformation of the soul, as in Plato, *Symposium* 210a–e, *Phaedrus* 249c, 250b, and 253c.

92. In *C. Acad.* 3:42 the philosophy of Plato and Aristotle, as combined by Plotinus (3:41), is not "the philosophy of this world, which our sacred rites rightfully detest, but of another, intelligible world." That this intelligible world (i.e., the world of Platonic Ideas) is contained in the divine Intellect (i.e., Christ) referred to several lines later is not explicit but is a doctrine so prominent in Plotinus that Augustine must have intended those in the know to pick up on it. In any case Augustine will soon explicitly teach that all Platonic Ideas are contained in the divine Intellect, *De Div. QQs 83*, 46.2.

93. *C. Ep. Fund.* 41, quoted at the end of "Authority and Reason," above.

94. See chapter 5, "Witnesses to Christ."

95. Brown, *Augustine of Hippo*, chapter 15.

96. Carol Harrison has recently issued a book-length challenge to the very notion of Augustine's "lost future" in *Rethinking Augustine's Early Theology*, insisting that there was never a major discontinuity in the development of Augustine's thought. While I agree with the consensus view in thinking there is a great shift in Augustine's thought when he abandons his earlier hope of arriving at happiness and understanding of God in this life (a hope that is central to his early philosophical work—so clearly in *Sol.* 1:14–15, for example, that Augustine explicitly corrects himself on this very point in *Retract.* 1:4.3—and which causes Harrison to find "a rather odd tension" in his early thought, which she doesn't quite know what to do with, pp. 45–46) I agree with Harrison in rejecting one prominent strand of this consensus (not in Brown), which contends that the early Augustine thought the soul could reach this happiness by its own unaided or autonomous efforts. No Platonist would believe that; cf. Cary, *Inner Grace*, chapter 1, "The Widening Scope of Inner Help."

97. *Civ. Dei* 10:29.

98. Ibid.

99. Cf. Goulven Madec's astute suggestions on this score, *Saint Augustin et la philosophie*, p. 70–71.

100. For the press-ganging, see Sermon 355:2 and Brown, chapter 14. For the aim of "becoming divine in leisure" (*deificari in otio*) and why it is not possible for ordained clergy busied with the care of their flock, see Ep. 10:2.

101. *De Ord.* 2:26.

102. See *De Grat. et Lib. Arb.* 20 and *De Fide et Oper.* 21 and 25, and the discussion of Augustine's rejection of "faith alone" in Cary, *Inner Grace*, chapter 1, "Connections of Love."

103. See the concluding image of *Conf.* 7:27, which plainly has this biblical precedent in mind.

104. See the beginning of "Christian Mysteries and Platonist Philosophy."

105. *De Quant. Anim.* 12.

106. *De Ord.* 2:27, quoted above, in "Christian Mysteries and Platonist Philosophy."

107. *De Quant. Anim.* 76. The Pauline reference is to 1 Cor. 3:2. "Distribute" is *dispensare,* which refers to the work of a *dispensator,* a household manager who distributes what is needed to various dependents serving in the house.

108. *Conf.* 7:24.

109. *Conf.* 10:6.

110. Sermon 117:15 (this passage is unaccountably omitted from Hill's otherwise excellent translation).

111. Ibid. 117:16.

CHAPTER 5

1. *Civ. Dei* 8:8. This view of beatitude is attributed specifically to Plotinus in ibid. 10:2.

2. Enjoying one's friend or neighbor in God is a key concept in Augustine's mature ethics, beginning with *De Doct. Christ.* 1:35. See the definition of the peace of the heavenly city, which includes "enjoying God and one another in God," in *Civ. Dei* 19:13. That this involves seeing one another's minds in the light of God is a thought developed at the end of ibid. 22:29. Cf. also *De Div. QQs* 83, 47, Ep. 92:2 and 95:8, and *De Bono Conjug.* 21. For a vigorous attempt to imagine what such seeing might be like, cf. Dante, *Paradiso* 8:85–90, 9:73–75, 15:61–63, and 21:49–50.

3. *De Bono Conjug.* 21. For the ontological basis of this unity see chapter 6, "Public Inner Wisdom" and "Shared Insight and Love's Union" as well as Cary, "United Inwardly by Love."

4. Ep. 147:7. In *Retract.* 2:41, Augustine lists this as a treatise *On Seeing God* (*De Videndo Deo*) and I will refer to it below under that title.

5. Shakespeare, *Othello,* III,iii,360.

6. For an extended argument to this effect, see Cary, "Believing the Word."

7. See chapter 3, "Fallen Language."

8. Ep. 95:8.

9. See chapter 4, "The *On the Teacher* Thesis" and "Learning Nothing from Scripture and Proof."

10. See Ep. 27:1f, 28:1, 40:1. In Ep. 232:6 Augustine urges a correspondent to get to know him through the *Confessions.* On the prospects of epistolatory friendship in Augustine's time see Conybeare.

11. *De Fide Rerum Invis.* 1f.

12. *Conf.* 10:11–38. The argument that this picture of memory as inner world is something new is presented in Cary, *Augustine's Invention,* chapter 10.

13. *Conf.* 2. I have translated Augustine's *voluntates* literally as "wills" in order to maintain the important verbal connection with the will (*voluntas*) and goodwill (*benevolentia*) of the friend. The usual translations, "wants" or "wishes," make for better English but less accuracy.

14. Ibid.

15. Ibid. 4.

16. See the end of the section, "The *On the Teacher* Thesis," in chapter 4.

17. Cf. *De Mor. Eccl.* 20. That Augustine in his earliest works did not make a clear distinction between the soul and the divine within it is argued in Cary, *Augustine's Invention,* chapter 7.

18. *De Fide Rerum Invis.* 2.

19. For *temporalis dispensatio* as equivalent of *oikonomia* in Augustine, see especially *De Fide et Symb.* 6 and 8 (where he indicates his awareness of introducing a technical term to his audience) and 18 (where he uses a more literal translation and expansion of the Greek term, *administrationem suscepti hominis;* cf. the earlier *suscepti hominis dispensationem,* Ep. 11:4). Cf. also his characterization of the temporal dispensation in *De Ver. Rel.* 13 and 19 and *De Doct. Christ.* 1:39.

20. *De Vera Rel.* 45. "Announce" (*nuntiat*) is a standard Augustinian (originally Ciceronian) metaphor for the deliverances of the senses.

21. *De Doct. Christ.* 1:20–39. O'Donovan's article remains the most detailed and insightful treatment of the way this formulation emerged from Augustine's earlier ethical formulations.

22. *De Trin.* 15:21.

23. Ibid. 12:21–25. The ensuing discussion of faith in 13:1–4 implicitly puts faith in the realm of *scientia* concerning temporal things.

24. *De Videndo Deo* (= Ep. 147:8).

25. Luther, 1535 *Lectures on Galatians* on Gal. 2:16 (LW 26:129). (This quotation is a keynote of the new approach to Luther research recently developed by Finnish scholars. See Maneermaa, as well as Braaten and Jenson for an introduction to this approach.) Much of what is most intensely paradoxical in Luther's theology stems from his teaching that Christ is present in the heart through faith, even though he is not inwardly seen. The paradox is that Luther's reliance on faith alone excludes the inner experience of vision, which is for Augustine the very goal of faith, while insisting that we are to believe that faith has in fact achieved (or rather been given) its goal, which is union with Christ himself. The intensity of the paradox stems from Luther's enthusiastic use of the Augustinian language of inwardness to articulate this effect of our dependence on the authority of an external word. For Luther, the inner presence of God is known secondhand; we do not see or experience it for ourselves but simply believe what we hear in the Gospel of Christ. (For this anti-experiential reading of Luther, which aligns him with medieval Catholic sacramental theology rather than with the more Augustinian form of inwardness characteristic of Protestantism, see also Cary, "Why Luther Is Not Quite Protestant.")

26. *Retract.* 1:14.1

27. *De Trin.* 15:21. Note how this unqualified affirmation of the truth of what is learned from the senses corrects Augustine's earlier use of sceptical critiques of empirical knowledge, as discussed in chapter 2, "The Two Kinds of Similarity."

28. See the discussion of Augustine in Auerbach's fundamental essay "Figura," pp. 37–43, as well as Mayer's treatment of the concept of *figura* in *Die Zeichen,* Part I, chapter 6, section 6.

29. See Mayer, *Die Zeichen,* Part II, chapter 6, section 9, and more recently the essay by Cameron as well as the discussion in Toom, pp. 223–245.

30. E.g., Mark 10:30, John 3:16, Romans 6:23, Titus 1:2, 1 John 5:20. The Greek phrase is often translated "everlasting life," but Augustine always sees it as something much more than a life that lasts forever: *aeterna vita* (the standard Latin translation) is for him a participation in divine eternity, entailing freedom from the changes, vicissitudes, and decay of time. See *Civ. Dei* 14:25, and for the underlying ontology of participation in divine eternity, *Conf.* 11:9–13. For Augustine's identification of the biblical concept of eternal life with the classical philosophical concept of happiness, see Cary, *Inner Grace*, chapter 1, "Beauty and Love."

31. *De Doct. Christ.* 1:39.

32. Auerbach articulates this point by noting that in Augustine the simple contrast of figure and fulfillment "is sometimes replaced by a development in three stages: the Law or history of the Jews as a prophetic *figura* for the appearance of Christ; the incarnation as fulfillment of this *figura* and at the same time as a new promise of the end of the world and the Last Judgment; and finally, the future occurrence of these events as ultimate fulfillment" ("Figura," p. 41). Replace "end of the world and the Last Judgment" with "eternal life," and I think Auerbach has it exactly right. The ultimate fulfillment of biblical and historical *figurae* is not any temporal event, not Christ in the flesh nor even the end of the world, but participation in divine eternity. This is why, as Auerbach puts it, there remains in Augustine "an idealism which removes the concrete event, completely preserved as it is, from time and transposes it into a perspective of eternity" (ibid. p. 42).

33. *De Doct. Christ.* 1:11.

34. See Cary, *Inner Grace*, chapter 1, "Wisdom and Virtue."

35. *Civ. Dei* 11:2.

36. Augustine sketches his program of purifying and educating the mind's eye for vision in metaphorical terms closely resembling the Allegory of the Cave in *Sol.* 1:12 and 23–25; see Cary, *Augustine's Invention*, chapter 5, "Education for Vision," and *Inner Grace*, chapter 1, "Conversion and Purification."

37. The contrast between Augustine's Neoplatonism, with its robust commitment to the intellectual vision of God, and the Neoplatonism of the Eastern church father now called Pseudo-Dionysius, with its powerful insistence on divine incomprehensibility, has far-reaching implications for the history of Western theology, which on this point did not follow Augustine. See Cary, *Augustine's Invention*, pp. 55–58 and 67–78, as well as "The Incomprehensibility of God and the Origin of the Thomistic Concept of the Supernatural."

38. *Retract.* 1:26, commenting on *De Div. QQs 83*, 12, which contains an excerpt from Fonteius's treatise *De Mente Mundanda ad Videndum Deum*.

39. *De Div. QQs 83*, 12.

40. *De Doct. Christ.* 1:11.

41. See chapter 4, "Authority and Reason," as well as the Plotinian view of how faith precedes understanding, discussed in Cary, *Augustine's Invention*, 40–44.

42. *Civ. Dei* 11:2, quoting from 1 Tim. 2:5.

43. For further discussion of this wordplay (consuming/assuming) and its basis in Nicene theology, see below, "Outward Voice and Inner Word."

44. The point that Christ is mediator as man not as God is an implication of Nicene theology to which Augustine frequently returns; see, e.g., *Civ. Dei* 9:15, *Conf.* 10:68, *De Grat. Christi* 2:33, Sermon 293:7.

45. *De Doct. Christ.* 1:38. For a discussion of this and the related passage in *Conf.* 4:18 about Christ running through his earthly race quickly so as to be found within, see Cary, *Augustine's Invention*, pp. 50–51.

46. *Civ. Dei* 11:3.

47. Ibid.

48. *C. Ep. Fund.* 41.

49. When the narrative of universal history in books 15–18 of the *Civ. Dei* gets to the chapter on the life of Christ (18:46), his death and resurrection are mentioned only in passing as Augustine gives an account of the unbelief of the Jews and its consequences.

50. *De Doct. Christ.* 1:38.

51. *De Dial.* 5. Writing consists of "signs of words" also according to *De Mag.* 8 and *De Doct. Christ.* 2:5.

52. See chapter 3, "The Ontological Ground of Convention."

53. *Conf.* 11:5.

54. Ibid.

55. Ibid. 12:33.

56. Ibid. 12:32–33. Once again I translate the noun *voluntas* and the verb *velle* with "will" rather than "wish" or "want," even at the cost of English idiom, so as to make key conceptual connections clear.

57. Ibid. 12:35.

58. *De Doct. Christ.* 1:43. As in the previous quotation, the verb here is *indigere*, to have need of.

59. *De Doct. Christ.* 1:38. The identification of Christ as "the beginning of ways" (*principium viarum*) stems from the standard patristic Christological reading of Prov. 8:22 (which Augustine quotes in this passage) though it is not so standard when Augustine identifies this beginning of God's ways not simply with Christ as eternal Wisdom but with Christ incarnate.

60. *De Ord.* 2:26. See chapter 4, "Authority and Reason."

61. That Augustine remains quite serious about the *On the Teacher* thesis throughout his career is one of the recurrent themes of Cornelius Mayer's scholarship. See his "Res Per Signa" for an examination of the early pages of *De Doct. Christ.*, the most important text where Augustine seems, verbally at least, to contradict the *On the Teacher* thesis.

62. *Conf.* 7:16.

63. Ibid. 7:1–2. The term "phantasm" appears once in the brief discussion of the possibility of glimpsing God as Truth at the end of *De Trin.* 8:3, which verbally echoes both *Conf.* 7:1–2 (stating the problem) and *Conf.* 7:16 (stating the solution). For the importance of this problematic of eliminating phantasms in order to gain a clear intellectual vision, see Cary, "Book Seven."

64. *De Trin.* 8:8.

65. See chapter 4, "Learning Nothing from Scripture and Proof."

66. Ibid. 8:7.

67. Ibid. 8:7–8.

68. Sermon 43:9.

69. *De Trin.* 8:3–4.

70. Sermon 117:3–14. For eternal generation as the original site of the Christian doctrine of divine incomprehensibility, see Cary, "The Incomprehensibility of God."

71. Sermon 117:15. This is part of the sentence that is omitted from the English edition of the sermons by E. Hill, as noted in chapter 4, "The Great Shift in Augustine's Teaching." This affirmation of divine intelligibility conflicts with the robust and widely accepted notion of divine incomprehensibility articulated by Pseudo-Dionysius, but not with Augustine's own weak notion of incomprehensibility. See chapter 6, "Words and Common Inquiry."

72. *De Trin.* 8:13.

73. Ibid.

74. Ibid. 8:9. "Form and Truth" (*forma et veritas*) is a hendiadys, two names for the same thing: the one going back to Plato, the other more characteristically Augustinian and used to remind us that (contrary what is suggested by Platonic texts like the Allegory of the Cave) Platonic Forms are to be found within the soul, though also above it.

75. Ibid.

76. Ibid.

77. Ibid.

78. Ibid. 8:10. Cf. the conclusion of 8:12.

79. Ibid. 8:12.

80. Ibid.

81. Ibid. 8:11.

82. See the systematic exposition of this point in Mayer, *Die Zeichen,* part II, chapter 6, especially sections 5–7, as well as Mayer's essay, "Philosophische Aussetzungen."

83. Sermon 288:3

84. *De Trin.* 15:9.

85. *De Quan. Anim.* 65–66.

86. Ibid. 66.

87. *De Trin.* 15:22.

88. *De Doct. Christ.* 1:12.

89. See Hanson, pp. 100–122.

90. Gregory of Naziansen, *Orat.* 29:19 (the third "Theological Oration"). For the role of this formulation in patristic soteriology as Augustine understands it, see Cary, *Inner Grace,* chapter 3, "The Grace of Participation."

91. See esp. Sermon 186:2, *Quod erat manentem, quod non erat assumentem.*

92. Sermon 187:4. He "is made" or "becomes" man (*homo factus est*) just as the Word "was made" or "became" flesh (*verbum caro factum est*) in John 1:14. The ambiguity in the Latin is impossible to retain in English but important for Augustine,

as it links temporal becoming with createdness. To become (*factus*) man means to be made (*factus*), in the sense of being created—becoming a creature that God has made. So in the Incarnation the Creator of all things becomes one of the things he has created or made. I will translate using the old idiom, "is made," to retain the resonance of createdness that would be lost in the colorless translation "became." The same idiom reappears below when the inner word is made or becomes voice (*fit vox*).

93. Sermon 121:5.

94. Sermon 117:16.

95. For the wordplay in *Civ. Dei* 11:2, see above, "Witnesses to Christ."

96. Sermon 187:3.

97. Augustine is quite aware that this distant ontological similarity between divine eternal Word and human inner word is the basis for his analogy; see esp. Sermon 119:7.

98. For this range of meaning of the term *vox*, see Augustine's discussion in Sermon 288:3.

99. Sermon 187:3. See also the development of the analogy in Sermon 119:6f and *De Doct. Christ.* 1:12.

100. On Augustine's rejection of the concept of life-giving flesh, which was being developed by his contemporary Cyril of Alexandria, see chapter 8, "Powerless Blood" and "Spiritual Eating."

101. Sermon 288:2, quoting Isa. 40:3–8. The reference to voice is in Isa. 40:3, the reference to Word in Isa. 40:8.

102. Sermon 288:3. On this sense of the term "sacrament," see chapter 6, "The Meaning of 'Sacrament.'"

103. Sermon 288:4, quoting John 3:30.

104. Sermon 288:5.

105. Ibid. Augustine takes "form of servant" and "form of God" from Phil. 2:6f, one of the most important sources of his Christological thinking.

106. See above, "Witnesses to Christ."

107. Sermon 288:5, quoting from Matthew 5:8.

108. Sermon 288:5.

109. Ibid., quoting John 14:9.

110. John 14:9–10. The first "you" is plural, referring to Jesus' time with the disciples; the second is singular (in Greek, the implicit subject of a second-person singular verb) referring to Philip's particular ignorance.

111. Sermon 288:5. A similar interpretation of Jesus' answer to Philip's question is found in Augustine's treatise *De Videndo Deo* (= Ep. 147:16).

112. Cf. *C. Max. Arian.* 2:24: "Now when it says, 'He who has seen me has seen the Father also,' who does not know that this is said because whoever sees the Son intellectually [*per intelligentiam*] in fact sees he is equal to the Father?"

113. Augustine is aware of joining a long Christian tradition when he reads the Platonist books as containing the same truth as John 1:1 in *Conf.* 7:13; cf. the conclusion of *Civ. Dei* 10:29.

114. E.g., 2 Cor. 4:18 (the temporal/eternal contrast), 1 Tim. 6:16 (God dwells "in light inaccessible" like Plato's sun), Heb. 8:5 (earthly things as "copy and shadow" of heavenly things). Though all of these passages use language and imagery derived from the Platonist tradition, none of them is a simple affirmation of Platonism; all of them, for instance, locate the flesh of the resurrected Christ in the eternal, heavenly realm of light, which is hardly what Plato had in mind in the Allegory of the Cave. Thus all of them call for interpretation, which could plausibly go in a Platonist direction but does not obviously have to do so.

115. Cf. Kierkegaard's way of distinguishing Christianity from Platonism in *Philosophical Fragments,* chapters 1 and 2.

116. For a fuller argument to this effect, see Cary, "Believing the Word."

117. For the soul as wax tablet for writing, see chapter 1, "Words Written on Platonic Souls." For the biblical picture of words written on the heart, see Prov. 3:3 and 7:3, Jer. 17:1 and 31:33f (an important passage quoted in Heb. 8:10 and 10:16), 2 Cor. 3:3.

CHAPTER 6

1. *Sacramentum* occurs in the Vulgate at Eph. 1:9, 3:3, 3:9, and 5:32, Col. 1:27, 1 Tim. 3:16, Rev. 1:20 and 17:7, covering a little less than a third of the occurrences of *mystērion* in the Greek.

2. In the Vulgate translation of passages in the New Testament in which *mystērion* appears twice within two verses (Eph. 3:3f and Col. 1:26f), *sacramentum* and *mysterium* are used in turn, as if they were wholly equivalent. Augustine likewise uses *sacramentum* and *mysterium* interchangeably in *De Cat Rud.* 32–35, a sample of which we shall see below. That Augustine employs these two terms "in absolutely equivalent fashion" is a fundamental and amply justified conclusion of Couturier's exhaustive study (p. 164). For a profound analysis of the history of the term *sacramentum* in patristic Latin up to and including Augustine, see Mayer, *Die Zeichen*, part I, chapter 6, section 4.

3. See Bornkamm. According to Raymond Brown, something like this rather bland sense of "secret" was what New Testament writers had in mind when they used the term *mystērion* to render a wide range of Semitic notions of divine secrets revealed, such as the access of the prophets to the deliberations of the divine court in heaven. If Brown is correct, then unlike the patristic writers, the term evoked for NT writers no associations with mystery cults.

4. See, e.g., Rom. 16:25, 1 Cor. 2:7, Eph. 1:9–11.

5. See Rom. 11:25, Eph 3:3–6, Col. 1:24–27.

6. E.g., 1 Cor. 13:2, 14:2, 15:51.

7. Rev. 1:20, 17:7. "Symbol" in this literary sense is one of the three major divisions of meaning of the terms *sacramentum* and *mysterium* for Augustine according to Couturier, along with "rite" and also "mystery" in the sense of doctrine (as in "mystery of the Trinity").

8. See chapter 4, "Christian Mysteries and Platonist Philosophy." This usage seems to afford us an indication of the historical origin of the use of the terms

sacramentum and *mysterium* to refer to central Christian doctrines—Couturier's third category of meaning.

9. Sermon 228.3.

10. *De Cat. Rud.* 32. Similar usages of both *sacramentum* and *mysterium* are scattered throughout the subsequent exposition of the Old Testament narrative in this treatise, ibid. 33–35.

11. Sermon 227.

12. *Sacramentum apellatur quandoque in sacra Scriptura res sacra et mystica*, in *Summa Sent.* 4:1.

13. *Sacramentum vero non solum significat, sed etiam confert illud cujus est signum vel significatio*, ibid.

14. Lombard, *Sent.*, 1:1.1. This passage follows immediately upon a quotation of the opening words of Augustine, *De Doct. Christ.* 1:2.

15. Lombard, *Sent.*, 4:1.4.

16. See *Summa Sent.* 4:1, as well as Hugh of St. Victor, *De Sacramentis* 1:9.2.

17. Aquinas, *ST* III, 60.1.

18. *Civ. Dei* 10:5.

19. For the importance of this definition of sacrament, "the most widespread throughout the whole high middle ages," see de Ghellinck, "Un chapitre," pp. 80–83.

20. Lombard, *Sent.* 4:1.2; Hugh, *De Sacramentis* 1:9.2; Aquinas, *ST* III, 60.2; cf. *Summa Sent.* 4:1, whose conceptual clarity on this issue is particularly instructive.

21. Aquinas, *ST* III, 62.1.

22. See chapter 5, "Secondhand Knowledge."

23. For this formulation (which is found in *Summa Sent.* 4:1 as well as in Lombard, *Sent.* 4:1.2), its sources, and its eventful career through the Middle Ages, see de Ghellinck, "Un chapitre," pp. 83–90.

24. *QQs in Hept.* 3:84.

25. Lombard, *Sent.* 4:4.4 and Aquinas, *ST* III, 68.2.

26. Ep. 105:12.

27. *De Bapt. c. Donat.* 5:29. The phrase "sacrament of grace" also occurs in Ep. 98:2, as well as the converse, "the grace of this sacrament," in Ep. 98:1. This important letter, in which the connection between sacrament and grace is perhaps clearer than anywhere else in Augustine, will be discussed extensively in chapter 7, beginning with "Unity in Adam."

28. *Civ. Dei* 10:5.

29. Ibid. 10:20.

30. Ibid. 10:3.

31. Ibid. Cf. *De Vera Rel.* 1f, as well as Cary, *Inner Grace*, chapter 1, "Dialogue with Plato."

32. *Civ. Dei* 10:2. Plotinus is actually named in the chapter and allowed to define the nature of happiness as Christians understand it.

33. Ibid. 10:19.

34. Ibid.

35. Ibid. 10:3.

36. Ibid. 10:6, quoting Rom. 12:5.

37. Phil. 2:6–7f. Designating Christ's humanity as "the form of the servant" is extremely common usage in Augustine; cf. chapter 5, "Outward Voice and Inner Word."

38. *Civ. Dei* 10:6. For the Nicene point that Christ is mediator according to his humanity, see chapter 5, "Witnesses to Christ."

39. Rom. 12:5–6a, translated from *Civ. Dei* 10:6, where Augustine quotes Rom. 12:3–6a.

40. *Civ. Dei* 10:5, quoting Hos. 6:6.

41. *Civ. Dei* 10:5, quoting Heb.13:16.

42. *Civ Dei* 21:27. Cf. Cyprian's treatise *On Works and Alms* 5: "by almsgiving our prayers become efficacious." For an introduction to Augustine's endorsement of this tradition, see Burnaby, *Amor Dei*, pp. 132–134.

43. *Civ. Dei* 10:5–6. Quotations from Heb. 13:16, Matt 22:40, and Sirach 30:24 (Vg.).

44. *Civ. Dei* 10:3.

45. *C. Faust. Man.* 19:11. "Seals" here translates *signacula*, which plays an important role in Western discussions of the sacraments because of its use in Rom. 4:11. The term means literally, "a little something used for a sign," and typically designates the mark of a signet ring on a wax seal.

46. See chapter 3, "Fallen Language."

47. See below, "Shared Insight and Love's Union."

48. In *De Dial.* 7 a whole chapter is devoted to the *vis verborum*, the "force of words," which has to do with how much they mean (*quantum valeat*) in terms of moving their hearer either by their sheer sound (as in poetry) or by their signification. But note: to speak of words moving their hearers is common parlance that Augustine is willing to adopt but does not think is perfectly accurate; see chapter 3, "Signs Moving Souls."

49. *Conf.* 7:7 and 7:11. See Cary, *Inner Grace*, chapter 2, "Reading Paul's Admonition."

50. *Conf.* 8:4. That Augustine does not regard himself as born again until he was baptized is clear from ibid. 9:14.

51. See ibid. 9:5–6, where both Verecundus and Nebridius are believers described as "not yet Christian" until they are baptized.

52. Ibid. 8:3.

53. Ibid. 8:4.

54. Ibid.

55. Ibid.

56. *De Ord.* 2:27. See chapter 4, "Christian Mysteries and Platonist Philosophy."

57. *Conf.* 8:5.

58. Ibid.

59. Ibid. 8:3.

60. Ibid. 8:4.

61. Ibid.

NOTES TO PAGES 171–174

62. Ibid. 8:3.

63. Ibid. 7:24. Thus I attempt to translate the untranslatable: *Non enim tenebam Deum meum Jesum humilis humilem.*

64. Ibid. 7:25. The point that he already believed in Christ despite his doctrinal deficiencies is explicit in ibid. 7:11; see Cary, *Inner Grace*, chapter 2, "Reading Paul's Admonition." His doctrinal deficiencies correspond to his description of what he "read" in the books of the Platonists in 7:13–14, which included "In the beginning was the Word...and the Word was God" (John 1:1) but not "the Word was made flesh" (John 1:14).

65. The allusion to Moses comes at the very end of the book, *Conf.* 7:27; the contrast between *via* and *patria* is found both here and near the end of 7:26.

66. *Conf.* 7:25.

67. The notion that *Conf.* 8 must narrate a conversion to faith—despite Augustine's explicit insistence that he already believed in Christ at that time (cf. *Conf.* 7:7 and 7:11)—results from reading Protestant notions of conversion back into *Confessions*, for reasons that have partly to do with later developments in Augustine's own thought concerning the decisive importance of the beginning of faith. See Cary, *Inner Grace*, chapter 4, "The Grace of Beginnings" and "Converting Paul's Will."

68. *Conf.* 9:5.

69. Ibid. 8:2.

70. This is the diagnosis of Augustine's situation presented in compact form in ibid. 8:17, and more elaborately in 6:18–20.

71. Augustine uses the phrase *studio sapientiae*, the pursuit of wisdom, which is Cicero's definition of philosophy, to designate what he longs for in both 6:20 and 8:17. The phrase has defined philosophy for him from the beginning of his writing career (*C. Acad.* 3:20). Cicero defines philosophy in these terms in *Tusc.* 1:1 and probably also in *Hortensius* (see Boethius, *De Diff. Top.* 2).

72. *Conf.* 6:21; cf. also the end of 6:19.

73. That true philosophy is love of God is explicit in *Civ. Dei* 8:1 and attributed to Plato in ibid. 8:8 and 8:11.

74. *Conf.* 6:24.

75. Ibid. 8:19.

76. *Conf.* 6:20, quoting Wisdom 8:21, which hovers in the background of the speech of Continence in *Conf.* 8:27 and recurs in ibid. 10:40, closely connected with the theological implications that most offended Pelagius (according to *De Dono Pers.* 53). This quotation subsequently becomes a leitmotif of the anti-Pelagian doctrine of grace; e.g., *De Pecc. Mer.* 2:5, *De Sp. et Litt.* 22, *De Dono Pers.* 43.

77. See *Conf.* 1:18 as well as 6:20, where I take it that baptism is meant by "the medicine of Your mercy for the healing of that infirmity."

78. *Conf.* 8:29.

79. Ibid. 9:14.

80. Ibid. 8:29. The *regula fidei* here refers both to Monica's dream in ibid. 3:19 and to the creedal instruction that is part of the catechesis preceding baptism.

81. Ibid. 8:4.

82. For this interpretation of the meaning of *Conf.* 8, see Cary, *Inner Grace*, chapter 2, "Reading Paul's Admonition."

83. See chapter 7, "Conversion and Perseverance."

84. See Cary, *Inner Grace*, chapter 4, "The Experience of Grace in Disarray."

85. For this account of conversion against the backdrop of Plato's Allegory of the Cave, see Cary, *Inner Grace*, chapter 1, "Conversion and Purification."

86. See chapter 7, "The Efficacy of Unity."

87. For young Augustine's precocious debating skills, practiced especially against unlearned Catholics, see the episode in *Conf.* 3:21 as well as the less well-known self-description in *De Duab. Anim.* 11, which is also reflected in the autobiographical remarks in *De Util Cred.* 2.

88. See chapter 4, "Authority and Reason."

89. *C. Acad.* 3:43, *De Lib. Arb.* 1:4, *De Util. Cred.* 1 and 20, *De Quant. Anim.* 12.

90. *De Ord.* 2:15, *De Quant. Anim.* 12.

91. *De Mor. Eccl.* 3 and 12 develop the metaphor of the "shade of authority"; cf. *De Quant. Anim.* 12 on authority as the safer route.

92. *Sol.* 1:13, 1:23; cf. *De Lib. Arb.* 2:36 (healthy eyes prefer to look at nothing so much as the sun) as well as *Sol.* 2:34 and *De Quant. Anim.* 25 on the aim of exercising the mind in order to see without being dazzled.

93. *De Ord.* 2:26.

94. The correlation is explicit in ibid.

95. *De Beata Vita* 10 and 27, *De Ord.* 1:31–32 and 2:45.

96. See chapter 4, "The Great Shift in Augustine's Teaching."

97. *Conf.* 6:8.

98. Sermon 52:16. The metaphor of "touching" (*ephaptein*) the intelligible goes back to Plato (e.g., *Republic* 6:484b, *Timaeus* 90c).

99. For this movement "in then up," see Cary, *Augustine's Invention*, chapter 3, "In Then Up" and chapter 5, "A Turning of Attention."

100. *Conf.* 9:24, quoting Wisdom 7:27 (a description of divine Wisdom, here applied to "Your Word"). Augustine and Monica proceed to reflect on this moment of shared insight in *Conf.* 9:25, for which see Introduction, "Shared Vision."

101. See for example *De Lib. Arb.* 2:37 and *Sol.* 1:22, as well as the discussion of Augustine's erotic imagery for the shared love of Wisdom in Cary, "United Inwardly by Love," pp. 12–13.

102. *Civ. Dei* 10:3; see above, "The Invisible Sacrifice."

103. *Conf.* 10:12–15; see Cary, *Augustine's Invention*, chapter 10.

104. *Conf.* 10:16–17.

105. Ibid. 10:34–37.

106. As in my discussions of *Conf.* 8, it is important for readers to bear in mind that this is a theological investigation of texts, not a historical investigation of events. The important issue for this investigation is not what the experience at Ostia was actually like, but what concept of inner unity Augustine had developed by the time he described the vision at Ostia more than a decade later in the *Confessions*. That is why *De Lib. Arb.* 2 is a literary *precursor* of the description of the vision at Ostia,

despite being written several years after events at Ostia. By the same token, we need not be concerned here with exactly which "books of the Platonists," if any, might have triggered the Ostia experience. It would be more useful to know which books of Plotinus Augustine had in front of him while he was writing *Conf.* 9 or *De Lib. Arb.* 2. O'Connell argues that *Ennead* 6:5.10 was especially important for the latter (in *Early Theory*, pp. 53–55). But still more important than any question of literary dependence is the issue of conceptual inheritance: there is no way anyone could have written *De Lib. Arb.* 2 or *Conf.* 9 who had not learned a great deal from the school of Plotinus, especially about how the intelligible is by its very nature common and shared by all, not private and proper to each.

107. *De Lib. Arb.* 2:8–12. On the common sense see Aristotle, *De Anim.* 3:2.

108. *De Lib. Arb.* 2:10.

109. Ibid. 2:17

110. Ibid. 2:18.

111. Ibid. 2:19.

112. Ibid. 2:20.

113. Ibid.

114. Ibid. 2:23.

115. Ibid. 2:34.

116. Ibid. 2:33.

117. Ibid. 2:32. Augustine actually uses the Nicene term *consubstantialis* here. It means that in the strongest possible sense Number shares the same divine being as Wisdom. Augustine hints at a Neopythagorean account of Number in his programmatic discourse in *De Ord.* 2:47–50 and develops one at length in book 6 of *De Musica*.

118. *De Lib. Arb.* 2:25.

119. Ibid. 2:37.

120. Ibid. Cf. the desire to have Wisdom naked in *Sol.* 1:22, where once again Augustine can share her with others free from jealousy, competition, or unchastity.

121. Boethius, *Consolation of Philosophy,* 4:6 (Prose), 15. The image is Boethian but the language of my translation is indebted (as is inevitable for anyone thinking in English) to T. S. Eliot's *Four Quartets* (Burnt Norton, line 62).

122. *De Lib. Arb.* 2:41.

123. Plotinus, *Ennead* 6:5.7. For the importance of this image for Augustine see O'Connell, *Early Theory*, pp. 62–63, and Cary, *Augustine's Invention*, pp. 29 and 121.

124. *De Quant. Anim.* 69. Much scholarly energy has gone into investigating the sources of this passage (e.g., Henry, pp. 73–75, and Pépin, "Une nouvelle source"), the most oft-mentioned candidates being Porphyry, *Sentences* 37, and Plotinus, *Ennead* 4:3.5. More important for philosophical purposes is that no one with any deep understanding of Plotinus could fail to notice this consequence of Plotinus's thought.

125. Augustine has a number of philosophical and theological uses for the underlying unity of all souls, including for instance in his thinking about the

psychological origin of time, but normally he discusses the Platonist notion of world-soul (a single soul that governs the movements of the whole cosmos but is distinct from our individual souls) and does not explicitly mention the more radical notion that all souls are one. On these topics see the investigations of Roland Teske, "The World-soul and Time" and *Paradoxes of Time*.

126. *C. Acad.* 3:42, *De Ord.* 2:16.

127. *De Lib. Arb.* 2:33.

128. See Cary, *Inner Grace*, chapter 2, "Divine Good Will."

129. Cary, *Augustine's Invention*, chapters 7 and 8.

130. *De Lib. Arb.* 2:34. Cf. the same distinction used for the same purpose in *Ep.* 18:2, *De Div. QQs 83*, 45.1, *C. Ep. Fund.* 21, *De Nat. Boni* 1, *Conf.* 7:23, *Civ. Dei* 8:5 (end). For the reasons in Augustine's development that lead to the mutability of the soul being the crucial mark of its non-divinity, see Cary, *Augustine's Invention*, chapter 8.

131. See, e.g., *Conf.* 7:16.

132. Cary, *Augustine's Invention*, pp. 71–73.

133. *De Lib. Arb.* 2:33.

134. Ibid., 2:32.

135. The "Ostia moments" in this treatise are *De Lib. Arb.* 1:29 and 2:39–40. In the former the joy of insight is described as ultimate happiness, using the Ciceronian term prominent in Augustine's early works, *beata vita*.

136. See especially the passage containing the famous saying, "My love is my weight," *Conf.* 13:10. But the metaphor of love, sin, or delight as a kind of weight in the soul is pervasive in Augustine's works; cf., e.g., *De Musica* 6:29 ("Delight is as it were the weight of the soul"), *De Gen. c. Man.* 2:34, *Ep.* 55:21, *De Gen. ad Litt.* 4:8, and *Civ. Dei* 11:28. For further discussion see Cary, "The Weight of Love."

137. E.g., *De Lib. Arb.* 1:33, *Conf.* 4:15, *Enarr. in Ps.* 62:13, *De Trin.* 10:7. On love as unitive force, see Burnaby, pp. 100–103, and Lienhard, " 'The Glue Itself Is Charity.' "

138. *Conf.* 4:11.

139. *Civ. Dei* 19:24. For a fuller exposition of Augustine's new social theory, see Cary, "United Inwardly by Love."

140. *De Doct. Christ.* 1:30. Cf. also *De Cat. Rud.* 49.

141. *De Cat Rud.* 33.

142. For an investigation of how Augustine's sermons instigate shared inquiry, in keeping with his long-standing philosophical convictions and practices, see Kolbet.

143. *Enarr. in Pss.* 33(1):1. Note also a little later in the same sermon: "Pay attention with me [*intendite mecum*]. . . . I'm knocking when I say these things; you also are knocking when you hear them. Let us continue to knock by praying, that the Lord may open to us" (*Enarr. in Pss.* 33(1):4).

144. Plato, *Timaeus* 27c and 48d, *Philebus* 61c, *Laws* 10:893b. See chapter 4, "The Great Shift in Augustine's Teaching."

145. Sermon 52:3.

146. Sermon 117:12.

147. Sermon 288:4.

148. Sermon 52. See Hill's helpful introductory note for reasons why this sermon should be dated before the related sections of *De Trin.*, the most important reason being the hesitancy with which Augustine here presents the notion of traces of the Trinity in the soul (esp. 52:23).

149. Sermon 52:8.

150. Ibid. 13.

151. Ibid. 20. *Vocibus* here could mean spoken words or inarticulate vocal sounds (see chapter 5, "Outward Voice and Inner Word"). The audience may not always be responding in words, but they are certainly responding vocally.

152. Sermon 52:21.

153. Ibid. 18.

154. Ibid. 16, quoting Ps. 31:22, based on the Septuagint.

155. Sermon 52:16.

156. Wisdom 9:14–15.

157. Sermon 52:16.

158. Sermon 117:5, quoted for instance in Aquinas, *ST* I–II, 4.3.

159. Sermon 52:16.

160. Sermon 117:5. This sermon, which contains Augustine's most extensive treatment of the theme of incomprehensibility, is the same one in which he affirms "we can see God with the mind or inward eye of the heart," 117:15 (this is the passage omitted in Hill's translation; see chapter 5, "Seeing Trinitarian Love," and chapter 4, "The Great Shift in Augustine's Teaching"). For the difficulties caused for Augustine scholarship by Augustine's belief in the power of the intellect to see God, see Cary, *Augustine's Invention*, pp. 67–71. For the ontological basis of these beatific "glimpses," which are intrinsic to all intellectual knowledge, see ibid., pp. 28 and 54.

161. Sermon 117:5. See the discussion of this passage in Cary, *Augustine's Invention*, p. 58. The fact that Augustine has so weak a doctrine of divine incomprehensibility has deep consequences for our understanding of the history of Christian theology; cf. Cary, "The Incomprehensibility of God."

162. *De Div QQs 83*, 54. To "maintain itself always the same way" is an idiom for immutability, as the context explains.

163. *De Lib. Arb.* 2:33.

164. Sermon 52:17.

165. Compare the first half of Sermon 52:17 with *Conf.* 10:15.

166. Sermon 52:15; cf. also Sermon 21, "return to yourself and take yourself away from all the noise; look inside yourself." For the verbal silencing at Ostia (*Conf.* 9:25) see also Introduction, "Shared Vision."

167. Sermon 52:20.

168. Ibid.

169. See chapter 5, "Outward Voice and Inner Word."

170. See Hugh of St. Victor, *De Sacramentis* 1:9.3; anonymous, *Summa Sent.* 4:1; Lombard, *Sent.* 4:1.5.

171. Such is the rationale for the institution of the sacraments given by that last great Augustinian theologian of the High Middle Ages, Bonaventure, in *Breviloquium*

6:1.3. This sums up the *propter humiliationem* theme going back to Hugh of St. Victor, who gives the most extensive explanation of it in *De Sacramentis* 1:9.3. The rationale is genuinely Augustinian: cf. the brilliant metaphor from *De Vera Rel.* 45, "in order to rise one must put weight on the very place one has fallen," discussed in chapter 5, "Testimony about Temporal Things."

172. See esp. Aquinas, *ST* III, 61.1, where the theme of humiliation is present but is subordinated to the theme of the natural human need to begin with corporeal and sensible things.

173. See Cary, *Augustine's Invention*, pp. 55–58.

CHAPTER 7

1. For a brief presentation of the key historical details, see Bonner, pp. 28–32, and Bright's article on the North African Church in Fitzgerald. For a full-length narrative, complete with social history, see Frend.

2. See Cyprian, *Ad Donatum* 4 (in the ANF edition this is Epistle 1).

3. The famous phrase is Cyprian's: *extra ecclesiam nullus salus*, in his Ep. 73:21 (= 72:21 in ANF).

4. At about the same time as Mary Douglas's groundbreaking study of the social meaning of purity (1st ed., 1966), Peter Brown saw the connection between concerns about purity and the maintenance of social boundaries among the Donatists in *Augustine of Hippo*, esp. chapter 19 (1st ed. 1967). This connection is prominent in recent work on North African Christianity such as Burns's *Cyprian the Bishop*.

5. Cyprian, *On the Lapsed*, 9: "we have done nothing," Cyprian imagines the little ones saying, "we are lost through the faithlessness of others." In his Ep. 98:3 Augustine reads this passage so as to uphold the necessity of individual will (contending that the children could not contract the guilt of idolatry without their own willing participation) but as an interpretation of Cyprian's intended meaning, Augustine's argument is unconvincing.

6. On this theology in Cyprian and his Donatist admirers, see Burns, *Cyprian the Bishop*, pp. 141–144 and 167–169.

7. See chapter 4, "Admonitions to Look Inside."

8. See chapter 3, "The Ontological Ground of Convention."

9. *De Bapt. c Donat.* 5:8.

10. *C. Cresc.* 1:27.

11. Augustine quotes Cyprian's dictum in *De Bapt. c. Donat.* 4:24 (in the NPNF edition, this is 4:25).

12. See chapter 6, "Taking Victorinus to Heart."

13. *De Bapt. c Donat.* 3:23, quoting 1 Cor. 2:15.

14. John 20:23 (translating from Augustine's Latin). In his exegesis Augustine switches from *remittere* to *dimittere* for the verb of forgiveness.

15. *De Bapt. c. Donat.* 3:22, commenting on Matthew 16:18–19.

16. *De Bapt. c. Donat.* 3:22, alluding to Cyprian, Ep. 75:2 (= 69:2), with its reference to Song of Songs 6:9.

17. *De Bapt. c. Donat.* 6:6.

18. As Burns notes (*Development,* pp. 59–71), this anti-Donatist point marks a subtle but important shift in Augustine's thinking about charity, which is no longer simply that which strengthens a good will but rather constitutes good-ness in the will. This ultimately makes a sharp distinction between faith and charity in the *ordo salutis* difficult to maintain; cf. Cary, *Inner Grace,* chapter 4, "The Expe-rience of Grace in Disarray."

19. In context, the biblical phrase is clearly all about unity: "Be careful to preserve the unity of the Spirit in the *bond of peace:* one Body and one Spirit . . . one Lord, one faith, one baptism, one God and Father of all . . ." (Eph. 4:3–5). Augustine's variations on the phrase include "bond of unity and peace" (*De Bapt. c. Donat.* 2:19), "bond of unity" (ibid. 3:23), "bond of charity and peace" (ibid. 1:14) and "bond of charity" (ibid. 6:7).

20. *De Mor. Man.* 8.

21. See Cary, "United Inwardly by Love."

22. Augustine actually uses the term *pseudochristiani,* e.g., in *De Bapt. c. Donat.* 3:26, 4:4(3), and 5:33.

23. Ibid. 4:5(4).

24. Ibid. 1:7.

25. 1 Cor. 13:3, which is a kind of leitmotif in Augustine's discussions of baptismal efficacy, e.g., *De Bapt. c. Donat.* 1:28, 3:19, 3:21, 4:24(23), and 5:33.

26. See chapter 1, "Reminders of Deeper Things."

27. *De Bapt. c. Donat.* 1:5 (where it is called *nota militaris*) and 6:1. Cf. also *C. Cresc.* 1:35.

28. The insufficiency of baptism without the intention of doing good works is the main thesis of Augustine's treatise *De Fide et Oper.*

29. *C. Ep. Parm.* 2:29.

30. Aquinas, *ST* III, 63.1 and 66.9.

31. *De Bapt. c. Donat.* 6:1.

32. That Augustine's theology tends in the direction of breaking the bond between baptism and regeneration (but stops short) is evident in *Enarr. in Pss.* 77:2, discussed in chapter 8, "The Virtue of the Sacraments."

33. *De Bapt. c. Donat.* 1:2.

34. Ibid. 1:11. Augustine is concluding a long discussion in which he justifies the fundamental principle we have quoted, by expounding in tandem the two do-minical sayings, "whoever is not with me is against me" (Matt. 12:30) and "whoever is not against us is for us" (Mark 9:40).

35. *De Bapt. c. Donat.* 1:14.

36. Ibid. 1:13.

37. Ibid. 1:14. The point at the end about the necessity of perseverance is one to which we will return below, "Conversion and Perseverance."

38. Ibid. 1:17–18.

39. Ibid. 1:19.

40. See, e.g., *Summa Sent.* 5:5, Lombard 4:4.2.

41. *De Bapt. c. Donat.* 5:9.

42. Sermon 293:10; cf. Sermon 176:2 and 294:18 as well as *De Pecc. Mer.* 1:23 and *De Gen. ad Litt.* 10:19, all using the verb "run" (*currere*) to describe how infants are brought to the church for baptism. The conviction that unbaptized infants were damned provided the premise of one of Augustine's main lines of argumentation against the Pelagians; see Cary, *Inner Grace,* chapter 3, "The Shape of the Controversy."

43. *De Gest. Pel.* 46.

44. *De Grat. Christi* 2:2.

45. See Sermons 174, 176, 293, and 294 for Augustine's appeal to this deep-rooted conviction.

46. It is perhaps necessary to underline the point that "guilt" in this discussion is a strictly objective concept, referring not to guilt-feelings or a sense of guilt but to the fact that one justly deserves punishment. Augustine's concern throughout is with the kind of guilt that is at issue in a court of law, not in psychotherapy.

47. This accounts for a striking about-face in Augustine's writing: in contrast to *Conf.* 1:11, where he suggests that infant misbehavior is actually sinful, in his anti-Pelagian works Augustine argues forcefully that babies are completely innocent except for their inheritance from Adam (e.g., Sermon 165:7, *De Pecc Mer.* 1:22 and 65–66).

48. See Goldbacher's discussion of the dating of Ep. 98 in his edition of the letters, vol. 5, p. 30.

49. Ep. 98:1 contains Boniface's questions; 98:3 contains Augustine's discussion of the treatise of Cyprian (mentioned above, "Validity without Efficacy"), which seems to say that baptized infants can lose their baptismal rebirth by involuntary participation in pagan rites to which they are brought by their parents.

50. Ep. 98:1, quoting both times from Ezek. 28:4.

51. See chapter 6, "Public Inner Wisdom."

52. For the point that *propria vita* includes *propria voluntas,* cf. *De Pecc. Mer.* 1:65.

53. O'Connell, *The Origin of the Soul,* pp. 187–197, 300–309, 325–326.

54. O'Connell, following Solignac, "La condition de l'homme pécheur," identifies five such passages in *The Origin of the Soul: De Pecc. Mer.* 3:14, *De Nupt. et Concup.* 2:15, *Civ. Dei* 13:14, *Enarr. in Pss.* 84:7, and *C. Jul. Op. Imp.* 2:177 (see also 1:178). I would add *De Pecc. Mer.* 1:11 and Sermon 165:7.

55. Plotinus, *Enneads* 6:4.14. See O'Connell's discussion of this and other relevant Plotinian passages in his treatment of the "Plotinian hallmark of Augustine's final theory of our relationship to Adam" in *The Origin of the Soul,* pp. 337–350.

56. See, for example, *De Pecc. Mer.* 1:21.

57. See Cary, *Inner Grace,* chapter 2, "Jacob and Esau."

58. *De Lib. Arb.* 3:24–28 and 32–35. O'Connell is clearly right in observing (*The Origin of the Soul,* pp. 132–133) that not until much later in book 3 do we get any signals that this presentation of the fallen soul theory is meant to be merely one hypothesis among several. For the controversy surrounding O'Connell's views on the fallen soul in Augustine, see Rhombs.

59. On the systematic priority of unity to division in Plotinus, see Cary, *Augustine's Invention*, pp. 24–30, and for the same priority in Augustine, see ibid., p. 136.

60. John 3:13, translated from Augustine's quotation in *De Pecc. Mer.* 1:60.

61. *Ep.* 137:4–12 (this long letter deserves to be called Augustine's treatise *De Incarnatione*). See the same reasoning summarized in Sermon 294:9–10.

62. *De Pecc. Mer.* 1:60.

63. Ibid.

64. Ibid., quoting 1 Cor. 12:12. See the similar use of Pauline imagery in *Civ. Dei* 10:6, discussed in chapter 6, "The Invisible Sacrifice."

65. *Ep.* 98:5. The dove is silver because of "the wings of a dove covered with silver" in Ps. 68:13, and also because this contributes to the metaphor of being "melted together," *conflatur.*

66. *Ep.* 98:2.

67. Ibid.

68. *Ep.* 98:10. Cf. *Civ. Dei* 21:16 for a fuller development of this teaching.

69. *De Bapt. c. Donat.* 1:24.

70. See Cary, *Inner Grace*, chapter 1, "Conversion and Purification."

71. See, e.g., *De Bapt. c. Donat.* 1:2, 6:7, and esp. 3:17, quoting Cyprian, *Ep.* 73:3, in which heretics "are converted to our church." For the early history of this ecclesial sense of "conversion" see Aubin, pp. 105–111.

72. *De Bapt. c. Donat.* 5:8–9.

73. Ibid. 4:33.

74. Ibid. 4:5(4).

75. Ibid. 5:24.

76. See above, "The Immediate Return of Sins."

77. *De Pecc. Mer.* 1:23, *C. Duas Ep. Pel.* 3:5.

78. *De Pecc. Mer.* 2:10, *Civ. Dei* 19:4.

79. *De Bapt. c. Donat.* 1:14. The quotation is from Matt. 24:13, the leitmotif of Augustine's doctrine of perseverance. Cf. also its use in *De Bapt. c. Donat.* 4:22(21).

80. *De Bapt. c. Donat.* 5:38.

81. Ibid., quoting 2 Tim. 2:19.

82. Ibid. 4:5(4), quoting Eph. 1:4 and Rom. 8:29.

83. A point clearly seen by Mayer, "Taufe und Erwählung."

84. *Conf.* 3:21.

85. Ibid. 5:17. The divine assurance given to Monica is of course exceptional: one does not normally know the particular effects of predestined grace in advance, and Augustine himself can only narrate the predestined answer to Monica's prayers in retrospect. What is not exceptional, in Augustine's reckoning, is that predestined prayers should lead to predestined conversion, both being outgrowths of divine grace. Aquinas explains the structure of this Augustinian point about predestination perfectly when, in answering *yes* to the question, "Can predestination be furthered by the prayers of holy people?" he argues that "providence, of which predestination is part, does not take away secondary causes but provides for effects in such a way that the order of secondary causes too comes under providence. . . . Thus the salvation of

persons is predestined by God in such a way that whatever promotes their salva-tion also falls under the order of predestination, be it their own or other people's prayers, other good works or anything else without which they would not attain salvation," *ST* I 23.8.

86. It is important to bear in mind that for Augustine conversion is not tanta-mount to salvation (see Cary, *Inner Grace,* chapter 4, "Problems of Perseverance"). Augustine's belief that he is converted by his mother's prayers but not yet saved is clear not just from his later insistence that no one knows whether they will be granted the gift of perseverance, but also from his description of the ineluctable perils and temptations he continues to face in *Conf.* 10:39–66, which leaves no room for the certainty that he will be saved in the end.

87. *De Grat. et Lib. Arb.* 29, *De Praedest. Sanct.* 22.

88. *De Dono Pers.* 15 and 63. On prayer for perseverance cf. also ibid. 4.

89. For baptism as a divine promise, see Luther, *The Holy and Blessed Sacra-ment of Baptism* 13–14 (LW 35:36–37) and *The Babylonian Captivity of the Church* (LW 36:58–61).

90. See Cary, *Inner Grace,* chapter 3, "Augustine's Evasiveness" and cf. chapter 8, below, "When Promising Is Giving."

91. For the centrality of Christ's intercession in Calvin's understanding of the distribution of grace, see Kendall, pp. 13–17, whose thesis is that for Calvin, "The decree of election . . . is not rendered effectual in Christ's death but in His ascension and intercession at the Father's right hand" (p. 16). Hence the later Calvinist doc-trine of limited atonement taught by the Synod of Dordt (in Schaff, 3:564–570) cannot be attributed to Calvin himself, who teaches rather a doctrine of limited interces-sion: Christ died for all but does not pray for all (pp. 13–14).

92. See chapter 6, "The Invisible Sacrifice," especially the discussion of the eucharistic theology of *Civ. Dei* 10:6.

93. *Civ. Dei* 10:20.

94. Ibid.: *se ipsam per ipsum discit offere.* This self-offering of the church is what Augustine proceeds to describe as the true sacrifice signified figuratively by all the Old Testament sacrifices.

95. This is a point Augustine repeatedly stresses when discussing Ps. 22:1. See *Enarr. in Pss.* 30(2):11 ("the Father did not ever forsake his Only one") and 34(2):5, as well as Ep. 140:6 ("the resurrection of one not forsaken") and the discussion in Cary, *Inner Grace,* chapter 3, "The Grace of Participation."

96. Ep. 140:15–17.

97. Acts 9:4. The point is often repeated; see, e.g., *Enarr. in Pss.* 30(2):3, 32(2):2, 34(1):1, and 37:6, as well as Ep. 140:18.

98. *Enarr. in Pss.* 30(2):3.

99. See chapter 8, "Powerless Blood."

100. See Cary, *Inner Grace,* chapter 2, "Jacob and Esau."

101. Ep. 164:19.

102. Ep. 190:25.

103. *De Gen. ad Litt.* 10:36.

104. The agonizing details of Augustine's permanent hesitation about accepting any particular theory of how our souls are derived (or not) from Adam's are a thread running throughout O'Connell's *The Origin of the Soul*. The story O'Connell has to tell is long and complex, but there are some constants: above all, the fact that Augustine's indecision is permanent, which is to say he never accepts either of the two major contenders for a theory about the origin of human souls, traducianism and creationism. Also constant is that the only explanations Augustine can think of for how we contract guilt from Adam depend on the idea that somehow our souls were all originally one in him.

CHAPTER 8

1. The formulation "sacraments of the New Law" becomes canonical for the Roman church in the Council of Florence in 1439 (Denz. 1310). It is the formulation under which Aquinas discusses sacramental efficacy throughout *ST* III, 62. For the addition of "confer" to "signify" in definitions of the church's sacraments, see chapter 6, "The Meaning of 'Sacrament.'"

2. Lombard, *Sent.* 1:1.1, quoted in chapter 6, "The Meaning of 'Sacrament.'"

3. Lombard, *Sent.* 3:40.3.

4. That this becomes Lombard's preferred designation is clear in *Sent.* 4:2.1, where he begins his discussion of the seven sacraments by saying, "Now let us proceed to the sacraments of the New Law..."

5. Lombard, *Sent.* 4:1.4. Lombard's definition of *sacramentum* is quoted in chapter 6, "The Meaning of 'Sacrament.'"

6. Lombard, *Sent.* 4:1.6, quoting Augustine, *Enarr. in Pss.* 73:2.

7. *Enarr. in Pss.* 73:2.

8. See below, "The Virtue of the Sacraments" and "Sacraments Promising Christ."

9. Calvin, *Inst.* 4:14.26; neither quotation is exact, but the one reflects accurately the vocabulary and argument of Augustine, Ep. 138:8, the other *C. Faust. Man.* 19:14. Calvin here is explicitly criticizing the interpretation of *Enarr. in Pss.* 73:2 given by the "miserable Sophists" (i.e., medieval scholastics) and probably has Lombard particularly in mind, whom he faults for an exaggerated view of sacramental efficacy in *Inst.* 4:14.16.

10. The contrast between *praenuntiare* and *annuntiare* is highlighted in *C. Faust. Man.* 19:16 (see below, "The Virtue of the Sacraments") as well as Ep. 138:8. The analogy with changes in verb tense is pointed out in these two texts as well as (more elaborately) in Augustine's argument that there is no change in faith from OT to NT, in *In Joh. Evang.* 45:9, from which Calvin quotes at length in *Inst.* 4:14.26.

11. *Enarr. in Pss.* 73:2.

12. Luther, *The Babylonian Captivity of the Church*, LW 36:65. For Calvin's reading of this passage of Luther, see the translation of the first edition of the *Institutes*, with Battles's helpful notes, *Institutes of the Christian Religion: 1536 Edition*, p. 91.

13. Luther, "A Brief Instruction on What to Look for and Expect in the Gospels," LW 35:120.

14. *Conf.* 10:40 (repeated 10:45 and 10:60). Cf. *De Sp. et Litt.* 22 and *De Dono Pers.* 53.

15. Luther, *The Freedom of a Christian*, LW 31:349. See Cary, *Inner Grace*, chapter 3, "Augustine's Evasiveness."

16. Luther, *The Freedom of a Christian*, LW 31:351f.

17. Descriptions of this late medieval sacramental economy, which included the sale of indulgences in connection with the sacrament of penance, may be found in most histories of the Reformation or biographies of Luther. For a vivid and sympathetic account of the piety supported and required by this economy, see Duffy, especially chapters 3–5 and 9–10.

18. Luther, *The Babylonian Captivity of the Church*, LW 36:65. Luther criticized this principle frequently in the early years of his career, when he was writing as a medieval theologian, a critic within the church of Rome. Cf. the conclusion to his important explanation of the seventh of his ninety-five theses in 1518 (LW 31:106–107) and his reply to the first article of the Papal Bull in 1521 (LW 32:12–17). Cf. also the pivotal but untranslated 1518 *Theses Pro veritate inquirenda et timoratis conscientiis consolandis*, Thesis 42, in WA 1:632, and the role this text plays in Luther's development according to Bayer, chapter 4.

19. Luther, *The Sacrament of Penance*, 1519 (LW 35:11). Cf. Luther's account of his interview with Cardinal Cajetan at Augsburg in 1518, where he describes this principle as a "common saying" (LW 31:274). A central bone of contention in the interview was Luther's affirmation of this principle in his explanation of his seventh thesis, where he puts it in place of the principle he rejects (LW 31:107).

20. Luther, *The Babylonian Captivity of the Church*, LW 36:66. Cf. also thesis 10 of *Theses Pro veritate inquirenda* (WA 1:631).

21. Denz. 1310.

22. From the reply to the first article of the Papal Bull, LW 32:17.

23. Augustine, *In Joh. Evang.* 80:3, which Luther quotes or paraphrases in many of the previously cited texts: cf. LW 31:193, 32:17, and 35:11. See below, "The Virtue of the Sacraments."

24. In Luther's Latin the formulation is literally "the faith of the sacrament" (*fides sacramenti*). But when he is speaking German he says, "the faith which believes the sacrament" (*der Glaub, der das sacrament glaubt*) in the 1519 sermon, *The Sacrament of Penance*, WA 2:715.

25. Calvin, *Inst.* 4:14.16. Cf. Calvin's instruction in the Geneva Catechism, "we are not to cling to the visible signs and there seek our salvation, or imagine the virtue of conferring grace to be fixed and enclosed in them" (*Calvin: Theological Treatises*, p. 132). This warning against clinging to external signs does not mean that Calvin disagrees with Luther about Christian faith being based on God's promises (to the contrary, see *Inst.* 3:2.7) but rather that Calvin thinks of the promise of God as less external than does Luther, for whom the Gospel is an external word because

it is a sacramental word. For an elaboration of this point see Cary, "Why Luther Is Not Quite Protestant."

26. Luther, Commentary on Psalm 51, LW 12:352.

27. Luther, *Large Catechism* (article on baptism), Tappert, p. 440.

28. It is important not to forget, throughout the discussion of Augustine's distinction between Old and New Testament, that what Augustine says about the moral failings of the Jews is not actually true. See Cary, *Inner Grace*, chapter 1, "Against Augustine on the Jews."

29. For this transition from life *sub lege* to life *sub gratia*, which is fundamental to Augustine's reading of Paul, see Cary, *Inner Grace*, chapter 2, "Four Stages."

30. *De Lib. Arb.* 1:15.

31. *Conf.* 3:13.

32. *De Div QQs 83*, 43.

33. The notion of proceeding upward to intellectual vision by "gradual steps" (*gradibus* or *passibus*) is prominent in Augustine's description of liberal education in *De Ord.* 2:39, *De Musica* 6:1f, *De Mag.* 21, and *Retract.* 1:6(5). Cf. Cicero's description of Platonic education as progressing *gradatim* in *Tusc.* 1:57, a passage that seems to have been a major inspiration in Augustine's thinking on education, according to Hagendahl, p. 143, and Courcelle, *Late Latin Writers*, p. 171; see also Cary, *Augustine's Invention*, p. 133.

34. *De Div. QQs 83*, 43.

35. We shall encounter an explicit analogy between the utterance of the word *Deus* and the performance of the sacraments in *C. Faust. Man.* 19:16 (see below, "The Virtue of the Sacraments"), although not to illustrate a point about historical change. Augustine elsewhere uses the utterance of the word *Deus* to illustrate the ontological gap between outward voice and inner word; e.g., Sermon 288:3 and *In Joh. Evang.* 1:8.

36. *De Div. QQs 83*, 44.

37. Ibid.

38. In Augustine's later, more elaborate seven-stage theory of universal history (*De Div. QQs 83*, 58.2 and 64.2, *De Gen. c. Man* 1:35–41, *De Cat. Rud.* 39) Christ comes rather in the sixth age, which is the old age of humanity, the senescence of the "outer man." In *Retractations* he offers an explanation reconciling the two accounts, which I find contrived. A simpler explanation is that as Augustine developed a more elaborate theory of the stages of human history, he changed his mind about where to locate Christ's coming in the sequence of stages. The earlier version, where Christ comes in the stage of young adulthood (*De Div. QQs 83*, 44 and 49), reflects a more straightforwardly educational view: Christ comes when humanity is grown up enough to learn intelligible things.

39. *De Div. QQs 83*, 49.

40. See chapter 6, "The Invisible Sacrifice."

41. *De Div. QQs 83*, 49.

42. See Cary, *Inner Grace*, chapter 1, "From Fear to Love."

43. For the genteel anti-Semitism in progressive theories of history the paradigmatic figure is Hegel (see the introductory chapters in "The Positivity of the Christian Religion" in *Early Theological Writings,* esp. pp. 68–71, an early and rather straightforward text that wears its Enlightenment convictions on its face); in liberal theology the paradigmatic figure is Schleiermacher (see *The Christian Faith,* §13 and 93.2–3).

44. See Cary, *Inner Grace,* chapter 2, "Four Stages."

45. *De Div. QQs 83,* 49. Cf. Lessing's "The Education of the Human Race" (in *Lessing's Theological Writings,* pp. 82–98), which picks up the analogy between the ages of a human being and the ages of humanity (§§1–3), as well as the notion that the Jews were not ready for Christ until they had grown up (§§16–19).

46. *De Div. QQs 83,* 53.

47. *De Ver. Rel.* 33.

48. Ibid., 33.

49. Exegetical inquiry as a form of intellectual delight (and hence of love) is a theme touched upon in this passage (*De Ver. Rel.* 33) and developed at length in *De Doct. Christ.* 2:7–8 and most vividly in Ep 55:12. For the gusto with which Augustine tackles an interpretive crux, see Peter Brown's insightful comments, pp. 250–251, 259–260, and 272–273.

50. *De Util. Cred.* 9.

51. See chapter 3, "Giving Signs."

52. *De Doct. Christ.* 3:9.

53. Ibid., quoting 2 Cor. 3:6.

54. *De Doct. Christ.* 3:9.

55. Ibid. 3:13.

56. Ibid. 3:10.

57. Ibid. 3:11.

58. Ibid. 3:12.

59. Ibid. 3:13.

60. See Cary, *Inner Grace,* chapter 1, "Wisdom and Virtue."

61. *Enarr. in Pss.* 77:2: *gratia, quae sacramentorum virtus est.*

62. Ibid. The key phrase is *ipsa gratia, cujus ipsa sunt sacramenta.* "Washing of regeneration" is a standard term for baptism taken from Titus 3:5.

63. See chapter 7, "The Immediate Return of Sins."

64. See especially Hugh of St. Victor, *De Sacramentis* 1:9, who identifies the virtue of the sacrament with the thing it signifies in describing the invisible, spiritual, and inward *res sive virtus sacramenti,* which he proceeds to identify as grace, in that the sacrament is a *signum ... spiritualis gratiae.*

65. For the fact that the description of sacraments as signs of grace stands in need of textual support in Augustine, see chapter 6, "Signs of Grace?"

66. For this two-track approach to sacramental efficacy, see chapter 6, "Signs of Grace?"

67. I would hazard the guess that the reason why Augustine here speaks of grace as the sacraments' *virtus* rather than using semiotic terminology like *res* is because

two sentences earlier he identified Christ in the flesh as the *significatio* of Old Testament sacraments; so here he wants at first to use a different, non-semiotic term to refer to a different thing that the sacrament was about. But one sentence later he speaks of "the grace of which these things are sacraments," which makes the semiotic connection anyway: grace in effect is the *res sacramenti* as well as the *virtus sacramenti*. None of this shifting vocabulary is particularly surprising in a sermon.

68. *C. Faust. Man.* 19:11. See chapter 6, "Taking Victorinus to Heart" (beginning).

69. *C. Faust. Man.* 19:12. Cf. Simon Magus as the example of unworthy reception of baptism in *De Bapt. c. Donat.* 1:17f, discussed in chapter 7, "The Immediate Return of Sins."

70. *C. Faust. Man.* 19:12. Augustine quotes 2 Tim. 3:5, which is accurately rendered in the King James Version, "having the form of godliness but denying the *power* thereof."

71. See chapter 6, "Signs of Grace?"

72. 1 Tim 1:5, as quoted in *C Faust. Man.* 19:12.

73. For Augustine's understanding of this traditional designation see Ep. 98:9.

74. See *De Doct. Christ.* 1:40, *De Cat. Rud.* 50, and *Conf.* 12:35.

75. *C. Faust. Man.* 19:13. I have translated Augustine's phrase *justitia fidei* with "the righteousness of faith" to remind readers who have no Latin of the standard language of older discussions of the doctrine of justification. Of course in Augustine's Latin (as in the New Testament's Greek) there is simply no difference between "righteousness" and "justice," both of which render *justitia*.

76. See for instance Aquinas, *ST* III, 61.4, *sed contra*. The older Dominican translation makes this interpretation explicit by rendering *virtute majora* as "more efficacious."

77. *C. Faust. Man.* 19:14.

78. Ibid. 19:16.

79. Ibid. 19:16. The italicized clause reads: *virtus tamen, quae per ista operatur, jugiter manet*. This is the same verb as the three virtues "that remain" in Augustine's quotations of 1 Cor. 13:13.

80. Aquinas, *ST* III, 62.2.

81. 1 Cor. 13:13. See Augustine's discussion in *De Doct. Christ.* 1:42, where it appears to be specifically charity, not faith, that lasts forever.

82. Cf. the usage of the verb *insinuare* in Sermon 52:20 (see chapter 6, "Words and Common Inquiry").

83. *In Joh. Evang.* 80:3. The italicized clause is quoted by Aquinas in the *sed contra* of *ST* III, 60.4 and 60.6, as well as by Luther, *Large Catechism*, pp. 438 and 448.

84. *In Joh. Evang.* 80:3.

85. Aquinas, *ST* III, 62.1, *sed contra* and 62.4, *sed contra*.

86. See Luther's description of his work as Reformer in one particularly vivid sermon, "I did nothing; the Word did everything," LW 51:77. On the power of the external word to bring about inward change, see Luther, *Against the Heavenly Prophets*,

LW 40:146–147 and 212–213. Note in the same connection Luther's warning against trying to distinguish too sharply between letter and Spirit, *Smalcald Articles* III, viii (p. 312).

87. *In Joh. Evang.* 80:3.

88. See chapter 5, "Outward Voice and Inner Word."

89. *De Sp. et Litt.* 54. See Cary, *Inner Grace,* chapter 3, "Augustine's Evasiveness."

90. See Introduction, "Downward Causality."

91. Aquinas, *ST* III, 62.5. Cf. Lombard, *Sent.* 4:2.1: "before the advent of Christ, who brought grace, there were to be given no sacraments of grace, which issued from the power [*virtutem*] of his death and passion."

92. Luther, *The Freedom of a Christian,* LW 31:351–352.

93. *C. Faust. Man.* 19:4.

94. Ibid.19:5.

95. Ibid. 19:1–6 (Faustus's speech).

96. *Lex per Moysen data est, gratia autem et veritas per Jesum Christum facta est.* Augustine's construal of the second clause is unusual, though grammatically more straightforward than the usual construal. Instead of construing the whole noun phrase, *gratia et veritas,* as the singular subject of the singular verb, *facta est,* he takes the subject to be *lex,* in the first clause. Hence instead of the usual rendering, "grace and peace came by Jesus Christ" he gets, in effect, "the Law becomes grace and truth by Jesus Christ." It should be noted that Augustine's Latin version, which is the same as the Vulgate, is an accurate translation of the Greek, which has the singular verb *egeneto* in the second clause.

97. *C. Faust. Man.* 19:7.

98. Ibid. 19:8.

99. *Prophetare, promittere,* and *praenuntiare* appear throughout Augustine's discussion of the sacraments in *C. Faust. Man.* 19:7–18. *Significare* is prominent in ibid. 19:17. *Praefigurare* is not present in the sacramental discussion of *C. Faust. Man.* 19 but common elsewhere, e.g., *De Div QQs 83,* 49 and *QQs in Hept.* 4:33.

100. See esp. *Enarr. in Pss.* 73:2, where after describing how the *sacraments* of the two Testaments differ (quoted above, "Sacraments Old and New") Augustine proceeds to describe how the *promises* differ: in the Old Testament "the land of Canaan is promised, abundant and fruitful, flowing with milk and honey, a temporal kingdom is promised, the felicity of this world is promised, the proliferation of children is promised, the subjection of enemies is promised, all of which pertains to earthly felicity."

101. *QQs in Hept.* 4:33.

102. *Enarr. in Pss.* 77:2. The contrast between veiling and unveiling as a way of explaining the relation of Old Testament and New Testament (cf. *Civ. Dei* 16:26) goes back to Augustine's reading of 2 Cor. 3:14–18 in *De Util. Cred.* 9, where it runs parallel to the contrasts of Law/grace, letter/Spirit, servitude/freedom, and fear/love. Augustine is probably indebted here to Tyconius, 3:8–10, who connects the unveiled faces in 2 Cor. 3:18 with the description of faith as "unveiled" (*revelari*) in Gal.

3:23–24, where prior to faith we are shut up under the guardianship of the Law as our disciplinarian (*paedogogus*).

103. See, e.g., *De Sp et Litt.* 18 (the righteousness of God) and 27 (grace), as well as the treatise *On the Grace of the New Testament* (= Ep. 140:6.15), where grace is veiled in the Old Testament.

104. *C. Faust. Man.* 19:9.

105. Ibid.

106. Ibid. 19:14.

107. Ibid.

108. Ibid. The phrase about being shut up under the guardianship of the Law (*conclusus . . . sub lege custodiebatur*) and the notion of faith being unveiled in the New Testament come from Paul's passage about the disciplinarian (*paedagogus*), Gal. 3:23–24.

109. Christ became incarnate as an example from which we learn humility, *De Musica* 6:7, *De Fide et Symb.* 6, *Conf.* 10:68, *Enarr. in Pss.* 33(1):4, *De Trin.* 8:7, *Ench.* 108, and in order to give an example of right living and loving, *De Div. QQs 83*, 25, 36.2, 43 (see also Cary, *Inner Grace*, chapter 1, "From Fear to Love"), *De Lib. Arb.* 3:76, *De Vera Rel.* 3 (see *Inner Grace*, chapter 1, "Dialogue with Plato"), *De Cat. Rud.* 40, Ep. 140:13–14, 25 and 43 (see *Inner Grace*, chapter 2, "The Grace of Participation").

110. *De Trin.* 4:6.

111. Luther's Christmas sermon of 1519 (WA 9:439–442), in which he identifies the Gospel as a sacrament (see Preface, "Powerless Externals"), begins with the distinction between Christ as example and Christ as sacrament, which in later works of Luther becomes the distinction between Christ as example and Christ as gift, which is parallel to the Law/Gospel distinction (see "Brief Instruction on What to Look for and Expect in the Gospels," LW 35:119). Luther is of course quite aware that the example/sacrament distinction stems from Augustine, as he shows in the *Lectures on Romans*, LW 25:309–310.

112. *De Trin.* 13:15, quoting Rom. 5:9. I am indebted to John Cavadini for pressing the question about the power of Christ's blood in "The Structure and Intention of Augustine's *De Trinitate*" (esp. pp. 108–109) though I doubt he will be happy with the answer that I think Augustine gives it.

113. See the discussion of the concept of mediation in chapter 5, "Witnesses to Christ."

114. See chapter 5, "Outward Voice and Inner Word."

115. The most crucial uses of the phrase by Cyril appear in his third letter to Nestorius and in the anathemas appended thereto (in Hardy, pp. 352 and 354, and Tanner, 1:54–55 and 61). For the role this document played in the council of Ephesus, see Grillmeier, pp. 414–415. For an introduction to the doctrinal issues under discussion at the council, see Young, pp. 213–229. For the contrast between Augustine's inward turn and Cyril's concept of life-giving flesh, see also Cary, *Augustine's Invention*, chapter 4, "Life-giving Flesh."

116. See chapter 6, "The Invisible Sacrifice."

117. I find the work of Karl Adam to be still the most helpful introduction to the nuances of these texts, though I propose a solution to their problems different from his.

118. Sermon 227, quoting 1 Cor. 10:17.

119. *In Joh. Evang.* 26, which expounds John 6:41–59, can be divided into three parts: paragraphs 1–7 on grace, 8–10 on the Incarnation, and 11–18 on the sacrament. The final paragraphs (19–20) are a conclusion that gathers up preceding themes and ties them together with the doctrine of the Trinity.

120. *In Joh. Evang.* 26:1. Cf. the similar account of the justice of God in *De Sp. et Litt.* 18. Readers without Latin or Greek may need to be reminded again that there simply is no difference between "righteousness" and "justice" in the New Testament, Augustine, or Luther—and that the English word "righteousness" only acquired its distinctive overtones of self-righteousness very recently, within the past century or two.

121. For the importance of this biblical term and its Augustinian interpretation in Luther's thinking, see the famous reminiscence in Luther's preface to the collected edition of his Latin writings published in his lifetime, LW 34:336–337. For a pivotal use of this term, see Luther's 1516 *Lectures on Romans*, LW 26:151–152, which quotes Augustine, *De Sp. et Litt.* 18.

122. *In Joh. Evang.* 26:19.

123. Ibid. 26:1. See Cary, *Inner Grace*, chapter 2, "The Grace of Participation," for the treatise *On the Grace of the New Testament* (= Ep. 140).

124. For the distinction between spiritual and sacramental eating, see *Summa Sent.* 6:7, Lombard, *Sent.*, 4:9.1–2, and Aquinas, *ST* III, 80.1–4.

125. John 6:44, as quoted in *In Joh. Evang.* 26:2. See Cary, *Inner Grace*, chapter 3, "Taught by God," for this and much of what follows concerning prevenient grace as inner teaching and delight.

126. *In Joh. Evang.* 26:2.

127. Ibid. 26:3. For the Plotinian sources of this idea of nonspatial movement of will, see Cary, *Inner Grace*, chapter 1, "Conversion and Purification."

128. See chapter 4, "The *On the Teacher* Thesis" (end).

129. *In Joh. Evang.* 26:4. On the noncoerciveness of a grace that gives the mind what it most deeply desires, see Cary, *Inner Grace*, chapter 1, "Beauty and Love."

130. *In Joh. Evang.* 26:4, quoting Virgil, *Eclogue* 2:65.

131. *In Joh. Evang.* 26:4.

132. Ibid. Cf. Plotinus, *Enneads* 1:6.4 (which picks up on Plato's description of the experience of falling in love) as well as 1:6.7 and 6:9.9, which both contain tag-lines very similar to Augustine's.

133. Cicero, *Acad.* 2:31. See also the very Augustinian line, "There is in our minds by nature a kind of insatiable longing to see the truth," in Cicero, *Tusc* 1:44. One wonders if some similarly "Augustinian" sentiment helped fire young Augustine's mind when he read Cicero's no-longer-extant exhortation to the philosophical pursuit of Wisdom, the *Hortenius* (see *Conf.* 3:7–8).

134. *In Joh. Evang.* 26:5.

135. Ibid.

136. Ibid. 26:7.

137. Ibid.

138. Ibid. 26:8. The Latin is one of Augustine's characteristic near-rhymes: *Filius dicebat, sed Pater docebat.*

139. Ibid. 26:9. On the analogy of inner word and eternal Word, see chapter 5, "Outward Voice and Inner Word."

140. Sermon 187:3; for extensive discussion of the analogy between flesh and voice (i.e., external word), see Sermon 288. Both texts are discussed in chapter 5, "Outward Voice and Inner Word."

141. *In Joh. Evang.* 26:10.

142. Ibid. 26:12.

143. Ibid. 26:12, commenting on Paul's passage on "spiritual drink," 1 Cor. 10:4.

144. *In Joh. Evang.* 26:12.

145. Ibid. 25:12. Cf. also Sermon 112:5, "Don't prepare your gut but your heart."

146. Karl Adam, in what remains a landmark study, agrees with the argument of this book to the extent of showing that through most of his career Augustine had little to say about the salvific efficacy of the external sacrament (*Die Eucharistielehre,* pp. 146–151). But in his anti-Pelagian period Augustine uses John 6:53 ("unless you eat my flesh and drink my blood, you shall have no life in you") to argue that participation in the Eucharist is as necessary for salvation as participation in baptism—and in the case of infants, just as efficacious, quite apart from their personal faith or virtue (see, e.g., *De Pecc. Mer.* 1:26–27, as well as further references in *Die Eucharistielehre,* pp. 156–159). I do not see, however, how this justifies Adam's conclusion that from this point in Augustine's career he treats the eucharistic flesh of Christ as salvific and life-giving. Rather, the lesson is the same for the Eucharist as for baptism: participation in the sacrament is necessary for salvation and eternal life because it is the indispensable outward sign of inner unity with the church, which is the true locus of salvific efficacy. Augustine never says anything to suggest that the rule is different for infants than for adults in this regard: the true salvific eating of Christ's flesh is inward, not literal; it means becoming what one eats, i.e., being incorporated into Christ's spiritual Body, the invisible church.

147. *In Joh. Evang.* 26:13.

148. Ibid.

149. *De Div. QQs 83,* 54.

150. Ibid.

151. *In Joh. Evang.* 26:13, quoting 1 Cor. 10:17. Cf. also Rom. 12:5, as quoted in *Civ. Dei* 10:6, discussed in chapter 6, "The Invisible Sacrifice."

152. *In Joh. Evang.* 26:13

153. Ibid. 26:19.

154. See chapter 7, "The Efficacy of Unity."

CONCLUSION

1. On ontotheology, see Heidegger, pp. 54–60. For a spirited critique of Heidegger by a very unintimidated Christian advocate of classical theism, see Hart, pp. 212–229.

2. Julian of Norwich, §19.

3. For this Christological criticism of Augustine's Christian Platonist soteriology see chapter 5, "Words Forming Persons?"

4. See chapter 5, "Secondhand Knowledge" and Cary, "Believing the Word."

5. See Cary, *Augustine's Invention*, chapter 5.

6. See ibid., chapter 9.

Bibliography

PRIMARY SOURCES: ANTHOLOGIES AND COLLECTIONS

Arnim, J. von, *Stoicorum Veterum Fragmenta* (Leipzig: Teubner, 1903).

Denzinger, H., *Enchiridion Symbolorum*, 33rd ed. (Freiburg: Herder, 1965).

Hardy, E., *Christology of the Later Fathers* (Philadelphia: Westminster, 1954).

Long, A. A., and D. N. Sedley, eds., *The Hellenistic Philosophers* (Cambridge: Cambridge University Press, 1987). Vol. 1: *Translations of the Principal Sources, with Philosophical Commentary*. Vol. 2: *Greek and Latin Texts with Notes and Bibliography*.

Schaff, P., *The Creeds of Christendom*, 3 vols., reprint ed. (Grand Rapids: Baker Book House, 1990).

Tanner, N., *Decrees of the Ecumenical Councils*, 2 vols. (Washington, DC: Georgetown University Press, 1990).

Tappert, T., *The Book of Concord* (Philadelphia: Fortress Press, 1959). Contains Lutheran confessional documents, including Luther's *Large Catechism* and *Smalcald Articles*.

Wehrli, F., *Die Schule des Aristoteles: Texte und Commentare* (Basel: B. Schwabe, 1944–1959).

PRIMARY SOURCES: EDITIONS AND TRANSLATIONS

Biblia Sacra Juxta Vulgatam Versionem (= Vulgate), 4th ed., ed. R. Weber (Stuttgart: Deutsche Bibelgesellschaft, 1994).

Ambrose, *Des Sacraments, Des Mystères, Explication du Symbole,* Latin and French, ed. and trans. D. Botte, SC series (Paris: Editions du Cerf, 1994).

Anonymous, *Physiognomics*, see under Aristotle.

————. *Rhetorica Ad Herrenium,* see under Cicero.

————. *Summa Sententiarum,* in PL 176:42–174.

Aquinas, *Summa Theologiae,* 3rd ed., 5 vols. (Salamanca: Matriti, 1961–1965).

————. *Summa Theologica* (ET of *Summa Theologiae*), 5 vols. (Westminster, MD: Christian Classics, 1981).

Aristotle, *Nicomachean Ethics,* trans. H. Rackham, Loeb series (Cambridge: Harvard University Press, 1947).

————. *On the Soul, Parva Naturalia, On Breath,* trans. W. S. Hett, Loeb series (Cambridge: Harvard University Press, 1957).

————. *Physiognomics,* in *Minor Works,* trans. W. S. Hett, Loeb series (Cambridge: Harvard University Press, 1936).

————. *Prior Analytics,* trans. R. Smith (Indianapolis: Hackett, 1989).

————. *The Works of Aristotle,* 12 vols., ed. W. D. Ross (Oxford: Clarendon Press, 1910–1952).

Augustine, *Against the Academics,* trans. J. J. O'Meara, Ancient Christian Writers series (Westminster: Newman, 1950).

————. *De Dialectica,* ed. and trans. B. D. Jackson (Dordrecht: Reidel, 1975).

————. *La doctrine chrétienne,* Latin-French, 1st ed., in *Le magistère chrétien,* BA series (Paris: Desclée de Brower, 1949), 149–541.

————. *La doctrine chrétienne,* Latin-French, 2nd ed., BA series (Paris: Institut d'Études Augustiniennes, 1997).

————. *Epistula,* ed. A. Goldbacher, 5 vols., CSEL series (Vienna: F. Tempsky, 1895–1923).

————. *On Christian Doctrine* (ET of *De Doctrina Christiana*), trans. D. Robertson (New York: Macmillan, 1958).

————. *On Christian Teaching* (ET of *De Doctrina Christiana*), trans. R. Green (New York: Oxford University Press, 1997).

————. *Opera Omnia* in PL, vols. 32–46.

————. *Sermons,* 11 vols., trans. E. Hill (Hyde Park, NY: New City Press, 1990–1997).

————. *Teaching Christianity* (ET of *De Doctrina Christiana*), trans. E. Hill (Hyde Park, NY: New City Press, 1996).

————. *Two Books on Genesis against the Manichees* (ET of *De Genesi contra Manichaeos*) in *Saint Augustine on Genesis,* trans. R. Teske (Washington: The Catholic University of America Press, 1991).

Barth, K., *Church Dogmatics,* trans. G. Bromiley et al. (Edinburgh: T. & T. Clark, 1956–1969).

Boethius, *The Theological Tractates* and *The Consolation of Philosophy,* trans. S. J. Tester, Loeb series (Cambridge: Harvard University Press, 1973).

————. *Boethius's De topicis differentiis,* trans. E. Stump (Ithaca, NY: Cornell University Press, 1978).

Bonaventure, *Breviloquium* (St. Louis: B. Herder, 1946).

Calvin, J., *Calvin: Theological Treatises* (Philadelphia: Westminster Press, 1954).

————. *Institutes,* trans. F. Battles and ed. J. McNeill, LCC series (Philadelphia: Westminster, 1960).

———. *Institutes of the Christian Religion: 1536 Edition,* trans. and ed. F. Battles (Grand Rapids: Eerdmans, 1986).

———. *Institutio Christianae Religionis,* CR, vol. 30, ed. G. Baum et al. (Brunswick: C.A. Schetschke et Filium, 1864).

Cicero, *De Finibus Bonorum et Malorum,* trans. H. Rackham, Loeb series (Cambridge: Harvard University Press, 1971).

———. *De Inventione, De Optimo Genere Oratorum, Topica,* trans. H. M. Hubbell, Loeb series (Cambridge: Harvard University Press, 1974).

———. *De Natura Deorum, Academica,* trans. H. Rackham, Loeb series (Cambridge: Harvard University Press, 1972).

———. *De Oratore,* books I and II, trans. E. W. Sutton and H. Rackham, Loeb series (Cambridge: Harvard University Press, 1967).

———. *De Oratore* III, *De Fato, Paradoxa Stoicorum, De Partitione Oratoria,* trans. H. Rackham, Loeb series (Cambridge: Harvard University Press, 1968).

———. *L'Hortensius de Ciceron: histoire et reconstitution,* ed. M. Ruch (Paris: Les belles lettres, 1958).

———. *Rhetorica Ad Herrenium,* trans. H. Caplan, Loeb series (Cambridge: Harvard University Press, 1968). This ancient textbook of rhetoric was long attributed to Cicero, but is almost certainly by someone else of about the same time.

———. *Tusculan Disputations,* trans. J. E. King, Loeb series (Cambridge: Harvard University Press, 1971).

Cyprian of Carthage, Epistles and Treatises in ANF 5:267–564.

———. *Opera Omnia,* 3 vols., ed. G. Hartel, CSEL (Vienna: C. Geroldi and Sons, 1868–1871).

Dante Alighieri, *Paradiso* (Italian and English), trans. J. Sinclair (New York: Oxford University Press, 1977).

Derrida, J., *Dissemination* (Chicago: University of Chicago Press, 1981).

———. *Of Grammatology* (Baltimore: Johns Hopkins University Press, 1974).

Diogenes Laertius, *Lives and Opinions of Eminent Philosophers,* trans. R. Hicks, Loeb series (Cambridge: Harvard University Press, 1950).

Eliot, T. S., *Four Quartets* (San Diego: Harcourt Brace, 1971).

Gadamer, H-G., *Truth and Method* (New York: Crossroad, 1985).

Galen, "On the Sects for Beginners" in his *Three Treatises,* pp. 1–20.

———. "On Medical Experience" in his *Three Treatises,* pp. 47–106.

———. *Three Treatises on the Nature of Science,* trans. R. Walzer and M. Frede (Indianapolis: Hackett, 1985).

Gregory Naziansen, *Discours,* ed. and trans. J. Bernardi, SC series (Paris: Cerf, 1978–1992). Greek text with French translation.

———. *Select Orations* and *Select Letters,* trans. C. G. Brown and J. E. Swallow, in NPNF, second series, vol. 7.

———. "The Theological Orations," trans. C. G. Brown and J. E. Swallow, in Hardy.

Gregory of Nyssa, *On Infants' Early Deaths* in NPNF, second series, 5:372–381.

Hegel, G. F. W., *Early Theological Writings,* trans. T. Knox (Chicago: University of Chicago Press, 1948).

Heidegger, M., *Identity and Difference*, trans. J. Stambaugh (Chicago: University of Chicago Press, 2002).

Hugh of St. Victor, *De Sacramentis*, in PL 176:173–518.

———. *On the Sacraments of the Christian Faith*, trans. R. Deferrari (Cambridge, MA: Medieval Academy of America, 1951).

Hume, D., *An Enquiry concerning Human Understanding* (Indianapolis: Hackett, 1977).

Justin Martyr, *Dialogue with Trypho* in ANF, 1:194–270.

Julian of Norwich, *A Revelation of Love*, ed. M. Glasscoe (Exeter: University of Exeter, 1976).

Kierkegaard, S., *Philosophical Fragments* and *Johannes Climacus*, ed. and trans. H. and E. Hong (Princeton: Princeton University Press, 1985).

Lessing, G., *Lessing's Theological Writings* (Stanford: Stanford University Press, 1956).

Locke, J., *An Essay concerning Human Understanding*, ed. P. Nidditch (Oxford: Clarendon Press, 1975).

Lombard, P., *Sententiae in IV Libris Distinctae* (Rome: Collegii S. Bonaverturae ad Claras Aquas, 1971).

Luther, M., *D. Martin Luthers Werke* (Weimar: H. Böhlau, 1883–1993).

———. *Large Catechism* in Tappert, pp. 357–461.

———. *Luther's Works*, 55 vols., ed. J. Pelikan and H. Lehman (Philadelphia: Fortress Press, 1958–1986).

———. *Smalcald Articles* in Tappert, pp. 287–335.

Milton, J., *Complete Poems and Major Prose* (Indianapolis: Bobbs-Merrill, 1957).

Philo of Alexandria, *On Mating with the Preliminary Studies* in *Philo*, vol. 4, trans. F. H. Colson and G. H. Whitaker, Loeb series (Cambridge, MA: Harvard University Press, 1949).

Philodemus, *On Methods of Inference* (= *De Signis*), rev. ed., ed. and trans. P. H. De Lacey and E. A. De Lacey (Naples: Bibliopolis, 1978).

Plato, *Platonis Opera*, complete works in Greek, ed. J. Burnet (Oxford: Clarendon Press, 1946).

Plotinus, *Enneads*, trans. A. H. Armstrong, Loeb series (Cambridge: Harvard University Press, 1966–1988).

Plutarch, "On Stoic Self-Contradictions," trans. H. Cherniss in *Plutarch's Moralia*, vol. 13, part 2, Loeb series (Cambridge: Harvard University Press, 1976).

Porphyry, *Sententiae ad Intelligibilia ducentes*, ed. E. Lamberz (Leipzig: Teubner, 1975).

Quintilian, *Institutio Oratoria*, 4 vols., trans. H. E. Butler, Loeb series (Cambridge: Harvard, 1969).

Schleiermacher, F., *The Christian Faith* (Edinburgh: T&T Clark, 1986).

Sextus Empiricus, *Against the Mathematicians*, translated under the title "Against the Logicians," books 1 and 2 (= *Adv. Math.* 7 and 8) by R. Bury in *Sextus Empiricus*, vol. 2., Loeb series (Cambridge: Harvard University Press, 1957).

———. *Outlines of Pyrrhonism*, trans. R. G. Bury in *Sextus Empiricus*, vol. 1, Loeb series (Cambridge: Harvard University Press, 1955).

Shakespeare, W., *The Riverside Shakespeare: Complete Works*, 2nd ed., ed. G. B. Evans (Boston: Houghton Mifflin, 1997).

Theophrastus, *Enquiry into Plants and Minor Works on Odours and Weather Signs*, 2 vols., Loeb series (Cambridge: Harvard University Press, 1949).

Tyconius, *The Book of Rules*, ed. F. C. Burkitt and trans. W. S. Babcock (Atlanta: Scholars Press, 1989). Latin and English; unfortunately lacking paragraph divisions.

———. "The Book of Rules, I–III" in K. Froehlich, *Biblical Interpretation in the Early Church* (Philadelphia: Fortress Press, 1985). Contains ET only, but includes paragraph divisions.

Varro, *De Lingua Latina*, 2 vols., trans. R. G. Kent, Loeb series (Cambridge: Harvard University Press, 1951).

Virgil, *Eclogues, Georgics, Aeneid 1–6*, ed. and trans. H. R. Fairclough, Loeb series (Cambridge, MA: Harvard University Press, 1998).

Wittgenstein, L., *Philosophical Investigations* (New York: Macmillan, 1953).

SECONDARY LITERATURE

Adam, K., *Eucharistielehre des heiligen Augustinus* (Paderborn: Ferdinand Schöningh, 1908).

———. "Zur Eucharistielehre des heiligen Augustinus" in his *Gesammelte Aufsätze* (Augsburg: Literar. Institut. P. Haas, 1936).

Annas, J., *Hellenistic Philosophy of Mind* (Berkeley: University of California Press, 1992).

Arnold, D., and P. Bright, eds., *De Doctrina Christiana: A Classic of Western Culture* (Notre Dame: University of Notre Dame Press, 1995).

Asmis, E., "Epicurean Semiotics" in Manetti, *Knowledge through Signs*, pp. 155–185.

Atherton, C., *The Stoics on Ambiguity* (Cambridge: Cambridge University Press, 1993).

Aubin, P., *Le Problème de la "Conversion"* (Paris: Beauchesne, 1963).

Auerbach, E., "Figura" in his *Scenes from the Drama of European Literature* (Minneapolis: University of Minnesota Press, 1984), 11–76.

Babcock, W., "*Caritas* and Signification in *De doctrina christiana* 1–3" in Arnold and Bright, pp. 145–163.

Barnes, J., J. Brunschwig, M. Burnyeat, M. Schofield, eds., *Science and Speculation: Studies in Hellenistic Theory and Practice* (Cambridge: Cambridge University Press, 1982).

Barnouw, J., *Propositional Perception: Phantasia, Predication and Sign in Plato, Aristotle and the Stoics* (Lanham, MD: University Press of America, 2002).

Bayer, O., *Promissio: Geschichte der reformatorischen Wende in Luthers Theologie* (Göttingen: Vandenhoeck and Ruprecht, 1971).

Bonner, G., *St. Augustine of Hippo: Life and Controversies*, 2nd ed. (Norwich: The Canterbury Press, 1986).

Bornkamm, G., "*Mystērion*" in G. Kittel, ed., *Theological Dictionary of the New Testament*, trans. G. Bromiley (Grand Rapids: Eerdmans, 1964–1976), 4:802–828.

Bourke, V., *Augustine's View of Reality* (Villanova: Villanova University Press, 1964).

Braaten, C., and R. Jenson, eds., *Union with Christ: The New Finnish Interpretation of Luther* (Grand Rapids: Eerdmans, 1998).

Bright, P., *Augustine and the Bible* (Notre Dame: University of Notre Dame Press, 1999).

———. "Church, North African" in Fitzgerald, pp. 185–190.

Brown, P., *Augustine of Hippo*, 2nd ed. (Berkeley: University of California Press, 2000).

Brown, R., *The Semitic Background of the Term "Mystery" in the New Testament* (Philadelphia: Fortress Press, 1968).

Burnaby, J., *Amor Dei: A Study in the Religion of St. Augustine* (London: Hodder and Stoughton, 1938).

Burns, J. P., *Cyprian the Bishop* (London: Routledge, 1991).

———. *The Development of Augustine's Doctrine of Operative Grace* (Paris: Études Augustiniennes, 1980).

———. "Grace" in Fitzgerald, pp. 391–398.

Burnyeat, M., and M. Frede, eds., *The Original Sceptics: A Controversy* (Indianapolis: Hackett, 1997).

———. "The Origins of Non-deductive Inference" in Barnes et al., pp. 193–238.

———. ed., *The Skeptical Tradition* (Berkeley: University of California Press, 1983).

———. "Wittgenstein and Augustine *De Magistro*," *Proceedings of the Aristotelian Society*, Supplement, 61 (1987) 1–24. Reprinted in Matthews, pp. 286–304.

Cameron, M., "The Christological Substructure of Augustine's Exegesis" in Bright, pp. 74–103.

Caputo, J., *Radical Hermeneutics* (Bloomington: Indiana University Press, 1987).

Cary, P., *Augustine's Invention of the Inner Self* (New York: Oxford University Press, 2000).

———. "Believing the Word: A Proposal about Knowing Other Persons," *Faith and Philosophy* 13:1 (1996) 78–90.

———. "Book Seven: Inner Vision as the Goal of Augustine's Life" in *A Reader's Companion to Augustine's Confessions*," ed. K. Paffenroth and R. P. Kennedy (Louisville: Westminster John Knox Press, 2003), 107–126.

———. "The Incomprehensibility of God and the Origin of the Thomistic Concept of the Supernatural," *Pro Ecclesia* 9:3 (Summer 2002) 340–355.

———. *Inner Grace: Augustine in the Traditions of Plato and Paul* (New York: Oxford University Press, 2008).

———. "United Inwardly by Love: Augustine's Social Ontology" in *Augustine and Politics*, ed. J Doody, K. L. Hughes, and K. Paffenroth (Lanham, MD: Lexington Books, 2005).

———. "Varro" in Fitzgerald, pp. 863–864.

———. "The Weight of Love: Augustinian Metaphors of Movement in Dante's Souls," in *Augustine and Literature*, ed. J. Doody, R. P. Kennedy, and K. Paffenroth (Lanham, MD: Lexington Books, 2006), pp. 15–36.

———. "Why Luther Is Not Quite Protestant," *Pro Ecclesia* 14:4 (Fall 2005) 447–486.

Cavadini, J., "The Structure and Intention of Augustine's *De Trinitate*," *AS* 23 (1992) 103–123.

Conybeare, C., *Paulinus Noster: Self and Symbol in the Letters of Paulinus of Nola* (New York: Oxford University Press, 2001).

Courcelle, P., *Late Latin Writers and Their Greek Sources*, trans. H. Wedeck (Cambridge: Harvard University Press, 1969).

Couissin, P., "The Stoicism of the New Academy" in Burnyeat, *The Skeptical Tradition*, pp. 31–63.

Couturier, C., "*Sacramentum* et *mysterium* dans l'oeuvre de saint Augustin" in H. Rondet, et al. *Études Augustiniennes* (Paris: Aubier, 1953), 161–332.

Davidson, D., *Inquiries into Truth and Interpretation* (Oxford: Clarendon Press, 1986).

Douglas, M., *Purity and Danger* (London: Routledge, 1991).

Duchrow, U., "*Signum* und *superbia* beim jungen Augustin (386–390)," *REA* 7 (1961) 369–372.

———. *Sprachverständnis und biblisches Hören bei Augustin* (Tübingen: J.C.B. Mohr, 1965).

Duffy, E., *The Stripping of the Altars: Traditional Religion in England, c. 1400–c.1580* (New Haven: Yale University Press, 1992).

Düring, I., "Aristotle and Plato in the Mid-fourth Century," *Eranos* 54 (1965) 109–120.

———. "Aristotle and the Heritage from Plato," *Eranos* 62 (1964) 84–99.

———. "Aristotle on Ultimate Principles from 'Nature and Reality'" in Düring and Owen, pp. 35–55.

———. *Aristoteles: Darstellung und Interpretation seines Denkens* (Heidelberg: Carl Winter Universitätsverlag, 1966).

———. "Did Aristotle Ever Accept Plato's Theory of Transcendent Ideas?" *Archiv für Geschichte der Philosophie* 48 (1966) 312–316.

———. and G. E. L. Owen, *Plato and Aristotle in the Mid-fourth Century* (Göteborg: Elanders Boktryckeri Aktiebolag, 1960).

Eco, U., R. Lambertini, C. Marmo, and A. Tabarroni, "On Animal Language in the Medieval Classification of Signs" in Eco and Marmo, pp. 3–41.

———. and C. Marmo, eds., *On the Medieval Theory of Signs* (Philadelphia: John Benjamins, 1989).

———. *Semiotics and the Philosophy of Language* (Bloomington: Indiana University Press, 1984).

Fitzgerald, A., ed., *Augustine through the Ages: An Encyclopedia* (Grand Rapids: Eerdmans, 1999).

Frede, M., "The Ancient Empiricists" in his *Essays*, pp. 243–260.

———. *Essays in Ancient Philosophy* (Minneapolis: University of Minnesota Press, 1987).

———. "The Method of the So-Called Methodical School of Medicine" in his *Essays*, pp. 261–278.

———. "Philosophy and Medicine in Antiquity" in his *Essays*, pp. 225–242.

———. "The Skeptic's Beliefs" in his *Essays*, pp. 179–200. Reprinted in Burnyeat and Frede, *The Original Sceptics*, pp. 1–24.

———. "The Skeptic's Two Kinds of Assent and the Question of the Possibility of Knowledge" in his *Essays*, pp. 201–222. Reprinted in Burnyeat and Frede, *The Original Sceptics*, pp. 127–151.

Fredriksen, P., "Paul and Augustine: Conversion Narratives, Orthodox Traditions, and the Retrospective Self," *Journal of Theological Studies*, NS, 37:1 (April 1986) 3–34.

Ghellinck, J. de, "Un chapitre dans l'histoire de la définition des sacrements au XIIe siècle" in *Mélanges Mandonnet* (Paris: Vrin, 1930).

———. *Le Mouvement théologique du XIIe Siècle* (Paris: Desclée, 1948).

Gilson, E., *The Christian Philosophy of Saint Augustine*, trans. L. E. M. Lynch (New York: Random House, 1960).

Glidden, D., "Skeptic Semiotics," *Phronesis* 28 (1983) 213–255.

Glucker, J., *Antiochus and the Late Academy* (Göttingen: Vandenhoeck & Ruprecht, 1978).

———. "*Probabile*, *Veri Simile*, and Related Terms" in Powell, *Cicero the Philosopher*, pp. 115–143.

Graeser, A., "The Stoic Theory of Meaning" in Rist, *The Stoics*, pp. 77–100.

———. *Zenon von Kition: Positionen und Problemen* (Berlin: de Gruyter, 1975).

Graham, D., *Aristotle's Two Systems* (Oxford: Clarendon Press, 1987).

Grillmeier, A., *Christ in Christian Tradition*, vol. 1, trans. J. S. Bowden (New York: Sheed and Ward, 1965).

Hacking, I., *The Emergence of Probability: A Philosophical Study of Early Ideas about Probability, Induction and Statistical Inference* (Cambridge: Cambridge University Press, 1975).

Hagendahl, H., *Augustine and the Latin Classics* (Göteborg: Elanders Boktryckeri Akteibolag, 1967).

Hanson, R. P. C., *The Search for the Christian Doctrine of God: The Arian Controversy 318–381* (Edinburgh: T&T Clark, 1988).

Harrison, C., *Rethinking Augustine's Early Theology* (Oxford: Oxford University Press, 2006).

Hart, D. B., *The Beauty of the Infinite: The Aesthetics of Christian Truth* (Grand Rapids: Eerdmans, 2003).

Henry, P., *Plotin et l'Occident* (Louvain: Spicilegium Sacrum Lovaniense, 1934).

Jackson, B. D., "The Theory of Signs in Augustine's *De Doctrina Christiana*" in Markus, pp. 92–147.

Jaeger, W., *Aristotle: Fundamentals of the History of His Development*, 2nd ed., trans. R. Robinson (Oxford: Clarendon Press, 1948).

Kendall, R. T., *Calvin and English Calvinism* (Oxford: Oxford University Press, 1979).

Kirwan, C., "Augustine against the Skeptics" in Burnyeat, *The Skeptical Tradition*, pp. 205–223. Reprinted in Kirwan, *Augustine* (London: Routledge, 1989), 15–34.

Kneale, W., and M. Kneale, *The Development of Logic* (Oxford: Oxford University Press, 1962).

Kolbet, P., "Formal Continuities between Augustine's Early Philosophical Teaching and Late Homiletical Practice," *Studia Patristica* 43 (2006) 149–154.

Kretzmann, N., "Aristotle on Spoken Sound Significant by Convention" in *Ancient Logic and Its Modern Interpretations*, ed. J. Corcoran (Dordrecht: Reidel, 1974), 3–21.

Lapidge, M., "Stoic Cosmology" in Rist, *The Stoics*, pp. 161–185.

Lienhard, J., E. Muller, and R. Teske, *Augustine: Presbyter Factus Sum* (New York: Peter Lang, 1993).

Lilla, S., *Clement of Alexandria: A Study in Christian Platonism and Gnosticism* (Oxford: Oxford University Press, 1971).

Lindbeck, G., *The Nature of Doctrine: Religion and Theology in a Postliberal Age* (Philadelphia: Westminster Press, 1984).

Long, A., "Cicero's Plato and Aristotle" in Powell, *Cicero the Philosopher*, pp. 37–61.

———. "Dialectic and the Stoic Sage" in Rist, *The Stoics*, pp. 101–124.

———. "Language and Thought in Stoicism" in Long, *Problems in Stoicism*, pp. 74–113.

———. "The Logical Basis of Stoic Ethics" in *Proceedings of the Aristotelian Society, Supplement*, 1971.

———., ed., *Problems in Stoicism* (London: Athlone Press, 1971).

———. "Stoic linguistics, Plato's *Cratylus*, and Augustine's *De Dialectica*" in *Language and Learning: Philosophy of Language in the Hellenistic Age*, ed. D. Frede and B. Inwood (Cambridge: Cambridge University Press, 2005).

———. "Stoic Psychology and the Elucidation of Language" in Manetti, *Knowledge through Signs*, pp. 109–131.

Lorenz, R., "Gnade und Erkenntnis bei Augustin" in *Zum Augustin-Gespräch der Gegenwart*, vol. 2, ed. C. Andresen (Darmstadt: Wissenschaftliche Buchgesellschaft, 1981), 43–125.

Louth, A., "Augustine on Language," *Journal of Literature and Theology* 3:2 (1989) 151–158.

Lozano-Miralles, H., "Sign and Language in Plato," *Versus* 50:51(1988) 71–82.

Mackey, L. "The Mediator Mediated: Faith and Reason in Augustine's *De Magistro*," *Franciscan Studies* 42 (1982) 135–155.

Madec, G., *Petites études augustiniennes* (Paris: Institut d'Études Augustiniennes, 1994).

———. *Saint Augustin et la philosophie* (Paris: Institut d'Études Augustiniennes, 1996).

Mannermaa, T., *Der im Glauben gegenwärtige Christus* (Hannover: Lutherisches Verlagshaus, 1989).

Manetti, G., ed., *Knowledge through Signs: Ancient Semiotic Theories and Practices* (Brepols, 1996).

———. *Theories of the Sign in Classical Antiquity*, trans. C. Richardson (Bloomington: Indiana University Press, 1993).

Markus, R.A., ed., *Augustine: A Collection of Critical Essays* (New York: Doubleday, 1972).

———. "St. Augustine on Signs" in Markus, pp. 61–91.

Marshall, B., *Trinity and Truth* (Cambridge: Cambridge University Press, 2000).

Mates, B., *Stoic Logic* (Berkeley: University of California Press, 1961).

Matthews, G. B., ed., *The Augustinian Tradition* (Berkeley: University of California Press, 1999).

Mayer, C.P., "Philosophische Voraussetzungen und Implikationen in Augustins Lehre von den *Sacramenta*," *Augustiniana* 22 (1972) 53–79.

———. " '*Res per signa*': Der Grundgedanke des Prologs in Augustins Schrift *De doctrina christiana* und das Problem seiner Datierung," *REA* 20 (1974) 100–112.

———. "Taufe und Erwählung: Zur Dialektik des *sacramentum*-Begriffes in der antidonatischen Schrift Augustins: *De Baptismo*" in C. P. Mayer and W. Eckermann, *Scientia Augustiniana* (Würzburg: Augustinus Verlag, 1975), 22–42.

———. *Die Zeichen in der geistigen Entwicklung und in der Theologie des jungen Augustins* [Part I] (Würzburg: Augustinus Verlag, 1969).

———. *Die Zeichen in der geistigen Entwicklung und in der Theologie Augustins, II. Teil: Die anti-Manichäische Epoche* (Würzburg: Augustinus Verlag, 1974).

Nussbaum, M., *Aristotle's De Motu Animalium* (Princeton: Princeton University Press, 1978).

O'Connell, R., *The Origin of the Soul in St. Augustine's Later Works* (New York: Fordham University Press, 1987).

———. *St. Augustine's Early Theory of Man* (Cambridge: Harvard University Press, 1968).

O'Donovan, O., "*Usus* and *fruitio* in Augustine, *De DoctrinaI*," *Journal of Theological Studies* 33:2 (Oct., 1982) 361–397.

Pacioni, V., "Liberal Arts" in Fitzgerald, pp. 492–494.

Pépin, J., "Une nouvelle source de saint Augustin" in "*Ex Platonicorum Persona*" (Amsterdam: Hakkert, 1957).

———. *Saint Augustin et la Dialectique* (Villanova: Villanova University Press, 1976).

Philip, G., "L'influence du Christ-Chef sur son Corps mystique" in *Augustinus Magister* (Paris: Études Augustiniennes, 1954) 2:805–815.

Polansky, R., and M. Kuczewski, "Speech and Thought, Symbol and Likeness: Aristotle's *De Interpretatione* 16a3–9," *Apeiron* 23 (1990) 51–63.

Powell, J. G. F, ed. *Cicero the Philosopher: Twelve Papers* (Oxford: Clarendon Press, 1995).

Press, G., "The Subject and Structure of Augustine's *De Doctrina Christiana*," *AS* 11 (1980) 99–124.

Ratzinger, J., *Volk und Haus Gottes in Augustins Lehre von der Kirche* (Munich: Karl Zink Verlag, 1954).

Rhombs, R., *Saint Augustine and the Fall of the Soul: Beyond O'Connell and His Critics* (Washington: Catholic University of America Press, 2006).

Rist, J., ed., *The Stoics* (Berkeley: University of California, 1978).

Ruef, H., *Augustin über Semiotik und Sprache: Sprachtheoretische Analysen zu Augustins "De Dialectica"* (Bern: Verlag K.J. Wyss Erben, 1981).

Schofield, M., "Aristotle on the Imagination" in Nussbaum and Rorty, *Essays on Aristotle's De Anima*, pp. 249–277.

Sedley, D., Aristotle's *De Interpretatione* and Ancient Semiotics" in Manetti, *Knowledge through Signs*, pp. 87–107.

———. "The Motivation of Greek Skepticism" in Burnyeat, *The Skeptical Tradition*, pp. 9–29.

———. "On Signs" in Barnes et al., *Science and Speculation*, pp. 239–272.

Solignac, A., "La condition de l'homme pécheur d'après saint Augustin," *Nouvelle Revue Théologique* 78 (1952) 385–416.

Tarrant, H., *Scepticism or Platonism? The Philosophy of the Fourth Academy* (Cambridge: Cambridge University Press, 1985).

Teske, R., "The Link between Faith and Time in St. Augustine" in Lienhard et al., *Augustine: Presbyter Factus Sum*, pp. 195–206.

———. *Paradoxes of Time in Saint Augustine* (Milwaukee: Marquette University Press, 1996).

———. "The World-Soul and Time in Augustine," *AS* 14 (1983) 75–92.

Testard, M., *Saint Augustin et Cicero* (Paris: Études Augustiniennes, 1958).

Toom, T., *Thought Clothed with Sound: Augustine's Christological Hermeneutics in De doctrina Christiana* (Bern: Peter Lang, 2002).

Watson, G., *Phantasia in Classical Thought* (Galway: Galway University Press, 1988).

Weidemann, H. "Grundzüge der Aristotelischen Sprachtheorie" in P. Schmitter., ed., *Sprachtheorien der abendländischen Antike* (Tübingen: Gunter Narr Verlag, 1991), 170–192.

Whitaker, C. W. A., *Aristotle's* De Interpretatione: *Contradiction and Dialectic* (Oxford: Clarendon Press, 1996).

Williams, R. "Language, Reality and Desire in Augustine's *De Doctrina*," *Journal of Literature and Theology* 3:2 (July 1989) 138–150.

Wolff, H. W., *Anthropology of the Old Testament* (Philadelphia: Fortress Press, 1974).

Young, F., *From Nicaea to Chalcedon* (Philadelphia: Fortress, 1983).

Index